Lecture Notes in Computer Science   3080

Commenced Publication in 1973
Founding and Former Series Editors:
Gerhard Goos, Juris Hartmanis, and Jan van Leeuwen

T0223613

Springer
Berlin
Heidelberg
New York
Hong Kong
London
Milan
Paris
Tokyo

Jörg Desel   Barbara Pernici
Mathias Weske (Eds.)

Business Process Management

Second International Conference, BPM 2004
Potsdam, Germany, June 17-18, 2004
Proceedings

 Springer

Volume Editors

Jörg Desel
Katholische Universität Eichstätt-Ingolstadt, Lehrstuhl für Angewandte Informatik
Ostenstr. 14, 85072 Eichstätt, Germany
E-mail: joerg.desel@ku-eichstaett.de

Barbara Pernici
Politecnico di Milano, Dipartimento di Elettronica e Informazione
via Beato Angelico 23/1, 20133 Milano, Italy
E-mail: barbara.pernici@polimi.it

Mathias Weske
University of Potsdam, Hasso-Plattner-Institute for Software Systems Engineering
Prof.-Dr.-Helmert-Straße 2-3, 14480 Potsdam, Germany
E-mail: mathias.weske@hpi.uni-potsdam.de

Library of Congress Control Number: 2004107855

CR Subject Classification (1998): H.3.5, H.4.1, H.5.3, K.4.3, K.4.4, K.6, J.1

ISSN 0302-9743
ISBN 3-540-22235-9 Springer-Verlag Berlin Heidelberg New York

Springer-Verlag is a part of Springer Science+Business Media

springeronline.com

© Springer-Verlag Berlin Heidelberg 2004
Printed in Germany

Typesetting: Camera-ready by author, data conversion by PTP-Berlin, Protago-TeX-Production GmbH
Printed on acid-free paper   SPIN: 11013068   06/3142   5 4 3 2 1 0

Preface

In recent years the management of business processes has emerged as one of the major developments to ease the understanding of, communication about, and evolution of process-oriented information systems in a variety of application domains. Based on explicit representations of business processes, process stakeholders can communicate about process structure, content, and possible improvements. Formal analysis, verification and simulation techniques have the potential to show deficits and to effectively lead to better and more flexible processes. Process mining facilitates the discovery of process specifications from process logs that are readily available in many organizations.

This volume of Springer's Lecture Notes in Computer Science contains the papers presented at the 2nd International Conference on Business Process Management (BPM 2004) which took place in Potsdam, Germany, in June 2004. From more than 70 submissions BPM 2004 received, 19 high-quality research papers were selected.

BPM 2004 is part of a conference series that provides a forum for researchers and practitioners in all aspects of business process management. In June 2003, the 1st International Conference on Business Process Management took place in Eindhoven, The Netherlands. Its proceedings were published as Volume 2678 of Lecture Notes in Computer Science by Springer-Verlag. A previous volume (LNCS 1806) on Business Process Management was based on four events devoted to this topic.

This book presents a significant view on the state of the art in business process management, ranging from formal approaches to descriptions of tools for the design of processes. The topics addressed by the contributions cover areas like business process modeling, formal models, as well as analysis and verification of business processes, process mining and workflow management, and, moreover, case studies from various domains including medicine, technology, and logistics.

Besides its research paper track, BPM 2004 hosted a keynote presentation by Christoph Bussler, Vice-Director of the Digital Enterprise Research Institute in Galway, Ireland. A tutorial on workflow modeling and analysis using Petri nets was given by Wil van der Aalst, Head of the Information Systems department in the Faculty of Technology Management, Eindhoven Technical University (NL). Rainer Ruggaber of SAP Corporate Research talked about SAP's involvement in European research projects. Thomas Volmering and Karl Wagner reported on a recently strengthened cooperation between SAP and IDS Scheer in the context of the new SAP software architecture, based on service technology. All these presentations are highly appreciated.

The organizers are thankful to SAP AG, IDS Scheer and Adesso AG as well as to the Hasso Plattner Institute for supporting this scientific event. A special thanks goes to Jörn Lauterjung and his colleagues from Geoforschungszentrum Potsdam, which provided the location of this year's BPM conference. We thank the local organization group at the Hasso Plattner Institute, including Hilmar Schuschel, Katrin Heinrich and Mirko Schulze, who provided the conference Web site and online registration system and also installed and maintained the Cyber-Chair conference management software that we used during the reviewing process. The group at KU Eichstätt-Ingolstadt, in particular Dorothea Iglezakis and Birgit Eisen, collected the final versions of the research papers and prepared the camera-ready copy of this Springer Lecture Notes in Computer Science volume.

We should like to acknowledge the excellent cooperation with Alfred Hofmann of Springer-Verlag and his colleagues in the preparation of this volume.

Finally, we are grateful to all Program Committee members and additional reviewers for their contribution to the success of the conference.

June 2004

Jörg Desel
Barbara Pernici
Mathias Weske

Program Committee

Wil van der Aalst, The Netherlands
Boualem Benatallah, Australia
Christoph Bussler, Ireland
Fabio Casati, USA
Piotr Chrzastowski-Wachtel, Poland
Leonid Churilov, Australia
Peter Dadam, Germany
Jörg Desel, Germany (Co-chair)
Jan Dietz, The Netherlands
Susanna Donatelli, Italy
Schahram Dustdar, Austria
Chiara Francalanci, Italy
Dimitrios Georgakopoulos, USA
Claude Godart, France
Kees van Hee, The Netherlands
Arthur ter Hofstede, Australia
Geert-Jan Houben, The Netherlands

Stefan Jablonski, Germany
Gerti Kappel, Austria
Ekkart Kindler, Germany
Akhil Kumar, USA
Ronald M. Lee, USA
Dan C. Marinescu, USA
Massimo Mecella, Italy
Andreas Oberweis, Germany
Barbara Pernici, Italy (Co-chair)
Manfred Reichert, Germany
Colette Rolland, France
Michael Rosemann, Australia
Heiko Schuldt, Austria
Edward Stohr, USA
Gottfried Vossen, Germany
Mathias Weske, Germany (Co-chair)
Leon Zhao, USA

Referees

Michael Adams
Rainer Anzböck
Danilo Ardagna
Xin Bai
Donald Baker
Giuseppe Berio
Sami Bhiri
Jaap Boender
Cinzia Cappiello
Gerome Canals
Eugenio Capra
François Charoy
Andrzej Cichocki
Vincent Chevrier
Enzo Colombo
Fabio De Rosa
Antonio Di Leva
Sebastian Eichholz
Pascal Fenkam
Thomas Gschwind

Rachid Hamadi
Bodo Huesemann
Alexander Kaiser
Markus Kalb
Markus Klemen
Agnes Koschmider
Jens Lechtenboerger
Kirsten Lenz
Beate List
Emily (Rong) Liu
Udo Mayer
Christian Meiler
Kees van der Meer
Marco von Mevius
Sascha Mueller
Amedeo Napoli
Phillipa Oaks
Ilia Petrov
Olivier Perrin
Frank Puhlmann

Stefanie Rinderle
Nick Russell
Monica Scannapieco
Orit Schwartz
Natalia Sidorova
Carla Simone
Quan Z. Sheng
Halvard Skogsrud
Justin O'Sullivan
Alexander Tararbrin
Farouk Toumani
Marc Voorhoeve
Liangzhao Zeng
Henricus M.W. Verbeek
Marc Voorhoeve
Peter Westerkamp
Darrell Woel
Moe Wynn

Table of Contents

Analysis and Verification of Business Processes

Process Mining

Workflow Management

Consistency in Model Integration

Kees van Hee, Natalia Sidorova, Lou Somers, and Marc Voorhoeve

Eindhoven University of Technology, Dept. Math and Comp. Science, P.O. Box 513,
5600 MB Eindhoven, The Netherlands
{k.m.v.hee,n.sidorova,l.j.a.m.somers,m.voorhoeve}@tue.nl

Abstract. We present a UML-inspired approach to modeling and analysis of
complex systems. Different stakeholders of a system may have different views,
modeled with different techniques. It is essential that the various aspect models
(use cases and life cycles) provide a complete and consistent description of the
total system. Our approach based on the composition and decomposition of
(colored) Petri nets allows the integration of aspect models. We illustrate our
approach by a case study.

1 Introduction

The analysis and engineering of complex systems cannot be performed by a single
person. So, several system architects are involved, modeling various subsystems. Also
the system will have several stakeholders with different views, which also requires
various models for being able to validate the proposals of the architects. Different
aspect models require different modeling techniques. UML [3] offers a wide range of
such techniques, most of them being diagram techniques. A UML description of a
moderate-size system contains hundreds of diagrams of various kinds. Each diagram
models one or more aspects of the considered system. By concentrating on a few aspects at a time, validation by stakeholders becomes possible.

As the project proceeds, the aspect models will be integrated, while adding detail
and rigor. This may lead to the discovery of inconsistencies. Early detection of such
inconsistencies will help to reduce development costs, so the software industry is
hard-pressed for methods to determine and preserve the consistency between the various models. We believe that there is no "silver bullet" for achieving this. The "honest"
way is by a single model that integrates all aspects modeled so far. From this integrated model, the aspect models are derived as projections. If and only if such an
integrated model can be found, the models made so far are consistent.

In this paper, we indicate how integrated models can be derived from aspect models in early stages of the development process. The key ingredients are Petri nets with
synchronization and projection operators. We start with various aspect models that are
combined by synchronization, resulting in an integrated model. From it, scenario's can
be derived by projection in order to allow validation. There exist many tools that support such an approach, some of them, e.g. ExSpect [7] and CPN [9], allow to add pre-
and postconditions, resulting in a functional prototype.

J. Desel, B. Pernici, and M. Weske (Eds.): BPM 2004, LNCS 3080, pp. 1–16, 2004.

The synchronization operator is closely related to the call mechanism for methods; the model thus can be used to support the design and implementation phases. We illustrate our proposal with a case study of the well-known library system, which is just large enough to illustrate the key aspects of our method.

In section 2, we introduce WF nets, a subclass of Petri nets used for our models and our operators for composing and decomposing them. In section 3, we describe the modeling, verification, and validation process. In section 4, we illustrate our process with a library case study, and we also show how our models can be extended, adding more functionality. We conclude with a comparison with related work.

2   Petri Net Models, Synchronization, and Projection

We assume the reader has some knowledge of "classical" place-transition nets (bipartite directed graphs), markings (distributions of tokens in places) and the interleaving firing rule. A transition may fire in marking M iff it can consume the necessary tokens from M; as a result of this firing, a new marking M' is reached, consisting of M with the consumed tokens removed and produced tokens added. A net defines a reachability relation between its markings: a marking M' is reachable from a marking M iff a finite sequence of firings exists starting in M and ending in M'.

Marked nets are too general for modeling. In [1], the class of **WF** (workflow) nets is defined, which can be compared to UML activity diagrams. A WF net possesses a unique source and a unique sink place. Every node of a WF net, seen as a directed graph, lies on a directed path from the source to the sink place. A WF net possesses an initial marking (one token in the source place) and a final marking (one token in the sink place). It is *sound* iff (1) from the initial marking it is possible for every transition t to reach a marking where t may fire and (2) the final marking is reachable from any marking M that is reachable from the initial marking. Sound WF nets are the very nets used for modeling use cases and object life cycles, c.f. [4].

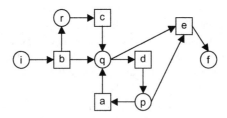

Fig. 1. Example of a WF net

In Fig. 1 a WF net is depicted. The places i,f are respectively the source and sink places. This net is sound, which can be verified by examining the reachable markings. For example, from the initial marking, a marking can be reached with only two tokens in p (e.g. by firing b, then c then twice d). From this marking, it is possible to reach the final marking by firing a, then e.

For convenience, we omit in this paper the source and sink place from the WF nets. Thus a WF net has one or more start transitions (without input places) and end transitions (without output places). The firing of transitions models the occurrence of events. If a transition bordering the source place fires, a "create" event occurs, since in a sound net this transition does not consume any tokens. Analogously, destroy events are firings of transitions bordering the sink place. The soundness property now states that whatever is caused by a single creation can eventually be undone by a single destruction.

For Petri nets there are several methods for analyzing the behavior. Some of these methods use only the structure of the Petri net and not the underlying state space. T-invariants provide such a method. A T-invariant can be computed by standard linear algebra and can be related to sequences of transitions that return the system to the state before the sequence was executed. We use T-invariants in the validation process.

The tokens in the places refer to objects; every place contains references to objects of one and the same class. Initially, we abstract from the attributes of the objects, allowing "classical" analysis of our nets. Eventually, our models will consist of high-level nets, e.g. colored nets [9], specifying pre- and postconditions for the firing of transitions. A transition will fire only if its consumption satisfies the precondition; it will then produce tokens in accordance with the postcondition.

We add operators for composing and decomposing net models, which are essential for the integration of models and for checking their consistency. The composition operator is called *synchronization* and is indicated by a dotted line connecting two transitions. When transitions synchronize in a high-level net, data may be exchanged in either direction. In Fig. 2, an example net with synchronization is shown at the left. The synchronization result is the net in the middle, which is obtained by transition fusion: the transitions participating in a synchronization are glued together. This mechanism resembles the synchronization within process calculi like CCS [10]. Synchronization between sound nets does not always result in a sound net; the middle net in Fig. 2 is not sound, since transition *cd* cannot fire.

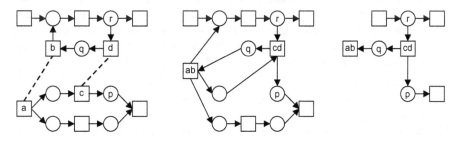

Fig. 2. Example of synchronization and projection

The decomposition operator is called *projection*. Projection of a net w.r.t. a subset S of the net's places is obtained by removing all the places not in S plus the edges leading to and from them. Transitions that become isolated are removed as well. The right-hand net shows the projection of the middle net w.r.t. the set $\{p,q,r\}$. If N is a connected net, P its set of places, and $S \subseteq P$, then N can be obtained by synchronizing its projections w.r.t. S and $P \setminus S$.

When creating WF nets for use cases, the transitions describe *events* that can occur. If a net models an object life cycle, the transitions represent *methods* of the object's class. In the design phase, the synchronization of methods will result in one of them calling the other. The following rule describes the essence of our approach: deriving an integrated model from aspect models and checking their consistency:

- The integrated model is derived from the aspect models (use cases and life cycles) by synchronization.
- All aspect models should be derivable from the integrated model by projection.

3 Modeling Process

We focus on deriving an integrated logical model that captures the functionality of the system, we have left out other engineering activities. In general, we have a succession of *elicitation, modeling, verification* and *validation* steps. We split the modeling step into three steps: *process* modeling, *data* modeling, and *transformation* modeling. In the elicitation steps the stakeholders play an important role. There are several techniques to obtain useful information from a group of stakeholders. Well-known are "brown paper sessions" where stakeholders write down individually the most important items, like issues, functions, scenario's, or objects. These items are stuck to a brown paper board and grouped by the moderator into related groups. Then the items are discussed and terminology is fixed. These sessions are repeated with different topics. Group decision support systems [11] provide computerized support. The modeling step is done by system architects, who also perform verification, possibly "on the fly" during modeling using "correctness by construction", sometimes after modeling (like verifying the integrated model). After modeling and verification comes validation with the help of stakeholders. As a result, a redesign may be needed.

The modeling, verification and validation steps are iterated until the stakeholders are satisfied with the logical model. At some stage when use cases have become stable, user interface designers can start to define screens containing forms and buttons. After having established the logical model, it is extended to accommodate for the designed user interface. We will describe the successive phases and steps in more detail. Remember that stakeholders are involved in phases 1 and 6 only.

Step 1: Elicitation
(a) Make a list of use cases, indicated by a name and some additional comments by the stakeholders.
(b) Define some allowed and explicitly forbidden scenario's (event sequences) for each use case.
(c) Identify the classes of objects that play a role in the scenario's.
(d) List relationships between object classes. The existence of these relationships is triggered by use case events that involve more than one object.
(e) Collect relevant attributes for the objects.
(f) Find static constraints that the system's state (the set of all living objects) should satisfy at all time.

Step 2: Process Modeling

(a) Create WF nets for the use cases. Each WF net should combine the allowed scenarios for one use case and disallow the forbidden ones.

(b) Create WF nets for the object life cycles. The transitions are the methods of the classes.

(c) Integrate the workflows by identifying the transitions in use cases and object life cycles that must be synchronized. If necessary, adapt use cases and/or life cycles.

Step 3: Data Modeling

(a) Construct the class model with relationships and attributes. We prefer functional relationships.

(b) Formalize the static constraints. Use logical predicates that can be translated back into natural language with increased precision. Add other common-sense static constraints.

(c) Define global variables. For each object class we define a global variable, called object store or object file. All objects that are active in the system reside in an object store. Also, other global variables like the current date or time are defined.

Step 4: Transformation Modeling

(a) Combine the process model and the data model. Establish the relationships between object classes and methods. For each class we determine whether the methods create, read, update, or destroy objects from it (a CRUD-matrix).

(b) Determine the input and output parameters of the methods: places, global variables and additional parameters, e.g. for the user interface.

(c) Determine pre- and postconditions of the methods. The end product is the high-level integrated model.

Step 5: Verification

(a) Check the soundness of all workflows: use cases, object life cycles, and the integrated model.

(b) Check that all use case nets can be derived from the integrated model by projection.

(c) Check that each relationship in the class model is created somewhere.

(d) Check the preservation of the static constraints. Some constraints may be temporarily violated during the execution of a certain sequence of transitions (a transaction) but they should be valid after the transaction.

(e) If necessary, return to modeling.

Step 6: Validation

(a) Validate the integrated model by spawning new scenarios from T-invariants of the nets.

(b) Validate all static constraints.
(c) Present the scenario's with data transformations added.
(d) If necessary, return to one of the modeling steps.

Step 7: User Interface Integration
(a) Make additional classes and methods to accommodate the user interface.
(b) Synchronize the additional methods with the existing ones. If necessary, adapt the logical model.

The steps are not executed in the order presented; it is important that verifications and validations are effectuated as soon as possible in order to reduce costs. For example, step 5a should immediately succeed steps 2abc for the modeled WF nets. Usually, the nets created in 2ab can be verified by hand; the net in 2c often needs tool support [14]. Step 6a can succeed step 2c after verification. Indeed, we have drawn a rather sizable WF net depicting the described process. Afterwards, the logical model is translated into specifications for software components. These components can be constructed from scratch or the can be assembled from existing components. For component selection, the scenario's are helpful.

The steps above apply to systems of moderate size. Large systems should be split into subsystems to which the above steps apply. By synchronization the subsystems are integrated as suggested in section 5 of this paper. This extra integration step should be verified and validated similarly to the description above, concentrating on the interface between the subsystems. We will illustrate the above approach with an example case study.

4 Case Study: A Library System

In the case study we consider a more or less standard library system. Stakeholders are personnel and members that lend books. Several copies of the same book may exist. Members can make reservations for books that are not available. We focus on the modeling steps, in particular the process modeling step. Therefore we treat the other steps rather superficially.

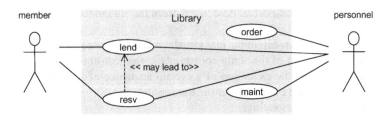

Fig. 3. Library use case diagram

4.1 Elicitation

Fig. 3 depicts typical use cases like lending a book, reserving and then lending a book, ordering books, and maintaining the member file and book catalogue. In Fig. 4 a loan/reserve use case net is given. The initial transition (event) is *s*, which creates a token in place *b* denoting the reservation by a member of a book in the catalogue. If the book is available, a loan is started (transition l_1). If the book is not available, the token stays in place *b* and if a matching book is returned, the reservation object can go to the notified state *d* by transition *n* (notification). From this state, transition l_2 can occur resulting in a loan (a token in *f*). A lent book can get lost (transition *lo*) or it will be returned (transition *re*).

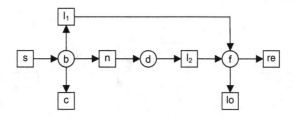

Fig. 4. Request / lend / reserve use case

Similar use cases can be found for maintenance and ordering activities. This is as complicated as it gets in our library case, but for other systems a use case may exhibit concurrent behavior, so it may have states that are distributed over various places. So far we encountered two object classes, reservations in places *b,d*, and loans in place *f*. When treating the other use cases, we encounter members, book orders, book copies, and book titles. It is necessary to distinguish book titles and copies, since several copies can exist for the same title. We determine the following classes (see Fig. 5):

MEM	library member
RSV	reservation **of** title **by** member
LOAN	loan **of** copy **by** member
TITLE	book title
BCPY	copy **of** title
ORD	order **of** title

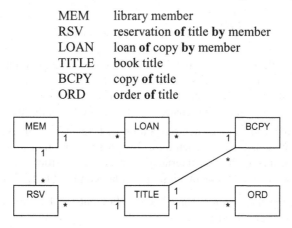

Fig. 5. Relations between object classes

4.2 Process Modeling

The next phase is the modeling of each object's life cycle. A life cycle is composed of create, update and destroy methods, drawn as transitions. The objects correspond to tokens within places; an object class ranges over a set of places. The simple MEM objects only have one state *a*. Other objects may have more states, e.g. BCPY objects may be available for lending (*h*) or not (*g*).

Life cycle modeling starts with projecting the use cases onto the places from one class. The transition l_1 of our example use case thus becomes split into *ln* (creating a loan), *regl* (recording the loan of a book title) and *stal* (creating a loan object). By concentrating on one class, one is likely to find "gaps" in the life cycles found so far, which need to be plugged by adding transitions.

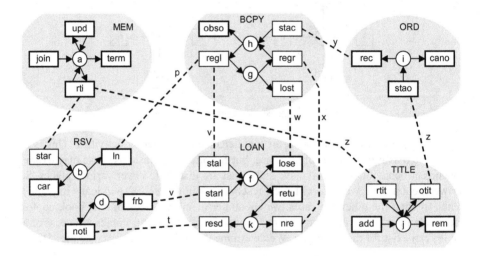

Fig. 6. Integrated library system model

The integrated model in Fig. 6 is obtained by synchronizing the transitions from life cycles that have been split (and some transitions that were added). Every life cycle produced so far should be obtainable by projection from the synchronization result. If not, the inconsistencies should be repaired (and discussed with the stakeholders).

The dashed lines indicating synchronizations are labeled; we will use these labels to identify the data exchanged in synchronization. Also, some transitions communicate with transitions from e.g. the user interface layer. These transitions have thick borders. The transitions, indicated by mnemonics, are explained in Table 1.

In Fig. 7, the synchronizations have been spelled out for the submodel without the classes MEM, ORD and TITLE.

Table 1. Mnemonics for the transitions in the model

MEM	join	start membership
	upd	update member details
	rti	request title
	term	terminate membership
RSV	star	start reservation
	ln	immediate loan
	car	cancel reservation
	noti	notify member
	frb	fetch reserved book
LOAN	stal	start immediate loan
	starl	start reservation loan
	lose	lent book lost
	retu	book return
	nre	title not reserved
	resd	title reserved
BCPY	stac	start copy
	regr	register return
	lost	register loss
	regl	register loan
	obso	write off
ORD	stao	start order
	cano	cancel order
	rec	receive
TITLE	add	add title
	rtit	read title
	otit	order title
	rem	remove

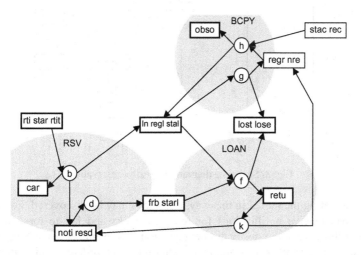

Fig. 7. Integrated model with spelled-out synchronizations (MEM, ORD, TITLE not shown)

4.3 Process Verification and Validation

A verification and validation step is possible before starting the data modeling. It is easy to see that all object life cycles are sound. For the use case in Fig. 4, this is also clear. Also, the use case in Fig. 4 can be obtained by projection on the places *b, d* and *f.*

We next turn to validation of the process model. It is possible to spawn "completed" scenarios by considering T-invariants of the net. A T-invariant is related to sequences of transitions that result in the same state before and after executing them. Each token produced is consumed and vice versa. T-invariant analysis is performed by standard linear algebraic techniques. Since completion of a T-invariant leaves no active token (case) in the net, all cases that were started have been completed, which makes T-invariants good candidates for validation. One rather intricate T-invariant is:

$$2(rti+req)+(ln+regl+stal)+(res+star)+retu+(resd+noti)+(frb+stal)+retu+(nre+regr).$$

This invariant indicates a scenario where two different members request the same book, one obtains a loan and the other a reservation. When the book is returned, the second member lends and finally returns it. The scenario is depicted as a sequence diagram in Fig. 8 and validated as such.

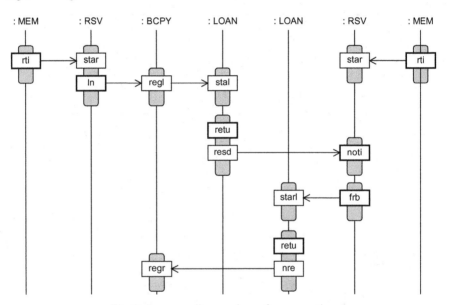

Fig. 8. Sequence diagram: loan after reservation

While validating the model in this way, omissions may be discovered. For instance, members may receive notifications for reserved books and fail to turn up to fetch them. After three days, the reservation expires and it is examined anew whether other reservations exist. Another omission is that after receiving ordered copies, they should be examined for reservations just like returned lent copies. This leads to a redesign of the model: a loan terminates when the book is returned and the BCPY class is extended with states and transitions. This redesign is displayed in Fig. 9. The states of BCPY now become:

e to be checked for reservations
k awaiting notified member
h free for lending
g lent.

The transitions *resd* and *nre* move from class LOAN to BCPY and BCPY is extended with the transition *lres*, a reservation becoming a loan.

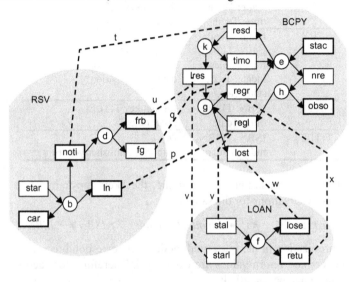

Fig. 9. Revised integrated model (MEM, ORD, TITLE not shown)

4.4 Data Modeling

After constructing and validating the "classical" Petri net model, it becomes appropriate to consider data. The use case models and the events (transitions) that occur in them are helpful in eliciting the data involved. Data can be input data: attribute values of objects related to consumed tokens and input parameters (e.g. from the user interface). Output data are attribute values of objects related to production and output parameters.

By looking at the transitions connected to a certain class, we can produce a list of attributes for each class (Table 2). The boldface attributes are the object's key attributes; many-to-one relations are implemented by including the (foreign) key of the "one" object within the "many" object.

Table 2. Attributes of library classes

MEM	**lcode**: Tcode	membership nr
	name : Tname	name of member
	address : Taddr	address
RSV	**lcode**: Tcode	foreign key MEM
	ISBN: TISBN	foreign key TITLE
	date: Tdate	date of reservation
	state: $\{b,d\}$	
LOAN	**bcode**: Tcode	foreign key BCPY
	lcode: Tcode	foreign key MEM
	date: Tdate	loan date
BCPY	**bcode**: Tcode	key
	ISBN: TISBN	foreign key TITLE
	free: Boolean	available indicator
	indate: Tdate	date of acquisition
	state: $\{e,g,h,k\}$	
ORD	**ISBN**: TISBN	foreign key TITLE
	date: Tdate	order date
TITLE	**ISBN**: TISBN	key
	titdat: Ttitdat	author(s)/publisher/year/title

We can formulate constraints: for example, the "key constraint" that a member cannot have two reservations for the same title:

$$\forall \, r,r' : RSV \mid r \neq r' \, \bullet \, r.lcode \neq r'.lcode \, \lor \, r.ISBN \neq r'.ISBN \, .$$

Each synchronization in the integrated model will correspond to some method call where parameters and return values are exchanged. Therefore, for each synchronization these values must be specified:

p,v	lcode + bcode
q,t,y,z	ISBN
r,u	lcode + ISBN
w,x	bcode.

(Note that in deriving method calls from synchronizations a choice has to be made which object takes the initiative.) By looking at synchronizations that connect objects from different classes, we can verify the modeled relations. An object is often related to objects that are involved in its creation. For example, an ORD object is created from a TITLE object, which accounts for their relation in Fig. 5. Relations can be transferred when creating an object involves destroying another one. For example, a BCPY object is created from an ORD object and it "inherits" its relation to TITLE. The existence of a relation is often the condition for synchronization. The synchronizations t,q and u between RSV and BCPY transitions all have the condition that the book's title matches the reserved title.

4.5 Transformation Modeling

The places in the WF nets contain tokens that correspond to objects. This makes it possible that one object corresponds to several tokens. When consumption and/or production of tokens occurs, the corresponding objects are created, destroyed, read or updated. When synchronization occurs, two or more objects can be accessed at the same time. In some cases, transitions (methods) must "globally" inspect all objects of a given class, which can be done by accessing a global variable containing all objects of this class. This variable has the same name as the class itself. It is not allowed to modify objects in this way; this should be done by the transitions.

For example, *resd* synchronizes with *noti* if a reservation exists and *nre* inspects the RSV variable to make sure that there are no reservations of the given title. If there are several reservations for the considered title, *noti* picks the oldest one, which also requires a global access. A third type of global access occurs when destroying MEM and TITLE objects, which may only occur if there are no other objects that refer to it. Another global variable is *day*, the current date. Table 3 lists which transitions create, read, update, and/or delete objects of each variable.

Table 3. CRUD matrix with transitions from the revised model

		MEM	RSV	BCPY	LOAN	ORD	TITLE	day
MEM	join	c						
	upd	u						
	rti	r					r	
	term	d	r		r			
RSV	star		c					r
	car		d					
	noti		u					r
	fg		d					r
	frb		d					
BCPY	stac			c				r
	resd			u				
	timo			u				
	nre		r	u				
	obso			d				
	regl			u				
	regr			u				
	lost			d				
	lres			u				
LOAN	stal				c			r
	star				c			r
	retu				d			
	lose				d			
ORD	stao					c		r
	cano					d		
	rec					d		
TITLE	add						c	
	otit						r	
	rtit						r	
	rem		r	r		r	d	

We are now in a position to specify every transition by giving pre- and postconditions. To this end we may use the Z language [8]. Each transition specification consists of a header and a body. The header describes the objects of the consumed and produced tokens, indicated by the place name decorated with a question mark (?) respectively exclamation mark (!) symbol. The synchronization labels are not decorated. Additional input and output parameters have been named *in* and *out* respectively. We do not mention global variables in the header.

Z requires that parameters are typed. Table 2 gives the types associated with the object attributes. In the body, conditions for the transition's occurrence are given. Unconnected conditions on different lines are interpreted as connected by conjunction ($\land$ symbol). Conditions only containing inputs must be preconditions; if they are not met, the transition will not occur. Many of the other conditions show how the output depends upon the input. Below we give the specifications for three transitions of the RSV class:

star

a reservation object is created from the synchronization *s*, with date and state added
$s : [l{:}Tcode, t{:}TISBN]$; $b! : RSV$
$(\nexists x : RSV \bullet x.lcode = s.lcode \land x.ISBN = s.ISBN)$ $b!.lcode = s.l \land b!.ISBN = s.t \land b!.date = day \land b!.state = b$

noti

the oldest RSV object matching synchronization *t* is selected and updated; the member and title id are output to the user interface
$t : TISBN$; $b?,d! : RSV$; $out : [l{:}Tcode, t{:}TISBN]$
$(\nexists r : RSV \bullet r.ISBN = b?.ISBN \land r.date < b?.date \land r.state = b)$ $t.ISBN = b?.ISBN \land d! = b? \oplus [state{:}d, date{:}day]$ $out = [l{:}b?.lcode, t{:}b?.ISBN]$

fg

an RSV object in state *d* waiting for more that 3 days is destroyed; its ISBN synchronizes via *q*
$q : TISBN$; $d? : RSV$
$d?.ISBN = q \land d?.date < day - 3$

Before validation, it can be e.g. verified that the reservation key constraint is preserved; when a new reservation id created by transition *star*, it is checked that no reservation with the same member and title code exists.

4.6   Extensions: User Interface Integration

While architects and stakeholders were busy with the logical model, another team of engineers has defined the user interface. It is now time to integrate the two models. For instance, the "request title" (*rti*) transition requires the ISBN number of the requested title as input parameter. The user interface engineers have designed title selection screens to achieve this. These screens do not directly interface to transitions in the logical model, but to an additional class TQRY that allows a user to find out the ISBN number of a book he or she is interested in. The class TQRY has the following transitions (methods):

mqry	make query	the user describes his wishes
dres	display results	a list of titles matching the query is displayed
rqry	refine query	the original query is modified
selt	select title	a title is chosen from the list.

The *selt* transition will synchronize with the *rti* transition defined earlier. In Fig. 10, the life cycle of a TQRY object is given. As attributes, it has a predicate and a set of titles found so far that satisfy the predicate. The "ports" r and z of the *rti* transition have been connected to the *selt* transition and *dres* synchronizes with the TITLE class to filter out the titles matching the predicate. Synchronization thus allows to integrate the different models, also in the technical design phase.

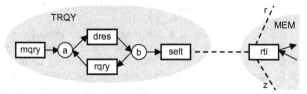

Fig. 10. The subnet for the request-title (*rti*) transition

5   Related Work and Conclusion

The use of Petri nets for the integration of UML models has been recommended by various authors. In all cases, some kind of composition operator is used to connect the various models. In [15], use case modeling with Petri nets is treated in conjunction with transition fusion (extended with place fusion). In [5], UML sequence diagrams that model scenarios are integrated within high-level Petri nets and used for prototyping. In [13], high-level nets are used for prototyping based upon state charts and collaboration diagrams. In [6], a thorough comparison of Petri nets and activity diagrams is given.

In our approach, the combination of synchronization and projection allows to move back and forth between aspect and integrated models, thus improving the consistency between the various aspect models. Current high-level Petri net tools like CPN [9] use token passing (i.e. place fusion) as composition operator. This operator adapts itself more easily to collaboration diagrams. The use of the synchronization operator (transition fusion) makes it easier to work with use cases, class and sequence diagrams. It also smoothens the transition to the design phases where method calls are implemented. Note that many modeling paradigms exist that allow synchronization and projection within Petri nets, c.f. [2,12]. Any such paradigm will do for the purpose described here.

Acknowledgements. We are thankful for the support of our colleagues Ad Aerts, Tim Willemse and Jaap van der Woude and for the efforts of many of our students. It was the teaching of systems analysis and design throughout the years that led to the insights of the present paper.

References

1. W.M.P. van der Aalst. Verification of Workflow Nets. In: P. Azéma and G. Balbo (eds) Proc. ATPN97, Lect. Notes in Comp. Science, Vol. 1248. Springer-Verlag, Berlin (1997)
2. E. Best, W. Fraczak, R.P. Hopkins, H. Klaudel, and E. Pelz. M-nets: an algebra of high-level Petri nets with an application to the semantics of concurrent programming languages. Acta Informatica Vol. 35, No. 10 (1998) 813-857
3. G. Booch, J. Rumbaugh, and I. Jacobson. The Unified Modeling Language User Guide. Addsion-Wesley, Reading (1999)
4. M. Chaudron, K. van Hee, and L. Somers. Use Cases as Workflows. In: W. van der Aalst, A. ter Hofstede, and M. Weske (eds) Proc. BPM 2003, Lecture Notes in Comp. Science, Vol. 2678. Springer-Verlag, Berlin (2003) 88-103
5. Mohammed Elkoutbi and Rudolf K. Keller. User Interface Prototyping Based on UML Scenarios and High-Level Petri Nets. In: M. Nielsen and D. Simpson (eds) Proc. ATPN 2000, Lect. Notes in Comp. Science, Vol. 1825. Springer-Verlag, Berlin (2000) 166-186
6. R. Eshuis and R. Wieringa. A Comparison of Petri Net and Activity Diagram Variants. In: Proc. Int. Coll. Petri Net Tech. Modeling Communication Based Systems (2001)
7. K.M. van Hee. Information Systems Engineering: a Formal Approach. Cambridge University Press, Cambridge (1994)
8. J. Jacky. The way of Z. Cambridge University Press, Cambridge (1997)
9. K. Jensen. Colured Petri Nets. Basic Concepts, Analysis Methods and Practical Use. EATCS monographs on Theoretical Comp. Science. Springer-Verlag, Berlin (1992)
10. R. Milner. Communication and Concurrency. Prentice-Hall, London (1989)
11. J. Nunamaker, A. Dennis, J. Valacich, R. Vogel, and J. George. Electronic Meeting Systems to Support Group Work. CACM Vol. 34, No. 7 (1991) 40-61
12. L. Priese and H. Wimmel. A uniform approach to true-concurrency and interleaving semantics for Petri nets. Theoretical Comp. Science, Vol. 206, No. 1-2 (1998) 219-256
13. J. Saldhana and S.M. Shatz. UML Diagrams to Object Petri Net Models: An Approach for Modeling and Analysis. In: Proc. SEKE'00 (2000) 103-110
14. H.M.W. Verbeek, T. Basten, and W.M.P. van der Aalst. Diagnosing Workflow Processes using Woflan. The Computer Journal, Vol. 44, No. 4 (2001) 246-279
15. J.L Woo, D.C. Sung, and R.K. Yong. Integration and Analysis of Use Cases using Modular Petri Nets in Requirements Engineering. IEEE Trans. on Software Engineering, Vol. 24, No. 12 (1998) 1115-1130

Using TimeNET to Evaluate Operational Planning Processes

Jörn Freiheit and Jonathan Billington

Computer Systems Engineering Centre (CSEC)
University of South Australia
Mawson Lakes, SA, 5095, Australia
{jorn.freiheit,j.billington}@unisa.edu.au

Abstract. In this paper we bridge the gap between performance evaluation and the modelling of business processes. On the basis of a case study from the field of operational planning processes we investigate the performance evaluation of human resource management processes. In particular we consider the affect of timing in operational planning processes. We use TimeNET for modelling. It provides methods needed to analyse the performance of the model.

Keywords: Operational planning processes, performance analysis, coloured stochastic Petri nets

1 Introduction

Performance evaluation of business processes is required to improve their efficiency. The first step in performance evaluation is to build an analysable model of the processes of interest. We thus need to integrate time into our models and aim to optimise the investigated processes using performance evaluation techniques. In military operational planning processes [8], staff members are the main shared resources. Hence, the performance of the process strongly depends on human resource management. We investigate the work load of staff members considering a certain allocation of the staff to the different tasks within the operational planning process. It is shown that coloured stochastic Petri nets [17] are suitable for the description and performance analysis of these processes.

Coloured Petri nets [14] are a well-known extension of Petri nets that provide a compact representation of complex structures and allow the hierarchical decomposition of processes. Stochastic Petri nets [3, 13] provide facilities for describing the time dependent behaviour of concurrent and complex systems. Moreover, there exist analysis methods to evaluate both the functional behaviour and performance of stochastic Petri nets. In this paper we use a dedicated Petri net class [17] that includes some of the modelling power of coloured Petri nets within the stochastic Petri net framework to model and analyse an operational planning process. Coloured stochastic Petri nets are chosen for two reasons. Firstly, as opposed to using only time-stamp based simulation as is currently possible with CPNs using Design/CPN, a simulation of the model's underlying

J. Desel, B. Pernici, and M. Weske (Eds.): BPM 2004, LNCS 3080, pp. 17–32, 2004.

stochastic process with an estimation of the approximation error becomes possible [15]. Secondly, the modelling and analysis tool TimeNET [18] supports the modelling and performance evaluation of coloured stochastic Petri net models. As opposed to other tools handling coloured stochastic Petri nets [4, 12] that only provide numerical analysis methods, TimeNET also contains a discrete event simulation component that allows the performance of models with more than one enabled deterministic transition at the same time [13] to be analysed. Moreover, stochastic *well-formed* nets [11], which are used in [12], require a certain kind of symmetry which renders them ineffective for our case study. For an introduction to the dedicated coloured stochastic Petri net class the reader is referred to [17].

Business processes are ordered sets of business activities. Activities are atomic amounts of work. In operational planning [8], the military staff complete different tasks to deliver a suitable plan. The goal of modelling and analysis of business processes is their optimisation. Performance evaluation of business processes allows several questions to be answered: What is the mean time for a process to be finished? How big is the utilisation of the resources? What are the bottlenecks? How will the above measures change if the available staff decrease e.g. due to leave? There are only few approaches [7,10,1,9] considering time, offering analysis or simulation as a means to evaluate the behaviour of the workflow model. Often the notion of time is limited to the control flow view and to deterministic delays and time constraints. Especially, stochastically distributed durations are mostly neglected [6]. However, employee absence due to sickness and failure of computer systems are common stochastic cases in business processes.

This paper builds on the work of Kristensen et al [16] who have provided the first model of the operational planning process that we wish to investigate. Their model used timed Coloured Petri nets and the tool Design/CPN to simulate the behaviour of the operational planning process. They derived results concerning staff utilisation and the identification of critical staff. In contrast, our model is at a higher level of abstraction and includes an updating mechanism to cope with intelligence reports occurring during the process. It also has flexibility to include stochastic or fixed durations for major activities of the process. We consider an allocation of 10 staff to the process. We assume that some staff (*required*) are essential for a particular activity, but that the process can be improved if further staff (*desired*) are allocated if they are available. We compute staff workload and mean process duration for both deterministic and stochastic cases and compare them.

The remainder of this paper is organised as follows: Section 2 briefly introduces the modelling methodology which is used in this paper. The model of the operational planning process is presented in Section 3. Section 4 presents the quantitative investigation of our model and Section 5 concludes the paper.

2   Methodology

Using TimeNET, a *resource model* and associated *workflow models* are required. The resource model describes the structure of the modelled process, the resources and their possible assignments within the process. A workflow model describes a certain behaviour of an object (staff member, document, etc.) within the process.

The resource model and the workflow models are merged automatically using the modelling and analysis tool TimeNET [18]. We shall explain the modelling methodology using a simple holiday reservation example. Dedicated Petri nets can be hierarchically structured. Figure 1 shows the highest level page of the booking resource model. Transitions with thick bars (see T1 in our example) are called *substitution transitions*, acting as place holders for submodels describing their behaviour in more detail on a lower level of the hierarchy. The places P1

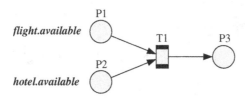

Fig. 1. Highest level page of the booking resource model

and P2 are initially marked with the tokens *flight.available* and *hotel.available*. *Object tokens* model staff, orders, commands, letters etc. inside the modelled system and consist of a name and a current state. *Elementary tokens* cannot be distinguished and are thus equivalent to tokens from uncoloured Petri nets. They are used to model states of the resources, for instance whether desired staff are available or not. Places can contain only tokens of one type. The model in Figure 1 only shows object places, i.e. places that contain object tokens only. Object tokens comprise the name of the token and a more detailed description, such as the state, separated by a dot (*string.string*). The token *flight.available* describes an available flight and the token *hotel.available* symbolises an available hotel. The submodel of the substitution transition T1 is shown in Figure 2. Places

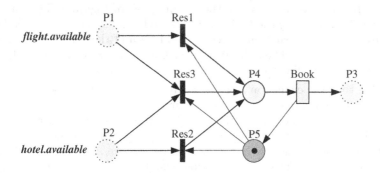

Fig. 2. Subpage of the resource model

shown as dotted circles are fused with the corresponding places on the higher level.

The place P5 is an elementary place containing an elementary token. This place models the sequential nature of reserving (Res1, Res2 and Res3) and booking (Book) flights and hotels. The exact behaviour of a transition is specified in a *workflow model*. The resource model describes all *possible* paths of tokens through the model while a workflow model specifies one certain path of coloured tokens through the resource model. Workflow models are hierarchically structured in the same manner as the resource model. The highest level page of our example's workflow model has the same structure as the resource model shown in Figure 1. Figure 3 shows the workflow submodel of transition T1. The work-

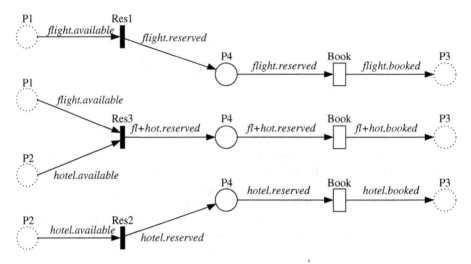

Fig. 3. Subpage of the workflow model

flow model in Figure 3 describes two different cases of booking. Either the flight and the hotel are booked separately or the flight and the hotel are booked together. The last case is shown in the middle path of Figure 3. The immediate transition Res3 reserves the flight and the hotel. The token *flight.available* and *hotel.available* disappear from places P1 and P2 and the token *fl+hot.reserved* appears on place P4. Then the transition Book can fire consuming the token *fl+hot.reserved* yielding the token *fl+hot.booked* on place P3.

Notice that the elementary places are not shown in the workflow model because they are only used to model the resources of the process but not the process itself. The resource model and the workflow models are merged resulting in a hierarchical model that has the same structure as the resource model (containing also the elementary places). In the merged model *binding tables* are associated with transitions. For example transition's Book binding table comprises three bindings (in TimeNET notation):

```
#in(P4):1'flight.reserved #out(P3): 1'flight.booked, #out(P5):1'e;
#in(P4):1'fl+hot.reserved #out(P3): 1'fl+hot.booked, #out(P5):1'e;
#in(P4):1'hotel.reserved #out(P3): 1'hotel.booked, #out(P5):1'e;
```

Moreover bindings are extended by further information. A binding of a transition depends on a *local guard*, which needs to be true to enable the binding. If the transition is a timed transition, the binding also contains the firing delay. Hence, it is possible to define different delays for different bindings of a transition. If the transition is an immediate transition the priority of the binding can be specified.

Merging the resource model and the workflow models is done automatically by TimeNET [18]. A detailed description of this compilation algorithm is given in [17].

3   A Coloured Stochastic Petri Net Model of JMAP

For the planning of operations the Deployable Joint Force Headquarters of the Australian Defence Force uses a process called the *Joint Military Appreciation Process* (JMAP) [2]. In [16] an overview of a detailed model of JMAP is presented using hierarchical timed coloured Petri nets [14]. Unlike [16], in our model an update strategy is integrated which introduces concurrency within the operational planning process. This strategy allows fast results of the entire process although the quality of the early results can be low. Another difference to [16] is that we investigate the underlying stochastic process of our model. While in [16] time stamps are used to analyse the numerical behaviour of the model, we use the discrete event simulation component of TimeNET [18] to analyse the stochastic behaviour of the model. This allows us to use not only deterministic but also exponentially distributed firing times.

In stochastic Petri nets (SPNs) [3] each transition has an associated distribution function describing its firing delay. Transitions depicted as a bar fire immediately without delay. Transitions drawn as empty rectangles have an exponentially distributed firing time, while transitions with deterministic delay are depicted as filled rectangles. The time dependent (stochastic) behaviour of the model is given by the initial marking and the subsequent transition firings, describing a stochastic process [5]. The type of process depends on the types of allowed firing delays and whether certain transitions are enabled together in one marking (state) or not. Further information on SPNs can be found in [13].

There are only a few tools for the analysis of coloured stochastic Petri nets [12, 4, 18]. However, [12, 4] do not provide a simulation component for coloured stochastic Petri nets but allow only the numerical analysis of them with the restriction that at most one transition with deterministic (or general) firing time may be enabled at the same time. Hence, models of the operational planning process with deterministic transitions are not analysable using these tools. Moreover, stochastic *well-formed* nets [11] that are handled in [12] require a certain kind of symmetry that is not found in operational planning processes.

3.1   Resource Model

Figure 4 shows the highest level page of the coloured stochastic Petri net resource model of JMAP. Figure 4 shows the four steps of JMAP: MissionAnalysis, COADevelopment, COAAnalysis and DecisionExecution. The process starts with a Preliminary Scoping Process. The places between these subtasks model their connection. The names of the places are constructed using the first letters of the names of connecting steps. The place P contains an initial token

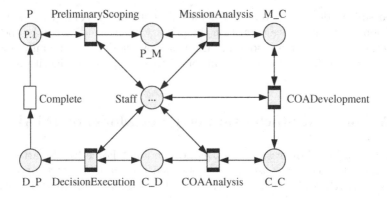

Fig. 4. Highest level page of the JMAP resource model

P.1 which symbolises the beginning of the process. The place Staff contains ten tokens S.1,... ,S.10 modelling ten staff members who are involved in JMAP. Due to the lack of space, the tokens are not depicted but instead three dots are shown. As the structures of the five substitution transitions are identical, we only explain the MissionAnalysis submodel in more detail.

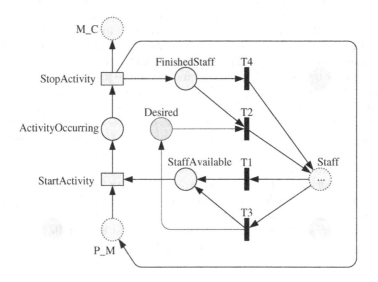

Fig. 5. Mission Analysis subpage – resource model

Figure 5 shows the detailed submodel (*subpage*) for Mission Analysis. It contains two timed (StartActivity and StopActivity) and four immediate transitions (T1,T2,T3,T4). StartActivity models the time spent preparing to start the Mission Analysis subtask, while StopActivity models the time taken to process the task until its completion.

In the submodel for **Mission Analysis** shown in Figure 5 there are three fusion places P_M, M_C, and **Staff** and one elementary place **Desired**. The elementary place is grey filled. This place is marked if desired staff members are available and appointed to the mission analysis task. Again, the initial marking S.1,...,S.10 of place **Staff** is not shown in detail. The immediate transitions T1 and T3 model the use of the required or desired staff members respectively. These transitions show the use of immediate transitions in stochastic Petri nets. They model a stochastic choice between two alternatives. Using priorities for immediate transitions the modeller can define which of the transition fires if both are enabled. Another concept for immediate transitions are weights that allows to specify the stochastic choice of either of the transitions. In our model we use priorities for transitions T1 and T3 to define that the task will be processed either by desired or by required staff members only. Note that we shall define a guard (**ready**) for transitions T1 and T3 that controls that these transitions can fire only if place P_M is marked adequately (see Figures 6-8) preventing withholding staff from other tasks that could be started. It must also be noticed that though the fusion places M_C and P_M belong to the postset of transition **StopActivity**, it is not necessary that both places are marked after the firing of the transition.

3.2 Workflow Models

The highest level page of the workflow model (not shown) of the JMAP is very similar to the highest level page of the resource model except the places **Staff** and P do not contain tokens initially. Workflow models can be described in the same hierarchical manner as resource models. Figure 6 shows a workflow model of the Mission Analysis in detail. Each element of the workflow model has a corresponding element of the resource model emphasised by identical names.

This workflow model describes the way of a token PM.1 taken from the place P_M through the Mission Analysis model. After the treatment of PM.1 a new token U.1 appears on P_M describing the start of the first update of the Mission Analysis step. Additionally, a token MC.1 is added to place M_C describing the start condition of the COA Development step. The digit 1 in PM.1 stands for the first treatment of the token PM. After a first update of the preliminary process (not shown), a token PM.2 appears in place P_M. For the token PM.2 another workflow model is specified which is explained later.

The immediate transition T3 models the appointment of the required (S.5+ S.6+S.7+S.8) *and* desired (S.9+S.10+S.1+S.2) staff members to the processing of the mission analysis task. Due to the definition of the resource model the elementary place **Desired** becomes marked (see Figure 5). If only the required staff members S.5,S.6,S.7,S.8 are available and the desired staff members S.9,S.10,S.1,S.2 are not, only transition T1 is enabled and T3 is disabled. After firing of T1, only the required staff are appointed to the task and the place **Desired** remains unmarked during the task is in progress.

Elementary places are not part of workflow models because their markings depend on the resources of the process. In our model, the place **Desired** is marked iff desired staff members are appointed to the task. However, it is possible to define boolean expressions which values depend on the marking of elementary

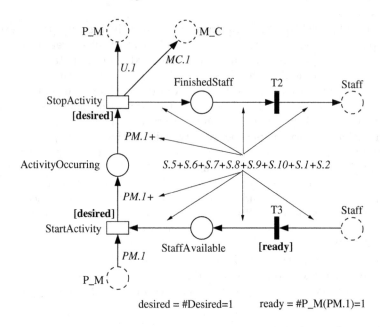

Fig. 6. Mission Analysis subpage – workflow model for desired processing

places. Such an expression is shown in Figure 6. The expression desired is true
if the place Desired is marked (let M be the current marking, then #Desired=1
stands for M(Desired)=1). This expression is used as a guard for the transitions
StartActivity and StopActivity. The reason for these guards is explained
later when the workflow model for the required processing is presented (see
Figure 7. In Figure 6 there is another guard, ready, which evaluates the marking
of place P_M. Only if there is a token PM.1 in place P_M, the appointment of staff
members starts. After processing the task, the staff members are added back to
place Staff by firing immediate transition T2.

In the centre of Figure 6 the arc inscriptions are shown. The arc inscriptions
are identical for all arcs except the arcs connected with transitions StartActivity and StopActivity. The arc connecting place P_M and transition Start-
Activity is inscribed with PM.1, describing that place P_M must be marked with
token PM.1 to enable transition StartActivity. Transition StartActivity is
enabled if place P_M is marked with token PM.1 and place StaffAvailable is
marked with tokens S.5, S.6, S.7, S.8, S.9, S.10, S.1, S.2 and the expression desired is true. After firing of transition StartActivity under this
assignment the tokens PM.1 and S.5, S.6, S.7, S.8, S.9, S.10, S.1, S.2
disappear from places P_M and StaffAvailable respectively and appear on place
ActivityOccurring. Hence, the presented workflow model describes *one* binding of transition StartActivity.

Another binding of that transition is modelled in Figure 7. This workflow
model describes the *required* processing of the task if token PM.1 marks the
place P_M. For the required processing of the Mission Analysis subtask, the staff

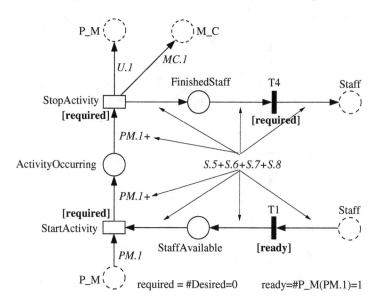

Fig. 7. Mission Analysis subpage – workflow model for required processing

members S.5, S.6, S.7, S.8 are allocated. The expression `required` is true
if the elementary place `Desired` (see Figure 5) is unmarked. The immediate
transition T4 can be enabled only if its guard, the expression `required`, is true.
If there would be no guard associated with transition T4, the transition would
be also enabled during the desired processing when the tokens S.5, S.6, S.7,
S.8, S.9, S.10, S.1, S.2 are in the place `FinishedStaff`. This explains why
we need the `Desired` place and related expressions and shows a weakness of the
approach compared to other high-level nets which allows the use of variables to
describe the behaviour of transitions.

After the desired and required processing of the Mission Analysis, a token
U.1 is added to place P_M and a token MC.1 is added to place M_C. The token U.1
symbolises the first update of the Mission Analysis process while the marking
MC.1 in place M_C symbolises the starting condition of the COA Development
subtask. The first update processing of the Mission Analysis subtask is shown
in the workflow model in Figure 8. After the first update of the Preliminary
Process, a token PM.2 appears in place P_M. If the staff members S.5, S.6,
S.7, S.8, S.9, S.10, S.1, S.2 are available (`StaffAvailable`), the transition `StartActivity` is enabled if the tokens PM.2 and U.1 mark the place P_M.
The firing of transition `StartActivity` under this assignment symbolises the
start of the first situation update of the Mission Analysis subtask. The model
in Figure 8 describes the process for the first situation update with the required
and desired staff members. There is another workflow model, describing the first
situation update of the Mission Analysis subtask using the required staff members only, which is not shown. This model also has workflow models for a second
and third situation update for both the desired and required processing. After
the third situation update no token U.4 is created but only a token MC.4 which is

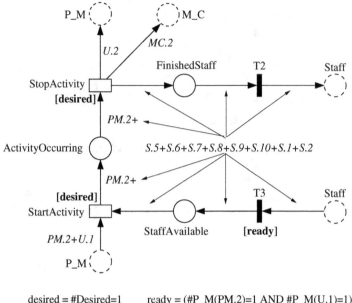

desired = #Desired=1   ready = (#P_M(PM.2)=1 AND #P_M(U.1)=1)

Fig. 8. Mission Analysis subpage – workflow model for first update of the Mission Analysis – desired processing

added to place M_C. Hence, after the third situation update of Mission Analysis, the task is completed.

4 Quantitative Analysis

In this section we present performance results for the JMAP model. The discrete-event simulation component of TimeNET [18] is used. The impact of different firing time distributions of the transitions is investigated. We consider certain staff allocations to the different tasks of JMAP. In our model ten staff members are initially available (S1,...,S10). It should be noticed that in a realistic JMAP about 130 staff members are involved. However, the model is easily extendable. We investigate the staff allocation presented in Table 1 which is arbitrarily chosen.

There are always pairs of staff members that are allocated for the same tasks (e.g. S1 and S2). Note that the tasks are processed under two different allocations, either only by required staff or by required and desired staff. That means that e.g. the Preliminary Process can be processed either by only S1, S2, S3 and S4 or by the staff members S1,...,S8. In the following we investigate the improvement of task processing by the latter allocation (*desired processing*) compared with task processing only by required staff (*required processing*).

Table 1. Staff Allocation

Step	Required Staff	Desired Staff
Preliminary Scoping	S1, S2, S3, S4	S5, S6, S7, S8
Mission Analysis	S5, S6, S7, S8	S9, S10, S1, S2
COA Development	S9, S10, S1, S2	S3, S4, S5, S6
COA Analysis	S3, S4, S5, S6	S7, S8, S9, S10
Decision&Evaluation	S7, S8, S9, S10	S1, S2, S3, S4

4.1 Questions of Interest

We want to answer three different questions. Firstly we investigate the utilisation of the staff members. As shown in Table 1, each staff member is twice required and twice desired to process tasks. The processing times (StartActivity and StopActivity) of each task are considered to be equal. Thus, we could conjecture that the utilisation of staff members will be equal. If the performance evaluation reveals that the work load of the staff members is not identical, we investigate which staff members are the most busy.

The second question we answer is: How much faster must the desired processing be compared to the required processing for it to be worthwhile? There will be times when staff could be used in a task for which they are required, or alternatively, that task could be postponed and the staff used in another task for which they are desired. Hence, we successively decrease the firing delays of the transitions which model the desired processing and consider a higher priority of the desired processing. That means that if not only the required but also the desired staff members for a subtask are available, the subtask is processed with the required *and* desired staff members.

Thirdly, we investigate if the results for the first and second questions are different if the firing times are fixed or exponentially distributed.

22 different models have been investigated, 11 models with only deterministic transitions and another 11 with exponential transitions. In ten of the models for each case, the firing delays vary from 1 to 10 minutes while the desired processing has higher priority than the required processing. The eleventh model describes the behaviour for prioritised required processing when the firing delays of the transitions are 10 minutes. Each simulation run took about 10 minutes on a PC with 2.4 GHz CPU and 512 Mb main memory. For all evaluations, a confidence interval of 99% and a relative error probability of 3% is chosen, to provide high accuracy for the simulation.

4.2 Deterministic Durations of Activities

In this section we evaluate the model under the consideration that all activities are of fixed duration. Hence, in the model the time transitions StartActivity and StopActivity of all tasks are associated with deterministic firing delays.

Firstly we assume that the immediate transition T1 has a higher priority than T3 for all tasks. This models that always the required staff will be chosen to process the task. The firing delays of the transitions `StartActivity` and `StopActivity` are set to 10 (minutes). Under these assumptions the mean processing time for the whole process is 256.4 minutes.

The whole process consists of processing the preliminary process and the four steps described in section 3 with three situation updates. After the third update of the Decision and Execution subtask, a token `DP.4` is generated on place `D_P` (see Figure 4). The transition `Complete` models the completion of the entire process and starts it again (taking tokens `DP.1+ ... +DP.4` from place `D_P` and adding a token `P.1` to the place `P`). The firing delay of transition `Complete` is set to 10. The throughput of transition `Complete` is derived by computing the performance measure `P[#D_P(DP.4)>0]/10` describing the probability that transition `Complete` is enabled divided by the transition's firing delay equals 10. The term $1/throughput(Complete)$ computes the mean processing duration of the whole process.

4.3   Varying the Firing Delays for Desired Processing

Each task processing by desired staff decelerates the process because the desired staff are not available for tasks which require them. Hence, we answer the following question: How much faster must the tasks processed by desired staff be, so that the mean processing duration of the complete process is less than or equal to that processed only by required staff? In other words: When is it worthwhile to chose not only required but also desired staff to process a task? To evaluate this, the model is changed into two directions. The immediate transition T3 of each task has higher priority than T1 to model that always T3 fires if both transitions are enabled concurrently (desired processing instead of required processing). This can be done by changing the priorities of the transitions T3 of each subpage in the resource model. Additionally the firing delays of transitions `StartActivity` and `StopActivity` vary between 1 and 10 (minutes) when they fire under the assignment for desired staff. This is done by changing the firing delays of the corresponding transitions in the workflow models.

Figure 9 shows the duration of the entire process for varied firing delays of the transitions `StartActivity` and `StopActivity` for desired processing. For the firing delays set to 10 and prioritising the desired processing the duration of the entire process is 357 minutes, 100 minutes longer than if only the required processing takes place. Each subtask must be processed about 40% faster for the desired case than for the required case to obtain any improvement by using the additional desired staff (i.e. when the delay of all tasks that are processed by required *and* desired staff members is 6 minutes, the total duration reduces to 244 minutes, which is less than 256 minutes for the required processing).

Figure 10 shows the idle times of the staff members for the deterministic case. Unexpectedly, idle times of staff members are different. While the idle time of staff members `S.9` and `S.10` is 27.5% for firing delays set to 6 minutes, it is only 24.0% for `S.5` and `S.6`, a difference of 3.5%. Although all staff members are desired for two subtasks each and required for two subtasks each and the tasks have the same delay distributions, their availability is different. It should be noticed that staff utilisation is identical for each staff member if we consider

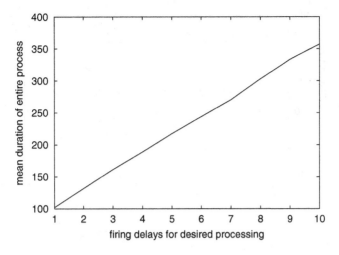

Fig. 9. Duration of the entire process for varying firing delays of desired processing – deterministic case

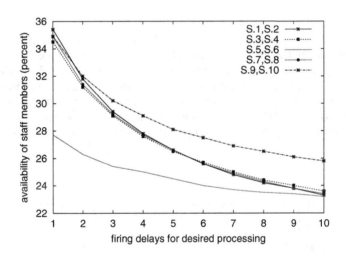

Fig. 10. Availability of staff members – deterministic case

purely required or purely desired processing, respectively. This is due to the sequential manner of the process. The order of subtasks to which staff members are allocated affects staff utilisation.

4.4 Exponentially Distributed Firing Times

Now we consider the process under the assumption that the processing times are exponentially distributed instead of deterministic which is yet less discussed in literature.

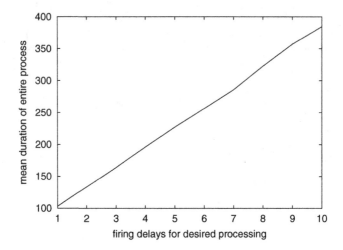

Fig. 11. Duration of the entire process for varying firing delays of desired processing
– exponential case

Figure 11 shows the duration until completion of the entire process for varying firing delays of the timed transitions if the desired processing has higher priority than the required processing. For the firing delays set to 10 and prioritising the required processing, the duration of the entire process is 277.8 minutes. For the firing delays set to 10 and prioritising the desired processing the duration of the entire process is 384.6 minutes. Only for firing delays equal to 6 or less the desired processing is worthwhile compared to the required processing.

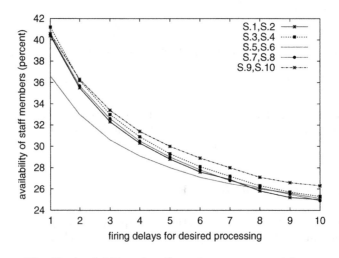

Fig. 12. Availability of staff members – exponential case

With the exponential distribution function, the average work load of all staff members is not as different as for the deterministic case, as shown in Figure 12. Again, the staff members S.5 and S.6 have the biggest work load, but this is e.g. for delays equals 6 only 1.8% higher on average than for S.9 and S.10.

5 Conclusions

In this paper an operational planning process is modelled and its performance is analysed. Using TimeNET, the proposed staff allocation is evaluated. Although each staff member is required for two tasks and desired for another two tasks, the work load of the staff members are different, even though each task has the same distribution and duration. Moreover, the difference between a purely deterministic model and the model with exponentially distributed firing rates is presented. The mean duration of the entire process is slightly bigger for the exponential model than for the deterministic one. However, the range of work loads of staff members for the deterministic model is significantly wider than for the exponential case.

In future we will investigate the modelling and analysis of different scheduling strategies for the Joint Military Appreciation Process using stochastic Petri nets.

Acknowledgements. The authors would like to thank Lin Zhang and Brice Mitchell of the Defence Science & Technology Organisation for their valuable discussions about JMAP and Armin Zimmermann of the Technische Universität Berlin for his support concerning TimeNET. The authors also gratefully acknowledge the helpful comments from the anonymous referees.

References

1. W.M.P. van der Aalst. Interval Timed Coloured Petri Nets and their Analysis. In M. Ajmone Marsan, editor, *Application and Theory of Petri Nets 1993*, volume 691, pages 453–472. Springer-Verlag, Berlin, 1993.
2. Australian Defence Force Publications (ADFP). *Joint Military Appreciation Process*. Operations Series 9, Joint Planning, Chapter 8, 1999.
3. G. Balbo G. Conte S. Donatelli Ajmone Marsan, M. and G. Franceschinis. *Modelling with Generalized Stochastic Petri Nets*. John Wiley & Sons, 1995.
4. F. Bause and P. Kemper. QPN-Tool for the qualitative and quantitative analysis of Queueing Petri Nets. In G. Haring and G. Kotsis, editors, *Computer Performance Evaluation, Modelling Techniques and Tools 94*, volume 794 of *Lecture Notes in Computer Science*, pages 321–334, 1994.
5. G. Ciardo, R. German, and Ch. Lindemann. A characterization of the stochastic process underlying a stochastic Petri net. *IEEE Transactions on Software Engineering*, 20:506–515, 1994.
6. J. Dehnert, J. Freiheit, and A. Zimmermann. Modeling and Evaluation of Time Aspects in Business Processes. *Journal of the Operational Research Society (JORS)*, 53(8):138–147, 2002.

7. J. Desel and T. Erwin. Modeling, simulation and analysis of business processes. In W. van der Aalst, J. Desel, and A. Oberweis, editors, *Business Process Management: Models, Techniques and Empirical Studies*, volume 1806 of *LNCS*. Springer-Verlag, 2000.

8. Deployable Joint Force Headquarters (DJFHQ). *SOP 310 – The Operational Planning Process*. 2001.

9. J. Eder, E. Panagos, H. Pozewaunig, and M. Rabinovich. Time Management in Workflow Systems. In W. Abramowicz and M.E. Orlowska, editors, *BIS'99 3rd International Conference on Business Information Systems*, pages 265–280. Springer Verlag, 1999.

10. C.A. Ellis, K. Keddara, and J. Wainer. Modeling Workflow Dynamic Change Using Timed Hybrid Flow Nets. In W.M.P. van der Aalst, G. De Michelis, and C. A. Ellis, editors, *Workflow Management: Net-based Concepts, Models, Techniques and Tools (WFM'98)*, volume 98/7 of *Computing Science Reports*, pages 109–128. Eindhoven University of Technology, Eindhoven, 1998.

11. G. Franceschinis G. Chiola, C. Dutheillet and S. Haddad. Stochastic well-formed coloured nets for symmetric modelling applications. *IEEE Transactions on Computers*, 42(11):1343–1360, 1993.

12. R. Gaeta G. Chiola, G. Franceschinis and M. Ribaudo. GreatSPN 1.7: Graphical Editor and Analyzer for Timed and Stochastic Petri Nets. *Performance Evaluation, special issue on Performance Modeling Tools*, 24(1,2):47–68, 1995.

13. R. German. *Performance Analysis of Communication Systems: Modeling with Non-Markovian Stochastic Petri Nets*. John Wiley and Sons, 2000.

14. K. Jensen. *Coloured Petri Nets. Basic Concepts, Analysis Methods and Practical Use, Volume 1-3*. EATCS Monographs on Theoretical Computer Science. Springer-Verlag, 1997.

15. Ch. Kelling and G. Hommel. Rare Event Simulation with an Adaptive RESTART Method in a Petri Nets Simulation Environment. In *4th Workshop on Parallel and Distributed Real-Time Systems*, pages 229–234, Honolulu, HI, USA, 1996.

16. Lars M. Kristensen, Brice Mitchell, Lin Zhang, and Jonathan Billington. Modelling and initial analysis of operational planning processes using coloured petri nets. In *Formal Methods in Software Engineering and Defence Systems 2002*, pages 105–114, Adelaide, Australia, 2002.

17. A. Zimmermann, S. Bode, and G. Hommel. Performance and Dependability Evaluation of Manufacturing Systems Using Petri Nets. In *1st Workshop on Manufacturing Systems and Petri Nets, 17th Int. Conf. on Application and Theory of Petri Nets*, pages 235–250, Osaka, Japan, 1996.

18. A. Zimmermann, J. Freiheit, R. German, and G. Hommel. Petri net modelling and performability evaluation with TimeNET 3.0. In *Proc. 11th Int. Conf. on Modelling Techniques and Tools for Computer Performance Evaluation*, pages 188–202, Chicago, USA, 2000.

Business Objectives as Drivers for Process Improvement: Practices and Experiences at Thales Naval The Netherlands (TNNL)

Jos J.M. Trienekens[1,2], Rob J. Kusters[1,3], Ben Rendering[4], and Kees Stokla[4]

[1]Eindhoven University of Technology, Den Dolech 2, 5600 MB Eindhoven, The Netherlands
{J.J.M.Trienekens, R.J.Kusters}@tm.tue.nl
[2]KEMA, Utrechtseweg 310, Arnhem, The Netherlands
[3]Open University, Valkenburgerweg 177, Heerlen, The Netherlands
[4]Thales NNL, Zuidelijke Havenweg 40, 7554 RR Hengelo, The Netherlands
{ben.rendering, kees.stokla)@nl.thalesgroup.com

Abstract. Over the last decade many organizations are increasingly concerned with the improvement of their hardware/software development processes. The Capability Maturity Model (CMM) and ISO9001 are well-known approaches that are applied in these initiatives. One of the major bottlenecks to the success of process improvement is the lack of business orientation. This paper reports on a process improvement initiative at Thales Naval Netherlands (TNNL). It presents an approach that has been followed to ensure a link between process improvement and business strategy. Main factors in this process improvement approach are goal decomposition and the implementation of goal-oriented measurement on three organizational levels, i.e. the business, the process and the team level.

Keywords: process improvement, goal decomposition, measurement

1 Introduction

Thales Naval Netherlands (TNNL) creates high-tech defence solutions for naval and ground based environments. This paper addresses a process improvement initiative in the business unit Radar & Sensors (R&S) that started in 2002. This business unit has an extensive expertise in the fields of radar, infrared, weapon control, display technology and communications equipment.

In 2001 a pre-assessment of the quality management system for the overall hardware/software production creation process, on the basis of the new ISO9001:2000 standard, showed that the current quality system didn't meet the new ISO requirements. Shortcomings were identified from different ISO9001:2000 viewpoints, respectively:

- Restricted business orientation of quality management and business process improvement.
- Lack of control loops.
- No feedback mechanism for continuous improvement (closing the control loops).

J. Desel, B. Pernici, and M. Weske (Eds.): BPM 2004, LNCS 3080, pp. 33–48, 2004.

Confronted with the new ISO-requirements and the actual shortcomings, the organization decided for a redesign of its quality management approaches and business improvement programs. The two main approaches at TNNL, that had been applied already for a period of 10 years, were respectively: ISO9001, as developed by the International Organization for Standardization [5], and the Capability Maturity Model (CMM) as developed by the Software Engineering Institute [9]. ISO9001 is related to business processes and specifies the minimal requirements for a quality system. This standard has been applied at TNNL to develop a quality management system for the overall hardware/software production creation process. CMM addresses explicitly concepts for continuous software process improvement. CMM has been applied at TNNL in particular in software development departments. One department in the R&S business unit reached the CMM level 3 (out of five levels, of that level one is the lowest and level five is the highest). This means that a reasonable level of maturity has been reached in the development process in terms of the formality and the structuredness of processes. Processes on level 3 are characterized as 'defined'. Both approaches, ISO9001 and CMM, can be considered to have complementary philosophies regarding quality and process management [9]. However, integration or combination of the two approaches is not easy because of the differences in business orientation, i.e. business processes in general versus software development processes. The kernel focus for integration or combination of the two approaches is the concept of continuous improvement. Regarding improvement ISO9001 can be considered to have an open 'loop control'. This means that the actions of a business system are independent of the control system output, i.e. there is no explicit feedback mechanism used for the tuning of actions and the continuous improvement of them. 'Closed loop control', as addressed in the CMM, is based on the application of metrics to modify actions on the basis of the control system output [4]. It was decided at TNNL to adopt the concept of 'closed loop control' and to elaborate this concept in the context of ISO9001:2000. The 'closed loop' concept, i.e. its explicit feedback mechanism, implies the application of business process measurement. Regarding measurement an approach that has been used already for a number of years in software development environments is Goal Question Metric (GQM) [6] [7]. GQM supports answering questions such as: how can be decided what needs to be measured, when should this be measured and where in the product creation process? In this way an ad-hoc and unsystematic application of metrics and the collection of irrelevant data is avoided. In order to get grip on the measurement problem two important assumptions are respectively (a) a metrics program should not be 'metrics based' but 'goal based' and (b) the definition of goals and measures need to be tailored to the individual organization. In particular the latter assumption was of interest at TNNL to link business improvement to the business strategy [1], [8].

Taking into account, both the identified shortcomings of the TNNL quality management system, and the need for measurement-based continuous improvement, a new process improvement initiative was launched. This initiative is aimed at ensuring a link between business strategy and the product creation process. Main issues in this initiative are respectively goal decomposition, continuous improvement and the development of goal-oriented measurement.

The structure of the paper is as follows. Section 2 introduces respectively: the business processes at TNNL, the identified problems and the directions for solution as formulated by the TNNL management. Section 3 presents a framework that acts as a basis of reference for the improvement initiative. Section 4 elaborates the framework and addresses goal decomposition and the development of goal-oriented measurement in the process improvement initiative. Examples from practice clarify the approach that has been followed. Section 5 contains conclusions and directions for future work.

2 Business Processes at TNNL, Practices, Problems, and Solutions

In the product creation process at TNNL two main primary process chains can be distinguished. Chain 1 reflects development of new and derivative products. Chain 2 describes the development of repeat products. In Chain 1 the processes, in particular requirements analysis and design, are strongly driven by specific customer requirements. In Chain 1 the processes are driven by the characteristics of existing product components. Both process chains are facilitated by a number of supporting process areas. For these areas, departments have been set up to support operational teams in the product creation process. Examples are a Configuration Management, a Data Management, and a Human Resource department. Furthermore outsourcing is supported explicitly. Because the main focus in the improvement initiative was on the two primary process chains, these are presented below.

2.1 Processes in Practice: The Chains

Chain 1. The most important chain 1 processes are depicted in Figure 1. We can distinguish Proposal & Contracting, System Requirements Analysis & Design, Product Development – Integration - Verification & Validation, System Integration - Verification & Validation, and Warranty. Each of these processes will be described.

Fig. 1. Chain 1: development of new and derivative products

Proposal and Contracting (P&C). This process consists of activities such as the intake of a request, i.e. the translation of requirements into a proposal, the tuning with the product portfolio, the response to the customer, and negotiation tasks.

System Requirement Analysis and System Design (SRA/SD). In the analysis part of this process the customer requirements are translated into a system concept that is the basis for a complete system requirements specification. The system concept is validated with the various stakeholders in the development process. In this process also a feasibility estimate is established. The system design part of the SRA/SD process refines the system concept, based on the availability of building blocks and well-founded make or buy decisions.

Product Development, Integration, Verification and Validation (PDIVV). This process realises the system according to the agreed specifications, assigns the work to be done to the production department or subcontractors and delivers the system components.

System Integration, Verification and Validation (SIVV). In this process the components are integrated. The final product is verified and validated against the original customer and system requirements.

Warranty. Regarding the warranty period of a product, activities are specified for system acceptation, receiving customer complaints on product failure, investigating defects and repairing defects.

Chain 2. The chain 2 processes describe the product creation activities of repeat products (see Figure 2). The Proposal, Contracting, and Warranty processes in this Chain are identical to those in Chain 1 and need no further introduction. The remaining processes are described below.

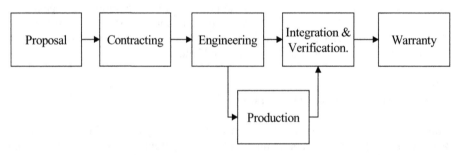

Fig. 2. Chain 2: development of repeat products

Engineering, Integration & Verification, Production. In these processes activities are carried out such as the determination of changes that have to be made to an existing product and of the validation of these changes. If reengineering is required of some parts of a product several sub processes or activities of chain 1 (mainly from the processes SRA/SD, PDIVV, SIVV) can be applied.

2.2 Problems and Directions for Improvement

In 2001 an independent quality assessment at TNNL based on the ISO9001:2000 standard was carried out. In this assessment the two primary process chains have been investigated together with the facilitating areas. ISO9001:2000 in particular emphasizes, in comparison with the previous ISO9001 standard:

- Business processes should be the basis for quality management. In particular those processes should be addressed in a quality management system, that are of critical importance for the business system as a whole,

- A quality management system explicitly focussed on continuous improvement, as opposed to the more static view of the previous standard,
- This continuous improvement should be (visibly) based on formal measurement,
- Management should be explicitly involved in the design and implementation of the quality management system.

The assessment results were summarized in three major problems that will be addressed below. For each of the problems the TNNL management defined a direction for improvement. The result is depicted below.

Table 1. Problems and associated improvement actions

Problem:	Improvement action:
There is a lack of insight in the critical parts of business processes. This is in particular caused by the absence of a clear link between primary processes and the business strategy.	The management at TNNL decided to introduce goal decomposition starting at the level of business strategy down to the level of primary processes and operational teams. In the improvement initiative only those processes, and their interrelations, will be addressed that contribute explicitly to the business strategy, see [1].
Continuous improvement, i.e. the specification, execution and control of improvement activities, is insufficiently addressed. In fact the emphasis in the current quality management system is on the specification of procedures for operational processes.	It has been decided that feedback and control loops will be developed and implemented to establish continuous improvement. These continuous improvement loops will be based on quantitative measurement. Implementation of continuous improvement into the business processes will be supported by the application of intranet-based tools, e.g. regarding the definition of metrics, the collection and analysis of data, and the definition of improvement activities, see [2].
Developing and implementing an improvement initiative is a process of organizational change. Until now the employees have not been involved sufficiently in the process of quality management	The management decided to carefully plan and control the new improvement initiative. The entire organization should understand the importance of continuous improvement. Therefore awareness on the importance of process improvement should be raised and operational teams should play a central role in the determination of their own improvement goals, which have to be derived from business and process improvement goals, see [10].

2.3 A Framework for the Improvement Initiative

Starting from the defined directions for improvement a framework has been developed to support the improvement initiative, see Figure 3. In this pyramid three management levels are recognized to link the improvement initiative to the business system, respectively the strategic, the tactical, and the operational level [1].

The Strategic Plan is positioned in the strategic top layer of the pyramid and acts as a basis for both a Process Management System (PMS) and a Quality Management System (QMS). In this plan management issues are addressed such as:

- The long-term vision of the management,
- The mission statement, and
- Organisational development issues.

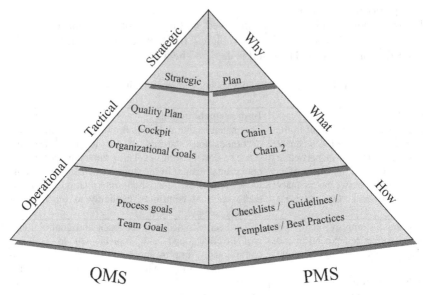

Fig. 3. A framework for the improvement initiative.

The PMS secures the product creation process. On the tactical level the product creation processes are described according to the two process chains (chain 1 for new products and chain 2 for repeat products). The processes are described by means of a format with guidelines regarding respectively: the description of the stakeholders of a process (such as the customer, the supplier, the owner), the process flow aspects (such as input, activities, output), and the performance of a process (such as process goals, improvement actions and metrics). For all processes a general description and detailed information (e.g. action lists) are available. On the operational level also supporting information is available such as checklists, templates, guidelines and best practices.

The QMS supports in particular the continuous (quality) improvement of the product creation process. Continuous quality improvement is based on goal decomposition, i.e. from business goals on the strategic level to process improvement and team improvement goals on the operational level. Regarding quality management, the Quality Plan and the so-called 'cockpit' are important concepts.

The Quality Plan, on the tactical level of the framework, forms a basis for the determination of improvement goals. The Quality Plan starts from the business strategy and specifies respectively the actual vision on continuous improvement, the short-term improvement goals and the accompanying improvement actions. The progress of the improvement program is monitored on the basis of performance indicators in the so-called management cockpit. The cockpit will be addressed in detail in section 4. Cockpit review by the management team takes place monthly. The Quality Plan is subject to management review at least twice a year.

3 Towards Goal-Oriented Improvement

The pyramid framework acts as a reference for the development and implementation of the improvement initiative. To develop the improvement initiative three important principles were taken from results of recent research in the domain of business improvement, respectively:

- Goal decomposition; business goals should be derived from overall business strategy. Based on these business goals operational process and team improvement goals have to be defined [1], [3], [8]. Both for business goals and for process improvement and team improvement goals, improvement actions have to be defined.
- Metric-based improvement. Management and control of improvement actions should be based on measurement. For each business goal, process improvement goal and team improvement goal a (set of) metric(s) has to be defined to be able to quantitatively control the effectiveness of improvement actions [11], [13].
- The decomposition of business goals into process improvement goals and team improvement goals, and the definition of metrics should be based on the needs and the requirements of the operational teams, that can be considered to be the main the stake-holders in the primary business processes [10], [12].

In accordance with these principles the improvement initiative was reformulated as a goal-oriented improvement initiative.

3.1 Goal-Oriented Improvement in the Business Model of TNNL

Starting from the pyramid framework the goal orientation in the improvement initiative has been elaborated into a high-level business model, see Figure 4.

In this business model the PMS is depicted as a horizontal dimension that reflects the transformation of materials and sub-products into products via process chains. It is aimed at maintaining operational control. The vertical dimension addresses the QMS, and is aimed at continuous improvement of the operational business processes. As stated before, in the horizontal PMS the operational processes and their interfaces are specified, authorities and responsibilities are defined, business rules e.g. for delivery on time are specified, etc. In the vertical dimension the improvement of processes, sub-processes and teams has to be managed (the QMS).

In order to link the business strategy (the vision and the mission statements of the management) to the product creation process, the business strategy is refined in terms of business goals and associated sub-goals. Subsequently process improvement and team improvement goals are derived. Based on this goal decomposition, improvement actions are defined both on the business level, the process level and the team level. To plan and control continuous improvement in the business model the plan-do-check-act cycle concept is implemented on the different levels of the goal hierarchy. For the sake of clarity of Figure 4 the plan-do-check-act cycle is only drawn in this figure on the lower level of the model. Of course the feedback mechanisms should also include feedback on the quality of the improvement goals itself. The lower layer teams should also report feedback about the quality of the higher-level process improvement goals, and the lower level processes should also report on the quality of the higher-level business goals.

To control the effectiveness of the improvement actions their efficiency and adequacy has to be measured. On the strategic level the business strategy is defined. On the tactical level business goals and performance indicators are defined which are derived from the business strategy. For each business goal one or more metrics are defined. Subsequently the business goals are decomposed into process improvement and team improvement goals. Also for these process improvement and team improvement goals, metrics are to be defined.

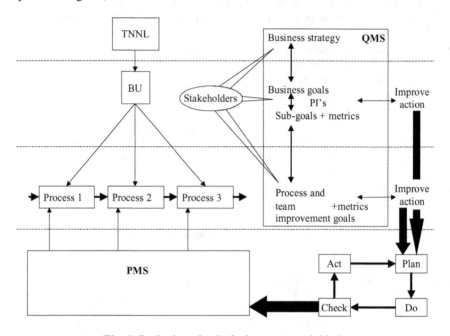

Fig. 4. Goal orientation in the improvement initiative

The decomposition of business strategy and business goals into process and team improvement goals, and the definition of accompanying metrics is not a straightforward, formal or deterministic process. Consensus building and inter-subjective decision-making is central. Therefore relevant stakeholders have to be involved in this process of goal decomposition, improvement action definition and metric determination. Stakeholders are parties that play a direct or indirect role in the product creation process. They can be both operational teams that develop the products, external customers, internal customers who use the output or deliver the input to a process. To organise this stakeholder involvement, workshops, brainstorm meetings and training sessions have to be planned carefully.

In the following section the development of this goal oriented improvement concept at TNNL will be presented. Here, concepts of goal decomposition and measurement play a central role. Regarding the involvement of stakeholders, we will focus on the operational teams that execute the actual process improvement goal decomposition, the team improvement goal definition and the metrics determination.

4 Development of Goal Oriented Business Improvement at TNNL

This section presents the approach that was followed and the (intermediate) results that were reached. Three phases can be recognized:

- A phase where top management defines the strategy, the business goals, business sub-goals, the performance indicators and the metrics, see the upper layers of Quality Management in Figure 4.
- A second phase in that the process improvement goals and the accompanying metrics are defined, see the lower layer of Quality Management in Figure 4, and
- A third phase in that the team improvement goals and metrics are defined (see also the lower layer of Quality Management in Figure 4).

In section 4.1 for the first phase only the results of the management discussions and the decisions that were made are reported. In fact this was a 'black box' strategic management process where only the outcome can be presented. Section 4.2 reports on a procedure that has been developed for process improvement definition and gives some examples of process improvement goals and metrics that have been defined. In section 4.3 the process of the definition of team improvement goals and metrics is described. This process is also clarified with practical examples.

4.1 Phase 1: Business Strategy, Objectives, and Performance Indicators

The high level management has defined five strategic objectives in the Management Handbook. These statements are based on the strategic objectives of TNNL and are taken as starting points for the development of the improvement initiative within the particular business unit R&S/JRS. The strategic objectives are respectively:

- Adequate profitability
- Delivering customer-oriented solutions
- Being the employer of choice
- Developing both existing and new markets
- Adequate and efficient knowledge- and technology management

These rather abstract objectives have been elaborated to make them more applicable on the tactical level or business level, see Table 2.

Table 2. Strategic objectives and their interpretation at the business level

Objective	Interpretation
Adequate profitability	To be reached via an efficient and effective executed creation process
Delivering customer-oriented solutions	Emphasis on meeting customer expectations and requirements (e.g. based on adaptability of products)
Being the employer of choice	Central is the stimulation, motivation, and improvement of the competencies of employees
Developing existing and new markets	To be reached via maintenance and improvement of relations with internal and external customers
Adequate and efficient knowledge- and technology management	Maintenance and development of all competencies regarding product development, including requirements determination, analysis and design and verification and validation, as well as various management and support competencies.

In order to measure whether or not these strategic objectives are met management has identified five performance indicator areas (PIA's). See also Table 3.

Table 3. The performance indicator areas at the business level

Efficient and effective executed creation process
Customer-oriented solutions
Employees
Customer satisfaction
Knowledge base

These five performance indicator areas are displayed in a so-called management cockpit that acts as a control mechanism to keep track of the improvement results. The management cockpit will be addressed further in the following of this section.

Strategic objectives and associated performance indicator areas act as guidelines. Using these, associated business goals and metrics can be derived. For each PIA a number of business goals can be defined, see Table 4.

Table 4. Business goals per PIA

Efficient and effective product creation process
Decrease the costs of adapting product or building blocks to customer requirements
Improve the quality of the order intake forecast
Improve customer confidence in critical process interfaces
Improve reliability of product delivery
Improve budget discipline
Customer-oriented solutions
Improve customer requirements specification regarding the match with TNNL product characteristics
Decrease the costs to adapt product or building blocks to the customer requirements
Employees
Satisfied employee
Improve the allocation potential of employees
Improve the motivation of employees
Customer satisfaction
Satisfied internal customer
Satisfied external customer
Knowledge base
Establish a critical level of knowledge
Improve the added value of the knowledge base
Spent sufficient effort into the organization's level of knowledge

The metrics can be used to decide whether or not specific business goals are reached, and subsequently what the score is of a particular PIA in the management cockpit at the strategic level. A distinction is made between hard and soft metrics, or quantitative and qualitative measures. A hard metric gives formal figures (e.g. illness rate, due date performance and spending rate). Soft metrics express confidence or satisfaction (e.g. confidence that goods will be delivered in time, confidence that the quality of baselines in the product creation process are adequate, customer satisfaction and employer satisfaction). Usually both types of metric are required to provide sufficient information. We give in table 5 some examples of metrics for the PIA's Efficient and Effective Product Creation Process, Customer-oriented Solutions, and Employees.

Table 5. Examples of goals and metrics

Example 1
Performance indicator area: Efficient and Effective Product Creation Process.
•   Business goal: reliability of product delivery.   •   Metric: in-time delivery with respect to operation planning.   •   Norm 80%.
•   Business goal: customer confidence in critical process interfaces.   •   Metric: appreciation score of the key stakeholders in the process, measurement based on questionnaire.   •   Norm: >7.
Example 2
Performance indicator area: Customer-oriented Solutions.
•   Business goal: customer requirements specification (CRS) match with TNNL product characteristics.   •   Metric: number of adjustments of CRS required with respect to existing product portfolio characteristics.   •   Norm: < 1.25*(reference data from experience base)/time.
Example 3
Performance indicator area: Employees.
•   Business goal: motivated employees.   •   Metric-1: staff turnover, norm: 5 %.   •   Metric-2: Average number of overtime hours per employee.   •   Norm: < x-hours per person.

Based on the application of the metrics, periodically the PIA-scores are being generated per performance indicator area (PIA) and shown in the management cockpit, as depicted in figure 5.

Based on the PIA-scores that are presented in the management cockpit the management can evaluate their strategic objectives. Subsequently the business goals act as starting points for improvements that have to be carried out on the process and the team level. In the next section the decomposition of the business goals into process improvement goals and the determination of accompanying metrics is presented.

4.2   Phase 2: Decomposition of Business Goals into Process Improvement Goals and Definition of Metrics

Starting from the business goals the areas in the product creation process have to be identified where specific (parts of the) processes should be improved. These improvements are then defined as process improvement goals. Each goal at the process level has to be provided with one or more metrics.

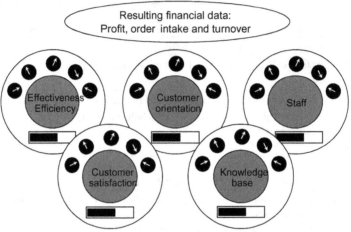

Fig. 5. The management cockpit

The decomposition of the business goals into process improvement goals for the operational teams on the one hand and facilitating departments on the other hand is performed in the following steps:
1. Per process of the product creation process a small team of stakeholders in the process is formed.
2. Each team makes an inventory of the improvement needs of the process and translates these needs into process improvement goals.
3. The process improvement goals are linked with one or more business goals. Goals that cannot be linked with any business goal are rejected.
4. The remaining process improvement goals are subdivided into three classes:
     a. Process improvement goals that can be assigned to operational teams, which execute the process.
     b. Process improvement goals on the interface between processes.
     c. Process improvement goals to be assigned to the departments, which facilitate the operational teams.

In the following paragraphs we will give some examples of the determination of process improvement goals. Because we restrict ourselves in this paper for the sake of clarity to the operational processes as stated in section 1, we will address in these examples only process improvement goals of the processes themselves and process improvement goals at the interface of processes. The process of that we will focus on in this example is the Product Development, Integration, Verification and Validation (PDIVV) process, see Figure 1 in section 2.1.

The PDIVV Process and its Stakeholders. The PDIVV process is a process in chain-1 that produces the system according to the agreed specifications, assigns the work to be done to the production department or subcontractors and delivers the system components, see section 1. The PDIVV process has interfaces with the processes SRA/SD and SIVV, which are considered as the most important stakeholders, together with the PDIVV-employees. The output of the SRA/SD process, and the input of PDIVV, is a validated and complete system requirements specification that is based on the availability of building blocks within TNNL. The output of PDIVV, and the input for SIVV, is a produced system and/or components that have to be integrated into a final product in the SIVV process. The final product is verified and validated against the original customer and system requirements. In the following table 6 we give examples of process improvement goals with respect to respectively the operational teams, the SRA/SD interface and the SIVV interface.

Table 6. Examples of process improvement goals

Process improvement goals with respect to the operational teams executing the process.
Process improvement goal: executing the work in accordance with the project plan.   • Related business improvement goal: efficient and effective product creation process (see 4.1).   • Metric: procentual time delay (t-real – t-plan)/t-real).
Process improvement goal: constructive feedback on personal performance.   • Related business improvement goal: improve the motivation of employees (see 4.1)   • Metric: questionnaire to determine a score for employee satisfaction regarding their interaction with Resource Management.
Process improvement goals with respect to the SRA/SD (interface at the input side)
Process improvement goal: improve the stability of the system requirements specification.   • Related business improvement goal: improve reliability of product delivery (see 4.1)   • Metric: changes over a period of time in (#requirements to work on)/ (#requirements total).
Process improvement goals with respect to the SIVV (interface at the output side)
Process improvement goal: improve satisfaction of the SIVV employees on the quality of the output by increasing frequency of reviews.   • Related business improvement goal: satisfied (internal) customer (see 4.1).   • Metric: (effort/time needed to react to complaints from SIVV)/(effort/time needed for the development of the output).

4.3   Phase 3: The Decomposition of Process Improvement Goals into Team Goals and the Definition of Metrics

The decomposition of the strategic objectives via the business goals into process improvement goals and the definition of accompanying metrics form the basis for actual business improvement. The improvement goals have to be embedded in the daily work of the operational teams. This section reports on the way workshops are carried out to determine team goals and metrics. The team improvement goals and metrics are registered in the QMS and serve there as a basis of reference for the day-to-day work of the various operational teams.

Workshop Objectives. The implementation of process improvement goals into the work of operational teams was supported by workshops. The objectives of the workshops for individual teams were to define its own set of team improvement goals, on the basis of on the one hand the process improvement goals, and on the other hand the teams own particular project objectives and the individual experiences of each team member. Team improvement goals can be related to one or more process improvement goals; just like process improvement goals can be related to one or more business goals.

Workshop Design. The workshops are being designed carefully in accordance with the size of the teams, which varies between 6 and 25 persons. The approach is to reach agreement on team improvement goals via dialog and mutual understanding. For a workshop relevant process improvement goals are pre-selected and act as a basis of reference during the whole workshop. The starting questions of a workshop are respectively:
- 'How do we contribute to the process improvement goals of the department',
- 'How do we measure team contribution', and
- 'What are individual roles in that'?

Subgroups of three to five persons are formed to discuss process improvement and team goals, both in parallel and sequential. They are provided with predefined templates that are based on the 'cockpit' and with the Goal Question Metric paradigm [7]. Team members can participate in more than one (sequentially) operating subgroup. Several iterations are used to derive team improvement goals and metrics from process improvement goals. The group's outcomes are reviewed each iteration by other subgroups. Finally, based on consensus building, the most suitable team goals and metrics are selected, and an action plan is proposed. Based on the iterations, the review mechanisms and the changing groups, maximum use of the variety of a team is reached, creating a large cohesion within the operational team.

Workshop Evolution. Over a period of eighteen months, monthly follow-up sessions are organized. In these sessions experiences are collected regarding the fit of the process improvement goals with the team improvement goals and the application of the team improvement goals and the metrics in practice.

Preliminary Workshop Results. Some examples of the results of the workshops are:
- Explicit team improvement goal definition provides teams with a clear focus on the major topics of their work
- Increased awareness of the teams on the impact of their work on the business as a whole. It provided teams with a "helicopter view" on their daily work.
- Clear contribution to the "team spirit" of the employees.

- Redesign of particular activities in the team, e.g. improving the efficiency of the work
- Follow-up workshops showed that specific important improvement topics could be kept on the agenda and didn't tend to disappear due to the day-to-day worries.

Some Examples of Metrics. In Table 7 two examples are given of the determination of team improvement goals, metrics and norms, on the basis of the process improvement goals as defined in section 4.2. For each of the examples a brief experience issue is given.

Table 7. Examples of team improvement goals

Process improvement goal: improve satisfaction of the SIVV employees on the quality of the output by increasing frequency of reviews, see section 4.2.
<ul><li>Team improvement goal: improve the quality of the specification.</li><li>Metric: objectiveness of the specification</li><li>Norms:<ul><li>○ >95% of the specification is described in quantitative terms</li><li>○ >95% of the essential specification is under control (determined on the basis of consensus of the team members)</li><li>○ >80% of non-essential requirements is under control (determined on the basis of consensus of the team members)</li></ul></li></ul>Experience issue: the distinction between essential and non-essential specifications supported the team members in getting a clear focus on main and side aspects of the specification.
<ul><li>Team improvement goal: improve communication with (internal) SIVV customers.</li><li>Metric: level of (internal) satisfaction, based on among others a number of contacts with internal customers and formal response given to questions.</li><li>Norm: >6 (on a scale of 1 to 10)</li></ul>Experience issue: the whole team was involved in the 'rating' and the team as a whole became aware of the number of contacts with the internal customers and the 'quality' of those contacts.

5 Conclusions

A pre-assessment on the basis of the ISO9001:2000 standard at TNNL showed shortcomings regarding quality management and continuous improvement. To improve the situation the management decided to set up an improvement initiative. Regarding the structure of this improvement initiative, a framework for goal-oriented quality improvement has been defined. Based on this framework, three directions for solving the problems have been defined, i.e. goal decomposition, metrification and stakeholder involvement. Regarding improvement three levels of improvement actions have been elaborated, respectively the business level, the process improvement level and the team improvement level. On each of these levels appropriate stakeholders played a role in the determination of metrics, e.g. top management, project or process leaders, and operational team members. Appropriate defined metrics, related to the improvement actions of a particular level, are used to determine the effectiveness of the improvement actions on a continuous basis. On the team level the team improvement goal definition and the determination of metrics is performed in workshops that are organized on a regular basis. Finally the evaluation of the improvement goals and the application of the metrics, e.g. the collection and the analysis of data, are supported by web-based intranet tools.

Acknowledgements. We would like to thank Sabine Te Braak of TNNL who has been helpful in the review process and the development of the figures in this paper.

References

1. Debou, C., Kuntzmann-Combelles, A.: Linking Software Process Improvement to Business Strategies: Experiences from industry, Software Process: Improvement and Practice 5 (2000) 55-64.
2. Balla, K. Bemelmans, Th., Kusters, R.J., and Trienekens, J.J.M.: QMIM: Quality through Managed Improvement and Measurement: towards a phased development and implementation of a quality management system for a software company, Software Quality Journal 9 (2001) 177-193.
3. Cattaneo, F., Fuggetta, A., and Sciutto, D.: Pursuing Coherence in Software Process Assessment and Improvement, Software Process Improvement and Practice 6 (2001) 3-22.
4. Dawson, D. and O'Neill, B: Simple Metrics for Improving Software process Performance and Capability: A Case Study, Software Quality Journal 11 (2003) 243-258.
5. International Organization for Standardization, http://www.iso.ch/iso/en/iso9000-14000/iso9000/iso9000index.html.
6. Latum F. van, Solingen R. van, Oivo M., Hoisl B., Rombach D., and Ruhe G.: Adopting GQM-based measurement in an industrial environment', IEEE Software (1998) 78-86.
7. Mellis W.: Software quality management in turbulent times: are there alternatives to process oriented software quality management, Software Quality Journal (2000) 277-295.
8. Neiger D., and Churilov L.: Structuring Business Objectives: A Business Process Modeling Perspective, in: Proceedings of the international conference BPM2003, Aalst W. van der, Hofstede A. ter, and Weske M. (Eds.), Eindhoven, The Netherlands, June 2003.
9. Paulk M.C.: How ISO9001 Compares With The CMM, IEEE Software (1995) 74-83.
10. Solingen R. van, Berghout E., Kusters R.J., Trienekens J.J.M.: From process improvement to people improvement, Information and Software Technology 42, (2000) 965-971.
11. Solingen R. van, Berghout E.: The Goal/Question/Metric Method, McGraw-Hill, 1999.
12. Stelzer D. and Mellis W.: Success Factors of Organizational Change in Software Process Improvement, Software Process: Improvement and Practice 4 (1998) 227-250.
13. Trienekens, J.J.M., Kusters R.J., Solingen R.: Product Focused Software Process Improvement: Concepts and Experiences from Industry, Software Quality Journal 9 (2001) 269-281.

Modeling Medical E-services

Rainer Anzböck[1] and Schahram Dustdar[2]

[1] D.A.T.A. Corporation,
Invalidenstrasse 5-7/10, 1030 Wien, Austria
ar@data.at
[2] Distributed Systems Group, Vienna University of Technology
Argentinierstrasse 8/184-1, 1040 Wien, Austria
dustdar@infosys.tuwien.ac.at

Abstract. On the one hand Web services are gaining increasing attention. A lot of standardization has improved their stability and range of application. Composition and coordination techniques for Web services enable an application integration effort beyond loosely coupled systems. On the other hand medical e-services are covered by the DICOM and HL7 communication protocols and profiled by the IHE (Integrating the Healthcare Enterprise) technical framework. Standardization is more extensive, most workflows are well defined and integration is tighter than in most other domains. Nevertheless standardization focused on conventional workflow systems. In an Internet-based medical environment with high security standards, communication is strongly restricted and conventional systems fail to deliver. This paper proposes a modeling process for medical Web services. The IHE *patient administration process flow* serves as a well defined example. Furthermore, the paper defines requirements of a Web service based middleware for the execution of medical e-services. The technique should enable building integrated medical applications for Internet-based workflow execution.

1 Introduction

With recent work in the field of workflows it is possible to define more flexible business models than in traditional workflows based on the Workflow reference model (WFMC) [1]. With the standardization of coordination, composition, transaction and security for Web services a new implementation method for Web service based scenarios is available. Especially the medical services domain is in a permanent evolution. Its workflows are complex and highly structured and a standardization of communication protocols has been covered by HL7 [2], DICOM [3] and the IHE framework [4]. Further standardization processes for health informatics are enforced by the European Union with the CEN/TC 251 work program [5].

One goal of our paper is to outline a modeling process for medical e-services. From the medical services domain initially introduced and the requirements defined subsequently, we conclude how to model such services based on the IHE *administrative process flow* sample in 5 steps. The modeling process should be refined in further research and result in a guideline or semi-automatic process for defining medical e-services' workflows using Web service based composition.

J. Desel, B. Pernici, and M. Weske (Eds.): BPM 2004, LNCS 3080, pp. 49–65, 2004.

Another goal of our paper is to show how recent work on protocols of the Web service stack and standardization efforts in the medical services domain (the IHE framework) help to solve application integration. First, we provide an introduction to the medical services domain. Then we outline requirements of a Web service oriented approach and use a specific example, the *administrative process flow*. When going into detail, we further focus on two IHE transactions, *patient registration* and *modality worklist provided*, as they are representative for HL7 and DICOM communication.

A third goal is the discussion of requirements for modeling medical e-services. Related to the example introduced we discuss Web service concepts and standards like SOAP [6], WSDL [7], WS-Coordination [8], WS-Transaction [9], WS-Security [10] and many more. From there we focus on the composition of Web services using BPEL [11] and define requirements to model IHE transactions as medical e-services. Finally, we conclude the results and provide topics for future work.

To summarize, our paper (i) suggests a modeling process for the *IHE administrative process flow* example and outlines implications for a general modeling process to implement medical e-services, (ii) introduces the medical services domain and the *administrative process flow* and (iii) defines requirements of a modeling process based on current Web service stack standards.

The paper is structured as follows. Section 2 introduces medical information systems, communication protocols and the IHE technical framework. Section 3 provides requirements of a modeling process for services like the IHE *administrative process flow*. Section 4 outlines a modeling process for medical e-services. Section 5 concludes the results and outlines future work.

2 Medical E-services

In this chapter we briefly introduce medical information systems, communication protocols and the IHE framework.

2.1 Medical Information Systems

Three types of medical information systems, the HIS (Hospital Information System), the RIS (Radiology Information System) and the PACS (Picture Achieving and Communication system) are the backbone of current information systems in the hospital and medical e-services environment. They are comparable to ERP (Enterprise Resource Planning) or SCM (Supply Chain Management) in business organizations. The HIS is an enterprise-wide system used for administrative services like patient and visit management, operation planning, billing, etc.. The RIS is a management system for medical imaging facilities (radiologists) and covers patient registration, examination scheduling and control, report generation, speech recognition, etc.. As can be concluded, both systems have overlapping services to fulfill: one on an enterprise the other on a department level. The second main software system category in medical e-services is called PACS and is responsible for all image management services. It transfers patient data to examination facilities (modalities), announces finished procedures and stores, prints, burns CDs, archives or transfers the generated image data.

These software systems are often integrated as departmental services for a larger hospital environment or spread across several locations. Because of their special storage, network and process performance requirements RIS and PACS systems are very important departmental services. Company related information on these systems can be found in [12-18], more theoretical work in [19-21].

2.2 Medical Communication Standards

The most relevant protocol standards for these services are HL7 for the RIS and DICOM for the PACS. PACS and RIS both implement a workflow model and cover implementations of the standard. Both systems have to be tightly integrated to perform services efficiently. The DICOM standard covers Client/Server communications used to exchange patient and examination information. The standard covers objects like patients, visits, medical procedures, images, etc.. Additionally, notifications, data query and exchange services based on these objects are defined. The HL7 standard is used for data exchange between different healthcare providers and is more suited for non-radiological institutions. Some functionality overlaps with DICOM for example the scheduling process or the patient and result management. Other functionality such as the exchange of image data is not part of HL7. More detailed information on HL7 can be found in [2] and on DICOM in [3, 22, 23]. Besides these protocols additional standards like CEN 251 [5] exist. Ambitions to converge these standards by using a common framework have led to the definition of IHE [4].

2.3 A Medical Workflow Framework

The IHE technical framework has been defined to extend the enterprise application integration to a level of scenario-based interaction. Over the years software products implemented the DICOM and HL7 standards by their own interpretation. This led to a situation of incompatibility and a lot of effort has to be put into application integration. The framework defines usage-scenarios with the goal that products conforming to the framework can be integrated seamlessly.

IHE defines transactions (workflow transactions) between applications by profiling DICOM and HL7 operations. Messages (domain activities) are selected and put into sequences to implement real-world scenarios. Additionally, flows (workflow services) are defined that correspond to a set of related transactions performed by different actors (administration application, image archive, etc.). Applications may perform the role of one or more such actors in one or more of these flows. To claim IHE conformity for a role in a workflow, a required set of flows and transactions has to be implemented.

IHE conformant applications can be integrated more tightly than applications in other domains. Nevertheless integration based on this framework is currently done using traditional workflow models in Intranet-based environments. An Internet-based infrastructure, as currently common in most environments, restricts interorganizational workflow [24] integration. In a real world scenario integrators have to deal with applications in a mixed Intranet and Internet environment. Workflow items like patient and image data are exchanged within and across organizational boundaries. Figure 1 shows an example of such an environment.

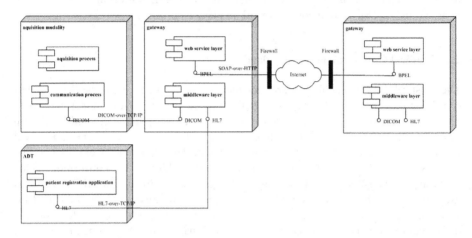

Fig. 1. Mixed Intranet/Internet environment for medical e-services

An Intranet-based environment consists of conventional HL7 and DICOM communication over a secure and reliable transport. Additionally, the IHE framework provides a solid foundation for defining medical workflows in this environment. Current solutions integrate applications based on conventional middleware. For example, gateways, acquisition modalities and patient registration applications are directly connected by their middleware layers. In contrast, we have to deal with interorganizational workflows, which are executed between nodes distributed over the Internet.

The gateways mentioned have two different responsibilities. On one hand, they implement IHE conformant Web service based workflow models for medical e-services. On the other hand, they enable internal nodes to participate in IHE conformant workflows, to attach their messages to XML workflow messages and to apply security and transaction support. In this paper we focus on the first functionality.

This scenario is beneficial for many reasons, like exchange of patient information which results in a reduced number of examinations, load balancing work between specialized physicians, etc. Through the standardization process related to the Web service stack [25] it is feasible to suggest a workflow implementation based on a separate layer that meets the requirements of an Internet environment on one hand, and supports standardization efforts of the industry, as outlined above, on the other.

Related to Web services, we have to consider the following aspects. First, we have to provide a transport mechanism, where SOAP-over-HTTP communication is a reasonable option. Next, we have to meet reliability and security requirements with additions like WS-Security [10], WS-ReliableMessaging [26] and others. To model workflows in a service-oriented computing (SOC) environment a composition language like BPEL is required. Furthermore, transactional behavior is beneficial for the quality of the business processes. For example, BPEL prefers the use of WS-Transaction [9], which we will focus on, when defining service modeling requirements. To summarize the aspects that have to be discussed when modeling medical e-services, we find

- a high degree of vertical standardization through DICOM, HL7 and IHE
- currently implemented systems based on conventional middleware
- lack of interorganizational workflow support as a common problem
- no current Web service based approach which tries to fill this gap

Therefore we suggest a Web service based workflow model that implements IHE conformant transactions to provide medical e-services functionality in a mixed Intranet/Internet environment.

2.4 Related Work

Most information related to medical e-services can be found in the corresponding standardization documents for HL7, DICOM and IHE. Similarly, all current standards related to the Web service stack are available. More specifically, a discussion of an interorganizational workflow in the medical imaging domain can be found in [27]. A first approach of Web service definition and middleware design for the medical imaging domain can be found in [28]. The paper covers the separation of the workflow layer, using BPEL [11] and WSDL [7], and the domain layer, using DICOM and HL7. Additionally, it performs a mapping between BPEL activities and DICOM and HL7 messages.

3 Requirements for Medical E-service Modeling

In this section we cover requirements that have to be met when modeling medical e-services. We outline the relationship of HL7, DICOM and IHE concepts to Web service modeling (especially BPEL) constructs. Additionally, we discuss the impact and usefulness of current Web service stack protocols.

3.1 HL7 and DICOM Encoding

When implementing medical e-services using Web service technology, we have to consider transferring HL7 and DICOM messages using XML and SOAP. One solution is a conversion of messages and binary data into XML. Another more advantageous approach is to simply attach original messages to SOAP messages and to only use identifiers and other attributes required for a proper workflow execution within the SOAP message. A third approach is to separate workflow and domain communication, with the disadvantage of an additional communication channel inappropriate for a firewall based Internet environment (see Figure 1). In this paper we focus on attaching HL7 and DICOM data, the second approach and on workflow modeling with attributes required for its execution.

When using attachments we have to consider techniques where HL7 and DICOM data has to be transferred together with the workflow messages. Because both standards define binary data types, an encapsulation and payload transfer should be supported. Several techniques are available like WS-Attachments [29] based on DIME [30] or SOAP Messages with Attachments (SwA) as described in [31]. More recently, the SOAP 1.2 [6] specification supports base64binary encoding [32] of data and is currently evolving as the standard mechanism for transferring binary data as it doesn't require additional protocol parsers. Furthermore, security as in WS-Security can be applied on binary data too. However, a modeling process has to provide techniques to transfer HL7 and DICOM messages over a Web service infrastructure.

3.2   Data and Service Identification

First, a clear identification of messages and data items is required. A necessary similarity between the HL7 and DICOM protocols is that they contain message identifiers (message ID for HL7 and association ID for DICOM). Furthermore, the data exchanged is identified by system wide identifiers (patient ID, visit ID, image ID). DICOM objects and HL7 messages use different definitions and identifiers for data items. Related to our example in section 4, the *patient registration* transaction messages are identified by the PID-3 (Patient identifier list) and the PV1-19 (Visit number) HL7 segment attributes. The DICOM *modality worklist* service uses patient UIDs, examination IDs and others.

Fortunately, IHE chooses the more specific protocol for a given situation. It defines a mapping between identifiers used in HL7 and DICOM and describes usage conventions to provide interoperability of the standards. The standardization effort lets us easily select the message segment IDs (HL7) or object modules UIDs (DICOM) suggested by IHE in each modeled IHE transaction. For service identification the unique IHE transaction name (e.g. patient registration) can be used. This identification is required by Coordination and Registration protocols as described in the next sections. A modeling process should select identifiers from the standard documents and provide a mapping between an IHE transaction and its Web service.

3.3   Web Service Coordination

When using Web services, the coordination of business partners is required for distributed activities. Currently, the main purposes of coordination protocols like WS-Coordination [8, 33] or other approaches [34-36] are reliable messaging, transactions and security. For medical e-services business partners are correlated by IHE transactions. Each of these transactions might be executed between two participants requiring transaction or security services. It has to be stated, that not every IHE actor might be a separate application. Therefore, participants are normally not 1:1 related to an actor. However, the IHE actor's name perfectly expresses the role in an IHE transaction.

To support coordination protocols unique identifiers are required. These identifiers are used by coordinators to define a coordination-context for the participants. As stated above, IDs for messages and transactions can be derived from the standards. Nevertheless, process instances that register coordination-contexts might use the same messages and transactions during their execution which makes these IDs improper. A unique ID generator must be used instead.

To coordinate service instances, information about used ports (service endpoint) can be extracted from the WSDL definition. Furthermore, specific roles, like master or slave in a 2PC transaction, might be required by the coordinator. However, BPEL uses a different transaction mechanism based on compensation, which better fits to the definition of an IHE transaction as outlined in the next section. For security purposes, service participants might define a security context. As for transactions, unique identifiers are required and have to be generated. For reliable messaging services, like WS-ReliableMessaging, there are additional message sequence numbers, which have to be generated by the middleware like context identifiers. Furthermore, medical e-services require delivery semantics of *ExactlyOnce* and *InOrder*, because the IHE framework only mentions messages delivered accordingly. The behavior for messages that are out of sequence is undefined. For example, the Collaxa BPEL Server [37] product contains support for reliable messaging in a delivery service module. Furthermore, it uses WS-Addressing [38] to handle the correlation of asynchronous messages.

A modeling process has to cover the appliance of transaction and security attributes to IHE transactions. Additionally, compensation activities have to be identified.

3.4 Web Service Transactions

Transaction protocols are used to increase the quality of a Web service based business process to the standards already provided by conventional middleware. Currently the most important standards are WS-Transaction and more recent but not yet widely used WS-TransactionManagement [39]. In general, there are different transaction models for direct, queued and compensation-based transaction processing [40]. For our infrastructure, we consider the use of BPEL and therefore a compensation-based approach. In Compensation-based Transaction Processing compensating actions are executed to "undo" the effects of actions that have been successfully completed [11]. More information on Web service transactions can be found in [41, 42].

DICOM and HL7 basically don't specify any transactional behavior. The application logic takes care that, for example, payments are not booked twice. With the introduction of an IHE based Web service middleware it is feasible to provide transaction services. As their name suggests, IHE transactions provide a granularity of activities useable for a transaction context. To implement a compensation-based model, compensation actions for IHE transactions have to be defined. Some transactions perform only read operations and therefore don't require any transactional semantics. A modeling process should provide a guideline to decide transactional behavior based on the operations executed in the IHE transaction.

As an example for compensation-based transaction processing, the *patient registration* transaction uses a HL7 ADT^A01 or A04 message to register a patient. In case of an error in the sending application, the registration process has to be undone with the A11 cancel message. If a patient is pre-registered (A05) the A38 cancel message is used. We provide a model of this example in section 4. As a second example, the *modality worklist provided* is read-only and therefore has no compensation activity. Models like the Direct Transaction Processing using the 2-phase commit (2PC) protocol and the Queued Transaction Processing used in queue-based middleware systems are currently inappropriate for the modeling of BPEL processes. For example, the Collaxa BPEL Server [37] contains support for WS-Transactions and executes compensation activities defined in the BPEL workflow model.

A modeling process has to integrate compensation activities into the composed Web service. Transactions should be part of the modeling phase and not applied afterwards.

3.5 Web Service Security

Several requirements for security have to be met when modeling medical e-services, because the data transferred is often highly confidential. For Internet-based infrastructures as outlined in Figure 1 existing standards in the medical industry [2, 3, 4, 5, 43] require strong encryption with a minimal key length of 128bit and authentication based on asymmetric keys. WS-Security supports username/password security, X.509 certificates, Kerberos authentication or SSL. It only defines the SOAP encoding of these standards. An established infrastructure for the authentication and encryption process has to be in place. If trust relationships as defined in WS-Trust [44] are used, an additional infrastructure for a Security Token Service is required. In WS-SecureConversation [45] Web service providers specify security requirements and requestors provide claims that can be matched prior to security establishment. The standard also states which parts of a SOAP message have to be signed and encrypted to avoid message tampering and ensure the privacy of the communication partners.

The gateways (Figure 1) used to transfer data via SOAP have to implement these security standards. An IHE transaction is performed between two actors; intermediaries are not mentioned in this context. For each transaction a security context has to be defined. For modeling purposes it is reasonable to use the same granularity of an IHE transaction as in WS-Transaction. In the case of using HL7 and DICOM as attachments in SOAP messages, WS-Security provides a specification of how this data has to be encrypted additionally. Because DICOM data can be very large (several 100MB) an application-level encryption using WS-Security might be infeasible. In such cases encryption can only be applied to the remaining part of the SOAP message. Another possibility is the use of transport layer security like TLS [46] or IP-sec [47], besides there are implementation difficulties in Internet-based scenarios.

On the other hand, the IHE standard itself defines transactions for a Kerberos service. The messages could be exchanged as supposed in 3.1. However, just few medical applications support this. Therefore, it might be necessary to provide an infrastructure based completely on Web service standards. A modeling process should at least identify security attributes for IHE transactions. How these transactions are secured in a specific scenario might be postponed to the implementation.

3.6   Web Service Registration and Binding

The UDDI standard [48] specifies Web services for service registration, subscription and binding. UDDI stores information about companies, services in general and Web services in particular in a 1:n relationship. For our purpose, the registry can provide yellow pages and green pages services. The former can be used to search for a service that implements specific IHE transactions. The latter is required to bind to the service at run-time. There is a private and a public model to distribute UDDI registries. We consider a private model where a registry is maintained by one participant of an IHE transaction. UDDI supports a security model for the communication with and the manipulation within the registry. Because the gateway (see Figure 1) already requires a security infrastructure, securing the registration service is reasonable.

For yellow pages, the IHE framework can be mapped to the registry by creating entries for IHE applications (services) and IHE Web services. Furthermore, a classification scheme is supported and can be used in the IHE context by classifying applications for their support of IHE actor (classes), and IHE Web services for their support of IHE transaction (classes). There is not necessarily a 1:1 relationship between a Web service and an IHE transaction. For green pages, the binding process can be implemented at design-time or at run-time. For workflows based on the IHE standard run-time binding is required, if a decision for a specific IHE actor is made on a process instance base. This is the case, for example, if a report for an examination is created by a physician based on the patient's diagnosis. The dynamic binding depends on attributes like modality name and requesting physician (DICOM) or referring doctor and assigned patient location (HL7). All attributes, required for dynamic binding, have to be modeled in BPEL.

There is currently no mechanism for service registration in IHE. A modeling process should address service binding requests for a selection beyond different IHE actors or run-time decisions within a process as mentioned above.

3.7   Web Service Composition

For Web service composition we have to consider the structure and granularity of a Web service to be a suitable part of the executed workflow. The following table provides a mapping between IHE concepts and BPEL language constructs that will be discussed further.

An IHE actor is modeled as a BPEL business partner. Applications might perform one or more roles and therefore participate in different BPEL processes. An IHE flow, like the *administrative process flow* is modeled as a BPEL process (see section 4). An IHE transaction is mapped on a BPEL service link, where only two business partners are communicating with each other over two BPEL ports. A single HL7 message or DICOM object is embedded in a SOAP message and transferred between the business partners using a BPEL invoke and receive activity. As stated above, BPEL uses WS-Transactions and a compensation mechanism. Compensation activities themselves are implemented as HL7 messages and DICOM objects.

Table 1. Relationship of IHE concepts and BPEL constructs

IHE concept	BPEL construct
IHE actor	BPEL partner
IHE flow	BPEL process
IHE transaction	BPEL service link, 2 BPEL ports
HL7 message/DICOM service	1 BPEL invoke+receive activity, 1 SOAP message
HL7 message/DICOM service	1 BPEL compensation activity

BPEL Variables. To specify a BPEL process, variables have to be defined, that are required for the workflow. For medical e-services they consist of the following four categories. First, we require environment attributes for the participating IHE actors and the implemented IHE transactions. This information is stored during composition in the BPEL server itself or for dynamic binding in a UDDI registry. For dynamic binding attributes suggested in section 4.6 (requesting physician, etc.) have to be stored additionally. The second category are attributes used to identify the message type (HL7 ADT^A01, etc.) and message content (patient UID, etc.). All message content identifying attributes are used to construct a BPEL correlation set. The third category consists of attributes used in state information and BPEL expressions. For example, the HL7 PatientClass is used to control the process flow of the patient registration transaction. The last category are the remaining attributes that reside only in the payload and are not part of the BPEL definition.

Basic Activities. BPEL uses basic activities to execute the workflow between business partners. In e-services IHE transactions are executed by performing HL7 and DICOM operations. For each operation between two partners the initiating part executes an *invoke* activity on a defined BPEL port and the receiving partner performs a corresponding *receive* activity on another port. The ports are related in a BPEL service link associating the business partners. The modeling process in section 5 provides a corresponding example. The paper in [28] provides details of this relationship for a medical workflow. Another approach focusing on a supply chain example can be found in [49].

Expressions and Structured Activities. BPEL uses expressions for conditions and variable assignment using extensions of the X-Path [50] standard. Variables of the first three categories can be used in expressions. For example, the HL7 PatientClass can be used in a boolean expression. BPEL supports among other things *sequence*, *switch* and *while* activities to structure the process. A model of these activities can be partially derived from the sequence diagrams provided in the IHE framework. As shown in the example of Figure 4 an A01, A04 and A05 message can be sent depending on the HL7 PatientClass, therefore a switch construct is used within the process. The modeling process in section 4 provides a corresponding example. For other examples refer to [28, 49]. A detailed analysis of BPEL patterns is given in [51].

Message Correlation and Correlation Sets. The messages sent and received in an IHE transaction have to be correlated by a unique identifier, a BPEL correlation set. This set can be constructed by appending all identifying HL7 and DICOM message attributes and depends on the structure of the underlying messages exchanged. The attributes are derived from the standardization documents for each transaction.

Scopes and Compensation Activities. A scope is a BPEL construct used for error or compensation handling. Compensation handlers can be defined on a scope level to perform compensation activities in case of application level errors. Compensation activities can also be used in error handlers for system level errors. As mentioned earlier, some of the IHE transactions activities require compensation and some do not. This information has to be derived from the respective standard documents. For the patient registration example the HL7 A01 message has to be compensated by an A11 message. The granularity of an IHE transaction is a candidate for defining scopes as its outcomes are defined clearly within the IHE framework. Further modeling examples should proof this assumption. Currently there is no evidence for the use of nested transactions.

3.8 Conclusions for a Modeling Process

For a mixed Intranet/Internet environment as introduced in Figure 1 we require a Web service infrastructure. However, IHE doesn't mention Web services. Nevertheless, IHE defines workflow transactions that can be mapped directly to a Web service composition language like BPEL. Furthermore, IHE defines compensation activities and a Kerberos infrastructure which narrows down modeling decisions related to security and transactions. As a first step to implement IHE transactions in a Web service infrastructure, we provide a modeling process for BPEL in the next section.

4 Outlining a Modeling Process

The modeling process is separated into four steps. First, we provide the four layer model to structure the content of the IHE framework. In the second step the process flow is defined and normalized. In the third step a similar approach is performed for the IHE transactions. Finally, based on the normalized descriptions BPEL and WSDL definitions are derived.

4.1 Definition of a 4 Level Use-Case Model

The first step for modeling medical e-services is the definition of 4-level UML [52, 53] Use-Case model, which has been introduced in [20] and is shown in Figure 2.

The layers used correspond to the definitions for profiles, flows, transactions and messages used in the IHE framework. On the top layer the IHE integration profiles are shown, a coarse grained overview of what an application performs. The *IHE Scheduled Workflow profile* we focus on is shown in the gray shaded area. These profiles are split into several flows. Each flow must be supported by an application that implements the profile (in our example the *administrative process flow*). IHE flows are defined as sequence diagrams in the IHE framework. Each IHE flow is further defined using several IHE transactions. These transactions are sequentially order and not all transactions of a flow have to be implemented by every participating actor. Finally, a transaction consists of one or several HL7 and DICOM messages that have to be sent or received. The upper three levels correspond to the workflow layer of the middleware, while the forth resides in the domain layer. While conventional workflow systems focus on the third and forth layer our approach takes the structure of the whole IHE specification into account. For readability different Use-Case models should be created to focus on the implemented IHE actors of a specific application. The IHE transactions that have to be modeled in the next step can be depicted from layer 3. For designing medical e-services we further focus on the *IHE administrative process flow*. The Use-Case model for medical workflows has been introduced in [20].

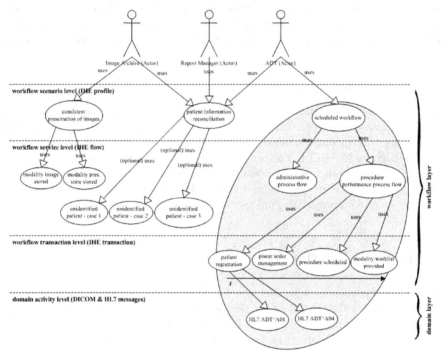

Fig. 2. Modeling process - 4-level Use-Case model

4.2   Selection, Definition, and Normalization of Process Flow

In a second step we can proceed to focus on the *administrative process flow* and provide an activity diagram (Figure 3) that corresponds to the public workflow for the department system scheduler / order filler IHE actor and is derived from the corresponding sequence diagram defined in the IHE framework [4].

UML activity diagrams are widely used as a representation language for workflows as discussed in [54]. The public process contains all activities (IHE transactions) performed by the IHE actor, internal operations are shown for readability. The diagram can be derived from the sequence diagram by performing several normalization operations.

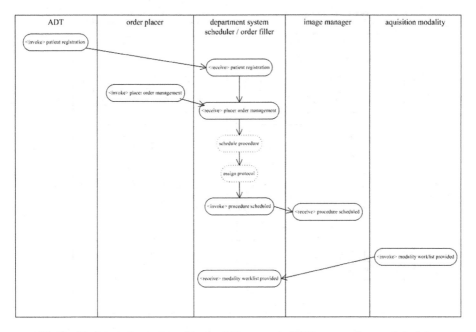

Fig. 3. *Administrative process flow* - public process of Department System Scheduler

First, an IHE actor, to define the public process for, is selected and actor independent and internal operations are deleted. Next, IHE transactions are translated into BPEL invoke and receive activities. Caution has to be taken, because IHE defines some of the transactions in the wrong direction. For example, the DICOM service used in the *modality worklist provided* transaction is shown as been executed from by department system scheduler on the acquisition modality. However, it is the client (acquisition modality) that queries a server during this operation, therefore the invoke activity is performed by the acquisition modality. Furthermore, the conversion results in two independent processes, therefore an IHE flow not necessarily corresponds 1:1 to a BPEL process. As another fact, an application might implement several roles in the IHE flow, therefore converting external transactions to internal which are not modeled in a BPEL process. To join two actors, the *invoke* and *receive* activities between them are converted to internal operations and omitted. The two sets of other activities are joined. The diagram outlines requirements of the process to implement. However, a BPEL process can not be directly derived because details of the underlying domain layer are omitted. These details are provided in the next step.

4.3 Selection, Definition, and Normalization of Transactions

In a third step we focus on the activities performed in an IHE transaction. The HL7 and DICOM messages exchanged between two systems in a *patient registration* transaction are outlined in Figure 4.

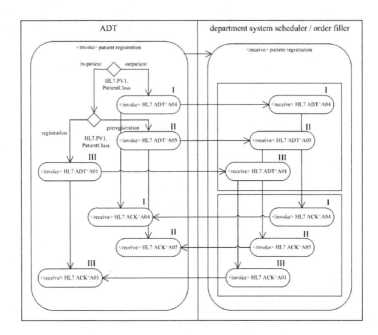

Fig. 4. *Patient registration* transaction - public process of Department System Scheduler

The activity diagram corresponds to the sequence diagram of the *patient registration* transaction defined in [4]. The diagram is a more detailed view of the IHE flow above. The simplified *invoke* and *receive* activities of Figure 3 might now be split into one or more BPEL activities. The *invoke* operation is annotated in the flow at the initial sender of the transaction (the ADT actor in our example).

Several implications for an implementation have to be depicted from the standard documents to normalize the activity diagram. For example, the patient registration distinguishes in-patient, outpatient and pre-registration. These cases depend on the PatientClass attribute of the PV1 segment of HL7 ADT messages. In the BPEL process this results in a *switch* structured activity. This implies several initiating *receive* activities for the process of the department system scheduler. BPEL supports multiple start activities by setting the *createinstance* attribute of these activities to "yes". Furthermore, HL7 requires acknowledge messages to be sent back to the initiator. These are modeled using an additional pair of *invoke* and *receive* activities.

As another example, Figure 5 shows the activities performed in a modality worklist provided transaction. The operation is simply converted into a pair of *invoke* and *receive* activities. No additional steps are necessary.

4.4   Definition of BPEL Process

In the next step we are able to derive a BPEL process specification from the provided activity diagrams for the *patient registration*. In short the following tasks are necessary. The BPEL specification contains definitions of *types*, *variables*, *messages* and *correlationSets* that can be derived from DICOM and HL7. Furthermore, business *partners* and a *process* using basic and structured activities are defined. The WSDL file contains a *portType* and a *serviceLinkType* section to define the Web services. Finally, compensation activities are provided using scopes and security issues are outlined.

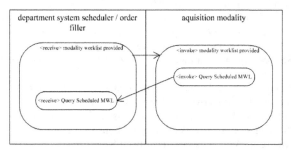

Fig. 5. *Modality worklist prov.* transaction - public process of Department System Scheduler

5   Conclusions and Future Work

In this paper we have introduced the medical services domain, defined requirements for designing medical e-services and outlined a Web service modeling process for IHE framework transactions.

However, several points remain unsolved in this context. First, the transfer and encryption of large binary data is an open issue. For Web service security it is not clear, whether a Web service or an IHE based infrastructure should be preferred. Next, some of the standard specifications of the Web service stack are not yet widely implemented or, especially for coordination services, competing standards exist. Therefore, this paper focused on the composition of medical e-services. Design implications for the areas of coordination, security, transaction and service binding have to be defined in more detail. Those standards are still subject to change and the implications on an infrastructure for e-services have to be revised subsequently. Finally, there are problems normalizing activity diagrams resulting of ambiguities in the medical industry standards.

From here, there are several directions to proceed in future work. On the one hand, one or more existing Web service infrastructures can be used to evaluate implementation specific issues of the BPEL process example. Further evaluations should add security, service binding and other features to show the usability in more complex scenarios. On the other hand, the modeling process, especially the mapping between IHE, HL7 and DICOM standard definitions on one hand and UML diagrams and BPEL constructs on the other, has to be defined formally. Finally, evaluation results and requirements for a Web service based infrastructure should result in an architecture for the execution of medical e-services.

References

1. Workflow Management Coalition: WFMC Reference Model, www.wfmc.org (1995)
2. HL7 Organization: Health Level 7, http://www.hl7.org (2000)
3. NEMA and Global Engineering Group: DICOM 3 Standard, http://www.nema.org (1998)
4. Radiological Society of North America: IHE Technical Framework 1.1, http://www.rsna.org/IHE/index.shtml (2003)
5. CEN/TC251 Health informatics - Medical data interchange: HIS/RIS-PACS and HIS/RIS Modality Interface - ENV 13939, http://www.centc251.org/ (2001)
6. W3C: SOAP Version 1.2, http://www.w3.org/TR/soap12-part1/ (2003)
7. W3C: Web Services Description Language (WSDL) 1.1, http://www.w3.org/TR/wsdl.html (2001)
8. BEA, IBM, Microsoft: Web Services Coordination (WS-Coordination), http://www.ibm.com/developerworks/library/ws-coor/ (2002)
9. BEA, IBM, Microsoft: Web Services Transactions (WS-Transactions), http://www.ibm.com/developerworks/library/ws-transpec/ (2002)
10. BEA, IBM, Microsoft: Web Services Security (WS-Security), www-106.ibm.com/developerworks/ webservices/library/ws-secure/ (2002)
11. BEA Systems, IBM, Microsoft, SAP AG and Siebel Systems: Business Process Execution Language for Web Services version 1.1, http://www-106.ibm.com/developerworks/library/ws-bpel/ (2003)
12. Siemens Medical e-services: http://www.medical.siemens.com
13. Philips: http://www.medical.philips.com
14. GE Medical Systems: http://www.gemedicalsystems.com
15. Agfa Healthcare: http://www.agfa.com/healthcare/
16. Kodak Medical: http://www.kodak.com/global/en/health/
17. Anzböck, R.: XR OPEN RIS Architektur, D.A.T.A. Corporation, http://www.data.at (2001)
18. Anzböck, R.: XR PACS Architektur, D.A.T.A. Corporation, http://www.data.at (2001)
19. Kreider, N.A., Haselton, B.J.: The Systems Challenge: Getting the Clinical Information Support You Need to Improve Patient Care, Wiley, John & Sons, Incorporated (1997)
20. Siegel, Eliot, Kolodner, Robert M.: Filmless Radiology, Springer (1998)
21. Huang, H. K.: PACS: Basic Principles and Applications, Wiley-Liss (1998)
22. Revet, Bas: DICOM Cookbook, Philips Medical Systems (1997)
23. Oosterwijk, H.: DICOM Basics, OTech Inc/Cap Gemini Ernst and Young
24. Aalst: Interorganizational Workflows: An approach based on Message Sequence Charts and Petri Nets, citeseer.nj.nec.com/vanderaalst99interorganizational.html (1999)
25. ebpml.org: The Web service stack, http://www.ebpml.org/webservices.htm (2003)
26. BEA, IBM, Microsoft, TIBCO: WS-ReliableMessaging, http://www-106.ibm.com/developerworks/webservices/library/ws-rm/ (2003)
27. Anzböck, R., Dustdar, S.: Interorganizational Workflow in the Medical Imaging Domain. Proceedings of the 5th International Conference on Enterprise Information Systems (ICEIS), Angers, France, Kluwer Academic Publishers (2003)
27. Anzböck, R., Dustdar, S.: Medical e-services workflows with BPEL4WS, http://www.infosys.tuwien.ac.at/Staff/sd/papers/MedicalServicesWorkflowsWithBPEL4WS.pdf (2003)
29. WS-Attachments: http://msdn.microsoft.com/library/en-us/dnglobspec/html/draft-nielsen-dime-soap-01.txt (2002)
30. Microsoft: Direct Internet Message Encapsulation (DIME), http://msdn.microsoft.com/library/en-us/dnglobspec/html/draft-nielsen-dime-02.txt (2002)

31. W3C, SOAP Messages with Attachments: http://www.w3.org/TR/2000/NOTE-SOAP-attachments-20001211 (2000)
32. "Base64 Content-Transfer-Encoding," RFC 2045, Section 6.8, IETF Draft Standard (1996)
33. Alonso, Casati, Kuno, Machiraju: Web Services, Springer (2004)
34. Bunting, Chapman, Hurley, Little, Mischkinsky, Newcomer, Webber, Swenson: Web Services Composite Application Framework Version 1.0 (WS-CAF), http://www.iona.com/devcenter/standards/WS-CAF/ (2003)
35. Arjuna, Fujitsu, IONA, Oracle, Sun, WS-CTX: Web Services Context, developers.sun.com/techtopics/webservices/wscaf/wsctx.pdf (2003)
36. Arjuna, Fujitsu, IONA, Oracle, Sun, WS-CF: WS-Coordination Framework, developers.sun.com/techtopics/webservices/wscaf/wscf.pdf (2003)
37. Collaxa Inc.: Collaxa BPEL Server 2.0: Reviewer's Guide, http://www.collaxa.com/pdf/cx-bpel-review-20.pdf (2003)
38. BEA, IBM, Microsoft: Web Services Addressing (WS-Addressing), http://www-106.ibm.com/developerworks/webservices/library/ws-add/ (2003)
39. Arjuna, Fujitsu, IONA, Oracle, Sun: Web Services Transaction Management (WS-TXM), http://developers.sun.com/techtopics/webservices/wscaf/wstxm.pdf (2003)
40. Tai, Mikalsen, Wohlstadter, Desai, Rouvellou: Transaction Policies for Service-Oriented Computing (2003)
41. Frolund, Govindarajan: Transactional conversations. In Proceedings of the W3C workshop on Web services, San Jose, CA, USA (2001)
42. Mikalsen, Tai, Rouvellou: Transactional attitudes: Reliable composition of autonomous Web services. In Workshop on Dependable Middleware-based Systems, WDMS 2002, Washington D.C., USA (2002)
43. STRING Kommission, Magda-Lena 2 Richtlinie: http://www.akh-wien.ac.at/STRING/ (2000)
44. WS-Trust, IBM, Microsoft, Verisign, RSA Security: www-106.ibm.com/developerworks/library/ws-trust/ (2003)
45. WS-SecureConversation, IBM, Microsoft, Verisign, RSA Security: www-106.ibm.com/developerworks/library/ws-secon/ (2003)
46. IETF, The TLS Protocol Version 1.1: http://www.ietf.org/internet-drafts/draft-ietf-tls-rfc2246-bis-05.txt (2003)
47. IETF, The IP Security Protocol: http://www.ietf.org/html.charters/ipsec-charter.html (1995)
48. IBM/Microsoft/SAP, et.al.: UDDI 3.0.1, http://uddi.org/pubs/uddi-v3.0.1-20031014.pdf (2003)
49. Mantell: From UML to BPEL, Model Driven Architecture in a Web services world, www-106.ibm.com/developerworks/webservices/library/ws-uml2bpel/ (2003)
50. W3C, X-Path: http://www.w3.org/TR/1999/REC-xpath-19991116 (1999)
51. Wohed, P., van der Aalst, W.M.P., Dumas, M., ter Hofstede, A.H.M.: Pattern Based Analysis of BPEL4WS, Department of Computer and Systems Sciences, Stockholm University/The Royal Institute of Technology, Sweden (2003)
52. Object Management Group: UML 2.0 Standard specification, http://www.omg.org (2003)
53. Fowler, Martin, Scorr, Kendall: UML destilled, Addison Wesley Professional (2000)
54. Dumas, ter Hofstede: UML Activity Diagrams as a Workflow Specification Language, Proceedings of the International Conference on the Unified Modeling Language (UML'2001), Toronto, Canada (2001)

OPCATeam –Collaborative Business Process Modeling with OPM

Dov Dori, Dizza Beimel, and Eran Toch

Technion, Israel Institute of Technology, Haifa, Israel
dori@ie, dizza@tx, erant@tx{.technion.ac.il}

Abstract. While collaboration has become a basic requirement for many development environments, solutions for collaborative modeling are far from being satisfactlory. OPCATeam, which relies on Object-Process Methodology (OPM), provides a collaborative modeling environment that can fit generic modeling purposes. OPM, a holistic, bi-modal visual and textual approach to the study and development of systems, integrates the object-oriented and process-oriented paradigms into a single frame of reference. This characteristic, combined with refinement and abstraction mechanisms, makes OPM ideal for business process modeling. OPCATeam features multi-user Client-Server architecture. The server holds a single OPM model for each system in a central repository. OPCATeam has three access permission levels: workgroup, OPM model, and diagram. The diagram permission, which is unique to OPM, aims to reduce the number of conflicts between concurrent updates and preventing modelers from affecting shared elements while allowing them to refine these elements. Users can simultaneously update the model through the clients according to their access permissions. The detailed design implementation is currently being tested.

1   Introduction

Collaborative design occurs "when a product is designed through the collaborative efforts of many designers" [1]. Collaborative modeling, which applies to a subset of these efforts, focuses on the architecting and design of processes and systems using a formal modeling methodology. This paper defines the requirements from a collaborative modeling environment, specifies architecture for this purpose that is based on Object-Process Methodology (OPM) [2], and describes OPCATeam – an application of these principles.

Collaborative modeling concepts have been known and implemented in such fields as business processes, systems modeling, CAD/CAM, software development, and ontology engineering. While applications in these fields operate under different conditions for different purposes, they do share a set of common requirements insofar as collaboration is concerned. Three guidelines help evaluate, compare and define collaborative system modeling solutions to the following common set of problems:

- *Concurrency*: The environment should allow team members to work on a shared system at the same time, based on a single integrated and consistent model that

J. Desel, B. Pernici, and M. Weske (Eds.): BPM 2004, LNCS 3080, pp. 66-81, 2004.

- describes it, throughout the development process. The model should be available to all the members in real-time, enabling them to get the most up-to-date view of the system.

- *Communication*: The environment should enable multi-way communication among the team members regardless of their physical whereabouts.

- *Security*: The environment should allow secure development, protecting the model under construction from unauthorized external entities and unauthorized changes by modelers.

OPCATeam, which relies on OPM, provides a collaborative modeling environment that can be used for a large variety of modeling purposes. OPM is a holistic, bimodal approach to the study, development and evolution of systems whose single model is represented both visually and in natural language. OPM integrates the object-oriented and process-oriented paradigms into a single frame of reference. Combined with elaborate built-in refinement and abstraction mechanisms, this structure-behavior combination in one model makes OPM ideal for business process modeling. An interesting application of OPM [24] is a generic reverse engineering process that captures the available alternatives at different application levels of an Enterprise Resource Planning (ERP) system. This is an example of a complex system for which the option of working in a collaborative environment is most beneficial.

Since an OPM model consists of a set of interrelated Object-Process Diagrams (OPDs), the main challenge of concurrent OPM-based collaborative development is maintaining the integrity of the OPM model that is manipulated by more than one modeler at the same time. Entities (objects or processes) in one OPD can be refined in a new OPD that contains their detailed descriptions. When an entity is refined, other entities that were directly connected to it in the source, abstract OPD are brought into the newly created OPD, and the modeler can add entities such as sub-processes inside an in-zoomed process and drag the links from the process to these sub processes. When more than one modeler is specifying details of the same entity they are bound to contradict. Moreover, since OPDs can share common entities, when two or more modelers work concurrently on two OPDs that share the same entity, each change in a common entity can potentially influence other OPDs.

Fig. 1 illustrates a simple example of an integrity maintenance problem. Two modelers are working on two different OPDs (SD1 and SD2), which are refined from a common OPD (SD). All three OPDs share a common entity (Object X), the type of which was determine in SD as "char[50]". Modeler A wishes to change the type of object X in SD1 to "date," while modeler B whishes to changes the type of object X in SD2 to "time." Since both modelers are working on the same model at the same time, they compromise the integrity of the OPM model. To avoid such situations, a method for maintaining the integrity and completeness of an OPD set needs to be developed. An important requirement of the collaborative system development environment is support of standard development processes, such as the spiral model. In such iterative development processes, each step in the process is based on refinement and modification of the output of the last step [3]. The architecture of our collaborative development environment takes advantage of OPM's built in refinement mechanism. As noted, security is a major challenge in multi-user environments.

Indeed, one of our goals is to protect the OPM model from unauthorized changes. We would like to ensure that the development of the OPM model is coherent with the organizational structure and authorizations of the development team.

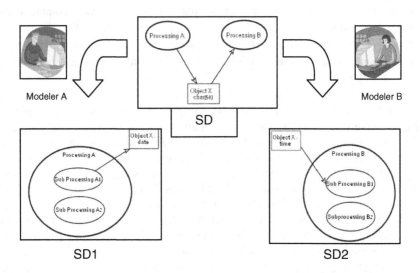

Fig. 1. An integrity problem created by concurrent OPM model development

OPCATeam has multi-user Client-Server architecture. The server holds, maintains and controls in a central repository a single OPM model for each business process or system. Users can simultaneously update the models through the clients according to their access permissions. Each client of OPCATeam sends update messages to the server, where the messages are synchronized and updated in the central repository. Communication services provide complementary infrastructure to the collaborative environment. An access control module enables organizations to implement a development process in a secure and moderated environment using the refinement features of OPM. The access control module enables users to define access permissions at three levels: Workgroup access level, OPM model access level and OPD access level. The Workgroup and OPM model are standard access control levels. They restrict access to resources for individual users or user groups. The third is a fine-grained OPD level that controls permissions to access individual OPDs. The creator of the OPD (the user who created the OPD) can grant viewing, editing, and refining permissions to other users. The viewing permission prevents modelers from being able to change the contents of an OPD. The editing permission grants full editing privileges to all the OPD elements, except those inherited from an ancestor OPD. The refining permission enables a modeler to refine a thing (object or process) in an OPD without changing its 'signature," i.e., the various links that are attached to it, including inputs, outputs, enabling and event links. This permission type, which is unique to OPM, helps reduce the number of conflicts between concurrent updates, preventing modelers from introducing contradictions into the model while still allowing them to refine common entities. Using the refinement permission type is one way to solve the problem exemplified in Figure 1. If the permissions of both modeler

A and modeler B are set to "Refine" on OPD SD, then both modelers can refine the processes and the connected objects, but they cannot commit to changes that may affect each other.

This paper specifies an implementation-independent collaboration model that is embedded in OPM and takes advantage of refinement ability.

2   Background

According to Webster dictionary, to collaborate means 'To work jointly with others or together especially in an intellectual endeavor." In the context of information technology, collaboration takes place whenever humans work together to accomplish a common goal or compatible goals using one or more computer applications. The collaboration concept is normally associated with groupware technology, which, according to [4], is designed to facilitate the work of groups. This technology may be used to communicate, cooperate, coordinate, solve problems, compete, or negotiate. During the past two decades, many organizations have been considering electronic collaboration of distributed teams as a means to achieve higher productivity and improve the quality of their work products. To this end, various collaboration technologies have been introduced to provide solutions in the areas of electronic communication, coordination, and content sharing. CSCW (Computer Supported Cooperative Work) was one of the first such technologies to encourage research collaboration projects. IBM Lotus Notes [5], for example, is one of these early research efforts results. In spite of such significant efforts, groupware products have failed to deliver anything more than marginal improvements to existing email and document management solutions. The current software industry offers significant variety of collaboration products in a number of domains. These include joint activity tools (e.g., audio communication, instant messaging, and content sharing tools) like NetMeeting [6], collaborative electronic presentations and meetings like Lotus Sametime [7], collaboration activities in ERP systems like SAP [8], and collaborative content management such as Documentum [9].

In this paper we focus on collaboration in the domain of formal engineering artifacts, which includes business process modeling, systems modeling, anthologies, CAD/CAM and software coding. A new approach to the capturing of Business Process Models, [10], is a collaborative business process modeling tool that combines Web discussion forums with MS VISIO drawing tool. However, the asynchronous tool's working mode potentially hinders its collaborative aspect.

Prominent systems for collaborative software coding include CVS [11], a large-scale open-source project, which provides a team of developers with a user-friendly, simple collaboration environment. TeamSCOPE [12] is a groupware solution that interfaces with development environments. An experiment that tested the effectiveness of TeamSCOPE concluded that features such as member list and chat improve teamwork efficiency.

Collaborative ontology engineering tools take a different approach. OntoEdit [13] uses client-server architecture to support a concurrent collaborative engineering process. The model under construction is duplicated through the client programs, and a locking mechanism enforces the model integrity. The users can lock a subtree of the ontology (which is specified as a tree) and edit it without interference. This approach could be implemented in a simple manner only under the assumption that there is no interconnectivity between the subtrees. Ontology classes may have relations between them, but in this system, working on a class assumes that it does not influence any related class. As explained, OPM cannot operate under this assumption, and must therefore employ a different approach.

In the field of systems modeling, Poseidon for UML [14] is in a process of upgrading to team-support edition. According to company announcements, this edition will include version control, multi-user support, and client-server architecture. Other UML-based tools, such as Rational Rose [15] and Cittera [16], base their collaborative features on standard version control software. Concurrency is achieved by breaking the system modules into separate files, which are then handled through the customary check-in/check-out mechanism. SoftDdoc [17] is an example of a distributed model management system that supports collaborative software development whose model descriptions are shared and managed through a middleware.

Extensive research and numerous projects, surveyed in [1], concern collaboration in the CAD/CAM domain. Eight future research opportunities were identified, including collaborative conceptual design modeling and data sharing. Another project [18] for computer-aided sequential control design tool deals with collaborative modeling problems and is based on client-server architecture. During a collaboration session, only the user who 'owns" a virtual token can modify the design, while others can only view it. This solution is missing the concurrency of teamwork, which is one of the basic building blocks of collaborative work. An interesting facet of collaboration is the social aspect, which relates to the influence of electronic collaboration on the team's relationship. The big challenge for managers is to recognize that both software and personal interactions contribute to successful collaboration [19].

3   Object-Process Methodology

Object-Process Methodology (OPM) is a holistic approach to the study and development of systems, which integrates the object-oriented and process-oriented paradigms into a single frame of reference. Structure and behavior, the two major aspects that each system exhibits, co-exist in the same OPM model without highlighting one at the expense of suppressing the other. Most interesting and challenging systems are those in which structure and behavior are highly intertwined and hard to separate. Due to structure-behavior integration, OPM provides a solid basis for modeling complex systems.

The elements of the OPM ontology are *entities* and *links*. Entities are of three types: *objects*, *process*es (which are *things*) and *states*. These are the basic building blocks of any system expressed in OPM. *Objects* are (physical or informatical) things that exist, while *processes* are things that transform objects. *Links* can be structural or procedural. *Structural links* express static relations between pairs of entities. Aggregation, generalization, characterization, and instantiation are the four fundamental structural relations. *Procedural links* connect entities (objects, processes, and states) to describe the behavior of a system. The behavior is manifested in three major ways: (1) processes can transform (generate, consume, or change the state of) objects; (2) objects can enable processes without being transformed by them; and (3) objects can trigger events that (at least potentially, if some conditions are met) invoke processes. OPM can be represented by two equivalent modalities: visual and lingual. The visual formalism is defines as a set of inter-related Object-Process Diagrams (OPDs), constitute the graphical representation of the designated model. In this article we focus on the visual representation. Because of the fact that the visual and lingual have a bi-directional mapping, all the assumptions and conclusions related to the visual representation apply to the lingual representation as well.

Three built-in refinement/abstraction mechanisms are built into OPM. They enable presenting the system elements at various detail levels without losing the comprehension of the system as a whole. In-zooming and out-zooming are one pair of refinement and abstraction mechanisms, respectively, which can be applied to entities (objects, processes and states). Zooming into an entity decreases the distance of viewing it such that lower-level elements enclosed within the entity become visible. Conversely, zooming out of a refined entity increases the distance of viewing it, such that a set of low-level elements that are enclosed within it become invisible.

Unfolding and folding are a second pair of refinement and abstraction mechanisms that can be applied on things –objects or processes. Unfolding reveals a set of low-level entities that are hierarchically below a relatively higher-level thing. The hierarchy is with respect to one or more structural links. The result of unfolding is a tree, the root of which is the thing being unfolding. Linked to the root are the things that are exposed as the result of the unfolding. Conversely, folding is applied to the tree, from which the set of unfolding entities is removed, leaving just the root.

4   OPCAT: Object-Process Case Tool

OPCAT[1] (Object-Process CASE Tool) [21] is an integrated system engineering environment that supports OPM-based system development and evolution. OPCAT has been under continuous development as an academic project since 1996. Designed to eventually support the entire system development lifecycle through OPM, OPCAT supports a bimodal graphical-textual view of the system under development, enabling increased OPM accessibility to heterogeneously skilled users engaged in the system development process. The environment already provides for many phases of the system lifecycle, including system specification, automatic analysis and design documentation generation, code generation into Java [22] and potentially any programming language, generation of various UML diagrams, including class, use-case, collaboration and Statecharts, and animated simulation of the OPM model. A major function not currently supported by OPCAT is collaborative concurrent development of a single system by different teams of users. The architecture of this collaborative OPCAT version, called OPCATeam, is the focus of this work.

---

[1] OPCAT can be freely downloaded from http://www.ObjectProcess.org

Definitions of Key Concepts

Element: A basic building block of any system expressed in OPM, which can be an entity or a link.

Entity: An element, which is not a link, which can be a thing or a state.

Thing: An object or a process.

Object: A thing that can exist for some time physically or logically.

Process: A thing that transforms an object by creating it or consuming it or changing its state (i.e., affecting it).

Link: a connector between two entities.

Structural link: A link denoting a persistent relation between objects.

Procedural Link: A link between a process and the object it transforms or a state of that object

OPM model: The OPD set that completely specifies a business process or system along with its OPL script, i.e., the set of all the OPDs that together specify the entire system, each with its corresponding OPL paragraph. In OPCAT, the information of an OPM model is saved in a single XML file.

System Map: A directed hypergraph in which each OPD in the OPM model is a node and each edge is directed from a node to another node in which one of the things is refined.

Scaling: refinement/abstraction, which can be in-zooming/out-zooming or unfolding/folding.

Consistency: A Boolean attribute of an OPM model denoting coherence and lack of any specification contradiction across the various OPDs in the OPD set of an OPM model.

Integrity: A Boolean attribute of an OPM model denoting completeness and lack of dangling elements in the database of the OPM model.[2]

5   Problem Specification

Since OPDs in the OPD set are interconnected in nature, a major challenge of collaborative OPM development is provision of reliable parallel collaborative OPM modeling. Since OPDs can share common entities (objects, processes or states), each change in a common entity potentially influences other OPDs. Therefore, a method for maintaining the integrity of an OPD set must be developed.

Following OPM conventions [2] we label OPDs hierarchically by SD (for System Diagram, the root), SD1, SD2, SD1.1, SD2.3.1, etc. A *refinement relation* between OPDs from SD1 to SD2 exists if and only if SD1 contains a refined (in-zoomed or

---

[2] A similar requirement in the database domain is referred to as "referential integrity."

unfolded) version of the same entity in SD2. A *commonality relation* between OPDs SD1 and SD2 exists if and only if SD1 and SD2 share at least one common entity.

In order to analyze the integrity problem, we extend the definition of the System Map hypergraph SM [2], in which each node represents an OPD. The edges of the augmented SM are of two kinds of labeled edges: directed and undirected. A directed edge represents a refinement (in-zooming or unfolding) relation, such that the edge is directed from the source OPD, in which the refined entity (object or process) is more abstract, to the destination OPD, in which that thing is more refined. The label indicates (1) the entity that is being refined and (2) the refinement type (in-zooming or unfolding).

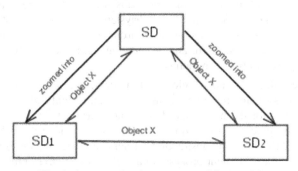

Fig. 2. An example of an augmented System Map

Fig. 2 illustrates an Augmented System Map, in which SD1 contains a refined version of an entity E1 (object or process) that appears in SD in its abstracted version. SD2 contains a refined version of another entity E2, which is also represented in SD in its abstracted version. In our example, the directed edges represent a refinement (in-zooming or unfolding) relation between SD to SD1 and between SD to SD2. Since a common entity (Object X) exists in SD, SD1 and SD2, an edge labeled 'Object X" connects each one of them to the two other nodes. The first group of directed edges forms a DAG. The second group of undirected edges may create a clique, as it does in our example. The formation of a clique depends on the appearance of the entities in the various OPDs.

Having created the Augmented System Map hypergraph, few kinds of complexity queries can be asked. A typical query for integrity checking is to find all the references to an object X that has just been updated by one team member. Fig. 2 illustrates that the response to this query can range from a simple graph to a clique. In this work we focus on a solution for evolving systems with OPM in a collaborative environment, Complexity analysis of such queries is a topic for a separate research.

Security and Access Control

Collaborative modeling requires addressing two security aspects. The first is protecting the model from inspection and changes by unauthorized entities, be they innocent or malicious. This aspect is applicable to various types of systems and the collaborative nature of the modeling environment per se does not complicate the problem any further. The second aspect, which is specific to collaborative environments, relates to the enforcement of regulations that team members must follow in order to maintain the integrity of the OPM model under development. To ensure this, the team must be coordinated and the model must be protected from damage caused by mistakes and uncoordinated changes by team members.

This regulation enforcement aspect is related to two characteristics of the system development process: organizational structure of the development team and the nature of the development process.

To understand the development team organizational structure aspect, consider a typical scenario of a team consisting of a team leader and two modelers. Each modeler is responsible for modeling one subsystem, while the team leader is responsible for the integration of the two subsystem models into a coherent system model. We require that our collaborative environment restrict each modeler to the subsystems she/he is responsible for and provide the team leader with tools to control the access permissions of his team members.

Regarding the nature of the development process, we note that many modern development processes are iterative in the sense that outputs of one development stage serve as inputs for the next stage. Furthermore, artifacts created in some stage can be refined and modified to produce a more concrete artifact in the next stage downstream. OPM's built-in abstraction/refinement mechanisms can naturally support this type of development process. In a collaborative environment, we require that only authorized team members who are responsible for a specific development stage will be able to refine artifacts created at that stage. For example, the domain expert representing the customer may define higher-level artifacts, mainly requirements, while the system architect may refine these artifacts, but not change them without the domain expert's approval.

6   OPCATeam Architecture

To realize our goal of creating a multi-user collaborative OPM-based system evolution environment, our proposed architecture, whose OPM model is presented in Fig. 3, tackles the aforementioned challenges of concurrent modeling, communications and access control.

Our solution is based on a client-server multi user environment architecture, in which a central server provides collaborative services to the OPCATeam clients. The Client-server architecture optimizes the workload distribution between the clients and the server: The server handles issues that are centralized in nature, while the client contributes visual and logical services that already exist in the single-user version of OPCAT. The OPCATeam client wraps the current single-user OPCAT implementation, offering a user interface for the services provided by the server. This way, any improved new version of the single-user OPCAT will automatically be incorporated into the collaborative environment. The server has three main modules:

- The **Model Manager** module handles concurrent development of OPM models using a central repository and a concurrent update mechanism. This mechanism allows simultaneous user updates to a single OPM model, which is shared by one or more authorized users, while its perfection is maintained at all times. The module includes a version control function that logs updates and enables revision control. It uses records of update history to ensure control over the collaborative development process.

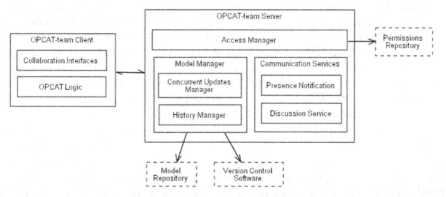

Fig. 3. OPCATeam architecture overview

- The **Access Manager** module controls access and restricts changes for reliable and secure collaborative development process. The permissions, managed by a central repository, impose access restrictions on the workgroup (a shared set of OPM models), on the entire OPM model, and on the OPM System Map.

- The **Communication Services** module is a set of communication applications, such as synchronized discussion (chat) option and a presence notification window.

Our solution is based on the existence of a **single** OPM model that is controlled and maintained by the server. Each OPD model is specified by its OPD set and saved in an XML format. OPCATeam users start a (potentially collaborative) session by downloading a copy of the OPM model to their local client workstations. Throughout their work, collaborating system modelers can send update messages, which are commensurable with their permissions, to the OPM model that resides on the server. The updates are synchronized and handled in the central OPM model repository.

The server inserts these synchronized updates into a queue and performs the following steps:

1. The server optionally rechecks the client permission to request the current handled update to boost the security level of the OPM model.

2. The server adds the authorized update to the OPM model.

3. The server checks the integrity of the OPM model immediately after introducing the change and performs any necessary adaptations of the OPM model database to maintain its perfection.

4. If the integrity of the OPM model database can be maintained, the server commits the update. After the commit execution, the updated model is accessible to all the authorized clients. Users can then initiate a request for the server to refresh their views and to inspect the changes introduced in the meantime by their collaborating team peers. If the integrity of the OPM model database cannot be maintained (e.g., a client has requested to update an object that no

longer exists in the OPM model) the server rejects the update, and sends a corresponding message to the client, specifying the reasons for the rejection. This process prevents imperfection problems. The module utilizes version control software that provides logging of updates, revision control, and rollback abilities. This enables system architects to manage and inspect the development process, and to implement utilities that may become standard in collaborative OPM-based system development. As noted, the server holds a single, most recently updated OPM model. Since the model is saved on the server, recovery from client crashing is simple. The only action the client needs to take is requesting a fresh copy of the OPM model from the server. However, the user does lose all the changes made since the last save operation (which can be either manual or automatic).

Access control enables users to define access permissions at three levels. The shallow access level is the *Workgroup access level,* the intermediate one is the *OPM model access level,* and the deep access level is the *OPD access level.* The first two levels follow the standard in many development environments, while the third is OPM-specific. The permissions are set individually at the user level and can be changed in real-time by an authorized users. *Workgroup* stands for a group of OPM models that a team of modelers takes an interest in. The workgroup access level exhibits the Boolean permissions *Create OPM model, View workgroup,* and *Admin* (which gives the user the permission to grant workgroup permission to unauthorized users). By default, every user can create a new workgroup, in which case he is defined as the *workgroup creator,* and gets the admin permission.

The OPM Model access level exhibits the Boolean permissions *View OPM model* (which gives the user the permission to view the OPDs in the OPD tree), *Commit OPM model* (which gives the user the permission to save the model in the Version Control Software repository), and *Admin.* The user who created the OPM model is defined as the *OPM model creator* and gets the admin permission. The corresponding workgroup administrator may add more Administrators to an OPM model.

The OPD access level exhibits the Boolean permissions *view OPD* (which gives the user the permission to view the OPD but not to update it), *Edit OPD* (which gives the user the permission to edit elements in his OPD, except for elements that were inherited from an ancestor OPD), *refine OPD* (which gives the user the permission to refine any OPM entity in his OPD by in-zooming or unfolding) and *Admin* (which gives the user the permission to grant OPD permissions to unauthorized users.) The user that created the OPD is defined as the *OPD creator,* and gets the admin permission. The OPM model Admin may add more Administrators to this OPD.

OPCATeam has at least one administrator, who is authorized to add or disable Administrators to a workgroup, disable users, etc. Fig. 4 illustrates the structure of the Access Control, and followed by the OPL that OPCAT generated. Fig. 5 illustrates the dynamic zoomed in server process for new OPD creation: a new OPD request message arrives to the server, which checks the user permission to apply for it. In case the checking results success, a new OPD is created, the user is acknowledged and the server updates the OPM Model.

The access control module helps reduce update conflicts. As noted, an OPM-model consists of a set of OPDs. The user can create, update or delete OPDs according to his permissions. Thus, in a restricted configuration of OPCATeam, conflicts can be totally prevented, while in other configurations, conflicts may occur, and will be handled by the server.

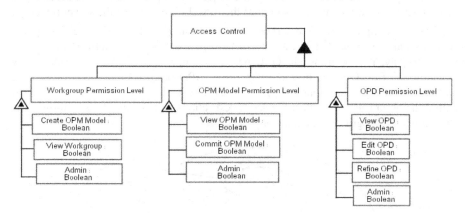

Fig. 4. Access control structure and OPL generation

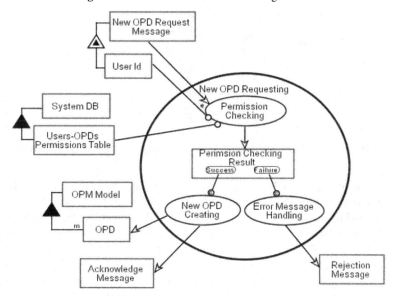

Fig. 5. A dynamic zoomed in server process for new OPD creation

Only one user, the *OPD creator*, is authorized to grant permissions to other users, but more than one user might have Edit permission to a certain OPD. The Edit permission allows the users to update, delete or create new OPD elements (except for elements that were inherited from an ancestor OPD). In such case, a conflict might occur if, for example, two clients request to update an OPM entity with two different attribute values. However, all client requests arrive at the server, which inserts them into a FIFO queue. The requests are handled one after the other, the sequence is legal, and therefore these two requests do not create any conflict. Another example is when two requests arrive at the server, the first request demands to delete an object, while the second one demands to update one of its attribute values. In this situation, the server accepts the first request, deletes the object, and updates the OPM model. The second request now results in violation of the model's integrity, so the server rejects it.

As these examples show, the server has appropriate tools to handle such cases, but conflicts can be prevented if the access control mechanism is defined in a more restricted way, i.e. by grant edit OPD permission to one user only at a time, or by replacing the Edit OPD permission with refine OPD permission, thereby preventing conflicts from occurring. Our design provides a host of access control mechanisms, letting the organization to select the set of restrictions that fits its needs. Following is an example of integrity maintenance by the server.

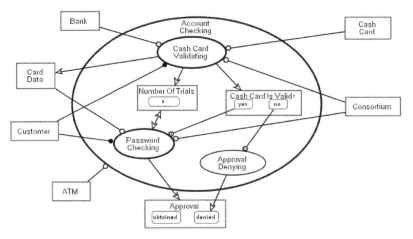

Fig. 6. The initial OPD describing an Account Checking process within an ATM system

Fig. 6 illustrates a zoomed-in process for account checking, which is an OPD taken from a description of an ATM system [2]. Fig. 7 illustrates the OPD after the server has committed an authorized user request to delete the object "**Consortium**". Fig. 8 illustrates the server rejection of an attempt to add an object that **Consortium** exhibits since **Consortium** does not exist any more in the OPM model.

The OPCATeam client is based on OPCAT (Object-Process CASE Tool) [21] and includes four major functions. The first two are inherited from the OPCAT, while the last two are OPCATeam-specific, designed to meet the collaborative system requirements. The first function is the visual support of draing and manipulating OPDs. The client offers the user a high-level and friendly graphical user interface that enables the user to model his required system fastly and clearly. The second function is the logical support in OPM. The client software prevents the user from performing illegal modeling actions that do not obey the methodology rules. The third function supplies the user with an interface to various standard collaboration utilities like server communication, chat, and presence window, while the fourth function supports the access control mechanism.

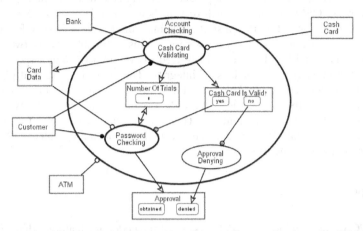

Fig. 7. The server accepts deletion of the object **Consortium** and updates the OPM Model.

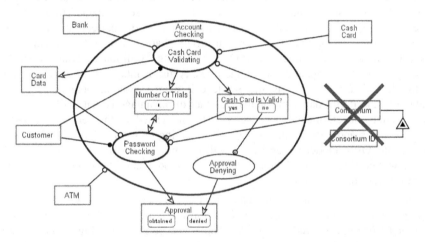

Fig. 8. The server rejects request to update a non-existing object

7   Implementation

The implementation of OPCATeam is divided into two phases. The first phase takes full advantage of OPCAT. OPCAT is able to get and return only a complete OPM model. Therefore, access control at this phase is limited to the workgroup and OPM model permission levels only. The more elaborate access control for individual OPDs will be implemented in the second phase. In the first phase, then, an additional type of permission, *Edit OPM model*, is defined. This permission temporarily replaces the Edit OPD permission. A user with Edit OPM model permission on a specific OPM model is equivalent to a user with Edit OPD permission to all the OPD-set of this OPM model. To speed up the development, users are able to work simultaneously on the same basic OPM model, but each one of them works in a separate *Session*. For example, two authorized users can start modeling from the same basic OPM model at the same time, but in two different sessions. This inevitably yields two different versions of the same OPM model, which need to be rejoined using a specific merge utility that eliminates potential lack of integrity. The goal of the second phase is to support the OPD permission level. To this end, two major functions have to be implemented. The first is relevant to the OPCATeam client granularity, which needs to be replaced by the OPD granularity. The second function is relevant to the server ability to get a partial OPM model and use it to update the complete OPM model white maintaining its integrity.

8   Conclusions

The OPCATeam architecture delivers system modeling features that meet the requirements of modern collaborative environments. It is concurrent, allowing teams of modelers to design a shared OPM model. The client-server paradigm enables real time modeling while eliminating risks of losing the model perfection. Furthermore, the architecture takes care of the interconnectivity characteristic of OPM, which poses a special challenge for collaborative OPM modeling. Additional advantages include security, central logging, and backup facilities. A disadvantage of the architecture lies in the fact that the server is the bottleneck of the system, potentially creating scalability and performance problems. Another disadvantage is that while engaged in OPM system development, users need to be connected to the server to allow for online updates and concurrent sessions. Augmenting OPCAT with the ability to add parts of the OPM model incrementally will remove this restriction as users working offline will be able to upload their updates to the model and the merge utility will take care of perfection constraints.

Our access control approach caters to the characteristics of OPM. Thus, for example, the introduction of the *refine* permission type, in addition to the standard *view* and *edit* ones, is unique to OPM. The *refine* permission allows users to refine entities generated by other users. Many established engineering disciplines apply refinement in large-scale projects or product development, but so far, software engineering and system modeling have made only limited use of this important principle. Our approach opens the door to full-scale adoption and application of refinement activities. Future research and development is planned to incorporate into the OPCATeam architecture new modules, such as workflow and peer-to-peer management. Orthogonally, principles applied in this work can be put to work in standard development approaches that use UML [23] and other modeling methodologies. We anticipate, however, that this will be more difficult since UML does not have built-in abstraction-refinement mechanisms like OPM.

References

1. Wang, L., Shen, W., Xie, H., Neelamkavil, J., and Pardasani, A., Collaborative conceptual design –state of the art and future trends. Computer Aided Design 34, 2002.
2. Dori, D. Object-Process Methodology – A Holistic Systems Paradigm. Springer Verlag, Berlin, New York, 2002.
3. Potok, T. E., Extensions to the spiral model to support joint development of complex software systems. Proceedings of the 30th Annual Southeast Regional Conference, ACM Press, 2002.
4. Usability First web site –http://www.usabilityfirst.com/groupware/intro.txl
5. IBM, Lotus Notes, http://www.lotus.com/products/product4.nsf/wdocs/noteshomepage
6. Microsoft, NetMeeting, http://www.microsoft.com/windows/netmeeting/
7. IBM, Lotus Sametime, http://www-1.ibm.com/servers/eserver/iseries/sametime/
8. SAP, http://www.sap.com/
9. Documentum, http://www.documentum.com
10. Kazanis, P. and Ginige, A. Asynchronous collaborative business process modeling through a web forum, Seventh Annual CollECTeR Conference on Electronic Commerce. Melbourne, VIC, Australia, in association with ACIS 2002.
11. CVS, http://www.cvshome.org/
12. Steinfield, C., Jang, C., and Pfaff, B., Supporting virtual team collaboration: the TeamSCOPE system. Proceedings of the international ACM SIGGROUP conference on supporting group work. ACM Press, 1999.
13. Sure, Y., Erdmann, M., Angele, J., Staab, S. Studer R., and Wenke, D. OntoEdit: Collaborative ontology engineering for the Semantic Web. Proceedings of the First International Semantic Web Conference 2002 (ISWC 2002), LNCS 2342, pp. 221-235, Springer 2002.
14. Gentleware , Poseidon for UML Enterprise Edition, http://www.gentleware.com
15. IBM, IBM Rational Rose - http://www.rational.com/products/rose/index.jsp
16. Canyon Blue Inc., Cittera UML collaborative tool. http://www.canyonblue.com/
17. Suzuki, J. and Yamamoto, Y. SoftDock: A Distributed Collaborative Platform for Model-based Software Development.
18. Yen, C., Li, W.J. and Lin, J.C., A web-based collaborative, computer-aided sequential control design tool. IEEE Control Systems Magazine, pp. 0272-1708, 2003.
19. Goldstein, H. Collaboration Nation, IEEE Spectrum, June 2003.
21. Dori, D., Reinhartz-Berger, I., and Sturm A. (2003). OPCAT –A Bimodal Case Tool for Object-Process based system development. 5th International Conference on Enterprise Information Systems (ICEIS 2003), pp. 286-291. Software download site: http://www.ObjectProcess.org/
22. Sun Microsystems, Inc. Java 2 Platform API Speciation. http://www.java.sun.com/products/jdk/.2/docs/api
23. Unified Modeling Language (UML) http://www.uml.org/
24. Soffer, P. Golany B., and Dori, D. ERP Modeling: A Comprehensive Approach. Information Systems 28, pp. 673-690, 2003.

On the Semantics of EPCs:
A Framework for Resolving the Vicious Circle

Ekkart Kindler

Computer Science Department, University of Paderborn, Germany
kindler@upb.de

Abstract. One of the most debatable features of *Event driven Process Chains* (EPCs) is their *non-local semantics*. Most non-local semantics for EPCs either have a formal flaw or no formal definition is given at all. It can be shown that a single transition relation cannot precisely capture the informal idea of the non-local semantics of EPCs. Therefore, we formalize the non-local semantics of EPCs as a pair of two corresponding transition relations by employing standard techniques from fixed point theory.

Actually, there are several choices when formalizing this semantics for EPCs. These choices, however, do not compromise the application of the underlying fixed point theory. Therefore, the mathematics applied in this paper can be considered as a semantical framework for formally defining different kinds of non-local semantics for EPCs. This framework can be used for the discussion and, eventually, for settling the discussion on the semantics of EPCs.

1 Introduction

Ever since the definition of *Event driven Process Chains (EPCs)* in the early 90ties [2], there has been a debate on their precise semantics. One feature recurrently provoking a debate is the *non-locality* of the semantics of the OR-join and the XOR-join connectors. On the one hand, a non-local semantics for these connectors helps simplifying many models. On the other hand, there is no satisfactory formalization of this semantics yet. Many formalizations simply ignore the non-local semantics of the OR-join and XOR-join connectors; others provide ad-hoc solutions. Rittgen [6] discusses some aspects of this problem and some approaches towards defining more satisfactory semantics for EPCs, which help resolving the problems. One concept proposed by Langner, Schneider and Wehler [4], for example, is some additional synchronization, which is similar to *dead path elimination* in IBM's MQ Series[1] process model [3]. Rittgen himself introduces some new syntax for EPCs in order to partially cure the problem [6].

One reason for the ongoing debate on the semantics of EPCs is inherent to the non-locality of the informal semantics for EPCs: In essence, a non-local semantics refers to itself in its own definition (see Sect. 2 for more details). Even worse,

---

[1] IBM MQ Series workflow was called FlowMark at that time.

J. Desel, B. Pernici, and M. Weske (Eds.): BPM 2004, LNCS 3080, pp. 82–97, 2004.

this self-reference occurs under a negation, which easily results in mathematical, conceptual, and technical 'short-circuits'[2]. In [8], we pinpointed these arguments and proved that there is no formal semantics (i. e. a single transition relation) fully compliant with the informal semantics of EPCs – the *vicious circle*.

From a theoretical point of view, this impossibility result should have settled the debate – against having non-local semantics for EPCs. In practice, however, there are many EPC models exploiting the non-local semantics. Moreover, constructs with non-local semantics are not specific to EPCs; there are other notations for modelling business processes with similar non-local semantics and with similar problems. Therefore, we set out to define a mathematically sound semantics for EPCs that comes as close as possible to the informal semantics[3]. This formal definition along with its underlying mathematics will be presented in this paper. In fact, we provide a framework for defining other versions of non-local semantics for EPCs. Technically, this framework resolves the vicious circle by distinguishing two corresponding transition relations for EPCs and by using fixed point theory for capturing self-references.

What is more, this framework comes with a characterization of *unclean* EPCs for each concrete definition of a semantics. These unclean EPCs are those that do not exactly capture the informal semantics and, therefore, are ambiguous. Within this framework we can investigate and, eventually, settle the debate about the most adequate semantics for EPCs – this way, resolving the vicious circle of never-ending discussions on the proper semantics of EPCs.

2   The Problem

In this section, we informally present the syntax and the semantics of EPCs and discuss the problem with its non-locality. Here, we can give a rough outline only. For a more detailed motivation of EPCs, their syntax, and their semantics, we refer to [2,5]. For a more detailed exposition of the problems with the non-local semantics of EPCs, we refer to [8].

Figure 1 shows an example of an EPC. It consists of three kinds of nodes: *events* graphically represented as hexagons, *functions* represented as rounded boxes, and *connectors* graphically represented as circles. The dashed arcs between the different nodes represent the *control flow*. The two black circles do not belong to the EPC itself; they represent a *state* of that EPC. A state, basically, assigns a number of *process folders* to each arc of the EPC[4]. Each black circle represents a process folder at the corresponding arc.

---

[2] In fact, it was a 'short-circuit' in the formal definition of a semantics for EPCs in [5] which, again, attracted our attention to this problem.

[3] Actually, there is not a single well-accepted informal semantics for EPCs. Here, we refer to the informal semantics presented by Nüttgens and Rump [5].

[4] In other formalizations, process folders are assigned to nodes rather than to arcs. Assigning folders to arcs significantly simplifies the technical presentation of our framework. Therefore, we have chosen to assign folders to arcs. But, this is not inherent to our framework.

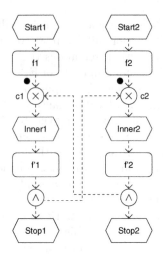

Fig. 1. An EPC

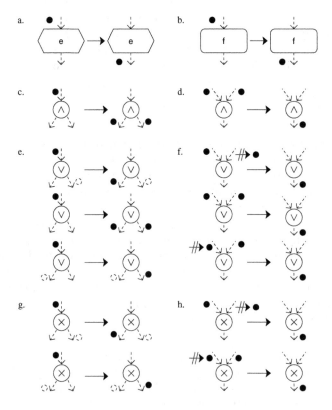

Fig. 2. The transition relation for the different types of nodes

The semantics of an EPC defines how process folders are propagated through an EPC. The corresponding state changes can be formalized as a *transition relation*. Clearly, the definition of this transition relation depends on the type of the involved node. For events and functions, a process folder is simply propagated from the incoming arc to the outgoing arc. The transition relation for events and functions is graphically represented in the top row of Fig. 2 (case a. and b.). For connectors, the propagation of folders depends on the type of the connector (*AND, OR*, resp. *XOR*) and whether it is a *join* or a *split connector*. Figure 2 shows the transition relation for the different connectors. For example, the AND-split connector (case c.) propagates a folder from its incoming arc to all outgoing arcs. The AND-join connector (case d.) needs one folder on each incoming arc; which are then propagated to a single folder on the outgoing arc. The OR-join and the XOR-join connector are similar, where a dashed circle indicates a possibly present process folder, which is not affected by the transition (case e. and g.).

The more interesting connectors are the OR-join and the XOR-join. Here, we focus on the XOR-join connector. An XOR-join connector (case h.) waits for a folder on one incoming arc, which is then propagated to the outgoing arc. But, there is one additional condition: The XOR-join must not propagate the folder, if there is or there could arrive a folder on the other incoming arc. In Fig. 2.h, this is represented by a label $\#\!\!\rightarrow\!\bullet$ at the other arc. Note that this condition cannot be checked locally in the considered state, because whether a folder could arrive at the other arc or not depends on the overall behaviour of the EPC. Therefore, we call the semantics of the XOR-join *non-local*. Likewise, the OR-join connector (case f.) has a non-local semantics. Note that, in both cases, the additional conditions refer to the transition relation itself (to its transitive closure to be precise) and that the transition relation occurs under a negation in this condition.

Basically, the non-locality results in two problems, a technical one and a conceptual one (see [8] for details):

1. In the definition of the transition relation, we refer to the transition relation itself. This self-reference easily results in definitions that are not mathematically sound. In principle, this problem could be avoided by using some kind of fixed point semantics – the standard trick for giving semantics to objects that refer to themselves such as recursive functions or recursive data types. The problem with the non-local semantics of EPCs, however, is that such fixed points do not always exist.

2. The conceptual problem is that, for some EPCs, there is no transition relation that exactly captures the informal semantics. The reason is that the self-reference occurs under a negation. For example, consider the EPC from Fig. 1 with one process folder on one of the incoming arcs of each XOR-join c_1 and c_2. For symmetry reasons, either both of them should be able to propagate this folder or both should not be able to propagate the folder.

But, either way contradicts the definition of the informal semantics of the
XOR-join.

One purpose of this paper, is to define a non-local semantics for EPCs that is
mathematically sound and comes as close as possible to the informal semantics
of EPCs. What is more, this definition allows us identifying problematic EPCs,
i.e. EPCs for which the informal semantics is ambiguous. We call such EPCs
unclean.

The main purpose of this paper, however, is the presentation of a framework
for defining and discussing different kinds of non-local semantics. The concrete
semantics defined here, serves as an example for presenting the framework. This
framework can then by applied to define different versions of non-local semantics
and to investigate them from a mathematical, conceptual, implementational and
pragmatical point of view. This way, we might, eventually, come up with 'the
semantics' of EPCs.

3   The Syntax of EPCs

In this section, we formalize the syntax of EPCs. Since the focus of this paper
is on a formalization of the semantics of EPCs, we will omit those syntactical
restrictions that are not relevant for our semantical considerations; moreover, we
consider *flat EPCs* only, i.e. EPCs without subprocesses.

Basically, an EPC is a graph, i.e. it consist of nodes and arcs connecting
those nodes. In order to express some of the syntactical restrictions of EPCs, we
first introduce a notation for denoting the ingoing and outgoing arcs of a node:

Notation 1 (Ingoing and outgoing arcs). *Let N be a set of nodes and let
$A \subseteq N \times N$ be a binary relation over N, the arcs. For each node $n \in N$, we
define the set of its ingoing arcs $n_{in} = \{(x, n) \mid (x, n) \in A\}$, and we define the
set of its outgoing arcs $n_{out} = \{(n, y) \mid (n, y) \in A\}$.*

An EPC consists of three different kinds of nodes, *events*, *functions*, and
connectors, which are connected by *control flow arcs*. A connector can be either
an AND-, an OR-, or an XOR-connector, which is indicated by labelling the
connector correspondingly. Each function has exactly one ingoing and one outgoing arc, whereas each event has at most one ingoing and at most one outgoing
arc. A connector has multiple ingoing arcs and one outgoing arc (a *join*), or it
has one ingoing arc and multiple outgoing arcs (a *split*):

Definition 1 (EPC). *An EPC $M = (E, F, C, l, A)$ consists of three pairwise
disjoint sets E, F, and C, a mapping $l : C \rightarrow \{and, or, xor\}$ and a binary
relation $A \subseteq (E \cup F \cup C) \times (E \cup F \cup C)$ such that*

- *$|e_{in}| \leq 1$ and $|e_{out}| \leq 1$ for each $e \in E$,*
- *$|f_{in}| = |f_{out}| = 1$ for each $f \in F$, and*
- *either $|c_{in}| > 1$ and $|c_{out}| = 1$ or $|c_{in}| = 1$ and $|c_{out}| > 1$ for each $c \in C$.*

An element of E is called an event, *an element of F is called a* function, *an element of C is called a* connector, *and an element of A is called a* control flow arc.

Note, that we have omitted the following syntactical restrictions for EPCs in our definition:

- Functions and events should alternate along the control flow.
- Each OR-split and each XOR-split connector should be preceded by a function, which determines to which direction the process folder is propagated.
- There should be no cycle of control flow that consist of connector nodes only.

Though these requirements are important from a pragmatical point of view, these restrictions are not necessary for defining the semantics of EPCs. So, we do not formalize these restrictions here. For a complete exposition of the syntax of EPCs, we refer to [5].

In the definition of the semantics, we need to distinguish among different types of connectors: AND-, OR-, and XOR-, each of which can be either a *split* or a *join connector*. The corresponding sets are defined below.

Notation 2 (Nodes and connectors). *For the rest of this paper, we fix the EPC $M = (E, F, C, l, A)$. We denote the set of all its nodes by $N = E \cup F \cup C$ and we define the following sets of connectors:*

	split connectors	join connectors
$\wedge$	$C_{as} = \{c \in C \mid l(c) = and \wedge |c_{in}| = 1\}$	$C_{aj} = \{c \in C \mid l(c) = and \wedge |c_{out}| = 1\}$
$\vee$	$C_{os} = \{c \in C \mid l(c) = or \wedge |c_{in}| = 1\}$	$C_{oj} = \{c \in C \mid l(c) = or \wedge |c_{out}| = 1\}$
$\times$	$C_{xs} = \{c \in C \mid l(c) = xor \wedge |c_{in}| = 1\}$	$C_{xj} = \{c \in C \mid l(c) = xor \wedge |c_{out}| = 1\}$

At last, we define the *states* of an EPC: An assignment of a number of process folders to each arc of the EPC. For simplicity, at most one folder at each arc is allowed in a state. But, we will see in Sect. 6 that this restriction can be easily released.

Definition 2 (State of an EPC). *For an EPC $M = (E, F, C, l, A)$, we call a mapping $\sigma : A \to \{0, 1\}$ a state of M. The set of all states of M is denoted by Σ.*

Note that, in our definition, we assign the process folders to the control flow arcs of the EPC, whereas most other formalizations (e. g. [7,6,5]) assign the process folders (or tokens) to the nodes of the EPC. Though this choice is not essential for the definition of the semantics, it allows us a smoother technical presentation of the semantics[5]. In addition, this choice makes the nodes of an EPC the active parts, whereas the arcs become the passive parts.

---

[5] For example, there is no need to extend an EPC with *pre-connectors* as introduced in [5].

4   The Transition Relation $R(P)$

Simplistically, the semantics of an EPC could be defined in terms of a *transition relation* between its states. In order to identify the nodes involved in the transitions, the transition relation is defined as a triple $R \subseteq \Sigma \times N \times \Sigma$. A single transition $(\sigma, n, \sigma') \in R$, represents a change from state σ to σ' that corresponds to node n.

In order to define and to argue on such transition relations, we introduce some notations:

Notation 3 (Restriction and reachability).   *For some transition relation $P \subseteq \Sigma \times N \times \Sigma$, and some subset $N' \subseteq N$, we define the* restriction of P to N' *as $P|_{N'} = \{(\sigma, n, \sigma') \in P \mid n \in N'\}$.*

By slight abuse of notation, we define the reachability relation P^* of P *as the reflexive and transitive closure of the binary relation $\{(\sigma, \sigma') \in \Sigma \times \Sigma \mid \exists n \in N : (\sigma, n, \sigma') \in P\}$.*

As discussed in Sect. 2, we need to refer to the transition relation in its own definition when defining a non-local semantics for the OR-join and the XOR-join connectors. Such cyclic references, however, are not possible in a sound mathematical definition. In order to resolve this cycle, we assume that some transition relation $P \subseteq \Sigma \times N \times \Sigma$ is given, and we define another transition relation $R \subseteq \Sigma \times N \times \Sigma$ where we refer to P whenever we would like to refer to R itself. In order to stress the dependency of R from the transition relation P, we denote it by $R(P)$. Formally, this reflects the fact, that R is a function that takes a transition relation P and gives another transition relation. This way, there is no cycle in the definition of $R(P)$. Later, in Sect. 5, we will use a standard technique of semantics, fixed points, for establishing a reference of R to itself. But, this need not bother us right now.

In the following definition, we first define a separate transition relation R_n for each node $n \in N$ of the EPC, which captures the behaviour of node n only. The overall transition relation $R(P)$ is the union of all the transition relations R_n. The details of this definition are not so important; but, we include it for completeness sake. Figure 2 from Sect. 2 gives a rough overview on the definitions of R_n for the different types of nodes. A more detailed explanation follows after the formal definition.

Definition 3 (Transition relation $R(P)$). *Let P be a transition relation for an EPC M. For each node $n \in N$, we define the transition relation $R_n \subseteq \Sigma \times N \times \Sigma$ as follows:*

a. *For $n = e \in E$ with $e_{in} = \{i\}$ and $e_{out} = \{o\}$, we define $R_e \subseteq \Sigma \times N \times \Sigma$ by $(\sigma, e, \sigma') \in R_e$ iff $\sigma(i) = 1$, $\sigma(o) = 0$, $\sigma'(i) = 0$, $\sigma'(o) = 1$, and $\sigma'(a) = \sigma(a)$ for each $a \in A \setminus \{i, o\}$.*

a.' *For $n = e \in E$ with $e_{in} = \emptyset$ or $e_{out} = \emptyset$, we define $R_e = \emptyset$.*

b. *For $n = f \in F$ with $f_{in} = \{i\}$ and $f_{out} = \{o\}$, we define $R_f \subseteq \Sigma \times N \times \Sigma$ by $(\sigma, f, \sigma') \in R_f$ iff $\sigma(i) = 1$, $\sigma(o) = 0$, $\sigma'(i) = 0$, $\sigma'(o) = 1$, and $\sigma'(a) = \sigma(a)$ for each $a \in A \setminus \{i, o\}$.*

c. *For $n = c \in C_{as}$ with $c_{in} = \{i\}$, we define $R_c \subseteq \Sigma \times N \times \Sigma$ by $(\sigma, c, \sigma') \in R_c$ iff $\sigma(i) = 1$, $\sigma(o) = 0$ for each $o \in c_{out}$, $\sigma'(i) = 0$, $\sigma'(o) = 1$ for each $o \in c_{out}$, and $\sigma'(a) = \sigma(a)$ for each $a \in A \setminus (\{i\} \cup c_{out})$.*

d. *For $n = c \in C_{aj}$ with $c_{out} = \{o\}$, we define $R_c \subseteq \Sigma \times N \times \Sigma$ by $(\sigma, c, \sigma') \in R_c$ iff $\sigma(i) = 1$ for each $i \in c_{in}$, $\sigma(o) = 0$, $\sigma'(i) = 0$ for each $i \in c_{in}$, $\sigma'(o) = 1$, and $\sigma'(a) = \sigma(a)$ for each $a \in A \setminus (c_{in} \cup \{o\})$.*

e. *For $n = c \in C_{os}$ with $c_{in} = \{i\}$, we define $R_c \subseteq \Sigma \times N \times \Sigma$ by $(\sigma, c, \sigma') \in R_c$ iff, for some $S \subseteq c_{out}$ with $|S| \geq 1$, we have $\sigma(i) = 1$, $\sigma(o) = 0$ for each $o \in S$, $\sigma'(i) = 0$, $\sigma'(o) = 1$ for each $o \in S$, and $\sigma'(a) = \sigma(a)$ for each $a \in A \setminus (\{i\} \cup S)$.*

f. *For $n = c \in C_{oj}$ with $c_{out} = \{o\}$, we define $R_c \subseteq \Sigma \times N \times \Sigma$ by $(\sigma, c, \sigma') \in R_c$ iff, for some $S \subseteq c_{in}$ with $|S| \geq 1$, we have $\sigma(i) = 1$ for each $i \in S$, $\hat{\sigma}(a) = 0$ for each $\hat{\sigma}$ with $\sigma(P|_{N \setminus \{c\}})^* \hat{\sigma}$ and for each $a \in c_{in} \setminus S$, $\sigma(o) = 0$, $\sigma'(i) = 0$ for each $i \in S$, $\sigma'(o) = 1$, and $\sigma'(a) = \sigma(a)$ for each $a \in A \setminus (S \cup \{o\})$.*

g. *For $n = c \in C_{xs}$ with $c_{in} = \{i\}$, we define $R_c \subseteq \Sigma \times N \times \Sigma$ by $(\sigma, c, \sigma') \in R_c$ iff, for some $o \in c_{out}$, we have $\sigma(i) = 1$, $\sigma(o) = 0$, $\sigma'(i) = 0$, $\sigma'(o) = 1$, and $\sigma'(a) = \sigma(a)$ for each $a \in A \setminus \{i, o\}$.*

h. *For $n = c \in C_{xj}$ with $c_{out} = \{o\}$, we define $R_c \subseteq \Sigma \times N \times \Sigma$ by $(\sigma, c, \sigma') \in R_c$ iff, for some $i \in c_{in}$, we have $\sigma(i) = 1$, $\hat{\sigma}(a) = 0$ for each $\hat{\sigma}$ with $\sigma(P|_{N \setminus \{c\}})^* \hat{\sigma}$ and for each $a \in c_{in} \setminus \{i\}$, $\sigma(o) = 0$, $\sigma'(i) = 0$, $\sigma'(o) = 1$, and $\sigma'(a) = \sigma(a)$ for each $a \in A \setminus \{i, o\}$.*

We define the transition relation $R(P) = \bigcup_{n \in N} R_n$.

Below, we briefly discuss the different cases of the above definition:

For an event e or a function f with exactly one ingoing arc i and exactly one outgoing arc o (cases a. and b.), the folder is propagated from the ingoing arc to the outgoing arc. Note that the folder is propagated only when there is no folder on the outgoing arc. The number of folders on all other arcs $a \in A \setminus \{i, o\}$ does not change. For start and end events (which have no incoming arc or have no outgoing arc) the transition relation is empty (a').

An AND-split connector (case c.) propagates a folder from an incoming arc to all its outgoing arcs. However, it will be propagated only, when there are no process folders on the outgoing arcs. Likewise, the AND-join (case d.) waits for a folder on each incoming arc and propagates it to the outgoing arc, provided that there is no process folder on the outgoing arc yet.

The OR-split connector (case e.) is similar to the AND-split. It can propagate a folder from the incoming arc to any (but at least one) of its outgoing arcs provided that there are no folders yet. The set of outgoing arcs to which the folders are propagated is denoted by S in the definition.

The OR-join connector (case f.) is more involved because of its non-local semantics. When there is a folder on at least one of its incoming arcs $S \subseteq c_{in}$ and no folder can arrive (according to P) on the other arcs without the occurrence of c, the folder is propagated to the outgoing arc. In order to formalize that no folder can arrive on the other incoming arcs $a \in c_{in} \setminus S$, the definition refers to the states $\hat{\sigma}$ that can be reached from σ (with respect to P) without the occurrence of c, i.e. the states $\hat{\sigma}$ with $\sigma (P|_{N \setminus \{c\}})^* \hat{\sigma}$.

The XOR-split operator (case g.) propagates the folder from the incoming arc to exactly one of its outgoing arcs. The formalization is similar to the one of the AND-split and the OR-split.

The XOR-join (case h.) is similar to the definition of the OR-join. Instead of selecting some set S of incoming arcs on which a folder must be present, we select exactly one incoming arc i. We require that no folder can arrive on the other incoming arcs (with respect to P) before the occurrence of c.

Altogether, the transition relation $R(P)$ is defined as the union of all individual transition relations R_n of the nodes n. Note that R_n depends on P only for the OR-join and the XOR-join, which are the only connectors with a non-local semantics.

Note that there are several options on how the transition relation for each node type could be defined. One option concerns the question whether a folder on an outgoing arc should block the propagation of a folder from the ingoing arc. Another option would be to define a local semantics for the XOR-join[6]. Actually, the purpose of this paper is not to discuss and to investigate all these options. Rather, the purpose of this paper is to provide a framework for formally defining a semantics for EPCs. The exact definition of the semantics for the individual connectors will be only the next step. In fact, the precise definition of $R(P)$ is not crucial for making the rest of our theory work (see Sect. 6 for details). There is only one crucial condition: $R(P)$ must be a monotonously decreasing function.

Lemma 1 ($R(P)$ is monotonously decreasing). *The operation $R(P)$ is monotonously decreasing; i. e. for two transition relations $P \subseteq P'$ we have $R(P) \supseteq R(P')$.*

Proof. The only relations that depend on P and P' in the definition of $R(P)$ and $R(P')$ are the relations R_c for the OR-join and the XOR-join connectors. For each state σ the set of states $\widehat{\sigma}$ reachable from σ with respect to P and P' must be checked for the additional condition ($\widehat{\sigma}(a) = 0$). With $P \subseteq P'$, we have $\{\widehat{\sigma} \mid \sigma\, (P|_{N \setminus \{c\}})^*\, \widehat{\sigma}\} \subseteq \{\widehat{\sigma} \mid \sigma\, (P'|_{N \setminus \{c\}})^*\, \widehat{\sigma}\}$, i. e. the set of states to be checked for P is smaller than the set of states to be checked for P'. Clearly, a smaller set means less restrictions because less states must satisfy the additional condition. Therefore, there are more transitions in R_c for P than for P'.

5 The Semantics of EPCs

As mentioned above, the semantics of an EPC should be some transition relation on the states of the EPC. In the previous section, we have not defined a transition relation, but we have defined a transition relation $R(P)$, which depends on some given transition relation P. In this section, we will use $R(P)$ for defining the semantics of EPCs. On a first glance, there are two different ways for defining this semantics:

---

[6] There is a debate whether the XOR-join should have a non-local semantics or not. For example, Rittgen [6] proposes a local semantics for the XOR-join connector. Here, we follow Nüttgens and Rump [5] in giving it a non-local semantics.

1. We could use some transition relation P and then calculate $R(P)$ as the semantics of the EPC. Actually, this idea is used in the semantics of YAWL [9]. The problem, however, is that we need to define P first. And it is by no means clear how P should be defined, and which definition is the best. YAWL, for example, uses a simple transition relation that ignores all OR-join connectors. Similar ideas came up in private discussions with Nüttgens and Rump during the discussions on [5,8]. But each choice appears to be ad hoc in some way.

2. A better solution would be to find some P such that we have $P = R(P)$ – i.e. P is some fixed point of R. In that case, P refers to itself in its own definition $R(P)$ – the fixed point trick. Therefore, a fixed point P of $R(P)$ would exactly meet our initial intension, which justifies to call a fixed point of $R(P)$ an *ideal semantics* of the EPC. The problem with this definition, however, is that for some EPCs such fixed points, resp. ideal semantics, P do not exist; for others there are several different ideal semantics, and it is impossible to characterize one distinguished semantics (e.g. the least fixed point with respect to set inclusion) among these ideal semantics. So, in some cases there wouldn't be a semantics at all; in other cases there would be 'too many' of them.

Since both of the above approaches are unsatisfactory, we try a combination of both: We are now looking for a pair of transition relations (P, Q), such that we have $Q = R(P)$ and $P = R(Q)$, i.e. one transition relation is the input for the definition of the other. We will see that such pairs exist for each EPC, and that there is a distinguished such pair that is used as the semantics of the EPC.

In order to prove the existence of such a pair, we use standard fixed point theory. To this end, we define the domain D of all pairs of transition relations and an order relation $\preceq$, which forms a complete lattice on this domain. Moreover, we define a function φ such that the fixed points of φ are exactly the pairs meeting the above requirement.

Definition 4. *For an EPC with nodes N and states Σ, we define the domain $D = 2^{\Sigma \times N \times \Sigma} \times 2^{\Sigma \times N \times \Sigma}$, and we define the relation $\preceq$ on D as follows: For two elements $d = (P, Q)$ and $d' = (P', Q')$, we define $d \preceq d'$ iff $P \subseteq P'$ and $Q \supseteq Q'$. On D, we define the function $\varphi : D \to D$ by $\varphi((P, Q)) = (R(Q), R(P))$.*

Note that $(D, \preceq)$ is a complete lattice on D, because $\preceq$ inherits this structure from $\subseteq$ and $\supseteq$. Moreover, the function φ is monotonic with respect to $\preceq$:

Lemma 2. *The function φ on D is monotonic, i.e. for each $d \preceq d'$, we have $\varphi(d) \preceq \varphi(d')$.*

Proof. Follows immediately from the fact that R is monotonously decreasing (Lemma 1) and the definition of φ and $\preceq$ (Def. 4).

A *fixed point* of φ is an element $d \in D$ such that $\varphi(d) = d$. Note that $d = (P, Q)$ is a fixed point of φ if and only if $P = R(Q)$ and $Q = R(P)$, which are exactly those pairs of transition relations we are heading for. What is more, we can show that φ has fixed points.

Proposition 1.

1. *The function φ has fixed points; in particular, it has a least fixed point and it has a greatest fixed point (with respect to $\preceq$).*
2. *If (P,Q) is a fixed point of φ then also (Q,P) is a fixed point of φ.*
3. *In particular, (P,Q) is the least point of φ, iff (Q,P) is the greatest fixed point of φ.*
4. *φ has a unique fixed point, iff the least fixed point has the form (P,P).*

Proof.

1. As mentioned above, $(D, \preceq)$ is a complete lattice and, by Lemma 2, we know that φ is a monotonic function on D (with respect to $\preceq$). By the renowned Knaster-Tarski-Theorem, φ has a least and a greatest fixed point.
2. Let (P,Q) be a fixed point of φ. In combination with the definition of φ, we have $(P,Q) = \varphi((P,Q)) = (R(Q), R(P))$, i.e. $P = R(Q)$ and $Q = R(P)$. Thus, we have $\varphi((Q,P)) = (R(P), R(Q)) = (Q,P)$. So, (Q,P) is also a fixed point of φ.
3. Let (P,Q) be the least fixed point of φ and (P',Q') be the greatest fixed point of φ. By 2., (Q,P) and (Q',P') are also fixed points of φ. Because (P,Q) is the least fixed point and (P',Q') is the greatest fixed point, we have $(P,Q) \preceq (Q,P) \preceq (P',Q')$ and $(P,Q) \preceq (Q',P') \preceq (P',Q')$. By the definition of $\preceq$, we have $Q \subseteq P' \subseteq Q$ and $P \subseteq Q' \subseteq P$. This implies $P' = Q$ and $Q' = P$.
4. Let (P,P) be the least fixed point of φ. By 3, we know that (P,P) is also the greatest fixed point. So, (P,P) is the unique fixed point of φ.
   On the other hand, if we know that there is a unique fixed point (P,Q), we know that this is also the least and the greatest fixed point. By 3., we know $(P,Q) = (Q,P)$, i.e. $P = Q$.

Proposition 1 says, that φ has two distinguished fixed points, the least and the greatest fixed point. Fortunately, if we know the least fixed point (P,Q), we know the greatest fixed point too: the reversed pair (Q,P). In particular, we have $P \subseteq Q$. P is the transition relation with the least transitions in it, and Q is the transition with the most transitions in its. So we can use the least fixed point for defining the semantics of the EPC.

Definition 5 (Semantics of an EPC). *Let M be an EPC and let (P,Q) be the least fixed point of φ (wrt. $\preceq$). Then, we call P the pessimistic transition relation of the EPC M, and we call Q the optimistic transition relation of the EPC M.*

Note that, according to this definition, the semantics of an EPC consists of two transition relations: The *pessimistic transition relation* P is the one that stops rather than doing something 'awkward'; the *optimistic transition relation* Q does something 'awkward' rather than stopping indeliberately. Both transition relations correspond to each other in such a way that $P = R(Q)$ and $Q = R(P)$ – so one is the input transition relation for the definition of the other.

When the pessimistic and the optimistic transition relation coincide, we know that we have an ideal semantics $P = Q = R(P) = R(Q)$. In that case, we call the EPC *clean*. Unfortunately, there are EPCs for which the pessimistic and the optimistic semantics do not coincide. We call these EPCs *unclean*.

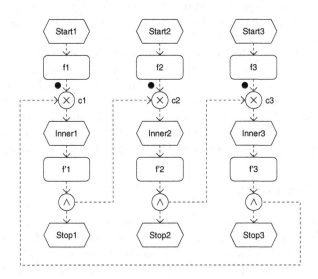

Fig. 3. An EPC with no ideal semantics

Figure 3 shows an example. We argue indirectly that this EPCs has no ideal semantics: To this end, let us assume that there is a transition relation P with $P = R(P)$ for this EPC. Now, we consider the state where there is a folder on each outgoing arc of the functions f_1, f_2, and f_3 as shown in Fig. 3. First, let us assume that according to P, connector c_i cannot propagate the folder on its incoming arc. Then, according to the definition of $R(P)$, the subsequent connector $c_{(i+1) \bmod 3}$ can propagate the folder according to $R(P)$ because no folder will arrive from the left incoming arc by assumption. By $P = R(P)$, we know that, according to P, connector $c_{(i+1) \bmod 3}$ can propagate the folder. Second, let us assume that, according to P, c_i can propagate the folder. By the same arguments, we can show that connector $c_{(i+1) \bmod 3}$ cannot propagate the folder according to P. Since we have an odd number of XOR-join connectors on the cycle, we can now argue that if c_1 can propagate the folder according to P, then it cannot propagate it and vice versa – a contradiction. So, our assumption that there is an ideal semantics $P = R(P)$ must have been wrong.

For some other examples, there are ideal semantics. But, there may be different ideal semantics, which are symmetric such that one cannot be preferred to the other. For the example shown in Fig. 1 in Sect. 2, we have two completely symmetric ideal semantics[7]. In the first semantics, connector c_1 propagates the folder and connector c_2 does not propagate it. In the second semantics, connector c_2 propagates the folder and c_1 does not propagate it. Since both ideal semantics are completely symmetric, one is as good as the other, there is no argument in favour of one of them.

These examples show that, in order to provide a semantics for all EPCs, we need to consider pairs of transition relations, as we did in our definition. Our definition gives a semantics to all (syntactically correct) EPCs – what is more, if the pessimistic and the optimistic transition relation coincide, we have an ideal semantics. These are the EPCs for which the formal semantics precisely captures the informal semantics – so we call them clean EPCs. On the other hand, EPCs for which the the pessimistic and the optimistic transition relation do not coincide, are unclean, because their formal semantics does not precisely capture the informal semantics. So, one benefit of our semantics is that not only every EPC has a semantics, but also that it identifies itself as clean or unclean.

6   The Framework

In the previous sections, we presented a semantics for EPCs. Actually, it is not our intension to propose this semantics as 'the semantics' of EPCs. There are still some aspects of this semantics that need to be discussed. The main purpose of this paper is to define a framework for formalizing the semantics of EPCs, which now allows us to discuss and to compare different semantics.

For defining a semantics for EPCs, it is now sufficient to define the function $R(P)$. The semantics of each individual node n of an EPC could be changed by changing the definition of relation R_n in Def. 3. As long as the resulting function $R(P)$ is monotonously decreasing, the rest of the theory will define a pessimistic and an optimistic transition relation in the very same way. Therefore, we can concentrate on the definition of $R(P)$ or even on R_n when discussing semantical issues. The soundness of this framework is captured in the following theorem:

Theorem 1 (Semantical framework). *Let $M = (E, F, C, l, A)$ be an EPC.*

1. *Let $\mathcal{A}$ be some set. Then, we call $\sigma : A \to \mathcal{A}$ a state of M. The set Σ denotes the set of all states. A subset $P \subseteq \Sigma \times N \times \Sigma$ is called a transition relation of M with respect to $\mathcal{A}$.*
2. *Let $R : 2^{\Sigma \times N \times \Sigma} \to 2^{\Sigma \times N \times \Sigma}$ be a monotonously decreasing function (with respect to $\subseteq$). We define the domain $D = 2^{\Sigma \times N \times \Sigma} \times 2^{\Sigma \times N \times \Sigma}$ and $\preceq$ on D as follows: For two elements $d = (P, Q)$ and $d' = (P', Q')$, we define $d \preceq d'$ if $P \subseteq P'$ and $Q \supseteq Q'$. Moreover, we define $\varphi : D \to D$ by $\varphi((P, Q)) = (R(Q), R(P))$.*

Then φ has a least fixed point (P, Q) and a greatest fixed point (P, Q) (with respect to $\preceq$).

---

[7] The argument is the same as in the previous example. But, in this example we have an ideal semantics because the cycle consists of an even number of XOR-joins.

Proof. The proof follows exactly the lines of the proofs of Lemma 2 and Prop. 1.

For defining a semantics for EPCs, we must first define some set $\mathcal{A}$, which represents the folders that are assigned to an arc of the EPC. In our example, $\mathcal{A}$ was the set $\{0, 1\}$; another reasonable choice would be the natural numbers[8], when we would like to have more than one folder on each arc.

Second, we must define a transition relation $R(P)$ (on the states derived from the set $\mathcal{A}$), which in fact defines a function from a transition relation to a transition relation. The only requirement is that this function is monotonously decreasing. Then, $R(P)$ defines the function φ, which according to the above theorem has a least fixed point. The least fixed point (P, Q) of this function defines the the pessimistic and the optimistic transition relation for the EPC.

As mentioned already, a careful discussion and evaluation of different semantics of EPCs is beyond the scope of this paper. We have only started with investigating some options and evaluating them. The evaluation covers different aspects such as modelling power, clarity, efficient analysis and simulation capabilities, etc.

It turned out that even subtle variations may have quite unexpected effects. Here, we give only one example: Apparently, the reason for an unclean EPC or an EPC with no ideal semantics are cycles in the control flow on nodes with non-local semantics. So, we would expect that EPCs without cycles in control flow will have an ideal semantics. But, it turns out that this is not true for the semantics as defined in this paper. The reason is that a folder on an outgoing arc may block the propagation of a folder on an incoming arc of an AND-split connector. Such a situation is present in the EPC of Fig. 4 for connectors c_1', c_2', and c_3'. We call these situations *contact situations* as they resemble the contact situations in Petri nets. Now, we show that there is no ideal semantics for this EPC. The arguments is very similar to arguments for the EPC from Fig. 3: Let us assume that this EPC has an ideal semantics. If connector c_i can propagate the folder on its incoming arc, the folder on the outgoing arc of connector c_i' can be removed, and connector c_i' can propagate the folder from its incoming arc to both its outgoing arcs. In particular, there will be folders on both incoming arcs of $c_{(i+1) \bmod 3}$. Therefore, $c_{(i+1) \bmod 3}$ cannot propagate its folder in that case. Vice versa, connector $c_{(i+1) \bmod 3}$ can propagate its folder if c_i cannot: because the folder on the outgoing arc of connector c_i' can never be removed, c_i' can never propagate a folder to the left incoming arc of $c_{(i+1) \bmod 3}$; so, $c_{(i+1) \bmod 3}$ can propagate its folder. Again, we end up in a contradiction. So, there is no ideal semantics for this EPC. Basically, the blocking of a connector in a contact situations can have effects in the reverse direction of the control flow. This results in cyclic dependencies even though there are no cycles in the control flow.

Altogether, the theorem we would have expected is not valid for our semantics. For resolving this problem with contact situations, we could either allow

---

[8] We did not choose natural numbers in our paper, because this introduces much more choices for the definition of $R(P)$. We could not make up our minds on these choices because good choices required more careful investigation that is beyond the scope of this paper.

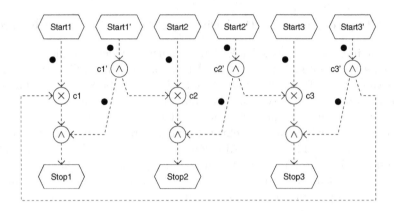

Fig. 4. An acyclic EPC with no ideal semantics

nodes to 'overwrite' existing process folders on their outgoing arcs, or we could use a semantics that allows multiple process folders per arc. Again, both choices have their advantages and disadvantages. From a pragmatic point of view, it is not clear, what 'overwriting' process folders should mean. From an implementational point of view, multiple process folders are problematic because it makes the calculation of the transition relation extremely inefficient; to be honest, we do not even know yet whether it is decidable.

This discussion gives just a glimpse on the many practical, mathematical, and implementational issues that have to be investigated before we can come up with the ultimate definition of 'the semantics' of EPCs.

7   Conclusion

In this paper, we have proposed a semantics for EPCs, which is mathematically sound. We have argued that this semantics must be a pair of transition relations, and that this semantics is as close to the informal semantics of [5] as it can be. Nevertheless, we do not claim that this is 'the semantics' of EPCs. The main contribution of this paper is a sound mathematical theory for defining all kinds of non-local semantics for EPCs. Other semantics can be defined by giving another definition for $R(P)$; when $R(P)$ is monotonously decreasing, the semantics comes for free. For defining different versions of semantics, we can concentrate on the definition of this relation. What is more, for any semantics defined in this framework, the framework clearly identifies clean and unclean EPCs. We hope that this framework helps to discuss different semantics and, ultimately, define 'the semantics' of EPCs.

In fact, there are many other notations for modelling business processes that have similar non-local semantics for some constructs. The framework presented in this paper can be easily adapted to most of these notations. For now, however, we are concentrating on the semantics of EPCs because there are enough problems left for EPCs. Currently, we are investigating different definitions in order to find the ultimate semantics of EPCs. As the simple problem from Sect. 6 has shown, this promises to be an interesting and exciting field of research. Moreover, we started some research on the efficient simulation of this semantics [1].

Altogether, we have shown that there is a sound mathematical foundation for the non-local semantics of EPCs. But, there are many pitfalls and unexpected effects. In fact, these are not only theoretical issues, but they concern quite practical aspects such as efficiency and analysis of inter-organizational business processes. Everybody using EPCs should be aware of that.

Acknowledgements. I would like to thank Markus Nüttgens, Frank Rump, and Peter Rittgen for many discussions on the semantics of EPCs, which inspired me to provide a sound definition of a non-local semantics for EPCs. In particular, the arguments with Markus Nüttgens encouraged me not to stop with an impossibility result. Moreover, I would like to thank Wil van der Aalst, Björn Axenath, and Nicolas Cuntz for discussions and comments on earlier versions of this paper, which helped to improve the presentation of the ideas.

References

1. N. Cuntz. Über die effiziente Simulation von Ereignisgesteuerten Prozessketten. Masters thesis (in German), University of Paderborn, June 2004 (in preparation).
2. G. Keller, M. Nüttgens, and A.-W. Scheer. Semantische Prozessmodellierung auf der Grundlage Ereignisgesteuerter Prozessketten (EPK). Veröffentlichungen des Instituts für Wirtschaftsinformatik (IWi), Heft 89, Universität des Saarlandes, January 1992.
3. F. Leymann and W. Altenhuber. Managing business processes as an information resource. *IBM Systems Journal*, 33(2):326–348, 1994.
4. P. Langner, C. Schneider, and J. Wehler. Petri Net Based Certification of Event driven Process Chains. In J. Desel and M. Silva, editors, *Application and Theory of Petri Nets 1998, LNCS* 1420, 286–305. Springer, 1998.
5. M. Nüttgens and F. J. Rump. Syntax und Semantik Ereignisgesteuerter Prozessketten (EPK). In *PROMISE 2002, Prozessorientierte Methoden und Werkzeuge für die Entwicklung von Informationssystemen, GI Lecture Notes in Informatics* P-21, 64–77. Gesellschaft für Informatik, 2002.
6. P. Rittgen. Quo vadis EPK in ARIS? *Wirtschaftsinformatik*, 42:27–35, 2000.
7. F. J. Rump. *Geschäftsprozeßmanagement auf der Basis ereignisgesteuerter Prozeßketten*. Teubner-Reihe Wirtschaftsinformatik. B.G.Teubner, 1999.
8. W.M.P. van der Aalst, J. Desel, and E. Kindler. On the semantics of EPCs: A vicious circle. In M. Nüttgens and F. J. Rump, editors, *EPK 2002, Geschäftsprozessmanagement mit Ereignisgesteuerten Prozessketten*, 71–79, November 2002.
9. W.M.P. van der Aalst and A.H.M. ter Hofstede. YAWL: Yet Another Workflow Language. Technical Report QUT Technical report, FIT-TR-2002-06, Queensland University of Technology, Brisbane, 2002.

Goal-Oriented Business Process Modeling with EPCs and Value-Focused Thinking

Dina Neiger and Leonid Churilov

School of Business Systems, Monash University, Victoria 3800, Australia
{Dina.Neiger,Leonid.Churilov@infotech.monash.edu.au}

Abstract. Goal-oriented business process modeling is driven by the need to ensure congruence of business processes and decisions with the values and vision of the business while meeting continuous demands for increased business productivity. However, existing business process modeling tools fail to address effectiveness and efficiency concerns in an integrated manner. Building upon the previous research by the authors aimed at addressing this gap through integration of process and decision modeling, in this paper, the links between process and decision modeling domains are formalized using a common semantic model that provides the bridge for future development of integrated tools.

Keywords: Business process modeling, Decision Sciences, Event-driven Process Chain, Value-Focused thinking framework, Goal-Oriented Business Process Modeling

1 Introduction/Motivation/Background

Within an efficient business process "things are done right", however the process must also be effective and "the rights things are done" otherwise the overall success of the business could be severely compromised [5]. Goal-oriented business process modeling aims to extend traditional business process modeling methodologies and tools that address the "how" of the business process concerned with the efficient execution of business processes to also include the "why" to ensure effectiveness of business processes.

To enable the "why" to be modeled each business goal has "to find expression in some aspects of the business process model" ([12], p. 20). This is achieved by developing goal models that describe business goals and relationships between them, and by using business goals to drive process decomposition. On the other hand, to facilitate efficient business processes, process decomposition drivers also need to take into account the "what" perspectives on process modeling such as activity and control flow, resource assignment, information and data flow, etc.

A review of goal-oriented business process modeling literature [15] identified three distinct perspectives on goal-oriented business process modeling: Decision Sciences, Requirements Engineering and Business Process Management perspectives. Each of these perspectives makes an important contribution towards goal-oriented business

J. Desel, B. Pernici, and M. Weske (Eds.): BPM 2004, LNCS 3080, pp. 98–115, 2004.

process modeling. Methods originating in Decision Sciences focus on modeling business goals and objectives with the aim of maximizing business effectiveness. Requirement Engineering methods provide a link between a variety of goal types and structures and activities and functions responsible for them. Within Business Process Management, frameworks that are able to represent various aspects of the business process, with the focus on its efficient execution have been developed and widely implemented. Individually these perspectives do not meet the requirements of goal-oriented business process modeling to address both efficiency and effectiveness constraints of the business as methodologies that are driven by the need to model an efficient business process are lacking in ability to ensure effectiveness of the process they model. On the other hand methodologies that are focused on modeling business goals and objectives are often not the best tools for assisting efficient process execution. This is easily illustrated by a brief analysis of the widely accepted methods within each perspective.

The i* framework [22], originating in the field of Requirements Engineering, provides the best compromise in the field of goal-oriented process modeling as it allows for complex goal classification structures according to goal types (e.g. functionality, verification, temporal, system state and goal level) and facilitates modeling of logical, causal and influencing relationships between goals whilst linking the goals to the activities and functions aimed at their achievement. However the complexity of the goal models within Requirements Engineering restricts their ability to adequately represent the sequential nature of the business process from the control flow perspective, thus limiting the usefulness of these models for optimizing efficiency of the executable processes.

An alternative way to represent goal structures has been adopted by Keeney [9], [10] within the scope of Decision Sciences, and is referred to as "value focused thinking" (VFT) framework. The focus of goals modeling within the Decision Sciences disciplines is to link the goal models to decision analysis methods in order to facilitate more effective decision-making within the business through a better understanding of the business dynamics, abstract and causal relationships between goals and links to optimization, simulation and other decision support modeling techniques (e.g. [20]).

ARIS House of Business Engineering is widely accepted within the business community and is considered to be one of the most comprehensive methodologies for process modeling [19], [21] as it enables description of the consolidated business model through different views of an extended Event-driven Process Chain (e-EPC) avoiding the complexity of an "all in one" meta-business process model whilst retaining all relevant information [18]. The e-EPC is a graphical representation of a business process that describes functional, organizational, target, output, human and information flows and corresponding objects. Despite an extensive modeling toolbox available within ARIS, it nevertheless lacks the comprehensive goal-modeling framework required for goal-oriented business process modeling [7], [12], [15], [22] .

It has been the contention of the authors, that the three perspectives are complementary from goal-oriented business process modeling point of view and through integration of the methodologies across the disciplinary boundaries it is possible to meet the requirements of goal-oriented business process modeling [14]. A conceptual model that enables such integration at an intuitive level was proposed in [14]. Within this model business goals are modeled using the VFT framework modified to take advantage of the logical structures present in Requirements Engineering; business processes are modeled with a hierarchy of e-EPCs; and the links between e-EPCs and goals within the VFT framework allow for each goal to be expressed within the business process model. To enable development of tools based on methods from different knowledge domains it is essential to accompany the intuitive model with a formalism that allows seamless transition between these domains.

The objective of this paper is to demonstrate how the VFT framework facilitates goal-oriented business process modeling. The contributions of this approach are 1) to introduce a common syntax to describe the e-EPC process model, hierarchy of e-EPCs and VFT goal model; and 2) to utilize this syntax for formal description of links between the VFT and e-EPC to enable goal-oriented business process modeling that addresses the gaps in the existing methodologies and tools. Rather than developing a new formal language, the existing formal constructs that describe EPC models [11] have been extended in this paper to allow formal expression of process decomposition and the VFT framework.

In accordance with these objectives, the paper is structured as follows. Background to the ARIS framework and EPC formal model is provided and modifications and extensions to the formal model are introduced in Section 2. In Section 3, the VFT framework and the proposed modifications are described and the syntax introduced in Section 2 is used to develop the formal goal-model. In Section 4, the e-EPC and the VFT goal model are linked to develop the goal-oriented business process model at conceptual and formal levels. The paper is concluded with a brief summary and directions for future research.

2   EPC Model within the ARIS Framework

According to the ARIS house of business engineering, an EPC can be formed at various levels of the business process [6]. At the highest level, relationship between key business processes is described with a "Value-Added Chain" model (p.264, [6]). Each process is described in detail with an EPC model that, at a minimum, include events, functions and rules and can be extended to an extended-EPC (e-EPC) to include other objects such as resources, information, etc., corresponding flows and links to other ARIS views such as organizational or data chart [18]. Without the loss of generality, goals are the only additional object types included in the e-EPC for the purposes of discussion in this paper. Within ARIS goals are not connected to each other within an e-EPC, rather the Objective Diagram tool is recommended for modeling goal structures [8]. However, the limited capabilities of the Objectives Diagram (e.g. lack of modeling tools for describing logical and influencing relationships between goals [15]) make it unsuitable for goal-oriented process modeling purposes.

In the ARIS modeling paradigm, the terms "function" and "process" are used interchangeably and synonymously with processes generally described as complex functions that can be divided into sub-functions to reduced complexity [13]. Functions are defined as "a technical task or action performed on an object to support one or more company goals" ([8] p. 4-1). The lowest level functions are defined as "functions which cannot be divided any further for the purpose of business analysis" ([8] p.4-2). Within this context, functions can support multiple goals and the association between functions and goals can be inherited by higher levels of the process hierarchy ([18] p.22).

Events, functions and rules are connected within an e-EPC by directional control flow links, while goals are connected to functions with non-directional goal assignment links. Process decomposition using an e-EPC model is defined by Davis ([6], p. 229) as either *horizontal segmentation* into "manageable chunks which link together" or *hierarchical decomposition* required for complex processes, to enable modeling at different levels of detail. Levels within the hierarchical decomposition are linked using directional process decomposition links. Within the horizontal segmentation, the functional flow is decomposed using the rules (also referred to as logical operators) summarized in Table 1.

Table 1. Interpretation of logical connectors within an e-EPC model ([6] p. 119)

Connector	Interpretation for a functional flow split
OR ⊗	one or more possible paths will be followed as a result of the decision described by the function immediately preceding the connector
XOR ⊗	one, and only one, of the possible paths will be followed
AND ⊗	process flow splits into two or more parallel paths

When a function is hierarchically decomposed it can be described within an e-EPC model as either a *hierarchically decomposed function* or a *process sign*. If a hierarchically decomposed function is used, the predecessor and successor events of this function are required to be the start and end events (respectively) of the subordinate EPC. If a process sign is used, the predecessor and successor events are not shown in the higher level EPC. Figure 1 illustrates a 2-level business process model using both alternatives for function one (f1) and its predecessor and successor events (e1 and e2 respectively). The model at the second level includes a horizontal decomposition into parallel branches using logical connector OR. Note that the above overview is not an in depth analysis of modeling in ARIS, rather it simply presents the context necessary for understanding the conceptual and formal model being discussed.

Formal Model for e-EPC. Keller and Teufel ([11] ch. 4.3) provided a declarative description of the syntax of the EPC models describing elements of the EPC graph and characteristics of a correct model ([11] p. 158). Not withstanding the limitations with respect to workflow correctness (e.g. [1], [3]), the resulting formal model is sufficiently generic to ensure consistency of business process with the overall business objectives as it enables description of:

- static objects (such as goals, functions, events, logical connectors, etc) and links between objects (including assignment, flow and decomposition links);
- relationships between levels of process and objectives decomposition structures; and
- guidelines for synchronized movement between levels of the process and goal models.

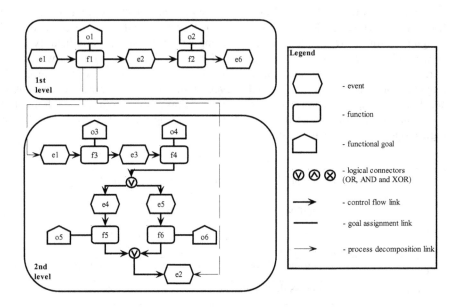

Fig. 1. An illustration of a 2-level business process e-EPC model [14]

As the formalism is based on a generic EPC model initially developed for SAP AG ([11] p. 149) and used as the core element of the ARIS framework [17], in acknowledgement of the people involved in developing and extending the EPC concept the formal model published by Keller and Teufel [11] is referred to in this paper as the Keller-Nuttgens-Scheer (KNS) model.

In this section, the KNS model is generalized to allow its application to the VFT model and modified to include additional objects and links to allow process objectives and decomposition to be described while excluding e-EPC objects that are not relevant in this context (e.g. organizational units). If required, the modified formalism can be extended to describe *all* objects of an e-EPC without difficulty.

Following the KNS model ([11] p. 159), a generic 7-tuple $g_t^{Id} = \left\langle Id_t, v_t, \kappa_t, \tau_t, \tau_t^\kappa, \alpha_t, \alpha_t^\kappa \right\rangle$ is defined as follows:

- t is type of the model being described by the tuple.
- Id_t is a unique identifier of a model type t.

- v_t is the non-empty, finite set of nodes of a model type t.
- κ_t is the link relationship, which describes the connections between the various types of nodes, κ is defined as $\kappa \subseteq V \times V$.
- τ_t, τ_t^κ are representations that assign a type to every node or link.
- $\alpha_t, \alpha_t^\kappa$ are representations that assign attributes to every node or link type.

The 7-tuple above will be used in this paper to describe two types of models – e-EPC model discussed in this section and the VFT model discussed in the next section. Therefore the t-subscript will take one of two values e (for an e-EPC) or o (for a VFT). In the context of the e-EPC model τ, τ^κ representations are defined as follows:

$$\tau_e : V_e \rightarrow \begin{cases} \text{function, event, process sign, AND connector,} \\ \text{OR connector, XORconnector, hierarchically} \\ \text{ranked function, process goal} \end{cases} \tag{1}$$

$$\tau_e^\kappa : \kappa_e \rightarrow \begin{cases} \text{control flow link, goal assignment link,} \\ \text{process decomposition link} \end{cases}$$

The representations are used to define the following sets of nodes (2) and links (3):

$$I_e = \left\{ u \in V_e \mid \tau_e(u) = \text{Id of an EPC} \right\} \tag{2}$$

$$E = \left\{ u \in V_e \mid \tau_e(u) = \text{event} \right\}$$

$$F = \left\{ u \in V_e \mid \tau_e(u) = \text{function} \right\}, F \neq \varnothing$$

$$F_H = \left\{ u \in V_e \mid \tau_e(u) = \text{hierarchically ranked function} \right\}$$

$$P = \left\{ u \in V_e \mid \tau_e(u) = \text{process sign} \right\}$$

$$B_1 = F \cup F_H \cup P$$

$$B_2 = F_H \cup P$$

$$O_P = \left\{ u \in V_e \mid \tau_e(u) = \text{process goal} \right\}$$

$$J_{AND} = \left\{ u \in V_e \mid \tau_e(u) = \text{AND connector} \right\}$$

$$J_{OR} = \left\{ u \in V_e \mid \tau_e(u) = \text{OR connector} \right\}$$

$$J_{XOR} = \left\{ u \in V_e \mid \tau_e(u) = \text{XOR connector} \right\}$$

$$J = J_{AND} \cup J_{OR} \cup J_{XOR}$$

$$B_J = B_1 \cup J$$

$$(u,v) \in \kappa \text{ is a link from node u to node v} \tag{3}$$

$$K_R = \{(u,v) \in (B_J \times E) \cup (E \times B_J) \cup (J \times J)\}$$

$$(u,v) \in K_R :\Leftrightarrow \tau_e^\kappa ((u,v)) = \text{control flow link}$$

$$K_O = \{(u,v) \in (B_I \times O_P) \cup (O_P \times B_I)\}$$

$$(u,v) \in K_O :\Leftrightarrow \tau_e^\kappa ((u,v)) = \text{goal assignment link}$$

In the context of goal-oriented business process modeling each function is linked to its goal(s) with the goal assignment links (4).

$$\forall u \in B_1 \ \exists v \in O_p : (u,v) \in K_O \tag{4}$$

Keller and Tuefel ([11] p. 159) use the concepts of positive and negative adjacency lists, input and output degrees and number, positive and negative incidence lists and the number of incidence nodes (5) to define start and end events of an EPC (6). These constructs can be also used to define events preceding and following hierarchically ranked functions (7) and connector nodes that follow a function (8) indicating a horizontal decomposition of a process flow.

Adjacency lists of a node v are the sets: $\qquad\qquad$ (5)

$$\text{adj}^+ (v,w) = \left\{ u \in V \middle| (v,u) \in \kappa_t \wedge \tau_t^\kappa ((v,u)) = w \right\}$$

$$\text{adj}^- (v,w) = \left\{ u \in V \middle| (u,v) \in \kappa_t \wedge \tau_t^\kappa ((u,v)) = w \right\}$$

Output and input degree of node v:

$$\gamma^+ (v,w) = \left| \text{adj}^+ (v,w) \right| \text{ and } \gamma^- (v,w) = \left| \text{adj}^- (v,w) \right|.$$

Incidence lists for node v:

$$\text{inz}^+ (v,w) = \left\{ (v,u) \in \kappa_t \middle| \tau_t^\kappa ((v,u)) = w \right\}$$

$$\text{inz}^- (v,w) = \left\{ (u,v) \in \kappa_t \middle| \tau_t^\kappa ((u,v)) = w \right\}$$

Number of incidence nodes for node v:

$$i^+ (v,w) = \left| \text{inz}^+ (v,w) \right| \text{ and } i^- (v,w) = \left| \text{inz}^- (v,w) \right|$$

$$E_s = \left\{ u \in E \middle| \gamma^- (u,w){=}0 \wedge \gamma^+ (u,w){=}1, \text{ where } w \in K_R \right\}, E_s \neq \varnothing \tag{6}$$

$$E_e = \left\{ u \in E \middle| \gamma^- (u,w){=}1 \wedge \gamma^+ (u,w){=}0, \text{ where } w \in K_R \right\}, E_e \neq \varnothing$$

$$E_{ps} = \left\{ u \in E \middle| \exists v, v \in B_2 \wedge u \in \text{adj}^+ (v) \right\} \tag{7}$$

$$E_{pe} = \left\{ u \in E \middle| \exists v, v \in B_2 \wedge u \in \text{adj}^- (v) \right\}$$

$$FC_{AND} = \left\{ u \in J_{AND} \middle| \exists v, v \in B_1 \wedge v \in adj^-(u) \right\} \tag{8}$$

$$FC_{OR} = \left\{ u \in J_{OR} \middle| \exists v, v \in B_1 \wedge v \in adj^-(u) \right\}$$

$$FC_{XOR} = \left\{ u \in J_{XOR} \middle| \exists v, v \in B_1 \wedge v \in adj^-(u) \right\}$$

$$FC = FC_{AND} \cup FC_{OR} \cup FC_{XOR}$$

To complete the description of an EPC model, it is necessary to introduce the concept of a path. The notation $u \xrightarrow{C} v$ is adopted from [11] p. 160 to describe a path defined as a connection from node u to node v by a chain of other nodes and connectors, where C represents the series of nodes and connectors included in the path. Notation $u \rightarrow v$ is used to describe the chain links between the adjacent nodes u and v. For any two nodes on an EPC path the following is true: $u,v \in C \, \exists \, (u,v) \Leftrightarrow (u,v) \in K_R$.

The constructs defined above are sufficient to describe a single e-EPC and local consistency criteria that when met ensure that an individual EPC model is correct ([11] pp. 161-165]. Keller and Teufel ([11] p. 167) stop short of defining global consistency criteria extending beyond the individual EPC model that are required to ensure that a business process model, which includes a set of e-EPCs linked to each other with process decomposition links, is correct.

Extensions to the KNS Formalism. In order to define global consistency criteria the KNS model has been extended in this section to include the space of all e-EPC tuples within a business process model (9), process decomposition links between e-EPCs (10), and a function Φ (11) that operates on that space of e-EPCs and allows selection of all objects of the same nature (e.g. links, nodes, etc) from a given e-EPC by enabling selection of elements from a given tuple. Tuple elements are numbered from one to seven as they appear in the initial tuple description g_e^{Id} : 1st element being an e-EPC ID, the next two elements being the sets of nodes and links respectively, and the remaining four elements referring to each of the four representations in the order of their appearance in the tuple.

$$G_t = \bigcup_i g_t^i, i \in I_e \tag{9}$$

$$K_H = \left\{ (u,v) \in (B_2 \times G_e') \right\} \tag{10}$$

$$(u,v) \in K_H :\Leftrightarrow \tau_e^\kappa ((u,v)) = \text{process decomposition link}$$

$$K_{EPC} = K_R \cup K_O \cup K_H$$

$$\Phi : \{G_t\} \times \{1,2,3,4,5,6,7\} \tag{11}$$

$$\Phi \left(g_t^{Id}, n \right) := n^{th} \text{ element of } g_t^{Id}$$

The above equations allow four global consistency criteria to be defined as follows:

D1. Process decomposition links cannot be used to connect nodes within an e-EPC to that e-EPC.

$$\forall i \in I_e, u \in \Phi\left(g_e^i, 2\right) \Rightarrow \not\exists\left(u, g_e^i\right) \in K_H \tag{12}$$

D2. If an e-EPC is a subordinate of another e-EPC it cannot also be its higher level e-EPC.

$$\forall i, j \in I_e, u \in \Phi\left(g_e^i, 2\right) \cap B_2, v \in \Phi\left(g_e^j, 2\right) \cap B_2, \left(u, g_e^j\right) \in K_H \tag{13}$$

$$\Rightarrow \not\exists\left(v, g_e^i\right) \in K_H$$

D3. Process sign doesn't include events in its adjacency lists

$$\forall i \in I_e, u \in \Phi(g_e^i, 2) \cap P, w \in \Phi(g_e^i, 2) \cap \left\{adj^+(u,w) \cup adj^-(u,w)\right\} \Rightarrow w \notin E \tag{14}$$

D4. The start event of a subordinate EPC corresponds to the predecessor event of the hierarchically ranked function that is linked to that EPC using process decomposition links. Similarly, the end event of a subordinate EPC corresponds to the successor event of the hierarchically ranked function linked to that EPC using process decomposition links.

$$\forall i, j \in I_e, i \neq j, u \in \Phi(g_e^i, 2) \cap F_H, e_s \in \Phi(g_e^i, 2) \cap E_{ps}, e_e \in \Phi(g_e^i, 2) \cap E_{pe,} \tag{15}$$

$$(e_s, u), (u, e_e) \in K_R, (u, g_e^j) \in K_H \Rightarrow e_s \in \Phi(g_e^j, 2) \cap E_s, e_e \in \Phi(g_e^j, 2) \cap E_e$$

The global consistency criteria D1-D4 describe the necessary characteristics of a multi-level business process model within the ARIS framework. The formal constructs use to described the business process model are adopted in the next section to goal models within the VFT framework.

3   Modified VFT Framework Goal Model

In this section, the term "objective" rather than "goal" is used to describe, "a statement of something that one wants to strive toward" ([10], p.34). This difference in terminology is adopted simply for ease of reference to the classical Decision Sciences sources rather than to highlight any differences in meaning.

According to Keeney [9], [10], objectives within the VFT framework are classified into two classes: *fundamental* objectives of the business that describe business values, and *means* objectives that describe the means of achieving fundamental objectives. The fundamental objectives within the VFT framework are structured as a hierarchy, while the means objectives are structured as a network referred to as the means-ends (or simply means) network.

The links between two structures and the objectives within them are non-directional links facilitating both top-down and bottom-up approaches for structuring objectives. The fundamental objectives do not have to be linked to individual means objectives ([10] p. 37) as long as it is established that means objectives *together* are sufficient to achieve fundamental objectives. Within the fundamental objectives hierarchy the links between objectives are always "one to many", "many to many" relationships are allowed for all other links within the VFT framework. Other tools such as System Dynamics causal loops and feedback diagrams can be used to explore the dynamics of individual relationships [20].

The simplicity of this structure enables functional and non-functional goals to be related to each other without the confusion present in the Requirements Engineering goal models ([7] p. 34). It also enables the VFT goal model to be linked to a generic process modeling framework (such as ARIS [6], [16], [17], [18]) for a better representation of the process modeling perspectives than is available within the Requirements Engineering process models. However, the absence of logical structures with the VFT framework hinders the use of the VFT goal model to guide process decomposition that includes synchronization, merging, split, choice and other patterns using AND, OR and XOR constructs [2] described in the previous section.

Modifications to the VFT Framework. To enable better synchronization between the VFT goal model and business process model decomposition, the VFT framework is modified to 1) include logical connectors within the means-ends [14], and 2) use directional links to connect objectives.

Adding logical connectors to the VFT framework (refer to Table 2) takes advantage of the logical structures present in the Requirements Engineering goal models while maintaining the benefits of the Decision Sciences methodologies thus resulting in a goal model that is better suited for linking to the generic business process modeling frameworks [14], [15].

Table 2. Interpretation of logical connectors within the VFT model ([14], p.5)

Connector	Interpretation for a objectives split
OR $\vee$	objective preceding the connector can be achieved by different non-mutually exclusive means
XOR $\otimes$	means objective preceding the connector can be achieved by different mutually exclusive means
AND $\wedge$	objective preceding the connector can be split into more than one objective, all of which have to be met

Similarly, modifying the VFT framework links to direct objectives structure from general objectives (corresponding to more complex processes) down to lower level means goals (of elementary functions) enables the VFT framework to guide the top-down decomposition of the business processes. Should a bottom-up approach be used to derive a process structure, links within the VFT framework and associated formalism can be easily modified accordingly. An example of a fundamental objectives hierarchy and means network is provided in Figure 2.

Within this example, there is one fundamental objective that can be decomposed into two lower objectives by asking a question "what do you mean by that?" ([4] p.49). The means objectives are derived from the fundamental objectives hierarchy by asking the question "how can you achieve this?" ([4] p.49). In the example provided in Figure 2, means objectives m3, m4 and m5 all have to be achieved in order for means objective m1 to be achieved. For example, to ensure that marketing competency is created within the organization to market a new product (m1), quality staff have to be recruited (m3), their training requirements need to be evaluated in a timely manner (m4), and training has to ensure that staff obtain key competencies (m5). Training goals can be met either through an up to date on-line documentation (m6) or expert personal training (m7). The marketing competency of the organization (m1) will influence level of customer demand for the product (m2).

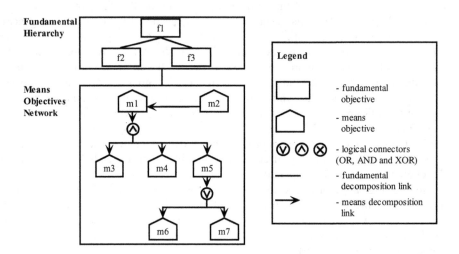

Fig. 2. An illustration of a VFT framework goal model with modified means-ends network.

Formal VFT Model. Similarly to the e-EPC formalism discussed in Section 2, objects and links within the VFT framework can be described with the 7-tuple $g_o^{Id} = \left\langle Id_o, v_o, \kappa_o, \tau_o, \tau_o^\kappa, \alpha_o, \alpha_o^\kappa \right\rangle$ by modifying τ, τ^κ representations (16).

$$\tau_0 : v_0 \rightarrow \begin{cases} \text{fundamental objective, means objective,} \\ \text{AND connector, OR connector,} \\ \text{XORconnector} \end{cases} \quad (16)$$

$$\tau_0^\kappa : \kappa_0 \rightarrow \begin{cases} \text{means decomposition link,} \\ \text{fundamental decomposition link} \end{cases}$$

Using these representations the sets of fundamental objectives, means objectives and logical connectors are defined in (17). The sets of fundamental decomposition links that are used to connect the fundamental objectives with each other and to the means-ends network; and means decomposition links that connect means objectives and logical connectors are defined in (18).

$$O_m = \left\{ u \in V_o \mid \tau_o(u) = \text{means objective} \right\} \tag{17}$$

$$O_d = \left\{ u \in V_o \mid \tau_o(u) = \text{fundamental objective} \right\}$$

$$J_{AND} = \left\{ u \in V_o \mid \tau_e(u) = \text{AND connector} \right\}$$

$$J_{OR} = \left\{ u \in V_o \mid \tau_e(u) = \text{OR connector} \right\}$$

$$J_{XOR} = \left\{ u \in V_o \mid \tau_e(u) = \text{XOR connector} \right\}$$

$$J = J_{AND} \cup J_{OR} \cup J_{XOR}$$

$$(u,v) \in \kappa \text{ is a link from node } u \text{ to node } v \tag{18}$$

$$K_M = \left\{ (u,v) \in (O_M \times O_M) \cup (O_M \times O_J) \cup (O_J \times O_M) \right\}$$

$$(u,v) \in K_M :\Leftrightarrow \tau_o^\kappa((u,v)) = \text{means decomposition link}$$

$$K_D = \left\{ (u,v) \in (O_D \times O_D) \cup (O_F \times O_D) \cup (O_D \times O_F) \right\}$$

$$(u,v) \in K_D :\Leftrightarrow \tau_o^\kappa((u,v)) = \text{fundamental decomposition link}$$

$$K_{VFT} = K_M \cup K_D$$

Path $u \xrightarrow{\ C\ } v$ is defined within the VHT model as:

$$u,v \in C \ \exists\,(u,v) \Leftrightarrow (u,v) \in K_{VFT} \tag{19}$$

where C represents a series of nodes and connectors included in the path

Similarly to an e-EPC model, there are a number of local consistency criteria (corresponding to local consistency criteria defined in [11] pp. 161-165) that apply to the VFT model that are defined using the constructs introduced in (5):

O1: Means objectives can have one inbound and/or several outbound means objective decomposition links.

$$\forall u \in O_M, v \in K_M : \left(i^-(u,v){=}0 \vee i^-(u,v){=}1 \right) \wedge \left(i^+(u,v){=}0 \vee i^+(u,v) \geq 1 \right) \tag{20}$$

O2: There are no loops.

$$\forall\, u \in O_m \cup O_d : (u,u) \notin K_{VFT} \tag{21}$$

O3: Connectors have one input and several outbound decomposition links.

$$\forall\, u \in J : \left(i^-(u,m){=}1 \wedge i^+(u,m){>}1 \right) \tag{22}$$

O4: Connections between connectors are acyclical.

$$\forall\, u \in J : u \xrightarrow{\ C\ } v \Rightarrow u \neq v \tag{23}$$

O5: Each means objectives is part of a path that starts at a fundamental objective.

$$\forall\, u \in O_M \;\exists v \in O_D: v \xrightarrow{\;\;C\;\;} u \tag{24}$$

As a single VFT goal-model describes a fully decomposed network of objectives for a business, global criteria do not need to be defined within the scope of a business.

4 Integrated Model for Goal-Oriented Business Process Modeling

Having described the ARIS and VFT frameworks individually it is now possible to link them. Firstly, the links are described at the conceptual and intuitive level, then the rules that formalize the links are introduced.

Conceptual Integrated Model. The answers to the following questions shape the conceptual goal-oriented business process model that links an e-EPC and a VFT framework:

(1) What is the relationship between the functional and process goals in an e-EPC process model and fundamental and means objectives in a VFT goal model?

(2) How do business vision and values (described within the VFT model) guide the design of the business process model?

(3) When does a business process model contain sufficient level of detail to ensure that business vision and values are met?

The answer to the first question lies in the definitions of functions and means objectives. Functional and (accordingly) process goals are ends towards achieving overall business objectives, as are the means objectives. Furthermore, the network of means objectives satisfies the requirements from functional and process objectives stipulated within the ARIS framework [13]. In other words, functional and process objectives satisfy the definition of means objectives and therefore they inherit the relationship to the fundamental objectives from the means objectives in the VFT framework.

Having established that functional and process objectives can be represented by means objectives within the VFT framework, it is easy to see how the business vision and values can guide the design of the business process model. The step-by-step guide introduced by the authors in [14] and reproduced in Figure 3 illustrates this process.

Steps 1 and 2 are contained within the VFT framework and are aimed at, firstly converting organizational values into specific fundamental objectives and subsequently using the fundamental objectives to derive the first level of the means objectives. The first level of means objectives usually corresponds to the first level of the process model (Step 3) that describes the relationships between broad organizational processes referred to as a Value Added Chain within the ARIS framework. The next two steps (4a and 4b) can be performed in parallel to enable decomposition within the means network and process, respectively taking into consideration other decomposition drivers such as level of detail required, resource allocation considerations etc. Step 5 provides the answer to whether the model contains sufficient detail as per the third question. When each of the means objectives within the network of means objectives are linked (directly or through other means objectives) to at least one function within the process model, it can be said that from the goal-oriented process modeling point of view, the business process model contains a sufficient level of detail.

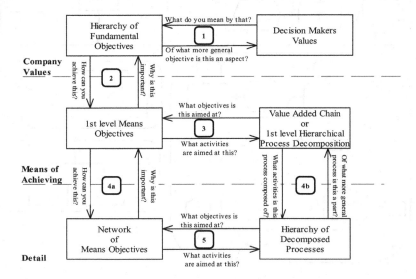

Fig. 3. Step by step guide to goal-oriented process modeling with VFT ([14], Fig. 4)

If required, additional levels of detail can be added to satisfy further process decomposition requirements by re-using objectives within the means network or by adding goals to the means network that correspond to new functions and processes. The formal model introduced later in this section provides the rules that allow this extension. The upward arrows in Figure 3 provide an intuitive guide for a bottom-up approach to goal-oriented business process modeling. To demonstrate how the two models link, the e-EPC in Figure 1 and the VFT in Figure 2 are combined in Figure 4.

Level 1 represents the first level of the means network and corresponding top level process e-EPC. Decomposition of the first function ("establish marketing department") demonstrates the relationship between the levels of the process and goal models. The horizontal decomposition within the process model, which allows a choice between the on-line and personal training, translates into an additional hierarchical level within the goal model, with objective m5 being achieved by either m6 or m7 objective and representing a broader level goal of staff training. As can be seen from this example, goals corresponding to a sequence of functions can be combined into a broader level objective using the AND logical connector. These and other rules are described in more detail at an intuitive level in [14] and are formalized below (M1-M5) using the constructs introduced in the previous sections. Functional and process objectives are referred to as process objectives in the description of the rules.

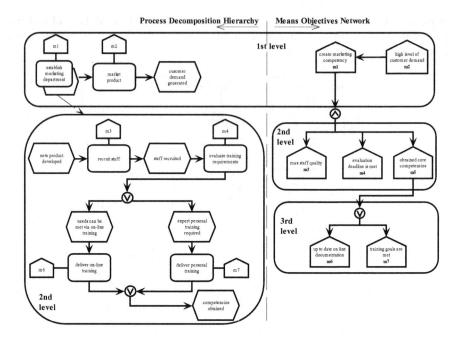

Fig. 4. Illustration of the integrated goal-oriented business process model (adopted from [14])

Formal Integrated Model. As discussed in the introduction, the objective of the integrated model is to ensure that process decomposition is guided by the business values, therefore the formalism assumes that both process and goal models are structured using the top-down approach. Rules below can be easily modified to allow a bottom-up approach to process modeling.

M1. Process objectives are a subset of means objectives. Consequently 1) the set of process objectives does not intersect with the set of fundamental objectives for the same business; 2) process objectives are linked to each other and other means objectives with means decomposition links; and 3) fundamental objectives linked to process objectives with fundamental decomposition links.

$$O_P \subseteq O_M \tag{25}$$

$$O_P \cap O_D = \varnothing$$

$$\forall\, u, v \in O_P\ \exists\, u \xrightarrow{\ C\ } v \iff \forall\, x, y \in C,\ (x, y) \in K_M$$

$$\forall\, u \in O_P, v \in O_M \setminus O_P\ \exists\, u \xrightarrow{\ C\ } v \iff \forall\, x, y \in C,\ (x, y) \in K_M$$

$$\forall\, u \in O_P, v \in O_D\ \textit{if}\ \exists v \xrightarrow{\ C\ } u \iff$$

$$\forall\, x, y \in C,\ (x, y) \in K_{VFT} \wedge \exists x, y \notin J,\ (x, y) \in K_D$$

M2. Functions within the highest level of the process hierarchy must be linked to at least one objective within the highest level of the means network.

$$\forall g_e^i \in L_{HE}, v \in \left(\Phi(g_e^i,2) \cap B_2\right): \exists u \in \left(L_{HM} \cap O_P\right) \wedge (v,u) \in K_O \ where \qquad (26)$$

$$L_{HE} = \left\{ g_e^i \in G_e \middle| \forall j \in I_e \not\exists v \in \Phi(g_e^j,2) \cap B_2 : (v,g_e^i) \in K_H \right\}$$

$$L_{HM} = \left\{ u \in O_M \middle| \not\exists v \in O_M : (v,u) \in K_M \right\}$$

M3. Means objectives that are not process objectives must be decomposed into process objectives [13], [14].

$$\forall u \in (O_M \setminus O_P), n \geq 2 \ \exists v_1,...,v_n \in O_P : \forall i = 1...n, n \in N_0 \ \exists v_i \xrightarrow{c} u \qquad (27)$$

M4. A means objective corresponding to a process path that consists of functions and events should be decomposed into process objectives using an AND connector.

$$\forall o \in O_M, o_1, o_2 \in O_P, j \in J, u_1, u_2 \in B1, e \in E: \qquad (28)$$

$$o_1 \rightarrow j \rightarrow o \wedge o_2 \rightarrow j \rightarrow o \wedge (u_1,o_1), (u_2,o_2) \in K_O \wedge u_2 \rightarrow e \rightarrow u_1 \Rightarrow j \in FC_{AND}$$

M5. A means objective corresponding to one or more path within a process flow split should be decomposed using the same connector as is used to split the process flow.

$$\forall o \in O_M, o_1, o_2 \in O_P, j_p \in FC, j_o \in J, u_1, u_2 \in B1, e_1, e_2 \in E: \qquad (29)$$

$$o_1 \rightarrow j_o \rightarrow o \wedge o_2 \rightarrow j_o \rightarrow o \wedge (u_1,o_1), (u_2,o_2) \in K_O \wedge$$

$$u_1 \rightarrow e_1 \rightarrow j_p \wedge u_2 \rightarrow e_2 \rightarrow j_p \Rightarrow j_o = j_p$$

The semantics model proposed in this section formalizes the relationship between an e-EPC process model within an ARIS framework and a goal model within the VFT framework. This extension of the process model takes business process modeling one step closer towards a holistic approach that utilizes process and decision modeling techniques to build an integrated framework for providing business solutions.

5   Summary

The motivation for the integration of the e-EPC and VFT framework methodologies has been the aspiration to address both efficiency and effectiveness business concerns. Does the integrated model meet these expectations? In essence, the integrated model connects Business Process Modeling and Decision Sciences using objectives as the link between the two disciplines. The common formalism allows seamless transition from one domain to the other thus breaking the artificial barriers between the disciplines and facilitating the use of complementary methods to deliver a more holistic approach to business process modeling. The ability of an e-EPC to represent multiple business process perspectives (with the aid of the ARIS framework) ensures that process efficiency concerns are addressed in the integrated model. The use of the VFT framework to guide the design of the business process and to structure process objectives ensures that the broader business objectives and values are expressed in the integrated process model and provides the links to decision support modeling tools allowing effectiveness concerns to be addressed.

The scope of this paper is restricted to formalizing the relationships between the two knowledge domains. The links between the two domains open the door to many interesting research questions yet to be addressed including, but not limited to:

- The implementation issues associated with the practical application of the model.
- Using objectives to provide formal links between an e-EPC and other decision models.
- Possibility of using dynamic objective structures to guide process execution.
- Incorporate complex relationships between objectives (e.g. partial satisfaction, conflict and trade-off) in the goal model using decision modeling tools.

References

1. van der Aalst, W. M. P.: Formalization and Verification of Event-driven Process Chains. Information and Software Technology Vol. 41 No. 10, 1999; pp. 639-650
2. van der Aalst, W. M. P.: Advanced Workflow Patterns. In Etzion O, Scheuermann P. (eds): 7th International Conference on Cooperative Information Systems (CoopIS 2000)., Springer-Verlag, Berlin, LNCS 1901 (2000) 18-29
3. van der Aalst, W. M. P., Desel, J., Kindler, E.: On the semantics of EPCs: A vicious circle. In Nuttgens, M., Rump, F., J.: EPK 2002 Proceedings. Trier, November 2002; http://www.epk-community.de (last accessed 20/8/2003)
4. Clemen, R. T., Reilly, T.: Making Hard Decisions with DecisionTools. 2nd rev. edn. Duxbury, USA (2001)
5. Daellenbach, H. T.: Systems and Decision Making: a Management Science Approach. Wiely, Chichester (1994)
6. Davis, R.: Business Process Modelling with ARIS: a Practical Guide. Springer-Verlag, London Berlin Heidelberg (2001)
7. Hurri, J.: Using Decision Tools in Deciding System Product Requirements: Literature Review and a Behaviourally Motivated Lightweight Tool. Licentiate Thesis, Department of Computer Science and Engineering, Helsinki University of Technology (2000), http://www.cis.hut.fi/jarmo/publications/hurri-licentiate.pdf (last accessed 11/12/2003)
8. IDS Scheer: ARIS Methods Manual. Version 5 IDS Scheer (2000)
9. Keeney, R. L.: Value-Focused Thinking: A Path to Creative Decision Making. Harvard University Press, Cambridge, Mass : Harvard University Press (1992)
10. Keeney, R. L.: Creativity in Decision Making with Value-Focused Thinking. Sloan Management Review Summer (1994) 33-41
11. Keller, G., Teufel, T.: SAP R/3 Process – Oriented Implementation: Iterative Process Prototyping. Addison Wesley Longman, Harlow, England (1998)
12. Kueng, P., Kawalek P.: Goal-Based Business Process Models: Creation and Evaluation. Business Process Management Journal , Vol. 3, No. 1 (1997) 17-38
13. Neiger, D., Churilov, L.: Structuring Business Objectives: a Business Process Modeling Perspective. In van der Aalst, W., ter Hofstede, A. and Weske, M. (eds.): Business Process Management. Springer-Verlag, Berlin Heidelberg, LNCS 2678 (2003) 72-87

14. Neiger, D., Churilov, L.: Goal-Oriented Decomposition of Event-Driven Process Chains with Value-Focused Thinking. In Proceedings of the 14th Australasian Conference on Information Systems (ACIS 2003), Paper #168, Perth, WA 26-28 November (2003)
15. Neiger, D., Churilov, L.: Goal-Oriented Business Process Engineering Revisited: a Unifying Perspective. accepted for The First International Workshop on Computer Supported Activity Coordination (CSAC 2004), Porto, Portugal, 13 April (2004) http://www.iceis.org/
16. Scheer, A.-W.: Business process engineering: reference models for industrial enterprises. Study edn. Springer-Verlag, Berlin, Heidelberg, New York (1998)
17. Scheer, A.-W.: ARIS – Business Process Frameworks. 3rd edn. Springer-Verlag, Berlin Heidelberg (1999)
18. Scheer, A.-W.: ARIS – Business Process Modeling. 3rd edn. Springer-Verlag, Berlin Heidelberg (2000)
19. Stein, A., Hawking, P., Foster, S.: ERP Post Implementation: a New Journey. In Proceedings of the 14th Australasian Conference on Information Systems (ACIS 2003), Paper #178, Perth, Western Australia 26-28 November (2003)
20. Sterman, J. D.: Business Dynamics: Systems Thinking and Modelling for a Complex World. The McGraw-Hill Companies, USA (2000)
21. Vernadat, F. B.:Enterprise Modelling Languages. ICEIMT'97 Enterprise Integration – International Consensus, EI-IC ESPRIT Project 21.859 (1997) (last accessed 1/12/ 2003) http://www.mel.nist.gov/workshop/iceimt97/pap-ver3/pap-ver3.htm
22. Yu, E. S. K., Mylopoulos, J.: AI Models for Business Process Reengineering. IEEE Expert, IEEE (1996) 16-23

A Workflow-Oriented System Architecture for the Management of Container Transportation

Sarita Bassil[1], Rudolf K. Keller[2], and Peter Kropf[1]

[1] Département IRO, Université de Montréal, C.P. 6128, succursale Centre-ville,
Montréal, Québec, H3C 3J7, Canada
{bassil, kropf}@iro.umontreal.ca
[2] Zühlke Engineering AG, Wiesenstrasse 10a, CH-8952 Schlieren, Switzerland
ruk@zuehlke.com

Abstract. In this paper, we introduce a workflow-oriented system architecture for the processing of client requests (CRs) for container transportation. In the context of multi-transfer container transportation, the processing of CRs can be achieved by specific sequences of interdependent activities. These sequences need to be just-in-time created. They also need to be adapted to deal with unexpected events that may occur. Workflow technology is used to model and to manage the processing of CRs. The creation and the adaptation of activity sequences require first, an optimized scheduling of a limited number of resources (by also respecting CRs constraints); and second, a number of special workflow concepts and functionality to correctly manage activity sequences. Optimization models are involved to take care of the resource management and of the activity scheduling. Enhancements of workflow concepts and functionality for workflow management systems are investigated to deal with an activity sequence creation and adaptation. Finally, the proposed architecture includes a rule processing part to reduce the time-consuming manual interaction with the system.

Keywords: system architecture, workflow management system, process planning, flexible workflow, transportation application.

1 Introduction

Workflow technology provides an appropriate support for the planning of activities. It allows for the coordination and the follow-up of tasks explicitly defined. Domains such as transportation can take advantage of this technology, in particular if its underlying challenging aspects are accommodated.

Nowadays, a growing number of transportation companies are facing fleet management (FM) issues and are forced to cope with highly constrained environments while maintaining a satisfactory level of efficiency. A definition of FM is given in [7]: "FM covers the whole range of planning and management issues from procurement of power units and vehicles to vehicle dispatch and scheduling of crews and maintenance operations". This type of management can be tackled under various lengths of planning horizons and levels of detail: the strategic, the tactical and the operational level. The latter involves a short planning horizon where the level of detail is relatively high.

J. Desel, B. Pernici, and M. Weske (Eds.): BPM 2004, LNCS 3080, pp. 116–131, 2004.

Among the sectors in which FM represents a particularly challenging issue, the *multi-transfer container transportation* (MTCT) – that could be extended to the multimodal freight transportation [17] – has gained in interest in recent years [7]. In MTCT a container is moved from terminal to terminal with the possibility to shift it from vehicle to vehicle before delivering it to the final destination. In this paper, we focus on MTCT at the operational level, in which a close follow-up of activities must be achieved in order to ensure a good client request (CR) satisfaction.

In the context of MTCT management, it appears that the processing of a CR can be achieved by a specific sequence of interdependent activities: e.g., attach an empty container to a vehicle, move the empty container to the origin location, load the container, move the container to the final destination, unload the container. Moreover, MTCT requires to just-in-time create the sequence of activities, or to just-in-time adjust a basic sequence of activities, needed to accomplish a specific request. It also requires a high degree of adaptation of ongoing activities' sequences to deal with unexpected events (e.g., new request arrival, delayed vehicles, crew member desistance).

Our approach exploits the workflow technology [28] to model and to manage the processing of CRs. Specific features of Workflow Management Systems (WfMSs) can result in positive effects for the transportation domain. These features include new concepts and functionality.

We are aware of the fact that workflow technology in the transportation domain is usually used to manage logistic activities where documents and information are passed from one participant to another according to a set of procedural rules [12]. However, the central issue related to workflows in our approach is the focus on supporting *flow of work* and not on supporting flow of "documents" [1]. Furthermore, we adopt the idea of emergent workflows described by Jørgensen and Carlsen in [15]: "emergent workflows provide an integrated support for planning, coordination and performance of work". The workflow definition and enactment are intertwined.

Taking into account a proposed extension of the Workflow Reference Model (WfRM) [30] that covers the support of particular workflow concepts and functionality [5], we already introduced an original transportation system framework adapted to the MTCT application [4]. This framework is conceptually divided into two main layers: a *workflow layer* and a *coordination layer*.

The workflow layer essentially gathers a set of concurrently running workflow instances, each of them being associated with a specific CR. Knowing that a workflow instance is composed of a sequence of activities, and that the state of these activities is known at any time, it is hence possible to determine the set of resources used such as vehicles, containers and drivers. Since we are dealing with activities to be achieved by humans, the dispatching of the appropriate crews at the appropriate time plays an important role. We take advantage of the worklist concept to ensure this task.

The coordination layer is responsible for a certain number of tasks that ensure the efficient allocation of resources. It is responsible to receive the new requests, to ask the workflow layer to instantiate new workflow instances and to react accordingly to unexpected events by sending modification orders to the workflow layer. In brief, the coordination layer gathers a set of optimization algorithms that are used for the management of resources and for the scheduling of activities.

Taking into account this framework, we propose in this paper a workflow-oriented system architecture applied in the MTCT context. This system – that we call the MTCT system – enables the user (called "system administrator" in the rest of the paper) to efficiently track and monitor the progress of many CRs in process. Moreover, the system allows crew members (called "drivers" hereafter) to identify at the right time their assigned activities and to transmit to the system administrator the state of each activity from its selection to its completion.

In the following, we explore the MTCT application (Section 2) and investigate workflow concepts and functionality for WfMSs to deal with this application (Section 3). We then present the architecture of the MTCT system (Section 4). This architecture is based on workflow technology, optimization engine technology and rule engine technology. Section 5 gives an example of a CR processing planning that illustrates the use and the characteristics of the developed architecture. Section 6 reports on the implementation of the MTCT system. Section 7 discusses related work and Section 8 concludes the paper.

2   The MTCT Application

Usually, a CR for container transportation gathers at least the following information: an origin location where goods are picked-up, a destination where goods are delivered, a pick-up and a delivery time window. To answer a CR, a number of activities of different duration are involved. These activities need to be performed in a certain order, and are scheduled within a given time window depending on the individual request information, on the resource availability and on the possible paths to follow.

We consider a set of transportation units that we call resources. This set is composed of a fixed number of containers with fixed wheels, trucks (i.e., vehicles) without loading space, crews and terminals. We suppose that the transportation company offers a full container-load, where one container carries at one time only merchandise related to one client. Besides the resources, we define a set of six activities, that we call *activity templates*. A composition of these activities provides a possible solution to satisfy a CR. An activity is assigned to a specific driver that becomes responsible for its execution within a specific time and by taking into account specific information that we call input attributes. Table 1 shows the six activity templates we defined.

Table 1. Activity templates involved in the processing of a CR for container transportation

	(1) Attach container to vehicle	(2) Detach container from vehicle	(3) Move vehicle to location	(4) Load container	(5) Unload container	(6) Wait at location
Input attributes	Container_ID Vehicle_ID Location_ID	Idem[1]	Container_ID Vehicle_ID O_location_ID[2] D_location_ID[3]	Container_ID Location_ID	Idem	Idem
Assignment	Driver_ID	Idem	Idem	Idem	Idem	Idem
Time	MinD/MaxD[4] WUT[5] EST/LST[6]	Idem	Idem	Idem	Idem	Idem

[1]The same as left, [2,3]The ID of the origin (resp., destination) location (it does not necessary correspond to the origin (resp., destination) location of a CR), [4]The minimum/maximum duration, [5]The warm-up time (time when the driver is informed about the activity to carry out), [6]The earliest/latest starting time.

A possible composition of these activities to answer a CR could be the following sequence: (1)-(3)-(6)-(4)-(3)-(2)-(6)-(1)-(3)-(6)-(5)-(3). Note that a "wait at location" activity is sometimes necessary before going further in the processing of a request.

The composition of activities should be based on a transportation network in which a number of nodes (i.e., locations) and edges (i.e., paths) between these nodes are defined. As a first configuration, we consider a transportation network with a central depot or terminal where resources are located and where a transfer is possible. A transfer is defined as the action of shifting a container from one vehicle to another vehicle. As an example, the sequence "(2)-(6)-(1)" in the composition presented above, represents a transfer.

Taking into account this configuration, a number of path scenarios are possible for the management of CRs. The simplest scenario would be to consider that the satisfaction of a CR consists to ask a couple container/driver (c/d – We consider that each driver is associated with a specific vehicle.) to leave the depot P at a specific time, to pick up the goods at the origin location O specified by the request, to deliver the goods at the final destination D and then to go back to P. In other words, answering a request consists of accomplishing the path P-O-D-P ("simple scenario").

Another scenario would be to ask a couple c/d to leave P at a specific time, to pick up the goods at O and to go back to P with the possibility to make a transfer at P (i.e., to change the driver and the vehicle at P) before delivering the goods at D and then to go back to P (i.e., P-O-P-D-P). This represents a "transfer scenario". It can be motivated by the non-availability of drivers. In this case, we hence need to plan a path P-O-P when a driver is just available to make this portion of the whole path.

In the first two scenarios, c/d should return to P before answering a new request. We may however, consider that a couple c/d is free to answer a new request as soon as the goods are delivered at a specific destination (i.e., $P-O_1-D_1-O_2-D_2-P$, where O_1/D_1 are related to a specific request and O_2/D_2 are related to another request). We talk about a "round scenario". A combination of the transfer scenario and the round scenario is also possible. Here is an example: $P-O_1-P-D_1-O_2-D_2-P$.

The scenarios presented above take into account a transportation network with a central depot. This transportation network configuration could be extended to a more complex one that gathers a number of distributed depots. Considering this configuration, a "multi-transfer scenario" of the kind $P_1-O-P_2-P_3-...-P_n-D$ (where $\{P_1, P_2, ..., P_n\} \in \mathcal{P}, \mathcal{P}$ being the partition of the set of depots) is possible.

An in-depth description of the MTCT application would involve the discussion of the different unexpected events (e.g., delayed vehicles, crew member desistance) that may occur, and their implication in our context. This however is beyond the scope of our paper. In the remaining of this paper, without loss of generality, only the "new request arrival" event will be considered to explain and discuss the MTCT System.

3   Workflow Concepts and Functionality for the MTCT System

The MTCT system we propose is workflow oriented and supports transportation processes. It should inform the drivers at the right point in time about the work to accomplish, while providing them the appropriate information. For transportation processes, it is sometimes impossible to fix all activity attributes as soon as a workflow instance is created/launched. It is also impossible to predict all events that may occur and that may necessitate a workflow structural deviation or an activity attribute updating. Our workflow-oriented system should provide the appropriate workflow concepts and functionality to support all these aspects. Otherwise, as stated in [9], the system would have to be "bypassed", which would cause (besides other problems) the problem of missing documentation. The following presents the list of special concepts and functionality for WfMSs necessary to deal with the MTCT application:

The Activity Template Concept. In order to introduce a standard way for defining activities, it is useful to define a set of activity templates related to the container transportation management. Activity templates are used by the system to schedule the different activities in a workflow model/instance. Each activity template consists of an elementary task with three types of attributes:

- *Input attributes*, which specify the (material) resources needed to accomplish a task.
- *Assignment attributes*, which specify the (human) actor responsible of accomplishing this task. This is mainly used by the system to let the task appear in the worklist where it should appear.
- *Time attributes*, which specify the (min/max) duration of the task, its (earliest/latest) starting time, and its related warm-up time.

Table 1 gives examples of activity templates related to the MTCT management.

The Warm-Up Time Concept (WUT). "Time" plays a crucial role in the transportation domain. Therefore, time attributes should be defined for each activity. Temporal aspects such as the duration and the starting time (fixed calendar date) are discussed in literature. The ADEPT project for instance, treats these two aspects in detail [9]. A differentiation should however be done between (1) the *planned starting time* of an activity, (2) the *activation time* of an activity (i.e., when the activity is due, taking into account the control flow of the workflow), and (3) its *assignment time* to a worklist. Usually, within current WfMSs an activity is assigned to a worklist as soon as it is due within the flow. However, crew members should not be surprised by activities, and they should know in advance about the next activity to carry out. Hence, the assignment time of an activity to a worklist should depend on the planned starting time of the activity and on the necessary warm-up time. Eder *et al.* tackle a similar problem by working on future personal schedules [10]. Their work is motivated by the need to provide early information about future tasks (i.e., forecasting of tasks). Their approach is based on probabilistic time management.

The Dynamic Setting/Updating of Attributes at the Workflow Instance Level. In the MTCT system, activity attributes are provided by a "Solution Provider" component that is external to the WfMS (see Section 4). Hence, no data flow between activities exists, and input attributes of all activities can be logically linked to the "start node" output attributes. However, we should be able at any time to set/update input attributes of activities not yet in a "running" state. It should also be possible to dynamically (re-)assign such activities to a valid workflow actor (i.e., late binding of resources [16]), and to dynamically set/update the time attributes of these activities by always respecting the temporal constraints.

The Dynamic Insertion of an Activity at the Workflow Instance Level. This insertion should be based on previously defined activity templates. During insertion, temporal constraints should be respected and input attributes of the inserted activity should be linked to newly generated data elements. This is well discussed in [22]. The dynamic insertion of an activity could be extended to the dynamic insertion of a sub-workflow. As an example from the MTCT application, the sequence of the two activities "detach container from vehicle" and "attach container to vehicle" should be inserted each time a container needs to be transferred from one vehicle to another.

The Dynamic Deletion of an Activity at the Workflow Instance Level. As an example, a deletion of the "move vehicle to the depot P" activity from a workflow instance should be possible in the special case where a round scenario is involved (refer to Section 2). In the context of the MTCT application, major verifications before permitting the deletion of an activity are related to the activity state (e.g., an activity in a "running" state cannot be deleted unless it is possible to preserve its context).

The Dynamic Management of Worklists. The reassignment or the deletion of an activity already assigned to a specific worklist should be complemented by a correct worklists management. Following a reassignment, the workitem that corresponds to the reassigned activity should be removed from its original worklist and it should appear in the appropriate worklist taking into account the new assignment (if not null). The workitem that corresponds to a deleted activity should be removed from its worklist. The updating of an activity input/time attribute should be complemented by a correct updating of the information provided by the worklists.

In short, there are a number of issues that arise from the list of workflow concepts and functionally just exposed. Insights from today's WfMS research projects [9, 10, 16, 22] are combined and contrasted, and an extension of the WfRM to accommodate these concepts and functionality is proposed in [5]. A discussion of the WfRM extension is beyond the scope of this paper.

4 Architecture of the MTCT System

We describe in this section the MTCT system architecture shown in Fig. 1, and give an overview of its underlying constructs. Two phases are distinguished in this system: the build-time phase and the run-time phase.

During build-time, a set of activity templates is defined using the Workflow Definition Tool. The latter is also used to design basic workflow models that capture the sequencing of the most likely required activities for the processing of a CR. Activity templates and workflow models are stored in the Workflow Repository as Workflow and Activity Template Definitions. Another component of the system is the Resource Definition Tool. It allows the definition of resources that make possible the accomplishment of the activities. The resources are stored in the Workflow Repository as Resource Definitions. The planned (fixed) availability of the human resources (i.e., shift) are defined via workflows using the Workflow Definition Tool. This will be detailed in Section 4.1. A third component of the system is the Optimization Model

Definition Tool. It allows for describing optimization models (OMs). These models are used to (re-)plan the processing of CRs. Refer to Section 4.2 for details. Another part of the definition deals with modification rules (MRs). These are usually defined using a rule editor (not shown in Fig. 1 for simplicity purpose). They go into the MR Repository. MRs and rule engines are discussed in Section 4.4. As a last part of the build-time phase, the Transportation Network Information is fixed within a specific database. It defines in particular locations/depots of the transportation network as well as the durations to move between two locations. This information, once it is specified, is rarely modified.

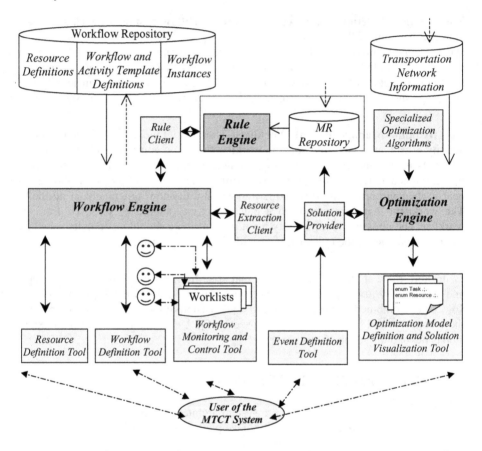

Fig. 1. Architecture of the MTCT System

At run time, when a new event appears, the system administrator of the MTCT system uses the Event Definition Tool to define this event (e.g., a new request arrival) as well as its related data. This triggers the selection of a specific OM. The Solution Provider module takes care of this selection. As long as no solution is found, a number of OMs may be solved. Specialized Optimization Algorithms are called by the Optimization Engine to solve a selected OM. Three data sources are used to initialize the OM:

1. The Event Definition Tool provides event information.
2. The Resource Extraction Client provides data related to the current reservation/unavailability of resources (reflected by the state of our workflow instances).
3. The Transportation Network Information database (already described in the build-time phase).

When an optimized solution is generated, it is interpreted and translated into a set of modifications that can be automatically applied, via the Rule Client, on the pool of currently running instances. We talk about modifying the pool of workflow instances when a new workflow instance is created as well as when a structural or an attribute modification is applied on an existing workflow instance. The interpretation of solution implications on this pool is the task of the Rule Engine and the MR Repository. The system administrator can also make manual modifications. Indeed, the optimized solution can be displayed to the system administrator via the Solution Visualization Tool, so that she can take decisions regarding the modification(s) to bring to the pool of instances. Manual modifications are applied from the Workflow Monitoring and Control Tool. Details about workflow management are given in Section 4.3. The Workflow Engine is responsible of applying modifications on the pool of workflow instances. It also executes the instances by enforcing the sequencing of the activities and by dispatching work at the appropriate time to the appropriate human resource. Worklists (which are part of the Workflow Monitoring and Control Tool) are used to show which activity needs to be carried out. Each human resource has her personal worklist to quickly identify her assigned activities.

4.1 Resource Management

The diagram of Fig. 2 describes the entities that are used for capturing the resource structure and the relations between them. A resource type (e.g., vehicle) gathers a set of resources (e.g., V101, V202). Unlike material resources, human resources (i.e., drivers) are not continuously available but only within their own shift. The planned unavailability (i.e., the complementary of the availability or shift) of the different drivers over a period of time is captured by a workflow with parallel branches. Each branch of the workflow corresponds to a specific driver and each activity of the branch defines a period of unavailability for this driver.

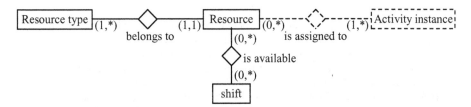

Fig. 2. Entity-relation diagram for the resource management

Resources can be assigned to activity instances. The tables corresponding to the dashed part of the entity-relation diagram (Fig. 2) are frequently updated. At a specific time, the reservation of the different resources is deduced from the set of activity instances where the state is different from "completed", "deleted" or "skipped".

4.2   The Optimization Part of the System

The need for an optimal management of resources when (re-)planning activities in the container transportation domain is well recognized [24] and can be answered by defining specific OMs. OMs can be defined as a data-independent abstraction of an optimization problem in which the aim is to find the best of all possible solutions. More formally, the goal is to find a solution in the feasible region (i.e., the set of all possible solutions), which has the minimum (or maximum) value of the objective function (i.e., a function which determines how good a solution is) [3]. In our context, we use OMs to plan the processing of CRs and to re-plan this processing when necessary. These OMs should assign resources to activities while satisfying the constraints of a CR as well as while respecting the information related to the transportation network. Our resource allocation problem is modeled as a constraint satisfaction problem that we resolve using constraint programming [27].

When modeling our problem, we leveraged the work reported in [26, 29]. Suitable strategies to answer a CR according to the different scenarios presented in Section 2 were developed. An example of a strategy consists of minimizing the duration of a request processing (i.e., minimizing the reservation of a set of resources). Taking into account this strategy, the following defines a model that picks an available resource and schedules the different activities to answer a CR according to the simple scenario:

- Given a set R of resources from a specific type.
- Given a set S of ordered triples $<r_i, st_{ij}, ft_{ij}>$, (st_{ij}, ft_{ij}) specifying a reservation block (starting/finishing time) for the resource r_i. Note that a number of reservation blocks can be associated with r_i at a specific time.
- Given information related to a specific request: origin location O, destination location D, pick-up time window (put_{min}, put_{max}) and delivery time window (dt_{min}, dt_{max}).
- Given transportation network information: duration(Move(P-O)), duration(Move(O-D)), duration(Move(D-P)) where P corresponds to the depot, and the durations of the specific operations at O and D: duration(Load), duration(Unload).
- We define the objective function Z as the duration of the request processing:
  Z = duration(Waiting_time(O)) + duration(Waiting_time(D)) + c
  Where c is a constant:
  c = duration(Move(P-O)) + duration(Load) +
       duration(Move(O-D)) + duration(Unload) + duration(Move(D-P))
- The problem to solve is the following:
  Minimize Z
  Subject to the following constraints (where t^* corresponds to the leaving time at P):
  (C1) t^* + duration(Move(P-O)) + duration(Waiting_time(O)) ≥ put_{min}
  (C2) t^* + duration(Move(P-O)) + duration(Waiting_time(O)) + duration(Load) ≤ put_{max}
  (C3) t^* + duration(Move(P-O)) + duration(Waiting_time(O)) + duration(Load) +
         duration(Move(O-D)) + duration(Waiting_time(D)) ≥ dt_{min}
  (C4) t^* + duration(Move(P-O)) + duration(Waiting_time(O)) + duration(Load) +
         duration(Move(O-D)) + duration(Waiting_time(D)) + duration(Unload) ≤ dt_{max}
  (C5) $\forall <r, st_j, ft_j> \in$ S where r ∈ R, $t^* > ft_j \lor t^* + Z < st_j$

When selecting a specific OM, such as the one defined above, the Solution Provider module provides to the Optimization Engine the necessary data to solve this model (i.e., the "given statements"). Once a solution is found, this module is also responsible of letting the Rule Processing part of the system "know" about this solution.

4.3 Workflow Management

The architecture of the MTCT system is based on WfMS modules that are compliant with the WfRM proposed by the WfMC [30]. We rely on workflow technology because it provides support in three broad functional areas [25]: (1) workflow definition: capturing the definition of the flow of work, (2) workflow execution: managing the execution of the workflow processes in an operational environment, sequencing the various activities to be performed, and (3) workflow monitoring: monitoring the status of workflow processes and dynamically configuring the runtime controller. We also rely on workflow technology because a number of today's WfMS research projects propose interesting and inspiring approaches to deal with dynamic modifications of workflow instances [2, 11, 18, 22, 23]. In the architecture of the MTCT system, the user can for instance adjust certain attributes or bring structural modifications to existing workflow instances at runtime. Examples include postponing the execution time of a specific activity, changing the driver responsible of an activity, adding a transfer to an already planned CR processing, and so on. Finally, once the execution of a workflow instance is completed, workflow technology allows for recording this instance as historical data (i.e., audit). Workflows are hence seen as providing a way to represent a blueprint of activities so that analysis becomes possible for the detection and for the prevention of bottlenecks at the operational level.

4.4 Modification Rules and Rule Engines

In the architecture of the MTCT system, we use rule engine technology to represent and exploit MRs. A rule such as: *'If a new request arrives, and if a solution is found when a specific optimization model is solved, and if a specific basic workflow model has already been defined, and if a workflow instance manager exists, then a new workflow instance related to the newly arrived request is instantiated from the basic workflow model"* can be nicely coded as a declarative statement [19]. The rules can be coded as standalone atomic units, separate from and independent of the rest of the application logic. This makes the rules easier to develop and maintain. Rule engines have already been applied for dynamic modification of workflows [21]. The idea is to use an automatic rule-based approach with a focus on cancer therapy workflow scenarios. The approach intends (1) to detect semantic exceptions, (2) to derive which instances and control flow areas are affected, and (3) to automatically adjust the affected areas. In the MTCT system, we intend to take advantage of this approach for the automatic structural modification of instances. At this level of our work, we only experimented with the automatic workflow instantiation and attributes setting.

5 An Example of a Client Request Processing Planning

In this section, we illustrate the different steps for answering a CR taking into account the simple scenario discussed in Section 2 and considered in Section 4.2. When a request is received, the system administrator uses a "request information" form (Fig. 3) provided by the Event Definition Tool to specify the related information. This information, the availability of the resources and the transportation network information are used to generate a solution if any.

If a solution is found (as in our case), the system administrator uses the Workflow Monitoring and Control Tool to instantiate a basic workflow model that captures a sequence of eight activities defined between a "start" activity and an "end" activity: (S) start, (A1) attach container to vehicle, (A2) move vehicle to O, (A3) wait at O, (A4) load container, (A5) move vehicle to D, (A6) wait at D, (A7) unload container, (A8) move vehicle to P, (E) end. Since the solution shown in Fig. 3 does not specify a waiting time at O, the activity (A3) is then deleted from the instance. Note that in this case, the activities constitute a simple sequence of actions. Other examples may yield to activities whose control flow is best captured in a state-transition diagram.

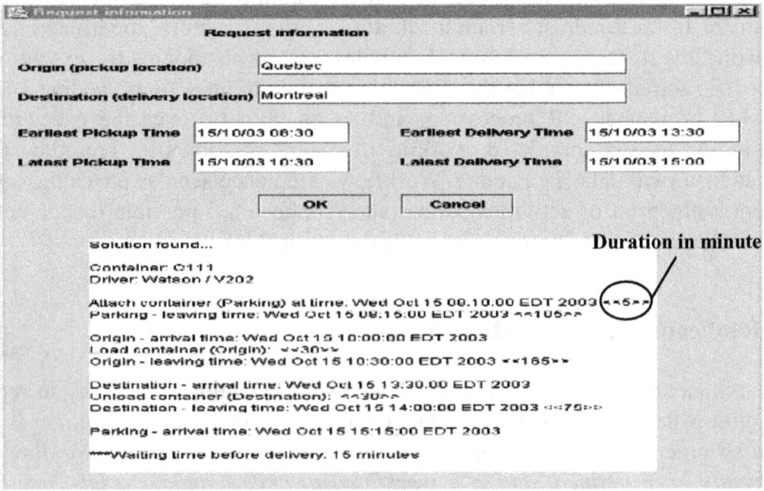

Fig. 3. "Request information" form

Two types of edges are used in our workflow model: the control edges and the time edges. The WfMS prototype we are using – ADEPT [8] – does not allow the specification of a fix calendar date for the activities' starting time. We use instead the "time edge" concept and we define a minimum and a maximum distance between the "start" activity (S) and each of the activities (A). The earliest and the latest starting time of (A) are specified taking into account the real starting time of (S).

The system administrator launches (S) to specify the five following output attributes (see Fig. 3): the CR origin location (Quebec), the CR destination location (Montreal), the central depot of our transportation network, and the container and vehicle IDs shown in the solution (C111 and V202). These attributes are given as input to the different activities of the workflow instance. The other elements of the solution (e.g., driver, starting time/duration of the activities) are used to set the assignment attribute and the time attributes for each activity.

The set of steps just accomplished by the system administrator (i.e., workflow instantiation, activity deletion, execution of (S) and attributes setting) can be automated so that time-consuming manual interactions with the system are reduced. For that reason, we need MRs such as the following, which applies to a workflow instantiation:

WHEN
    there is a **RequestInformation** called *?ri*
    there is a **OptimizationModel** called *om*   such that *OM_ID=1* and *Solution_Found=true*
    there is a **ProcessTemplate** called *?pt*   such that *PT_Name.compareTo('Simple')=0*
    there is a **ProcessInstanceManager** called *?pim*
THEN
    Apply *?pim*
      so that assert(*createProcessInstance(?pt, ?ri.Request_ID, 'Standard', 'Administrator'*)   )

The notation used above stems from ILOG JRules [13]. It is based on an English-like syntax. Four class instances are involved in the rule shown above: RequestInformation and OptimizationModel are classes from our implemented application; ProcessTemplate and ProcessInstanceManager are classes provided by the ADEPT API.

6 Implementation of the MTCT System

Part of the presented architecture has already been implemented (MTCT System version 0.1). This version includes an extended WfMS and an optimization system.

We use ADEPT, a WfMS prototype developed at the University of Ulm [8]. Two main criteria were applied to retain this system among other WfMSs. The first and foremost criterion is its compliance with the basic WfRM, as well as its support for the "activity template" concept, for temporal aspects (except the WUT concept), and for two structural modifications (the insertion and the deletion of an activity). The second criterion refers to the availability of its API.

A *Mediator* component that extends the existing ADEPT API was implemented. This component provides functions for the dynamic setting/updating of attributes (input attributes, assignment attributes and time attributes) and for the dynamic management of worklists. The WUT concept is not supported yet.

We use OPL Studio from ILOG [14] to define OMs that are solved using the CPLEX optimization algorithms. Since our implementation is based on ADEPT which is implemented in Java and which uses an Oracle relational DB, the advantage of OPL is twofold: (1) We can access its C++ API from Java code, relying upon the Java Native Interface (JNI). So, once a model is designed, compiled and tested in OPL Studio, it can be easily solved from a Java application by interfacing with OPL. (2) We can establish a connection to a database and initialize the model by reading the appropriate relational tables. Having this in mind, we implemented in Java the ADEPT Resource Extraction Client and the Solution Provider.

In a standalone fashion, we have incepted integrating rule engine technology (ILOG's JRules) into our MTCT system. The integration with the MTCT system will be accomplished at a later stage, once we are satisfied with the results of applying MRs on the pool of workflow instances. Since rules for the transfer scenario, the round scenario and the multi-transfer scenario are much more complex than those for the simple scenario, we will deal with them in later versions.

In Fig. 4, we present a screenshot of the MTCT system. The main window in (a) shows the Workflow Monitoring and Control Tool. It provides functionality the system administrator can use to modify the pool of the workflow instances. The first two windows (top right) are monitoring windows and show running workflow instances: a planned unavailability workflow instance, and one of the CR processing instances that is going on. The three windows at the bottom right show the current reservation of the different resources. This information is automatically extracted and used by the Solution Provider component; however, the system administrator is also able to visualize it at any time. The last window here (bottom left) shows one of the possible windows the system administrator can access to make manual modifications to the pool of instances – the "Activity (re-)assignment" in this case. In fact, each time she chooses one of the six possible functionality options, the corresponding window is opened. The two windows in (b) show the worklists of two specific drivers. All necessary information is available for the execution of an activity related to a request processing instance. As we can see, activities related to a planned unavailability workflow instance are also communicated to drivers via their worklists.

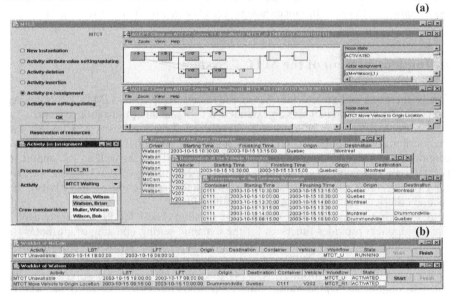

Fig. 4. Screenshot of the MTCT System version 0.1. **(a)** The environment of the system administrator; **(b)** The environment of the drivers

As a final note in this section, the performance of the system shall be briefly discussed. A performance evaluation may be performed in terms of answering questions such as "how much time does it take to generate a solution using OMs?" and "how much time does it take to modify the pool of instances (e.g., to instantiate a new workflow instance, to update already planned/instantiated ones)?". Based on our current prototype implementation, we expect to encounter a performance problem which is mainly related to the continuously access to the database. In fact, some of the ADEPT API functions useful in our context are not implemented yet. Consequently, we sometimes had to manipulate the ADEPT database directly, especially when implementing the *Mediator* component. The performance of the system would be considerably enhanced if the functions of this component were inherently provided by the WfMS (e.g., ADEPT).

7 Related Work

The MTCT system is, to our knowledge, the first workflow-based system to support the processing of CRs for container transportation. Planner systems in the transportation domain usually use planning languages such as PDDL (Planning Domain Definition Language) [20] to describe a logistic problem and its solution, represented as a sequence of ordered activities (a plan). These systems do not however allow for plan monitoring and control during execution – an inherent characteristic of the workflow technology on which the MTCT system is based.

TeleTruck [6] is a prototype software system that is probably the closest related one to the MTCT system. This prototype has been developed for planning, optimizing, and monitoring of road haulage. The underlying approach is based on multi-agent technology: physical objects (e.g., trucks, drivers, trailers, load spaces) are modeled by intelligent agents. Those agents are able to reason and plan on the basis of their individual resources and means provided by the corresponding physical objects. For TeleTruck, the work is not described for a specific CR but for a specific vehicle (i.e., each vehicle's plan is represented separately). In the MTCT system, however, workflows are used to provide a complete description of the work process to be enacted for a particular request. Consequently, the processing of each request is separately documented and can easily be tracked. If necessary, the client can be quickly informed about the state of her request. The originality of the MTCT system in respect of the TeleTruck system stems from the fact that the reservation of the resources is reflected by the workflows, and that the support for dispatching drivers in their daily work is smoothly provided by worklists, a concept tightly associated with the workflow technology. In the TeleTruck system, the traditional timetable approach is used. Finally, in this system, the emphasis is put on the on-line re-planning to cope with highly dynamic environment, whereas in our system we take advantage of already existing optimization algorithms, by only defining simple OMs.

8 Conclusion

In this paper, we studied the *multi-transfer container transportation* (MTCT) application and we described an architecture with all its underlying concepts to deal with client requests (CRs) for container transportation. It is based on workflow management, optimization engine technology and rule engine technology. We claim that the processing of CRs and the management of human resources availability can be adequately and profitably dealt with using workflows. Since a workflow instance is composed of activities and the state of these activities is known at any time, the reservation of resources can be deduced. Optimization models (OMs) take care of the management of resources and the scheduling of activities following the occurrence of an unexpected event such as the arrival of a new CR. Solutions from the optimization part of the system are translated into a set of modifications that are applied on the pool of workflow instances. The use of the rule engine technology considerably reduces the time-consuming manual interactions with the MTCT system in an obvious way.

We believe that the MTCT system provides an environment that can easily help on the one hand, a user of a container transportation company to efficiently manage the processing of CRs, and on the other hand, a crew member to just-at-the-right-time identify the work to do.

We feel that the architecture proposed can also be applied in the context of transportation applications other than the MTCT application. We may think about local express-mail services and dial-a-ride services where the planning of activities can be solved as a Pick-up and Delivery Problem. Moreover, production systems in which assembly lines are involved could take advantage of this architecture. Indeed, in such systems, two issues are interrelated: the management of limited (shared) resources and the management of processes.

As future work, we aim to further investigate several issues that are central to our system. Among them is the support of unexpected events such as delayed vehicles, crew member desistance and technical problems. The only event supported up to now by the MTCT system is the "arrival of a new CR". Another issue is the distributed worklists we would like to investigate in order to dispatch work on a network of several computers, which could be located at different terminals/vehicles. Finally, modification rules are an important research issue for us. We will have to come up with rules that would bring structural modifications to workflow instances. We will also have to define more complex OMs taking into account the different path scenarios (simple and complex scenarios). Solutions coming from these OMs will potentially be translated into structural modifications of workflow instances.

Acknowledgments. The completion of this research was made possible thanks to funding provided by the NSERC (CRD-224950-99), Bell Canada's support through its Bell University Laboratories R&D program, and support by the CIRANO. We thank Benoît Bourbeau from CIRANO, who has given valuable thoughts regarding the MTCT application.

References

1. Abbot, K.R. and Sarin, S.K., Experiences with Workflow Management: Issues for the Next Generation. In *Proceedings of the 5th Conf. on Computer Supported Cooperative Work (CSCW'94)*, 113-120, Chapel Hill, NC, Oct 1994.
2. Agostini, A. and De Michelis, G., Improving Flexibility of Workflow Management Systems. In van der Aalst, W., Desel, J., and Oberweis, A. (Ed.), *Business Process Management: Models, Techniques, and Empirical Studies. LNCS 1806 Springer*, 218-234, 2000.
3. Algorithms and Theory of Computation Handbook, *CRC Press LLC*, 1999. Appearing in the Dictionary of Computer Science, Engineering and Technology, *CRC Press LLC*, 2000.
4. Bassil, S., Bourbeau, B., Keller, R.K., and Kropf, P., A Dynamic Approach to Muli-transfer Container Management. In *Proceedings of the 2nd Int'l Workshop on Freight Transportation and Logistics (ODYSSEUS'03)*, Palermo, Sicily, Italy, May 2003. On-line at <http://www.unipa.it/Odysseus/Odysseus2003_file/odysseus-main_file/pdf/Programma.htm>.
5. Bassil, S., Rolli, D., Keller, R.K., and Kropf, P., Extending the Workflow Reference Model to Accommodate Dynamism. *Technical Report GELO-155*, Software Eng. Lab, University of Montreal, Quebec, Canada, Feb 2003. On-line at <http://www.iro.umontreal.ca/~bassil/>.
6. Bürckert, H.-J., Fischer, K., and Vierke, G., Transportation Scheduling with Holonic MAS – The TeleTruck Approach. In *Proceedings of the 3rd Int'l Conf. on Practical Applications of Intelligent Agents and Multiagents (PAAM'98)*, 577-590, London, UK, Mar 1998.
7. Crainic, T.G., Long-Haul Freight Transportation. *Handbook of Transportation Science*, R.W. Hall (Ed.), 2nd Edition, Kluwer Academic Publishers, 2002.

8. Dadam, P. and Reichert, M., The ADEPT WfMS Project at the University of Ulm. In *Proceedings of the 1ˢᵗ European Workshop on Workflow and Process Management (WPM'98) (Workflow Management Research Projects)*, Zürich, Switzerland, Oct 1998.
9. Dadam, P., Reichert, M., and Kuhn, K., Clinical Workflows – The Killer Application for Process-oriented Information Systems? In *Proceedings of the 4ᵗʰ Int'l Conf. on Business Information Systems (BIS'2000)*, 36-59, Poznan, Poland, Apr 2000.
10. Eder, J., Pichler, H., Gruber, W., and M. Ninaus, Personal Schedules for Workflow Systems. In *Proceedings of the Int'l Conf. On Business Process Management (BPM'03)*, 216-231, Eindhoven, The Netherlands, Jun 2003.
11. Ellis, C.A. and Keddara, K., A Workflow Change Is a Workflow. In van der Aalst, W., Desel, J., and Oberweis, A. (Ed.), *Business Process Management: Models, Techniques, and Empirical Studies. LNCS 1806 Springer*, 201-217, 2000.
12. E-Workflow – the Workflow Portal, Workflow Case Studies (Transportation). 1997-1998. On-line at <http://www.e-workflow.org/case_studies/transportation/index.htm>.
13. ILOG JRules. On-line at <http://www.ilog.com/products/jrules/>.
14. ILOG OPL Studio. On-line at <http://www.ilog.com/products/oplstudio/>.
15. Jørgensen, H.D. and Carlsen, S., Emergent Workflow: Planning and Performance of Process Instances. In *Proceedings of the 1999 Workflow Management Conf. –Workflow-based Applications (WFM'99)*, 98-116, Münster, Germany, Nov 1999.
16. Kammer, P.J., Bolcer, G.A., and Bergman, M., Requirements for Supporting Dynamic Adaptive Workflow on the WWW. In *Proceedings of the Workshop on Adaptive Workflow Systems at CSCW'98*, Seattle, WA, Nov 1998. On-line at <http://ccs.mit.edu/klein/cscw98/>.
17. Kinnock, N., EU Commissioner for Transport, Task Force Transport Intermodality Brochure, Oct 1995. On-line at <http://www.cordis.lu/transport/src/taskforce/src/intbrch2.htm>.
18. Kradolfer, M., A Workflow Metamodel Supporting Dynamic, Reuse-Based Model Evolution. *Doctoral thesis,* University of Zürich, Switzerland, 2000.
19. McClintock, C. and Berlioz, C.A., Implementing Business Rules in Java. In *Java Developers Journal*, 5(5):8-16, 2000.
20. McDermott, D., Ghallab, M., Howe, A., Knoblock, C., Ram, A., Veloso, M., Weld, D., and Wilkins, D., PDDL - The Planning Domain Definition Language. *Technical Report*, Department of Computer Science, Yale University, New Haven, CT, 1998.
21. Müller, R. and Rahm, E., Rule-Based Dynamic Modification of Workflows in a Medical Domain. In Buchmann, A.P., (Ed.), *Datenbanksysteme in Büro, Technik und Wissenschaft (BTW'99)*, Freiburg im Breisgau. Springer, 429-448, Berlin, 1999.
22. Reichert, M. and Dadam, P., ADEPTflex: Supporting Dynamic Changes of Workflow without Losing Control. *Journal of Intelligent Information Systems*, 10(2):93-129, 1998.
23. Sadiq, S.W. and Orlowska, M.E., Architectural Considerations in Systems Supporting Dynamic Workflow Modifications. In *Proceedings of the Workshop on Software Architectures for Business Process Management at CAiSE'99*, Heidelberg, Germany, Jun 1999. On-line at <http://www.itee.uq.edu.au/~shazia/Publications/CAISE99.pdf>.
24. Taleb-Ibrahimi, M., de Castilho, B., and Daganzo, C.F., Storage Space Versus Handling Work in Container Terminals. *Transportation Research B*. 27(1):13-32, 1993.
25. The Workflow Automation Corporation, Workflow Automation: New Opportunities for Dramatic IT Results. *White Paper*, 1998. On-line at <http://www.workflow.ca/>.
26. Trilling G., Génération automatique d'horaires de médecins de garde pour l'hôpital Côte-des-Neiges de Montréal. *CRT-98-05*, University of Montreal, Quebec, Canada, Jan 1998.
27. Tsang, E., Foundations of Constraint Satisfaction. *Academic Press*, London, 421 pp., 1993.
28. van der Aalst, W. and van Hee, K., Workflow Management: Models, Methods, and Systems. *The MIT Press*, 368 pp., 2002.
29. Weil, G., Heus, K., François, P., and Poujade, M., Constraint Programming for Nurse Scheduling. *Engineering in Medicine and Biology*, 14(4):417-422, 1995.
30. Workflow Management Coalition, The WfRM. *WFMC-TC-1003*, Version 1.1, Jan 1995.

Business to Business Transaction Modeling and WWW Support

Mateus Barcellos Costa[1], Rodolfo Ferreira Resende[1],
Mírian Halfeld Ferrari Alves[2], and Marcelo Vieira Segatto[3]

[1] Universidade Federal de Minas Gerais
{mcosta,rodolfo}@dcc.ufmg.br
[2] Université François Rabelais Blois-Tours-Chinon/LI - Antenne de Blois
mirian.halfeld@univ-tours.fr
[3] Universidade Federal do Espírito Santo segatto@ele.ufes.br

Abstract. The information systems that support Electronic Commerce on the Internet are becoming more common and complex. The complexity of these systems increases the need for new models with different degrees of abstraction in order to simplify the visualization of different aspects of the structure, constraints and operation of the software. In this paper we discuss some aspects of the Electronic Commerce transactions presented in the literature. Our first contribution is to organize in a conceptual and logical level some models presented in the literature. We describe an Electronic Commerce application using these models and we discuss some aspects of a prototype that we are currently developing. The proposed models are useful not only to describe but also to support the adoption of new aspects in the applications. Another contribution is to demonstrate, in the context of the proposed models, the use of Automated Trust Negotiation.

1 Introduction

Business to Business Electronic Commerce - B2B E-Commerce, from the technological point of view, aims ideally at enabling autonomous business applications to cooperate, using each other functionalities conveniently. Some of the challenges reside in the integration and interoperability of the applications and the problems of reaching this goal are related to scalability, dynamism, autonomy, heterogeneity and legacy systems [12]. These issues increase the need for B2B E-Commerce models that can be used to realize system design and implementation.

Several models have been proposed to support the development of B2B E-Commerce applications[8,16,17,21], in particular models for commercial transactions. The term commercial transaction is used here as a commercial interaction or an operation among two or more partners. In this paper we discuss these transactions under a conceptual view from the model presented by Trastour et al[21], which defines commercial transactions in terms of a life cycle composed of four phases.

J. Desel, B. Pernici, and M. Weske (Eds.): BPM 2004, LNCS 3080, pp. 132–147, 2004.
© Springer-Verlag Berlin Heidelberg 2004

To discuss the life cycle model we use as a working example the Electronic Inverted Auction of the Procurement Portal of the Brazilian Federal Government - ComprasNet[19]. The ComprasNet Electronic Auction enables suppliers to check each other bids and is used for procurement of ordinary products and services such as office supplies, fuel, security services, cleaning supplies and transportation. These products and services can be auctioned using a simple rule based on the smallest price. There are two forms of the ComprasNet Auction: live and electronic. In both cases, there are public sessions for tender presentation. In the live form, these sessions occur in a place where the suppliers must be physically present. In the electronic version, public sessions are performed through the Internet, using the interactive system available at the ComprasNet Portal [19,20].

From the concepts presented by Trastour et al[21] and Bartolini et al[3], we discuss a logical model, based on the Negotiation Host. Again, we use as an example the ComprasNet Electronic Auction.

The conceptual and logical models are usefull not only for the description of system requirements but they also facilitate the addition of new concepts and mechanisms. To illustrate the addition of a new concept and mechanism, the theme of Automated Trust Negotiation [18,25], is discussed in the context of the proposed models.

The development of B2B E-Commerce applications can be facilitaded with the support of a framework [3,9]. However the development of a framework is a difficult task. Therefore we decided to first develop a prototype that is helping us in eliciting the framework requirements. Our prototype is based on Web services technology [23], and can be tailored as a specific B2B E-Commerce application. In this prototype B2B E-Commerce transactions are translated into message exchanging between autonomous and distributed elements.

The remainder of this paper is organized as follows. In Section 2, we discuss some issues about Web based E-Commerce. In Section 3 we discuss the life cycle model as the base for a conceptual model. Section 4 describes the Negotiation Host as a logical model. In Section 5 we present our prototype called SONAR - Web Service for Remote Negotiation. In Section 6 we discuss the theme of Automated Trust Negotiation and Section 7 concludes the paper and presents some future work.

2   Web Based E-commerce

In the beginning of the Web, major advances in Electronic Commerce took place in Business to Customer - B2C - applications based on *Hypertext Markup Language - HTML*. Typical B2C applications are virtual malls such as **www.amazon.com** and air travel systems such as   **www.voegol.com.br**. These applications are characterized by the human-computer interaction based on the use of Web forms. Business to Business Electronic Commerce, in its turn, has its focus on the integration and interoperability of applications [7]. In these early years of the Web, attempts to automatize B2C applications to use them in the B2B scenario were made through the simulation of the human behavior in a screen-scrapping approach and reverse-engineering the Web Application. This approach had some technical problems [7] and restrictions related to the needs of negotiation mechanisms in B2B applications [21].

Web based B2B E-Commerce shows far more promising economical consequences than B2C. B2B applications allow procurement, billing, accounting, human resources, supply chains and manufacturing transactions. In fact, companies and governments have expressed great interest to turn theirs B2B operations into operations supported by E-Commerce transactions over the Internet [12]. Other examples of Electronic Procurement systems beyond ComprasNet are the Websupply [24], *Martins* [11] and *Mercado Eletrônico* [13]. Almost all of these systems claim to generate electronic versions of traditional and widely used commercial operations. Procurement systems, for example, are usually based on operations such as auctions, contracts and quotations [21].

In order to enhance the B2B E-Commerce Application development some consortia define standards and technological frameworks. One of these initiatives is the RosettaNet [15], founded in 1998 to develop XML based standards to describe products and business processes of Information Technology supply chains [6].

3   A Conceptual Model for Commercial Transactions

A conceptual model enables application requirements description in terms of problem domain concepts. We considered the use of several works as the base of a conceptual model for commercial transactions. Schmidt and Lindermann[17] for example, suggest a transaction model composed of three phases: Information, where participants search for potential partners, Agreement: characterized by the negotiation and an agreement formation, and Settlement: that describes payment and delivery logistics. However, we have decided to adopt the life cycle model described by Trastour et al[21] and Bartolini et al[3] because of its comprehensiveness. We demonstrate the model informally describing the ComprasNet Electronic Auction. We do not describe the ComprasNet Auction stages, since they follow the traditional structure of auctions [14].

The life cycle model has the following phases:

1. Matchmaking;
2. Negotiation;
3. Contract Formation and
4. Contract Fulfillment.

In the Matchmaking phase a participant locates other participants. The goal of this phase is to group potential business partners. This can be done, for instance, using advertisements and querying over them.

The ComprasNet stages of Announcement, Registration of Proposal and Qualification can be mapped on the Matchmaking phase. The announcement partially describes the object that will be negotiated. The complete description is listed in an official contract or official negotiation rule. The *negotiation locality* is uniquely defined by the specific auction. A supplier needs to gain access to a negotiation locality in order to participate in the negotiation. Suppliers have to register in advance in order to participate in any auction. After the registration, the suppliers receive login names and passwords that will grant access to the negotiation locality. To participate in an auction, a supplier acquires an announcement or negotiation bill and sends an initial proposal on the date and time defined by the negotiation rule.

The sending and receiving of the proposals are the activities of the Proposal Formation Stage. The auction administrator determines who is able to participate in the negotiation from the group of interested suppliers. This activity is performed in the Qualification Stage.

In the Negotiation Phase participants negotiate with each other trying to reach as a result an agreement. The terms of the agreement define, for example, goods, prices and delivery dates. The ComprasNet stages of Presentation of Bids and Habilitation can be mapped in the Negotiation Phase. In the Presentation of Bids, suppliers, possibly considering the other bids published, send new bids which may be accepted or rejected by the auction administrator who also determines when the Presentation of Bids closes. After closing the bid presentation the habilitation of the participant who gave the smaller accepted bid is checked. This checking involves the verification of juridical, technical and economic documents.

If a winning supplier is disqualified the next better accepted proposal is checked. This process continues until a suitable supplier is found and declared to be the winner or, less likely, the auction is cancelled. The other participants may oppose to the result. If there is no opposition the auction object is granted to the winner.

In the Contract Formation Phase the agreement produced in the Negotiation Phase is transformed in a legal contract. The ComprasNet stages of Granting and Homologation can be mapped in the Contract Formation Phase.

In the Contract Fulfillment Phase the parties carry out the contract. The contract execution stage of the ComprasNet can be mapped in the Contract Fulfillment Phase.

As discussed above the stages of the electronic auction in the ComprasNet can be put in correspondence to the presented life cycle model. Table 2 summarizes the mapping presented.

Although the ComprasNet Electronic Auction has significantly improved the government procurement system, its commercial transactions are not totally automatic and its stages often need human intervention. Several approaches to automatize Matchmaking and Negotiation phases have been proposed. However the effectiveness of these approaches in all the different scenarios were not analysed yet.

The use of abstract levels to capture the system's requirements and introduce useful mechanisms in the commercial transactions is the basic contribution of this paper. We adopt the presented life cycle as our high level description model and in the next sections we describe a logical model based on the concept of a Negotiation Host that incorporates logical mechanisms and coordinates an implementation model.

Table 1. Mapping between life cycle and ComprasNet Stages

Life Cycle Phases	ComprasNet Stages
Matchmaking	Announcement, Registration of Proposal and Qualification
Negotiation	Presentation of Bids and Habilitation
Contract Formation	Granting and Homologation
Contract Fulfillment	Contract Execution

The use of the presented life cycle as a conceptual model provides the first description of Electronic Commerce applications. We were able to describe not only the ComprasNet Auction but several other applications. This conceptual model is focused in the problem domain. In the next section, we discuss a logical model that bridges the problem and solution domains.

4   A Logical Level: The Negotiation Host

In this section, we introduce the concept that a Negotiation Host as presented by Bartolini et al[3] and Trastour et al[21] can be used as a logical modeling element that further describes the elements discussed in the conceptual level.

In the life cycle model participants of commercial transactions are categorized as *clients* that demand goods and services and *suppliers* that provide goods and services. Trastour et al[21] defined a model element called *Negotiation Host - NH* that mediates and governs the actions that take place in the life cycle phases. The Negotiation Host corresponds to a logical entity that can be implemented in many different ways. In this section we describe this element. We will continue to use the ComprasNet Electronic Auction in order to illustrate some of the aspects of the Negotiation Host.

The tasks of the NH range from the Matchmaking to the Contract Formation phases. Here we limit the description of the tasks to the first two phases: Matchmaking and Negotiation. They are the following [3,21]:

- *Apply the admission rules to the participants*: The NH must group the potential business partners. In the ComprasNet Electronic Auction this function is performed in the stages of Announcement, Registration of Proposal and Qualification. The information needed to conduct the transaction can be represented by means of a *Negotiation Template* [3]. Its function is to represent the set of information and instructions that rule the negotiation.
- *Apply the protocol of bid presentation*: This protocol depends on the negotiation schema used. In the ComprasNet Electronic Auction, the initial bid

presentation has a specific date and time. New offers may be sent until the end of the Presentation of Bids stage.

- *Bid validation*: During the negotiation, participants submit their bids representing current agreements and specify restrictions over the parameters expressed in the Negotiation Template. The bid validation takes into account the follow criteria:

  - the bid must have a valid restriction over the parameters defined in the Negotiation Template;
  - the bid must be submitted according to the rules of the negotiation;
  - these rules specify, among other things, who can make bids, when they can do that and what kind of bids can be made.

  In the ComprasNet Electronic Auction a new proposal is accepted only if the offered value is smaller than the currently winning proposal.

- *Form the Agreement*: The result of the Negotiation phase is an agreement which defines an unambiguous parameter configuration that can be used in the Contract Formation Phase. Then the NH must record the agreement that might be transformed in the legal contract.

- *Apply presentation and visibility rules*: The NH must notify the participants about the current negotiation status according to a set of presentation and visibility rules;

- *Terminate the Negotiation*: The NH controls the end of negotiation according to the established termination rules. In the ComprasNet Electronic Auction the end of the Bids Presentation stage is decided by the auction administrator.

We view the Negotiation Host as a set of functional units that support the negotiation. These units may be implemented using different technologies. In the ComprasNet Electronic Auction the Qualification Stage is performed by the auction administrator, i.e., a human element.

Participants can be modeled in the external or internal environment of the Negotiation Host. Both type of participants can start a commercial transaction. During the transaction, the NH may represent the roles of clients and suppliers. The NH executes the actions based on resolutions decided by the participants. As we see in Figure 1, in negotiations mediated by the NH, we define four possible cases. In Figure 1.a, the NH plays the client role and the suppliers are external elements. Figure 1.b shows the case in which the NH plays the roles of the suppliers and the client is external. In the third case, Figure 1.c, client and suppliers are external and in the fourth case, Figure 1.d the NH plays the role of both client and suppliers.

In the ComprasNet suppliers are external elements and they communicate with the NH by means of documents such as the official negotiation rules and by sending bids. Its negotiation model is consistent with the first case (Figure 1.a).

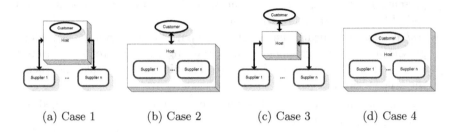

(a) Case 1   (b) Case 2   (c) Case 3   (d) Case 4

Fig. 1. Negotiation Cases

5 A Prototype Supporting Procurement Transactions

We have been developing some electronic commerce applications using the models presented in the earlier sections. This experience showed us that having a framework to support these developments would be an important asset. We decided to first develop a prototype to help us in defining the framework requirements since such type of design is a challenging task. This section presents a partial description of SONAR - the Web Service for Remote Automatic Negotiation that supports the phases of Matchmaking and Negotiation of procurement transactions involving one customer and many suppliers.

5.1 Service Oriented Architecture

Our description is mainly based on the definitions found in Graham et al[7] and W3C [23,22]. Web services are an implementation model for *Service Oriented Architecture - SOA*. W3C defines a Web Service as a software system identified by an URI, whose public interfaces and bindings are defined and described using XML. Its definition can be viewed by other software systems. These systems may then interact with the Web service in a way prescribed by its definition, using XML based messages conveyed by Internet protocols. The SOA model has three entities: (1) the *Service Requester*, (2) the *Service Provider* and (3) the *Service Register*. Service providers interacts with service register by advertising theirs services in the registers. Service requesters use registers to find the services that they want. Finally, requesters and providers associate with each other to perform the specific tasks of the application. The technology that support SOA has been organized in three stacks: *Wire Stack, Description Stack* and *Discovery Stack*. In the current status of our investigation we consider the interactions between the requester and the provider. These interactions are supported by the Wire Stack. The base of this stack can be built by standard Internet protocols such as HTML, SMTP and FTP and the higher level protocols are based in XML/SOAP. Our implementation uses HTTP and the messages are XML documents posted in SOAP envelops.

5.2   Some Implementation Aspects

The current version of SONAR offers support for procurement transactions based on the smallest price. In the Matchmaking phase, participants interact with SONAR transferring information needed to start the negotiation. Currently SONAR only supports a Negotiation phase as showed in Figure 1.d. To support this model, the interactions among customer, suppliers and SONAR occur as follows:

- Matchmaking phase:
  - The customer sends the announcement to SONAR;
  - SONAR advertises the announcement in SONAR's Yellow page system;
  - The suppliers search for announcements browsing SONAR's yellow page system;
  - Suppliers interested in a specific invitation for a bid, send the initial proposals to SONAR;
  - SONAR notifies suppliers about the acceptance or rejection of the proposal;
- Negotiation phase:
  - SONAR starts the automatic negotiation;
  - SONAR notifies the participants about the negotiation status;
  - SONAR notifies the participants about the result of the negotiation;

Figure 2 shows the interactions among the elements.

The initial interaction of the customer with SONAR authorizes it to publish the announcement. Then, interested suppliers can send initial proposals. The proposals consist of messages documents that obey a predefined shared XML-Schema. When an initial proposal is received, it can be accepted or not. The acceptance criterion is in conformity with the template adopted for the proposals. Particularly, a restriction of acceptable minimum price exists, and it prevents that SONAR accepts proposals formulated with error by the suppliers. Each initial proposal possess as attributes the offered value, the boundary-value , and a value or function of displacement. The offered value is the initial supplier's bid value. The boundary-value is the smallest value that the supplier can offer. This value, as in a real situation, is known only by the corresponding supplier. The displacement value or function is used to compute the customer's next bid, considering the current winning bid as a parameter. The function may be, for example, a percentile function. SONAR can restrict the displacement value to a lower bound.

The period for receiving initial proposals ends at a specific time published at the announcement. When this time finishes, the automatic negotiation starts. SONAR establishes for each participant a private negotiation process that adopts the initial proposal as reference for launching the suppliers processes, which simulate SONAR negotiation supplier's side. Figure 3 shows the interactions of SONAR negotiations. A negotiator for the customer is also simulated. Its goal is to control a particular negotiation and to execute the necessary functions. The terms customer and supplier in this phase are related to SONAR processes

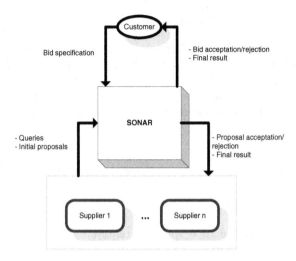

Fig. 2. Actors and its interactions in a transaction supported for the SONAR

that represent and execute the relative actions for the real customer and the suppliers.

The communication between customer and suppliers take place through the exchange of messages and by the shared access to the bids repository illustrated in Figure 3 for the Proposal Bank. The suppliers have permission to modify its bids and the customer has access only for reading it.

The behavior of the negotiation protocol is illustrated by the algorithms in Figure 4. First, the customer (Figure 4.a), classifies the initial proposals and determines the current winner (variable Win). After that, it informs all the suppliers, except the current winning supplier, that they had not been successful. This acknowledgment corresponds to the message NOT_WIN. Later, the customer verifies its message input buffer, to test if it had some change in the bank of proposals. This buffer has size 1 and the messages sent by the suppliers are overwrote. When the message is read, it is consumed from the buffer. When the suppliers update their proposals in the proposal bank SONAR sends the message PROPOSAL_CHANGE to the customer. In case it has received a message PROPOSAL_CHANGE, the customer reclassifies the proposals possibly establishing a new current winner and sending the message NOT_WIN for the suppliers that are not winning. This process executes in busy wait mode and the classification of the proposals occurs in a critical section, protecting the simultaneous access to the Proposal Bank by the suppliers. When the customer is reading the Proposal Bank, no supplier can write a new proposal. Suppliers in turn, can have simultaneous read access to the Proposal Bank.

Customer executes during the time established for the negotiation. The NegTimeOut() function is used to determine the end of the execution. The suppliers learn about the end of the negotiation when they receive the messages TERMINATE_NEG or /WIN . Message TERMINATE_NEG is sent by the customer to all the suppliers, except to the winner, who receives the message WIN. The call of the AgreementFormation() function illustrates the change to the next phase of the transaction life cycle.

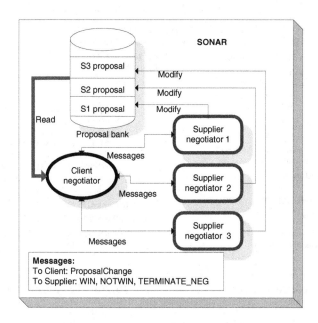

Fig. 3. Supplying interaction between the negotiating customer and three negotiators during the process of negotiation

The suppliers remain waiting for messages of the customer. The messages sent by the customer can be: NOT_WIN, WIN and TERMINATE_NEG. When a supplier receives a message NOT_WIN, it tries to produce a new bid using the RelaxProposal() function and, if successful, it modifies the proposal of the supplier in the Proposal Bank through the ModifyProposal() function . This function executes in a critical section, preventing the simultaneous access to the Proposal Bank. When a supplier receives messages WIN or TERMINATE_NEG, the process finishes. The Report function illustrates a communication to the real supplier on the result of the negotiation.

The support to the other negotiation models (Figure 1.a, b and c), implies the existence of interactions between independent negotiating elements and, a standard for exchange messages with security and trustworthiness is required for this phase. Currently, for the interactions carried out in the Matchmaking phase, the communication between participants and SONAR is through SOAP envelops that do not offer support to specific security mechanisms. We are considering the use of ebXML Messaging Service.

The ebXML is an initiative of the OASIS and UN/CEFACT (United Nations Centre for Trade Facilitation and Electronic Business), it intends to define a set

```
Procedure ClientNegotiator() {

MaxScore=Minimal_Score;
Win=No_One;
m= PROPOSAL_CHANGE
Do

        If (m== PROPOSAL_CHANGE)
        Begin Critical Section
            For All sp_i ∈ ProposalBank
                Score_i = Measure(sp_i);
                If (Score_i ≤ MaxScore)
                    MaxScore=Score_i;
                    Win=s_i
        End Critical Section
        For All s_i ≠ Win
            SendMessage(s_i,NOT_WIN)
        m=CheckMailBox();
While Not(NegTimeout());
For All s_i ∈ s,   s_i ≠ win
    SendMessage(s_i,TERMINATE_NEG)
If (Win ≠No_One)
    SendMessage(Win, WIN)
    Call AgreementFormation()
}
```

```
Procedure SupplierNegotiator() {

Terminate=FALSE;
While (Terminate == FALSE) Do
        m=CheckMailBox();
        If (m ≠ NULL)
            Switch(m)
            Case NOT_WIN:
                NewProposal=RelaxProposal()
                If (NewProposal ≠ NULL)
                    Begin Critical Section
                        ModifyProposal(NewProposal);
                    End Critical Section
                    SendMessage(ClientNeg,PROPOSAL_CHANGE);
            Case WIN:
                Report(WIN);
                Terminate=TRUE;
            Case TERMINATE_NEG:
                Report(NOT_WIN);
                Terminate=TRUE;
}
```

(a) Client Negotiator   (b) Supplier Negotiator

Fig. 4. Algorithms of the Negotiation

of specifications whose objective is to make possible the exchange of electronic business-oriented data in B2B and B2C transactions. The specifications ebXML has a modular architecture composed of independent functional units that can be used separately. One of these functional units is the Messaging Service, that provides a standard for exchange messages in a trustworthy and reliable form [6]. However, the security aspects of SONAR also are being considered in its logical model, as we will see in Section 5.

5.3   Querying Support

The querying support is a SONAR module that is still in specification. The goal of this module is to provide automatic consultation to the repository of invitations for bids. Generically this problem consists in determining a function $F(P) \rightarrow R$, where $P = \{p_1, p_2 \ldots p_n\}$, and p_i, $1 \leq i \leq n$ are descriptive parameters of the information. For example, suppose some supplier is searching for invitations for bids that will accur in january, 2004, to acquire office supplies. Then, P would be represented by the set $P = \{Invitation\_for\_Bids, January, 2004, supplies, office\}$. The set $R = \emptyset$ or $R = \{R_1 \ldots R_k\}$ where R_i, $1 \leq i \leq k$ is a description that takes care of the parameters of D. Chang et al[4] discuss a Top-K query processing implementation to find and establish a ranking of joined occurrences. Decker et al[5] suggest the use of *middle agents*, as connection elements between suppliers of information and requesters in a scene of distributed multi-agents. Li and Horrocks[10], guided to the Semantic Web, consider a system for matchmaking based on a repository of information where agents can publish and search for announcements described in Daml-S (DARPA Agent Markup Language - Web Service Based Ontology), a description language based on ontologies, and a reasoner based on Description Logic [1]. These approaches can also be used in the case where customers look for potential suppliers.

6   Automated Trust Negotiation

Models are important not only because they simplify the description of the applications but also because they give support in the description of aspects that are common to the modeled applications. In this section we discuss some aspects of Automated Trust Negotiation in the context of the presented models.

In the ComprasNet Electronic Auction and in several Web applications the security model is based on centralized security domains. The participants gain access to the resources typically through an user name and password and their access rights are rigidly determined by the domain. The Internet is becoming a marketplace with an increasing number of sales and procurement services. Therefore centralized security domains are not flexible enough to deal with automatic interactions among these systems. A more flexible mechanism for commercial transactions are the techniques related to Automated Trust Negotiation [?,25].

Based in the TrustBuilder protocol [25], we consider the use of these techniques in some security aspects of the Matchmaking and Negotiation phases of the life cycle. Bartolini et al[2] discuss some aspects of security and the use of digital credentials in commercial transactions. However they consider only support to the systems whose security is already based on credentials mechanisms.

In the Automated Trust Negotiation the access concession and attainment to a determined resource occurs through the exchange of digital credentials and by the use of access control policies that specify which combinations of credentials a participant must disclose. The participant that possess the resource is called server and the one that requisite it is called client.

The central idea of the TrustBuilder is the separation of the negotiation protocol from specific negotiation strategies of each participant. This separation allows interoperation of participants with different negotiation strategies. Formaly, a message in TrustBuilder is a set $m = R_1, \ldots, R_k$, where R_i, $1 \leq i \leq k$, is a disclosure of a local credential, a local policy or a local resource. A failure message is represented by $m = \emptyset$. A sequence of disclosures of protected resources is safe if each resource of the sequence is unlocked at the time it is disclosed. To guarantee the safe ending of a negotiation, independent of negotiation strategies, the TrustBuilder protocol requires that the strategies obey the following conditions:

1. if a message contains a denial disclosure policy $C \leftarrow false$, then C must appear in a previously disclosed policy;
2. a credential or policy can be disclosed at most once;
3. every disclosure must be safe.

Before the negotiation starts, the client sends a request message to the server indicating that he wants to gain access to a resource. Next, server and client change messages until the resource is disclosed or one of them send a failure message.

When business partners do not share the same security domain, Automated Trust Negotiation becomes a viable alternative. We show its flexibility to deal with commercial transactions by analyzing the use of its techniques with the Negotiation Host.

In the Negotiation Host security requirements can be established independently of the actions of (1) admission in the negotiation, (2) negotiation and (3) applications of visibility and presentation rules.

6.1   Admission in the Negotiation

A mechanism for the admission in the negotiation is the establishment of criteria that will enable the participants to adhere to the Negotiation Template. Therefore, an option related to negotiation access control is the introduction in the Negotiation Template of a set of credentials that must be disclosed by the participant who wants to gain access to the negotiation, i.e., the set of disclosures to be done by the participant must be a solution for the resource. The resource in this case is the access to the negotiation. The introduction of the set of credentials is consistent to the Negotiation Template, since this set can be considered a descriptive piece of the negotiation's object. It is possible that due to some system requirement the Negotiation Template itself becomes a resource to be protected. In this case, a previous set of credentials must be disclosed by the participant to gain access to the Negotiation Template. Therefore we must consider two moments: (1) gaining access to the Negotiation Template and (2) gaining access to the negotiation.

6.2   Negotiation Phase

Considering that negotiators are external to the Negotiation Host, the interactions among them will take place in a decentralized fashion. Therefore there must be a control of which participant can send a proposal and when he can do so. After the participants admission to the negotiation we can consider that they start to share a common security domain. Thus an option to guarantee some of the security aspects of the Negotiation Host is implementation of control algorithms that take advantage of this common security domain. With this approach different protocols can be established to control the proposal sending.

When we apply Automated Trust Negotiation in the Negotiation phase, the control of proposals sending and the validation become the same task. To send a proposal, the participant must attach to it, a set of credentials that must be disclosed in order to validate the proposal. The Host must disclose the control policy to the participants and can control the credential distribution according to the protocol.

6.3   Visibility and Presentation Rules

Another function of the credentials disclosed by the participant is the mapping of the visibility domain and presentation of the negotiation state. Given a set of credentials disclosed by a participant, the Host will determine which and how the elements of the current state of the negotiation will be presented.

6.4   Introducing Automated Trust Negotiation in the Logical Model

As discussed previously, our logical model describes mechanisms to support the Matchmaking and Negotiation phases. We describe these mechanisms according to the phase that they are related.

1. Matchmaking: we can identify two cases. A participant searches for another participant to enter into his negotiation process or, a participant searches for other participant in order to enter its negotiation. In both cases it is the responsibility of the Host:
    - To reveal the set of credentials that the participant must disclose to access the Negotiation Template. This set can be empty indicating that the Negotiation Template is an unprotected resource.
    - To publish the Negotiation Template. The Negotiation Template in its turn, incorporates the set of credentials whose disclosure gives access to the negotiation process. The disclosure strategies must respect the rules of the TrustBuilder protocol.
2. Negotiation: the Negotiation occurs with the exchange of proposals among participants driven by the Negotiation Host. The participants can send proposals at any time. The function of the Negotiation Host is to validate the proposals based on the:
    - Compatibility of the proposals with the Negotiation Template.
    - Permission for sending: if the proposal doesn't incorporate the set of necessary credentials for its sending at that time, this will not be a proposal valid.

7   Conclusion

The development of applications based on B2B E-Commerce transactions is a complex endeavour. We need models to help developers in the description of these applications. Based on the work of Trastour et al[21] we described a life cycle for interactions among entities that want to acquire products and services and entities that want to supply them. This life cycle can be the base of a high level model for applications that support B2B transactions. From the idea of the Negotiation Host [3,21] we describe a corresponding logical model. We used the ComprasNet Electronic Auction to illustrate these different levels of description. We described the Electronic Auction in these two levels showing the different degrees of abstraction.

We not only demonstrated the utility of these two levels of abstraction in the description of the ComprasNet Electronic Auction, but we also showed how they facilitate the introduction of concepts and mechanisms, discussing the addition of the Automated Trust Negotiation.

Currently we are making experiments with SONAR, a prototype that supports B2B transactions. We describe in this paper some of the decisions related to this prototype. Our future work includes the development of a framework that will help the development of B2B E-Commerce applications, a better formalization of B2B transactions description models, the support of more complex negotiation protocols and the incorporation of standards such as ebXML.

We want to adopt a software development process and customize it with our models. This customization will allow us to inherit several aspects of the process, in particular, a modeling language, which will enrich our expressiveness.

We would like to thanks Fundação São João Batista - FSJB, for supporting Mateus Barcellos da Costa. LECOM-DCC/UFMG was instrumental in providing resources for this investigation.

References

1. F. Baader et al. *The Description Logic Handbook: Theory, Implementation and Applications*. Press Syndicate of the University of Cambridge, Cambridge, UK, 1 edition, 2003.
2. C. Bartolini and M. C. Mont. Digital credentials and authorization to enhance trust in negotiation with e-services. HP t. paper, Trusted E-Services Laboratory - HP Laboratories, HP T. Paper - Bristol -UK, Jun. 2000.
3. C. Bartolini, C. Preist, and N. R. Jennings. Architecting for reuse: A software framework for automated negotiation. In *Third International Workshop on Agent Oriented Software Engineering*, 2002.
4. K. C.-C. Chang and S.-W. Hwang. Minimal probing: Supporting expensive predicates for top-k queries. pages 346–357, Madison, Jun. 2002. SIGMOD Conference, ACM.
5. K. Decker, K. Sykara, and M. Williamson. Middle-agents for the Internet. pages 465–466, Boston, July 2000. International Conference on MultiAgent Systems, IEEE Computer Society.
6. A. Dogac et al. An ebXML infrastructure implementation through UDDI Registries and RosettaNet PIPs. pages 346–357, Madison, Jun. 2002. SIGMOD Conference, ACM.
7. S. Graham et al. *Building Web Services with Java: making sense of XML, SOAP, WSDL and UDDI*. Sams Publishing, Indianapolis, USA, 2002.
8. N. R. Jennings et al. Agent-based business process management. *International Journal of Cooperative Information Systems*, 5(2 e 3):104–130, 1996.
9. Ralph E. Johnson. Frameworks = (components + patterns). *Communications of the ACM*, 40(10):39–42, October 1997.

10. L. Li and Ian Horrocks. A software framework for matchmaking based on semantic Web technology. Budapest - Hungry, May 2003. International World Wide Web Conference, ACM.
11. Martins-B2B. [Online] Available: http://www.martins.com.br.
12. B. Medjahed et al. Business-to-Business Interactions: issues and enabling technologies. *The VLDB Journal*, 12(1):59–85, 2003.
13. Mercado-Eletrônico. [Online] Available: http://www.me.com.br.
14. P. Milgrom. Auction and bidding: a primer. *Journal of Economic Perspectives*, 3:3–22, 1989.
15. RosettaNet. [Online] Available: http://www.rosettanet.org.
16. A. Scharl, J. Gebauer, and C. Bauer. Matching process requirements with information technology to assess the efficiency of Web information systems. [Online] Available: www.citeseer.nj.nec.com/scharl00matching.html.
17. B. Schmid and M. Lindermann. Elements of a reference model for electronic markets. Kohala Coast, Jan. 1998. Annual Hawaii International Conference on System Sciences, IEEE Computer Society.
18. K. E. Seamons, T. Yu, and M. Winslett. Limiting the Disclosure of Access Control Policies During Automated Trust Negotiation. San Diego, Feb. 2001. Network and Distributed System Security Symposium, Internet Society.
19. Secretaria de Logística do Ministério do Planejamento - Governo do Brasil, Brasília- Brasil. *Manual do ComprasNet*, Jan. 2002.
20. Secretaria de Logística do Ministério do Planejamento - Governo do Brasil, Brasília - Brasil. *Manual do Pregão Eletrônico*, Jan. 2002.
21. D. Trastour, C. Bartolini, and C. Preist. Semantic Web Support for the E-Commerce B2B Life Cycle. Honolulu, May 2002. International World Wide Web Conference, ACM.
22. W3C. Web services architecture W3C working draft, Nov. 2002. [Online] Available: http://www.w3.org/TR/2002/WD-ws-arch-20021114/.
23. W3C. Web services glossary: W3C Working Draft 14, May 2003. [Online] Available: http://www.w3.org/TR/2003/WD-ws-gloss-20030514/.
24. Websupply. [Online] Available: http://www.websupply.com.br.
25. T. Yu, M. Winslett, and K. E. Seamons. Interoperable Strategies in Automated Trust Negotiation. Philadelphia, Pennsylvania - USA, Nov. 2001. Conference on Computer and Communications Security, ACM.

Integration of Multi-attributed Negotiations within Business Processes

Carlo Simon[1] and Michael Rebstock[2]

[1] University Koblenz-Landau, 56070 Koblenz, Germany,
simon@uni-koblenz.de,
[2] Darmstadt University of Applied Sciences, 64295 Darmstadt, Germany,
rebstock@fh-darmstadt.de

Abstract. For the integration of electronic negotiation systems within information systems, it is essential to model both using the same modelling paradigm to avoid frictions. We develop a generic model of electronic negotiations using Petri nets as a formal base focussing especially on the underlying processes. We introduce a negotiation scenario from which we derive the relevant processes, protocols and information objects, explaining the motivation for negotiations as well. Our approach is modular and allows an extension in various dimensions - however in this paper we concentrate on the idea of integrating electronic negotiations within business processes. As such, our models can be used as formal guide for integrating negotiation environments within workflow management systems and for simulating and verifying electronic negotiation scenarios.

1 Introduction

Negotiations are important activities within business processes and are themselves processes. Their execution (not exclusively) depends on the information available for the negotiation partners, and consequently on their information system. However, this can also be used to integrate negotiation processes within existing information systems such as workflow management systems [14] in order to automate them [2].

So far, research on electronic negotiations has concentrated on single attributed negotiations, such as auctions or stock exchanges [10,4]. Although non-electronic negotiations are typically multi-attributed, their formalization has not yet been discussed extensively.

Also multi-agent systems base on formal negotiation processes. Since they are typically only described in terms of source code [1,3] the integration of the related concepts into business environments can hardly be done.

Our aim is to develop a generic model of electronic negotiations which can be integrated into business process models - therefore, we use Petri nets. We restrict our considerations to bi-literal negotiations which serves to simplify the explanations and means no restriction to our approach. Our models can be used for simulating and verifying negotiation scenarios - a prerequisite for the development of automatic electronic negotiation systems. Our focus is on describing a

J. Desel, B. Pernici, and M. Weske (Eds.): BPM 2004, LNCS 3080, pp. 148–162, 2004.

generic framework instead of specific scenarios. The modules described are kept simple provided that this allows a better understanding of the overall concepts.

This paper is structured as follows: after introducing a negotiation scenario, we consider business processes and information objects required. We continue with the motivation for negotiation situations and introduce a negotiation protocol. Negotiation processes and the strategy of the negotiation partners are developed independently and are integrated. Finally, we discuss our results.

2   Negotiation Scenario

Rebstock and Thun call the first partner of a (bi-lateral) negotiation scenario *requester*, the second *responder* [14]. They aim to establish a *contract* with one another for trading goods or services. Following a *negotiation protocol* and depending on *individual strategies* and *abilities* the parties exchange *binding offers* until a contract is established or one of the parties terminates the negotiation.

We consider negotiations to be special business activities which must be integrated within a company's business processes. The entire set of all business processes and the available resources restrict the offers that can be issued or accepted by the negotiating partners. As such, for a decision on changing or accepting an offer both must be known. Since fulfilling a contract means to instantiate new business processes, this is an additional relation between negotiations and other business processes.

The scheme in Fig. 1 visualizes this interweaving showing processes as rectangles, and information as circles. Negotiation partners are assumed to act independently, and their only communication channel is the binding offer. We will discuss the elements of this diagram in more detail in the next sections.

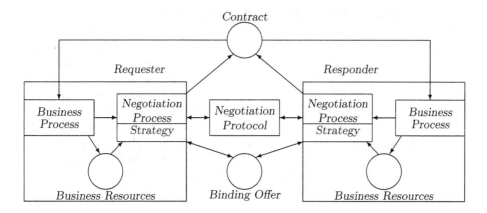

Fig. 1. Bi-literal, multi-attributed negotiation of independent negotiation partners

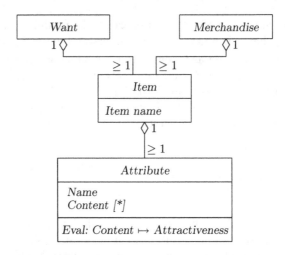

Fig. 2. Class diagram of want and merchandise

Not only business environments but also multi-agent environments require an integration of the negotiating parties within such a scenario which helps to specify interfaces and implies an overall process of possible negotiations. Exemplarily, we consider the negotiation phases described by Kersten [9]: the *pre-negotiation* phase, the *negotiation* itself, and the *post-settlement* phase. In our scenario of Fig. 1, the pre-negotiation phase corresponds to the transition from business process to negotiation process/ strategy where a negotiation is initiated. The negotiation itself is described by the negotiation protocol in conjunction with the negotiation processes of requester and responder. The post-settlement phase corresponds to fulfilling the contract by initiating new business processes.

3   Business Information and Processes

One prerequisite for negotiations is a *want* for goods, services, or money of one negotiation partner and a *merchandise* which can be offered by the other. Both consist of *named items* which themselves consists of *named attributes* with a *content*. Different want or merchandise vectors allow the description of acceptable trade goods from the perspective of each negotiation partner. The *attractiveness* of these vectors is determined individually. Figure 2 shows the respective diagram in UML notation [16]. Want and merchandise can also be represented in the simple form of relational database tables having the schemas **Want:** *(Name, Content, Item name, Attractiveness* and **Merchandise:** *(Name, Content, Item name, Attractiveness)*.

Although our data models are in UML notation, this notation is not appropriate for the business process modelling. And since we consider negotiations as business processes we prefer a notation which is typically used for business process modelling. There exist several Petri net-based approaches to business process modelling, for example [13,22,21,20] and event driven process chains (EPC) [17], and therefore we use Petri nets for modelling negotiations as well.

All approaches mentioned above use a common notation for business processes, information, and resources where activities are modelled as transitions, information and resources as places. A marking is used to indicate the current state of execution and the overall system's state. Principle process patterns for *sequence, alternative, independence,* and *iteration* on which more complex processes are defined are used within these notations.

The different approaches to modelling business processes using Petri nets typically vary in details like the type system used to specify the marking of the places or the interface of the nets. In accordance with Simon [19], we use transition bounded Petri nets where processes are firing sequences reproducing the empty initial marking beginning with firing the *start* and ending with firing the *goal* transition. This representation allows to indicate processes with the aid of T-invariants, a structural property of Petri nets. If required - however - this representation can simply be transformed into place bounded nets like for example those used by van der Aalst [22,21].

High-level Petri nets like Predicate/Transition Nets (Pr/T nets) introduced by Genrich and Lautenbach [6] or Colored Nets [8] defined by Jensen allow the representation of complex information and resources. Places are marked with sets of tuples and transitions access these places like transactions database tables as shown in Fig. 3. Marx extended the definition of Pr/T nets such that transitions are firing for sets of tuples [11] indicated by the use of braces.

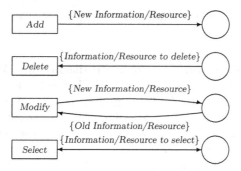

Fig. 3. Operations on information from top to bottom: add, delete, modify, and select

We do not repeat the formal definitions of Pr/T nets, but explain their main concepts while discussing our models.

4   Binding Offer and Contract

The motivation to negotiate is to find a *contract* which is acceptable for both negotiation partners. *Binding offers* are issued playing the role of a communication channel between independent negotiation partners. Consequently, they are central for our negotiation scenario.

A binding offer consists of a set of *offer attributes* describing the offer in general (like terms of payment or delivery) and a set of *offer items* (descriptions of goods or services) specified by a set of *item attributes*. Each attribute (both offer and item attribute) is given by its *name* and *content*, offer items by their *name* and the *direction* of exchange. An exchange from a requester Q to a responder P is indicated by $Q{\to}P$ and the other direction by $P{\to}Q$. In money based trade, all goods or services are exchanged from one partner to the other while money is exchanged back. Barter trade means an exchange of goods or services in both directions.

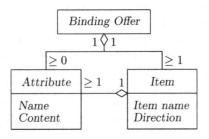

Fig. 4. Class diagram of binding offer

Figure 4 shows the corresponding static diagram in UML notation [16]. It generalizes the data model of Rebstock and Thun [14] allowing to consider barter trade as well. Alternatively, binding offers can be represented as relational database tables, too. *Item name* and *direction* of offer attributes are assumed to have null values, i.e. in general we are considering a scheme **Binding Offer:** *(Name, Content, Item name, Direction)*.

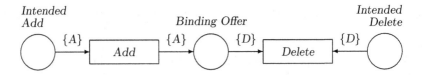

Fig. 5. Petri net model for changing a binding offer

Binding offers change throughout negotiations which is implemented in the Pr/T net of Fig. 5. The typing of place *Binding Offer* is as specified by Fig. 4.

Transitions *Add* and *Delete* apply changes to a binding offer as intended by the negotiation parties which fill the respective places in accordance with their individual strategy. Initial offers are implemented as initial changes. Afterwards, responder and requester mutually specify their intended changes ruled by a negotiation protocol which is considered in the following section. A modification of items can be realized by a combined *Add* and *Delete* operation.

5   Negotiation Protocol

Negotiation protocols rule the exchange of offers and counter-offers. We assume a symmetric structure for this protocol, except for the start of the negotiation.

A Petri net implementation of a simple protocol is given in Fig. 6. Places *Responder* and *Requester* indicate the active negotiation partner. Transitions *Initial Offer*, *Change Offer$_P$* and *Change Offer$_Q$* correspond to the initial definition and the modification of existing binding offers. Transitions *Accept$_P$* and *Accept$_Q$* represent the acceptance of the last given offer, *Terminate$_P$* and *Terminate$_Q$* the termination of the negotiation by the responder (P) or the requester (Q), respectively.

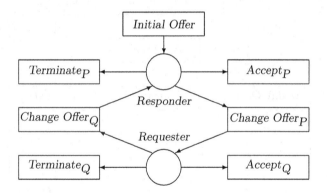

Fig. 6. Negotiation protocol for a bi-literal negotiation of independent partners

Since the initial offer is made by the requester, the responder is the active negotiation partner after firing transition *Initial Offer*. S/he can accept this offer as a contract, might terminate the negotiation, or might modify the offer. In the last case, the requester has the same option to react to the counter-offer s/he receives. We thus describe an iteration of interactive negotiation phases.

The protocol we have chosen is probably one of the most simple that can be found. However, the existence of this module within our generic structure allows to extend this part by a more complex one.

6   Negotiation Processes of Requester and Responder

Negotiation processes describe the independent behavior of the negotiation partners. Although we are able to model the behavior of each participant differently,
we assume that requester and responder behave the same way in the following
(except that the requester starts by making an initial offer while the responder
reacts to this).

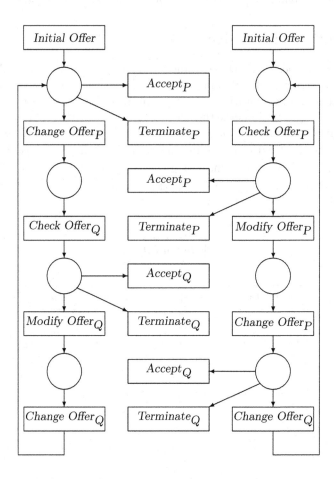

Fig. 7. Processes of requester (left) and responder (right)

The requester process starts with formulating and making an initial offer.
The responder accepts this offer, terminates the negotiation, or makes a counter-
offer which has to be evaluated by the requester. As a result of this evaluation,
the requester accepts the current binding offer, terminates the negotiation, or
readjusts the current binding offer. In the last case, the responder reacts to

this modification and we are iterating on the previously observed behavior. The responder process is in principle the same, however, starts with receiving and evaluating an initial offer.

Figure 7 shows an implementation of both negotiation processes as Petri Nets which are independent from each other and from the negotiation protocol. This allows us to detail the models modularly if this is required.

We use the join operator for Petri nets defined by Simon in [19] to verify whether both processes and the protocol can be successfully synchronized. We merge equally named transitions of all participated nets. Figure 8 shows the result of this join. Simulating this net shows that each requester and responder process is still realizable in the joined net. Consequently, the negotiation processes are such that the negotiating parties can communicate with each other and that this communication is compliant with the negotiation protocol.

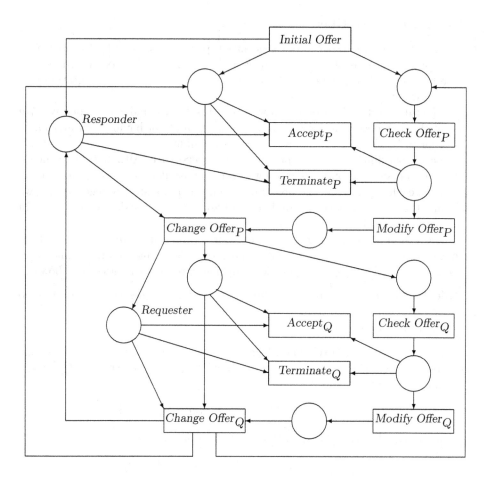

Fig. 8. Join of negotiation protocol, requester and responder processes

7   Negotiation Strategy

Negotiation strategies have been widely discussed in auction theory [10], game theory [15,7,12], and software agents [1,2,3]. Decision making processes within these theories consist of a series of alternatives leading to a specific strategic behavior. In the remaining, we describe such decision-making processes with the aid of Petri nets and integrate these resulting models within our framework. As an example, we choose the *negotiation plan* described by Carabelea [1] which we adapt to our problem.

Within the negotiation processes of requester and responder (as shown in Fig. 7) the decision making is located within two transitions each: for the requester *Check Offer$_Q$* and *Modify Offer$_Q$*, for the responder *Check Offer$_P$* and *Modify Offer$_P$*. They are abstractions of more complex net structures and processes. We consider both types of transitions in more detail.

7.1   Checking an Offer

The negotiation processes of the negotiation parties described by Carabelea [1] correspond to those of Sec. 6: they can *accept*, *reject* or *modify* orders. We therefore chose this specific formalization for demonstrating the integration into our framework.

The rules for the decision are described from the responder's perspective. We adapt this perspective as well as the simplification of not having offer attributes in order to be as close to the given rules as possible.

Carabelea differs actors in *persuader* and *persuadee*. Although our concept of requester and responder is more general because it allows both participants to act in each role (in real life both buyer and seller can start a negotiation), we assume that persuader corresponds to requester and persuadee to responder in the remaining section.

A decision on continuing a negotiation or terminating it bases on a want for goods. In our environment negotiation partners have wants and merchandise. A decision for terminating a negotiation can therefore be formulated as follows:

Rule 1: The responder is not willing to trade any requested item or has no want for any offered item
⇒ Terminate the negotiation

For describing the exchange of goods, services, and money we choose the perspective of the responder P (and abbreviate the requester with Q). For a binding offer O we define

$$O_{Q \to P} := \{o \in O \mid o.Direction = (Q \to P)\}$$

as the set of all items offered to the responder and

$$O_{P \to Q} := \{o \in O \mid o.Direction = (P \to Q)\}$$

as the set of all items offered by the responder.

Figure 9 shows a Petri net implementation of *Rule 1*. Tokens on places *Want* and *Merchandise* are typed as specified by Fig. 2 and those on place *Binding Offer* as specified by Fig. 4. Transition *Rule 1* is enabled if none of the wants or merchandise are contained in the binding offer and there seems to be no chance to find a contract.

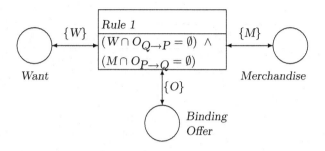

Fig. 9. Petri net implementation of *Rule 1*

A responder will try to substitute items if *Rule 1* is not fulfilled however there are items of the current offer which are not part of want or merchandize:

Rule 2: If *Rule 1* is not fulfilled but there exist requested items the responder is not willing to trade or there exist offered items he has no want for
⇒ Try to substitute these items

Substitute: If the responder has a substitution for the items affected by *Rule 2*
⇒ Modify the offer

¬Substitute: If the responder finds no substitution for the items affected by *Rule 2*
⇒ Terminate the negotiation

A formal specification of *Substitute* and *¬Substitute* requires a definition of the items which can be substituted. The description of this substitution relation can simply be done in another table and can therefore be integrated within our framework. However, we do not want to conceal that filling this table is labor intensive for real world domains.

A final rule describes the want of the responder to trade the goods specified by the binding offer.

Want: If *Rules 1* and *2* are not fulfilled
⇒ the responder has a want to trade the offer items.

The negotiation balance *NB* defined by

$$NB := \frac{\text{Attractiveness of all items being negotiated}}{\text{Attractiveness of all items being traded for it}}$$

is a measure for the success of a negotiation. A negotiation partner subjectively profits from a negotiation if $NB > 1$ holds true.

In contrast to other approaches using on *value* or *profit* as measures, our concept of *attractiveness* allows us also to model strategies which do not try to maximize these parameters and are discussed in experimental economics [5,18].

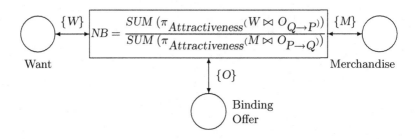

Fig. 10. Net implementation for determining NB

Figure 10 shows a Petri net implementation of a calculation of NB. The places have the same meaning and typing as in Fig. 9. If the transition fires, NB is instantiated with the quotient of the attractiveness of all goods offered to the requester and the attractiveness of all goods offered by the requester.

Carabelea introduces two parameters controlling the strategic behavior of the negotiation partners relatively to their current negotiation balance NB. Informally speaking, these parameters have the following meaning:

ulfa: Upper limit for acceptance A responder can only accept an offer if $NB < ulfa$.

ulfnp: Upper limit for new proposal A responder tries to modify an offer if $ulfa \leq NB < ulfnp$. In this case the responder sees a chance to successfully finish the negotiation. Otherwise, if $NB \leq ulfnp$, the offer is rejected and the negotiation terminates.

Upon these parameters, Carabelea defines six rules specifying the responder's reaction from which we have taken five rules.

Rule 3: If $NB < ulfa$
    $\Rightarrow$ Accept
Rule 4: If $ulfa \leq NB < ulfnp$ and there exists is an offer item X which would lower the responder's NB
    $\Rightarrow$ Try to adjust the offer
Adjust: If the responder can adjust offer items affected by *Rule 4*
    $\Rightarrow$ Modify the offer
¬Adjust: If the responder cannot find offer items to adjust
    $\Rightarrow$ Terminate the negotiation

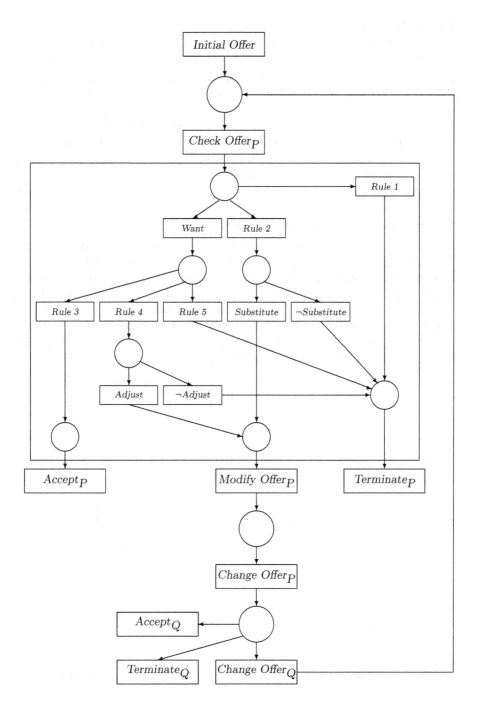

Fig. 11. Decision making integrated within the negotiation process

Rule 5: If $ulfnp \leq NB$
   $\Rightarrow$ Terminate the negotiation

An implementation of these rules as Petri nets can be based upon the Petri net elements we have defined so for. Figure 11 visualizes the entire decision-making process and integrates it into the implementation of the responder's negotiation process.

Beside the structure of the decision process which is visualized in Fig. 11, all transitions of the decision process must be connected to the places *Want*, *Merchandise*, and *Binding Offer* as described above. Transitions *Rule 3*, *Rule 4*, and *Rule 5* must also instantiate *NB* and compare its value in accordance with the rule conditions given above.

7.2 Formulating a (Counter-)Offer

The final aspect of electronic negotiations for which we have not demonstrated so far that it can also be formalized within our framework, is the modification of the binding offer. In our environment, a responder has two options to modify an offer: increasing or lowering the attractiveness of items offered. The selected strategy depends on assumptions concerning the preferences of the negotiation partner and the availability of resources. However, since we are not including assumptions within our model in this paper, we are only interested in how to model the actual modification of the offer.

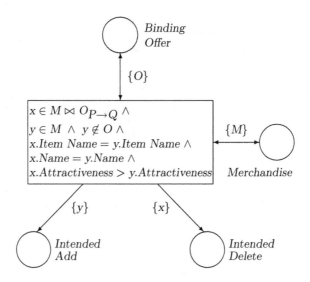

Fig. 12. Modify an offer by lowering the attractiveness of an offered item

Figure 12 shows a Petri net model for formulating intended changes when lowering the attractiveness of an offered item. For this, an offered item x (i.e.

$x \in M \bowtie O_{P \to Q})$ is substituted in O by an item y merchandized by the responder (i.e. $y \in M$). Items chosen for modification are of the same kind and therefore supposed to be substitutable but are having a lower attractiveness for the responder ($x.Item\ Name = y.Item\ Name \wedge x.Name = y.Name \wedge x.Attractiveness > y.Attractiveness$). Finally, we assume that the new item y is currently not part of the binding offer ($y \notin O$).

As already mentioned above, the selection of items x and y for substitution could be improved by extending the responder's model by a memory.

8   Conclusion

Starting with an schematic overview over the entire scenario, we developed a process model of bi-lateral multi-attributed negotiations. Within this, we identified major activities for issuing binding offers and finding a final contract. We demonstrated how to implement these activities within Petri nets as a formal language.

Our framework is a generic model of electronic negotiations because of its modularity and the possibility to refine and change each of the modules our framework is based upon. The resulting overall model as well as the single modules can be simulated and analyzed with the formal methods already known in Petri net theory. Since most approaches to business process modelling are also Petri net based, our methodology is open to seamlessly integrate such models.

The described negotiation scenario is only an example. Our approach can be used to describe different protocols, processes and strategies which we can analyze with respect to their consistency upon each other. Since our methodology is based on a mathematical formalism, it can be implemented within a negotiation simulation environment, one of the topics we will work on in the future. This does not only increase the quality of electronic negotiation environments. Further, by exchanging specific modules we can compare existing approaches to electronic negotiations on a formal basis.

References

1. C. Carabelea. Adaptive agents in argumentation-based negotiation. In Marik, editor, *Conference MASA 2001*, Lecture Notes in Artificial Intelligence 2322, pages 180–187. Springer, 2002.
2. R. Davis and R. G. Smith. Negotiations as a metaphor for distributed problem solving. *Artificial Intelligence*, 20(1):63–109, 1983.
3. D. Deschner, F. Lang, and F. Bodendorf. Strategies for software agent based multiple issue negotiations. Lecture Notes in Computer Science 2115, pages 206–216. Springer, 2002.
4. B. Dietrich and R. V. Vohra, editors. *Mathematics of the Internet - E-Auction and Markets*, volume 127 of *The IMA Volumes in Mathematics and its Application*. Springer, New York, 2002.

5. E. Fehr and K. Schmidt. Theorioes of fairness and reciprocity - evidence and economic applications. Institute for Empirical Research in Econimics 75, University of Zurich, 2001.

6. H. J. Genrich and K. Lautenbach. System modelling with high-level petri nets. *Theoretical Computer Science*, 13, 1981.

7. M. J. Holler and G. Illing. *Einführung in die Spieletheorie*. Springer, Berlin, 1996.

8. K. Jensen. *Coloured Petri-Nets*. Band 1. Springer Verlag, Berlin, 1992.

9. G. E. Kersten. The science and engeneering of e- negotiation: An introduction. In R. H. Sprague, editor, *Proceedings of the 36th Annual Hawaii International Conference on Systems Sciences*, Los Alamitos, CA, 2003.

10. V. Krishna, editor. *Auction Theory*. Academic Press, San Diego, 2002.

11. T. Marx. *NetCase - Softwareentwurf und Workflow-Modellierung mit Petri-Netzen*. PhD thesis, Universität Koblenz-Landau, 1998.

12. P. Morris. *Introduction to Game Theory*. Springer, New York, 1994.

13. A. Oberweis. *Modellierung und Ausführung von Workflows mit Petri-Netzen*. Teubner Studienskripte, Stuttgart, 1996.

14. M. Rebstock and P. Thun. Interactive multi-attribute electronic negotiations in the supply chain: Design issues and an application prototype. In R. H. Sprague, editor, *Proceedings of the 36th Annual Hawaii International Conference on Systems Sciences*, Los Alamitos, CA, 2003.

15. G. Romp. *Game Theory - Introduction and Applications*. Oxford University Press, Oxford, 1997.

16. J. Rumbaugh, I. Jacobson, and G. Booch. *The Unfied Modeling Language Reference Manual*. Addison Wesley, Reading, Mass., 1999.

17. A.-W. Scheer. *Wirtschaftsinformatik - Referenzmodelle für industrielle Geschäftsprozesse*. Springer-Verlag, Berlin, 1994.

18. R. Selten. Rethinking rationality. In R. Selten and G. Gigerenzer, editors, *Bounded Rationality: The Adaptive Toolbox*. Cambridge, MA, 2001.

19. C. Simon. *A Logic of Actions and Its Application to the Development of Programmable Controllers*. PhD thesis.

20. C. Simon. Verification in factory and office automation. In *IEEE International Conference on Systems, Man and Cybernetics (SMC)*, Hammamet, Tunesien, 2002.

21. W. van der Aalst and K. van Hee. *Workflow Management - Models, Methods, and Systems*. MIT Press, Cambridge, Massachusetts, 2002.

22. W. M. P. van der Aalst. The Application of Petri Nets to Workflow Management. *The Journal of Circuits, Systems and Computers*, 1998.

Management of Knowledge Intensive Business Processes

Norbert Gronau[1] and Edzard Weber[2]

[1] University of Potsdam, Germany
[2] University of Oldenburg, Germany

Abstract. Knowledge processes and business processes are linked together and should be regarded together, too. Business processes can be modeled and analyzed extensively with well known and established methods. The simple signs of static knowledge does not fulfill the requirements of a comprehensive and integrated approach of process-oriented knowledge management. The Knowledge Modeler Description Language KMDL is able to represent the creation, use and necessity of knowledge along common business processes. So KMDL can be used to formalize knowledge-intensive processes with a focus on certain knowledge-specific characteristics and to identify weak points in these processes. For computer-aided modeling and analyzing the tool K-Modeler is introduced.

1 Introduction

Knowledge management has gained importance since the 1990s. Companies hope for an improvement of innovation capability and an increase of process efficiency. Not at last globalization, emerging competition, increasing market dynamics and shorter product development and life cycle times require an increased adaptability of companies to a dynamic environment [PRR98]. These requirements cause an adaptation and consequent aligning of business processes to existing and future market demands.

A process flow is determined by given rules as regulation or at least as constraint for a certain proceeding [KH93]. These rules schedule the subprocesses and tasks resp. functions. Summarized there is a logically coherent chain. In the managerial context this chain is also called business process. Within the process occurs a combination of certain material or immaterial input objects, which are transformed into an output object according to the given process rules [SF96]. The procurement of the needed material input or information objects is often fulfilled by other well defined processes. These can easily be specified because the type and characteristic of the required objects will remain nearly unchanged for different process flows. Whereas the demand of knowledge as process input cannot be predetermined easily. It depends on the dealing employee and environmental situation the process is embedded in.

Variations or divergence from a used reference business process, inadequate or impractical process rules or the missing of a well structured process model

J. Desel, B. Pernici, and M. Weske (Eds.): BPM 2004, LNCS 3080, pp. 163–178, 2004.

can only be overcome by the employee's knowledge for keeping the process flow going on. Neither the quality or quantity of a knowledge demand nor the point of time can be forecasted. These processes of knowledge exchange have to find their own way and cannot be completely captured by common business process models. Thus undesigned and unscheduled knowledge conversion processes are running in parallel to common business processes. And the long time aim of a comprehensive process oriented knowledge management approach must be to discover these processes, to model, analyze and optimize them.

Knowledge processes and business processes are linked together and therefore should be regarded together. Business processes can be modeled and analyzed extensively with well known and established methods. Some more approaches exist that consider knowledge as a component of a company or an organization [Goe02][Rem01]. The simple mapping of static knowledge (typically in an explicit manner as information) does not fulfill the requirements of a comprehensive and integrated approach of process-oriented knowledge management. Only the coordination of business processes with the processes of knowledge processing guarantees an efficient general knowledge flow [Rem02a, p. 2].

The above mentioned problems and challenges have been the trigger for the development of the Knowledge Modeler Description Language KMDL and a software tool basing on KMDL to model knowledge-intensive business processes [Arb03a][Arb03b]. Within KMDL the term knowledge is understood as bound to persons. This kind of knowledge named from Nonaka and Takeuchi as tacit knowledge is personally and cannot be transferred to a formal notation. It is anchored in the activities and skills of the knowledge bearer and additionally in her/his ideals, values and experiences [NT95]. Therefore also knowledge can be modeled and analyzed that is not necessary for the fulfillment of an operative business task in a business process. Furthermore with KMDL the different possibilities of knowledge conversion can be modeled, so that the flow of knowledge between persons can be visualized. Knowledge flows in a process and the different kinds of knowledge conversion can be used in the model to retrieve information on the generation of new knowledge and possible weak spots.

2   Definition of Knowledge Intensive Business Processes

Some authors accentuate the ability to plan the knowledge requirement and determine the knowledge intensity on the basis of variability and exceptional conditions [Hei02]. Other sources name processes as knowledge intensive if an improvement with conventional methods of business reengineering is not or only partially possible [Rem02a]. Davenport recognizes the knowledge intensity by the diversity and uncertainty of process input and output [Dav95].

A process is knowledge intensive if its value can only be created through the fulfillment of the knowledge requirements of the process participants. Clues for a knowledge intensive process are apart from the above mentioned criteria:

- Diversity of information sources and media types
- Variance and dynamic development of process organization [Hof02]

- Many process participants with different expert's reports
- Use of creativity
- High degree of innovation
- An available degree of decision scope.

Common business processes are characterized by a predefined process structure and repeated tasks that are fulfilled basing on the underlying process model, which contains information, tasks and user roles.

Knowledge-intensive business processes are only partially mapped by the process model due to unpredictable decisions or tasks guided by creativity. Typically knowledge flows and knowledge transfers between media and persons are necessary to achieve a successful process completion.

3   Knowledge and Knowledge Conversion

KMDL uses the understanding of tacit knowledge according to Nonaka/Takeuchi. They argue that knowledge cannot exist on information media like documents or database entries, because this media is not bound to persons. Knowledge that can be expressed on handbooks, papers, patents or software is named as explicit knowledge following a term coined by Polany [NT95,Neu99].

New objects of knowledge or information are created by transformation of objects existing in the process. This transformation is performed by an interaction of knowledge and information objects. As an analogy to Nonaka and Takeuchi four types of knowledge conversion are distinguished. Explicit knowledge and information are modeled as information object, while tacit knowledge is represented as knowledge object. So a strict separation of knowledge bound to persons from knowledge not related to persons and from information can be achieved. KMDL distinguishes the following types of knowledge conversion:

- **Internalization** means the conversion of information in tacit knowledge. A knowledge object is generated with the help of one or more information objects.
- **Externalization** is understood as the transformation of tacit knowledge in information objects. Other information objects do not participate in this conversion.
- The transmission of tacit knowledge from person to person is called **socialization**. This is handled normally by means of direct personal communication. In the K-Modeler description language socialization is represented by the interaction of knowledge objects.
- During a **combination** one or more information objects are used to create new information. Knowledge objects can participate in the combination, but have only a coordinating role and are not created by the information to be combined.

4   KMDL – The Knowledge Modeler Description Language

The result of the modeling process should be an idealistic, simplified and similar mapping of a subject, system or other part of the world. The main aim is to study some characteristics of the original system using the model [HBvB+94]. To guarantee the completeness of the modeling method, certain elements, relations and their qualities have to be considered to be able to grasp the knowledge intensity of a process and the usage of knowledge.

4.1   Common BPM Tools

The occurrence of knowledge and its flow and transfer between media and persons is not well modeled in common business process management tools. At least the following requirements have to be fulfilled for modeling knowledge-intensive business processes [GPSW03, p. 316f][DK04]:

Goal: Which goal shall be reached with the modeling? Are there only documentation purposes or are a weak spot analysis and the definition of a new process necessary?

Integration of process and knowledge modeling: There should be a unique approach that combines or integrates the process definition with the flow and transfer of knowledge.

Tacit knowledge: Which definition and appreciation of knowledge is used by the model's approach? Is there a differentiation between explicit and tacit knowledge? Is it possible to express different levels of tacit knowledge [Sno00]?

Knowledge conversion: Are different mechanisms of knowledge conversion considered and expressed separately in the process model?

Knowledge flow: Is there a differentiation between information flow and knowledge transfer?

Offer and demand: Is it possible to show differences in the model between the offer of knowledge and its demand?

Person-related knowledge: Is the modeling of knowledge restricted to organizational units or is it possible to show knowledge bound to persons?

Comparison of intended and actual level of knowledge: Is it possible to compare the knowledge levels required for posts with the knowledge persons actually have?

View representation: Is it possible to navigate through the models using different views, e.g. an organizational or a process flow view?

Knowledge maps: Is it possible to generate knowledge maps from the results of modeling?

With this set of requirements some commonly used process modeling approaches like ARIS [All98][Sch98], INCOME [Rem02b] and PROMOTE [KW02] were judged (see table 1).

Table 1. Suitability of common tools for modeling of knowledge-intensive business processes

Requirement	ARIS	INCOME	PROMOTE
Goal	Documentation	Documentation	Planning
Integration of process and knowledge modeling	++	++	++
Tacit knowledge	o	o	o
Knowledge conversion	−	−	-
Knowledge flow	−	-	++
Offer and demand	−	−	−
Person-related knowledge	−	−	−
Comparison of intended and actual level of knowledge	−	−	−
View representation	++	+	+
Knowledge maps	++	++	++

The comparison of the investigated approaches had shown that no common approach separates tacit knowledge form explicit information. This lack was one of the main reasons for the development of KMDL, which was designed to fulfill all above mentioned requirements modeling business process.

4.2 Requirements for Describing Knowledge Intensive Processes

If knowledge intensive processes are regarded it has to be accounted for further weak spots concerning the properties of knowledge:

- Knowledge monopolies
- Unsuitable knowledge profiles of employees
- Dissatisfied demand for knowledge objects
- Acquisition and generation of unnecessary knowledge
- Multiple generation of similar knowledge
- Barriers against knowledge transfer
- Media breaks
- Missing actualization of knowledge

Knowledge monopolies exist if only a few people have the knowledge about a certain domain. This could be intentionally because it is classified knowledge, but it could also become a problem if the knowledge owner quits his job and so this knowledge gets lost for the company. For preventing organizational knowledge leakage by employee turnover upcoming knowledge shortages or monopolies should be detected at an early stage.

Employees have to be qualified for their post. An under-qualification should be avoided because the effort of the incorporation into the task would be to high. And an over-qualification should be avoided because that person could work more efficiently on another task.

The mapping of following aspects has to be demanded from a description language:

- Knowledge is bound to persons (knowledge bearer).
- Knowledge itself cannot be coded. Therefore a paraphrase of the knowledge or a description of the knowledge domain is necessary (knowledge descriptor).
- The required or available knowledge of a person can cover an arbitrary set of an arbitrary common defined knowledge domain (class of competency).
- The knowledge of a person can only be modeled as a reference to a section of a domain (knowledge object)
- The usage of knowledge depends on its context (pragmatic aspect)
- Knowledge can be inquired or offered (knowledge demand and knowledge offer).
- Knowledge can be externalized, internalized, socialized or combined (knowledge flow).

4.3   Elements of KMDL

KMDL provides an object library containing information, task, position, position requirements, person, knowledge object and knowledge descriptor (see fig. 1).

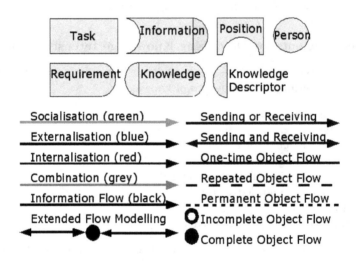

Fig. 1. Elements of KMDL

Information: Information is next to existing knowledge a base for the creation of new knowledge. Information can be externalized in an easy manner. It is stored on data media or written down in documents. The creation of new information is done by externalization or combination. The understanding of information within KMDL corresponds with the description of explicit knowledge given by Nonaka and Takeuchi. They argue, referring to Polyani, that two kinds of knowledge exist, tacit and explicit knowledge. Tacit knowledge is bound to persons, context specific and difficult to communicate. Explicit knowledge can be represented in a formal, systematic language [NT95, p. 72].

Tasks: Tasks are the basic framework for models of business processes. The order of the tasks determines the temporal structure of the process. A task is defined as an atomic transfer from input to output, represented as information objects.

Positions: Tasks are related to and be fulfilled by positions. Positions are manned by persons and have the necessary knowledge objects of all persons assigned to them. Relating employees and tasks to a position the functional and organizational structure of a company can be represented.

Requirements: Performing tasks makes demands on the positions, that are modeled as task requirements. The totality of requirements defines the tacit knowledge that is necessary for a position working on a concrete task. Every needed tacit ability is represented by a knowledge object. More than one requirement can be associated to a position, because normally more than one ability is necessary to accomplish the task.

Person: Persons are the owners of knowledge objects that are necessary to fulfill tasks. The totality of knowledge objects of a person should be equal to the requirements of the task the person has to do.

Knowledge: A knowledge object contains tacit knowledge of persons. Knowledge objects can be available or asked. Available knowledge objects can be used for task fulfillment immediately. Asked knowledge objects are necessary for the task fulfillment, but must be generated by the person responsible for the task. This can be done by internalization or socialization.

Knowledge descriptor: A knowledge descriptor describes the borders of a knowledge domain and defines partial domains, if necessary. It is no codification of knowledge. Task requirements and knowledge objects refer to a certain knowledge descriptor. In the attributes of the task requirement it is noted, which domain part in which quality is required. The knowledge object says, which domain part it covers in which quality.

4.4   Knowledge Conversion

KMDL supports all four expressions of knowledge conversion (combination, internalization, externalization and socialization. A socialization occurs, when people exchange tacit knowledge directly. This can be done during a personal talk, on a conference, during exchange of experiences or by imitation. These examples show that a knowledge conversion can have varying appearances. Depending on the intention of the model it can be sufficient to represent a socialization as a directed relation between knowledge objects of two persons. KMDL also offers extended representation possibilities to grasp further characteristics. These can be transferred to other expressions of knowledge conversion.

Frequency: The contact between two persons for the exchange of knowledge is possible once, often or permanent. The last possibility occurs especially during an imitation. The other cases can be explained with single or multiple telephone calls.

Completeness: The completeness of the socialized knowledge has to be considered. Different or supplementary contents can be given in different contacts. In addition a complete transfer of the actual knowledge is possible in every contact.

Number of participants: A conversion can take place with multiple participants. A talk given to three people is a single act of socialization. If this is modeled as three different relations between speaker and listener, it is meant that three different contacts with three different acts of socialization exist.

Direction of conversion: A discussion, a brainstorming meeting or a personal suggestion of one of the participants implicates a multitude of knowledge flows. These are not directed. Every participant can be either sender or receiver. Otherwise the acts of socialization had to be represented on the level of single sentences. Such a degree of detail is not efficient and no real gain of information. Therefore a representation of expressions of knowledge flows is necessary, where the participants can be sender, receiver or both.

The graphical representation of these qualities in KMDL is shown in Fig. 1. The conversion is represented as a node, with that all participants (knowledge or information objects) are linked. These relations are directed and show the status of the element as sender or receiver. The line style shows the frequency of participation while the completeness of the conversion is represented by the shape of the node symbol.

4.5   Scaling and Comparability

The coverage of a knowledge domain is coded in an interval from 0 to 100. 100 means that be described knowledge domain is totally covered. A value of zero means that no knowledge from this domain is available. A knowledge descriptor always describes an ideal status of 100. Within the attributes of a knowledge descriptor are divided in different subclasses. Possible names of the intervals are

- no knowledge available
- basic knowledge
- working knowledge
- management knowledge and
- expert knowledge

With a position requirement it has to be mentioned, which competency class is required. The position requirement can also use an own classification or a numeric scale. The expressed accuracy is in this case lower than the exact number feigns. The accuracy of the model is the higher, the more detailed the knowledge domain is split up. It has to be mentioned that all these classifications and categories depend on subjective assessments or from hidden objective information. Competency classes are also assigned to the knowledge objects. By comparison with the position requirements of a task, filled with a person, it is possible to recognize over or under qualifications. Learning measures or personal reassignments can be derived from these results.

The main function of the knowledge descriptor is the preservation of the semantic correctness of a model and for internal comparisons of knowledge objects, demands and requirements with each other. The knowledge descriptor delivers an ideal requirement satisfaction for a part of a knowledge domain. Knowledge objects and position requirements need a content alignment from a link to a knowledge descriptor. They are not allowed to define or categorize knowledge by themselves. These have to reuse the prior defined descriptor. By this way and in combination with the competency classes a semantic comparison is possible.

Without knowledge descriptors each modeler would have to describe the knowledge domain of a knowledge object anew. It could happen that knowledge objects or knowledge requirements concerning the same knowledge domain would get different descriptions by different modelers or users. The similarity would not be recognizable. Also different knowledge objects and requirements could get a similar or the same description by different (or even the same) modelers. The use of knowledge descriptors prevents these inconsistencies. Modeling tools can support the user by offering a set of predefined descriptors. The semantic similarity and comparability of knowledge objects and requirements can be automatically detected by references to the same knowledge descriptor.

Because the similarity and comparability are identified by a reference to another object, independence exists from the textual definition of the knowledge descriptors. So a knowledge domain can de described in any way. Different models and model intentions need different comprehension of a knowledge domain. A knowledge descriptor needs not to describe the knowledge of a domain itself. This would only be possible in special cases when the knowledge domain solely consists of explicit knowledge that is also used as the descriptor's textual definition. But it should be an abstract concerning a certain part of a knowledge domain with a user-defined accuracy. So even tacit knowledge can be specified in a model. This is the recommended way for using knowledge descriptors in KMDL. KMDL does not want to model the knowledge itself. It only models a personal knowledge object as references to a knowledge domain that is characterized by a knowledge descriptor.

4.6   Using KMDL

An editorial process is taken as example. There is a set of research areas. A topic of one of these areas has to be selected and a concept for a publication has to be written for it by a scientific project leader. Based on this concept another person has to do further research and write the final scientific paper.

It is a very simple example and a process like this could very easily be reused as a reference process by any organization. But there are also a lot of implicit assumptions and concurrent activities for serving those two tasks of encouraging

and creating a publication. In figure 2 it is shown how the knowledge requirements and knowledge processes of a concrete editorial process could be represented by KMDL. The visualization of knowledge descriptors and requirements
has been neglected in the example.

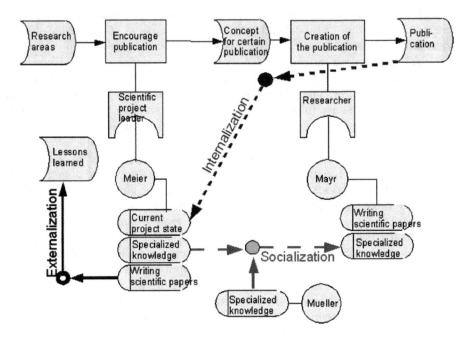

Fig. 2. Process modeled with KMDL

In this case knowledge of scientific writing includes the writing itself as well
as the review of scientific literature. If it should not be a random or cyclic
topic selection for the publication, the project leader needs an overview over
the existing literature and has to recognize the necessity for selecting a certain
topic. He needs specialized knowledge about the selected topic and because of
his responsibility for the publication he needs to know the current state of the
publication. The researcher needs skills in writing and specialized knowledge
about the considered topic, too.

In this example the required knowledge of the project leader and the researcher was insufficient for doing their job. Therefore the researcher was taught
in several sessions by the project leader and a further person. (Of course there
might be some more external information objects as sources, too.) These sessions
(maybe a weekly personal meeting) are represented as a knowledge conversion.

Although the reference process has not proposed it, the project leader took a
permanent view on the arising publication. This is an internalization to acquire
knowledge of the qualitative and quantitative state of the paper.

After all the project leader took a moment and wrote down some lessons learned about writing a scientific paper (externalization). In this case the researcher knew how to write using a scientific style. If there will be another one without this knowledge he could use the externalized knowledge for teaching himself.

This example is too small for analyzing complicate coherence. But even if this reference process for writing a paper is reused for some times, some special concurrence activities may be identified. If there are the same informal sessions for knowledge socialization in every writing process, these meetings should be integrated formally in the reference process or at least be supported technically or organizationally. So an expensive reorganization for each new writing process would not be necessary.

4.7 Model Views

The classification of model elements along a time validity allows partial models that can be used in different manners.

Output-specific process model. A model containing tasks, information objects and information flows has no company specific expression. It can be declared as a reference model without problems and used in different companies. Time validity means in this context that a different arrangement of the model elements creates another reference model. Shall a specific element arrangement be used, so is this arrangement principally invariant.

Company-specific process model. By adding positions and position requirements a company specific adaptation takes place. The organizational structure of the company is modeled by the positions. The output-specific process model is not influenced by this (constancy). Obviously necessary adaptations have to be done on the level of the company structure. The position requirements weight and detail the process in the direction of a specific company. Companies are allowed to define different position requirements for the same task in a process, if this process has different contributions to the value creation in the companies. Weighting, contextual alignment and organizational structure change seldom. Therefore this process model has a long-term validity as a company-specific process model.

Pass-through-specific process model. The participating persons and therefore also the knowledge objects can change with every single process pass-through. Of course new instances of information objects occur every time to be created in the process. The validity of the model membership of these elements is over the medium term. Such a model has to be considered as a pass-through-specific process model.

Conversion-specific process model. The modeled knowledge conversion has only a limited time validity. These flows occur only selective during a whole process pass-through. The actuality of knowledge is to be grasped. The time aspect has to be modeled with other attributes, so that the validity of these process models is over the medium term, too. It is not possible to model or predict the specific content expression, but a framework can be given by the position requirement.

Every of these models can be used as a reference model. A pass-through-specific process model is the basic structure for modeling concrete expressions of knowledge conversion. The company-specific process model is the base for the pass-through-specific process model. An output-specific process model in turn is the framework for a company-specific process model.

5 K-Modeler – The Modeling Tool for Knowledge Intensive Business Processes

Basing on the concept of KMDL a tool is under development that allows to store the modeled knowledge-intensive business processes in a database and to analyze them [Arb03a].

5.1 Features of K-Modeler

The software is completely developed in JAVA, while the data is stored in an relational database management system. For interactive modeling a modeling pane is available. Needed objects can be placed on the work pane with drag and drop. Afterwards the edges between the objects are drawn with the mouse to create logical connections. The modeling process is watched by an intelligent agent. Objects can only be placed agreeing with the defined syntactical rules. Furthermore a function *Syntax check* exists, that is able to recognize errors in the model. Fig. 3 shows the graphical user interface and the model of a process example.

The separation between information and tacit knowledge is another important benefit of K-Modeler. Information are at the disposal of the whole organization. They incorporate the intellectual assets and are available in different manners like patents, organization diagrams, handbooks and so on. They exist independently form the persons in an organization and are therefore often named as *organizational memory* [BP98]. In contrary knowledge can only be created by individuals. Organizations should foster create persons [NT95]. Fostering can be the availability of information or the connection of people for knowledge exchange.

This idea was realized with K-Modeler. The organization, with processes running in it, puts information and infrastructure for the administration of information at the disposal of the members of the organization. Persons enrich the information pool of the organization by creating new information. The information (and also new tacit knowledge objects) is created by combination with tacit knowledge objects.

5.2 Process Analysis with K-Modeler

Additionally the K-Modeler tool offers functions to analyze the modeled processes. Queries for some problem classes are pre-defined. It is not possible to

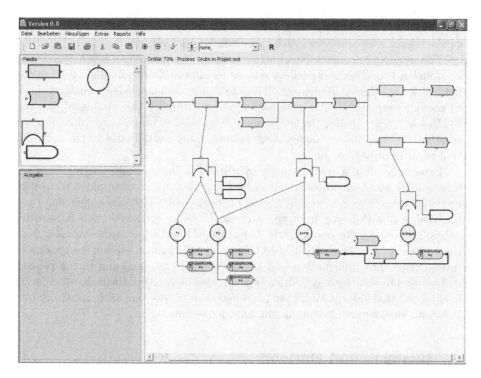

Fig. 3. User interface and example process of the K-Modeler tool

pre-define all possible queries but further queries for individual reports can easily be added.

General weak spots have been introduced above (4.2). Context-sensitive weak spots must be individually defined. For example, assignment of personnel to a couple of task could be an overwork in special cases. But it is not a generally admitted weak spot. Furthermore those queries can be abstract (For example: Which persons are overqualified?) or refer to concrete elements of a process model (For example: Which persons in position X are overqualified?). Again only the abstract ones can be pre-defined. Query patterns for element-sensitive queries can be pre-defined but have to be adapted by concrete values.

The analyzes are not only basing on the actual modeled process but on the process database. Information on all existing and on former processes and process elements are taken into consideration. In the meaning of a process warehouse the variety of possible evaluation and reports is unlimited. This requires that additionally reports based on non-general or non abstract weak spot queries have been identified by the user and translated in SQL statements.

If K-Modeler is used with person-related data, a well-directed comparison is possible between the qualification of employees and the process requirements.

So employees can be supported, because matching teachers for specific abilities can be found and connected with these employees easily.

The usage of information technology used in companies can be analyzed with K-Modeler, too. This is especially related to information technology used in the field of knowledge management. The main aim of knowledge management is to provide employees with information and to simplify the finding of experts. K-Modeler judges using the attributes of knowledge and information objects, whether the knowledge management system really participates in the distribution of these objects or not.

Especially after a restructuring of a process the ensemble acting between information and tacit knowledge can be disturbed. As an example it is mentioned the attempt to cut cost by laying off personnel. With the dispensing tacit knowledge is withdrawn from the process. If a former model with K-Modeler exists, it is possible to predict, whether relevant knowledge was withdrawn from the process or not and which knowledge and information cannot be generated furthermore. The information and knowledge objects remaining in the process will be used in another way. Which way can also be predicted with K-Modeler. It is expected that information that is no longer used, become antiquated because it can no longer participating in the knowledge flow.

6   Summary and Outlook

The description language KMDL and the K-Modeler tool were developed to model and analyze knowledge-intensive business processes especially considering the aspects of flow and conversion of knowledge bound to persons.

First experiences in practice, for instance during the concept of a new large governmental Intranet or during the creation of a corporate university show, that typical advantages of business process modeling can be reached also with K-Modeler. A certain proceeding model assures the efficient collection of additional qualities and attributes, that are necessary to generate statements concerning the quality of the knowledge management in the investigated process.

One of the next steps will be the reimplementation of the interactive graphical tool, which is actually in the status of a prototype. The conceptual defined automated weak spot analysis will be implemented then. Another step is the usage of all collected process elements for the documentation of the process and for a navigation through all participated elements, perhaps with a knowledge map. Furthermore the usage of KMDL and K-Modeler for skill management is actually in preparation.

References

[All98]   T. Allweyer. *Knowledge Process Redesign*. Saarbrücken, 1998.

[Arb03a]   Arbeitsgemeinschaft Wissensmanagement. K-Modeler, 2003.
            http://www.k-modeler.de (Last accessed: January 2004).

[Arb03b]   Arbeitsgemeinschaft Wissensmanagement. KMDL - Knowledge Modeler Description Language, 2003. http://www.kmdl.de (Last accessed: January 2004).

[BP98]   Uwe M. Borghoff and Remo Pareschi, editors. *Information Technology for Knowledge Management.* Berlin, 1998.

[Dav95]   Thomas H. Davenport. Improving Knowledge Work Processes, 1995. http://www.kmadvantage.com/docs/KM/Improving_Knowledge_Work_Processes.pdf (Last accessed: 25. Sept 2002).

[DK04]   Stefan Dilz and Andre Kalisch. *Anwendungen und Systeme für das Wissensmanagement. Ein aktueller Überblick,* volume 3 of *Wirtschaftsinformatik: technische und organisatorische Gestaltungsoptionen.* GITO-Verlag, Berlin, 2004.

[Goe02]   T. Goesmann. *Ansatz zur Unterstützung wissensintensiver Prozesse durch Workflow-Management-Systeme.* Berlin, 2002.

[GPSW03]   N. Gronau, U. Palmer, K. Schulte, and T. Winkler. Modeling of knowledge-intensive business processes with the declaration language KMDL. In U. Reimer, A. Abecker, S. Staab, and G. Stumme, editors, *Professional knowledge management - Experiences and visions,* pages 315–322. Bonn, 2003.

[HBvB+94]   W. Hesse, G. Barkow, H. v. Braun, H.-B. Kittlaus, and G. Scheschonk. Terminologie der Softwaretechnik - Ein Begriffssystem für die Analyse und Modellierung von Anwendungssystemen. *Informatik-Spektrum 17.1 und 17.2,* 1994.

[Hei02]   P. Heisig. GPO-WM - Methode und Werkzeuge zum geschäftsprozessorientierten Wissensmanagement. In A. Abecker, editor, *Geschäftsprozessorientiertes Wissensmanagement.* Berlin Heidelberg New York, 2002.

[Hof02]   M. Hoffmann. Analyse und Unterstützung von Wissensprozessen als Voraussetzung für erfolgreiches Wissensmanagement. In A. Abecker, editor, *Geschäftsprozessorientiertes Wissensmanagement.* Berlin Heidelberg New York, 2002.

[KH93]   G. Knolmayer and H. Herbst. Business rules. *Wirtschaftsinformatik,* 4(35):386–390, 1993.

[KW02]   D. Karagiannis and R. Woitsch. The PROMOTE approach: Modelling Knowledge Management Processes to describe Knowledge Management Systems. In N. Gronau, editor, *Knowledge management strategies, processes, communities.* Aachen, 2002.

[Neu99]   H. G. Neuweg. Könnerschaft und implizites Wissen. Zur lehrlerntheoretischen Bedeutung der Erkenntnis- und Wissenstheorie Michael Polanyis, 1999.

[NT95]   I. Nonaka and H. Takeuchi. *The Knowledge-Creating Company. How Japanese Companies Create the Dynamics of Innovation.* Oxford University Press, New York, 1995.

[PRR98]   G. Probst, S. Raub, and K. Romhardt. *Wissen managen, wie Unternehmen ihre wertvollste Ressource optimal nutzen.* Frankfurter Allgemeine, Gabler, Frankfurt a. M., 2. edition, 1998.

[Rem01]   U. Remus. Towards a framework for Knowledge Management Strategies: Process- Orientation as Strategic Starting Point. Maui, Hawaii, January 2001. Proceedings of the 34th Hawaii International Conference on System Sciences [HICSS-34].

[Rem02a]   U. Remus. Integrierte Prozess- und Kommunikationsmodellierung zur Verbesserung von wissensintensiven Geschäftsprozessen. In A. Abecker, editor, *Geschäftsprozessorientiertes Wissensmanagement*. Berlin Heidelberg New York, 2002.

[Rem02b]   U. Remus. *Process oriented knowledge management. Concepts and modeling*. PhD thesis, University of Regensburg, Germany, Regensburg, 2002.

[Sch98]   A.-W. Scheer. *ARIS From business process to the application system*. Berlin Heidelberg, 3rd edition, 1998.

[SF96]   A. C. Schwickert and K. Fischer. Der Geschäftsprozess als formaler Prozess. Definition, Eigenschaften und Arten. Technical Report WI Nr. 4/1996, Universität Mainz, Lehrstuhl für ABWL und Wirtschaftsinformatik, 1996.

[Sno00]   D. Snowden. The ASHEN Model an enabler of action in Knowledge Management. 3(7):14–17, April 2000.

SMART: System Model Acquisition from Requirements Text

Dov Dori, Nahum Korda, Avi Soffer, and Shalom Cohen

Technion, Israel institute of Technology
{dori@ie, korda@tx, asoffer@tx, shalom1@tx}.technion.ac.il

Abstract. Modeling of a business system has traditionally been based on free text documents. This work describes an elaborate experiment that constitutes a proof of concept to the idea that a system model can be acquired through an automated process whose input is a corpus of technical free text requirement documents and whose output is an OPM model, expressed both graphically, through a set of Object-Process Diagrams, and textually in equivalent Object-Process Language. Our experiment has yielded a high quality system model that required a much smaller effort than what would have been needed in the traditional approach.

1 Introduction

Architecting systems in general and software systems in particular is a tedious task that consumes significant time and expertise resources. Systematically transforming unstructured, free text business specification and user requirements into precise and formal system specifications is a laborious and complex operation, where instead of focusing on the overall design, one often gets lost in a clutter of details. Automation could be of great assistance here, not only because it can significantly lower the overall effort, but also because it allows system designers to focus on the system overview, get the "big picture" much more quickly, and ultimately maximize the overall efficiency of the system while minimizing its time to market.

While the vision of automating the modeling and architecting processes by extracting semantics from requirements expressed in free text may seem to make a lot of sense, a wide semantic gap stands in the way of such automation. On one side of the gap that we seek to bridge is free natural language text, while on its other side is a formal, machine "understandable" and processable character stream. Documentation that serves as a basis for architecting new systems or improving existing ones, such as business process specifications or user requirements, is formulated in natural language that is not even in a machine-readable, let alone machine-understandable format.

While formalization of freely expressed ideas, concepts, intentions, and desires into rigorous specifications seems to be beyond the reach of current computing technologies, not all hope is lost. The emergence of the Semantic Web and ontology engineering technologies may point the way to eventually bridge the semantic gap obstacle. Although it still seems unrealistic to expect complete automation of the system

J. Desel, B. Pernici, and M. Weske (Eds.): BPM 2004, LNCS 3080, pp. 179–194, 2004.
© Springer-Verlag Berlin Heidelberg 2004

design, partial, semi-automatic solutions that operate under human supervision may already be feasible and may prove to be extremely useful.

Our proposed strategy is to start bridging the semantic gap in parallel from its two sides—the formal side and the natural language (NL) side—as follows:

1. On the formal side of the semantic gap, the need is for a paradigm and a tool that is capable of human-oriented intuitive expression of complex system function, structure, and behavior while at the same time being formal to a degree that a machine can unambiguously process it. Object-Process Methodology (OPM) [1] is obviously an excellent candidate for the task at hand, since Object-Process Language (OPL), the textual modality of OPM, utilizes a constrained subset of English, which brings it a significant step closer to the unconstrained natural language that exists on the other side of the gap. The additional advantage of using OPM is that its two semantically equivalent modalities, one graphic (Object-Process Diagram) and the other textual (Object-Process Language), jointly express the same OPM model. Accordingly, every verbal formulation (OPL) is automatically paralleled by its graphic presentation, (OPD), and vice versa, such that complete equivalence between the two presentations is guaranteed at any point in time.

2. On the NL side of the semantic gap, information extraction technologies will be utilized in order to achieve the following benefits:
    *   Extracting from unstructured text elements—entities and links—that are key concepts for the domain and the problem at hand,
    *   Detecting and mapping alternative formulations of relevant ontological relations, and
    *   Deriving a semi-formalized presentation of the underlying documentation that could be manually organized into a rigorous formal model of the required system.

To prove the concept of deriving an OPM model from unstructured technical text, this paper describes an experiment in which we utilized information extraction techniques in order to automatically generate OPL script—a structured subset of natural English—from which the corresponding diagrammatic specification in the form of a set of Object-Process Diagrams (OPDs) was constructed semi-automatically utilizing the OPM-supporting CASE tool (OPCAT) [2]. The automatically derived OPL sentences served as a basis for modeling the initial requirements. The automatically-generated initial specification was elaborated upon by the system architect conferring with the domain expert—the representative of the system beneficiary or user, and obtained the expert's blessing. This initial OPM-based system specification can be further developed into a complete formal system design with OPCAT, and automatically documented, converted into a set of UML diagrams if so desired, and implemented as a set of JAVA classes.

The experiment described in this paper is, to the best of our knowledge, a first successful attempt to construct a system model in a semi-automatic way from the system's free text documentation of the requirements. The experiment was based on GRACE (Grid Search and Categorization Engine), a European Community Information Society Technology (IST) project [3]. This complex software development project combines

Grid, ontology engineering, and knowledge management. GRACE was found to be suitable for our experiment due to its extensive background documentation, which includes user and system requirements. A subset of this documentation corpus served as the free natural language text on which the automatic content extraction and OPM model building was performed.

The rest of the paper is structured as follows: Section 2 includes a review of the state-of-the-art in automating modeling from free text. This is followed by a description of OPM in Section 3 and application of OPM to model the architecture of our SMART system in Section 4. The experiment is described in section 5, and section 6 presents our conclusions.

2   Automating Modeling from Text: State of the Art

Architectures of systems and their underlying software provide high-level abstractions for representing the function, structure, behavior, and key properties of the system. A first and crucial phase in system architecting is eliciting, gathering, analyzing, and engineering the stakeholders' requirements. In spite of the clear and direct relationships between requirements engineering and system architecture modeling, these two activities have traditionally been pursued independently from one another.

2.1   From Requirements to Architecture

System requirements include the customer's expectations and vision of the desired solution of the business problem at hand, and constraints on the solution. The requirements documentation reflects interests of the different system's stakeholders—customers, endusers, developers, and managers [4]. Requirements deal with concepts, intentions (both explicit and implicit), goals, alternatives, conflicts, agreements, and above all—desired functional and non-functional system features and properties.

Architecting a system from its requirements has not yet fully been understood. The task of system architecting from its requirements is difficult due the complex nature of the interdependencies and constraints between architectural elements and requirement elements. A number of techniques have been proposed, though, to assist in this effort-consuming and poorly understood task .For example, the Component Bus System, and Properties (CBSP) approach [5, 6], also supported by tools [7, 8], is an analysis method that operates through classification of system features and properties as reflected in the requirements and altering their representation using an intermediate language.

Techniques that have been proposed so far to bridge the requirements-design gap commonly involve human-driven conceptual analysis of the requirements—an iterative, error-prone, and resource-consuming effort for extracting domain-knowledge related information from the requirements. The CREWS project [9], which makes use of language processing in scenario-based requirements engineering approach [10], promotes guidance of the elicitation and validation of requirements that is based on textual scenarios.

2.2 Working from Business Specification and User Requirements

Another approach to supporting the requirements engineering (RE) process is based on the fact that natural language plays an important role during the requirements stage. It is argued [11] that acquisition of application domain knowledge is typically achieved through language manipulation, either through document and text analyses or by means of interviews. It has therefore been suggested there that RE should be supported by a CASE tool that is based on a linguistic approach. Such RE support environment would generate the conceptual specification from a description of the problem space provided initially through natural language statements.

A complete and effective RE process, which naturally involves language manipulation, includes the following steps: (1) *acquisition* of domain-dependent knowledge using NL statements, an automated version of which [12] applies NL-processing-based metadata extraction to automatically acquire user preferences, (2) *graphic representation* of the semantic contents of the NL statements, which should be easy to understand and manipulate, and (3) *mapping* of the real-world description to a conceptual schema, or a requirements-level system model. Based on this analysis, an approach for tackling the inherent complexity of the RE process is proposed [13] that is based on a CASE tool for the requirements engineering process. This CASE tool is essentially a rule-based expert system, which is a highly technical environment that requires substantial support in rule generation, adaptation, and checking.

2.3 Natural Language Processing

Industrial practice has shown that NL requirements are easier to evolve, maintain, and discuss with (possibly non-technical) stakeholders. Recognizing the potential role of natural language processing (NLP) in the requirements engineering process, efforts (e.g., [14]) have been made to identify tasks where NLP may be usefully applied. At the same time, however, a note of caution is sounded by noting the limitations of NLP in requirements engineering [15].

A number of experiments have been reported on the use of NLP techniques in the context of systems development. Lexical analysis was used [16] to find abstractions in unstructured and un-interpreted text. Other studies applied NL parsing and understanding techniques to automatic extraction of models from NL requirements [17, 18, 19]. Several specific NLP tools and techniques, including [20, 21], have been introduced for the purpose of analyzing and controlling software requirements. These techniques rely on lexical analysis to extract abstractions from natural language text [22]. The use of NLP has also been reported in analogical reasoning technology for specification reuse and validation [23]. Although the application of NLP techniques to handling system requirements is appealing, it is often difficult to check and prove properties, such as correctness, consistency, and completeness on those requirements [24]. Abstract systems were suggested for detecting such ambiguities and under-specifications [25] as well as requirement redundancies [26].

When moving from early requirement gathering, in which ideas, concepts, and intentions are expressed with NL, to the analysis phase, the freely expressed NL-based requirements need to be formalized. They need to be replaced by rigorous specifications, so coherence, consistency, and feasibility can be reasoned about, at least semiformally. Lightweight formal methods were used in [27] for partial validation of NL requirement documents. Checking properties of models obtained by shallow parsing of NL-expressed requirements, they concluded that automated analysis of requirements expressed in natural language is both feasible and useful.

The conclusion drawn from current research is that the RE process should be supported by a CASE tool that incorporates a linguistic approach. The tool should facilitate an RE-support environment that generates a conceptual specification from a description of the problem space provided through natural language statements. We distinguish between two different types of NL sentence analyses. One is the syntactic analysis, which is based on finding the parts-of-speech in a sentence, including object, subject, verb, adjective, adverb, etc. A notable method of syntactic analysis of this form is Knowledge Query and Manipulation Language (KQML) language, proposed by ARPA Knowledge Sharing Effort in 1992. It uses Knowledge Interchange Format (KIF) [28] for content description through an ASCII representation of first order predicate logic using a LISP-like syntax [29]. The other sentence analysis type is the semantic approach, in which we seek the deep, underlying meaning of what the sentence expresses in terms of detecting objects in the sentences and relations between them, or a transformation to an object (its generation, consumption, or change of state) that a process causes through its occurrence. These two different types of NL sentence analyses were adopted by [30] to form their Word Class Function Machine aimed at both the syntactic analysis and semantic analysis of NL. Performance of these analyses has been an issue for Samuelsson [31] who optimized the analysis and generation machinery through the use of previously processed training examples [26].

This paper suggests the use of NLP in conjunction with Object-Process Methodology (OPM) [1] and its supporting CASE tool (OPCAT) [2] for acquisition of application domain knowledge. The proposed approach seeks to extract as much semantics as possible automatically from a given corpus of related technical documents, such as requirement documents, and build from this extracted semantics an initial conceptual model in a semi-automatic way using OPM and its OPCAT support environment. We next focus on OPM.

3   Object-Process Methodology

Most interesting and challenging systems are those in which structure and behavior are highly intertwined and hard to separate. Object-Process Methodology (OPM) is a holistic approach to the modeling, study, and development of systems. It integrates the object-oriented and process-oriented paradigms into a single frame of reference. Structure and behavior, the two major aspects that each system exhibits, co-exist in the same graphic-NL bimodal OPM model without highlighting one at the expense of suppressing the other.

The elements of the OPM ontology are entities (things and states) and links. A thing is a generalization of an object and a process—the two basic building blocks of any system expressed in OPM. Objects are (physical or informatical) things that exist, while processes are things that transform objects. In a specific point of time, an object can be exactly in one state, and objects states are changed through occurrences of processes. Links can be structural or procedural. Structural links express static relations between pairs of entities. Aggregation, generalization, characterization, and instantiation are the four fundamental structural relations. Procedural links connect entities (objects, processes, and states) to describe the behavior of a system. The behavior is manifested by processes that interact with objects in three major ways: (1) processes can transform (generate, consume, or change the state of) objects; (2) objects can enable processes without being transformed by them; and (3) objects can trigger events that invoke processes.

3.1 The Bimodal OPM Model Representation

Two semantically equivalent modalities, one graphic and the other textual, jointly express the same OPM model. A set of inter-related Object-Process Diagrams (OPDs) constitute the graphical, visual OPM formalism. Each OPM element is denoted in an OPD by a symbol, and the OPD syntax specifies correct and consistent ways by which entities can be linked. The Object-Process Language (OPL), a subset of English formally defined by a grammar, is the textual counterpart modality of the graphical OPD-set. OPL is a dual-purpose language, oriented towards humans as well as machines. Catering to human needs, OPL is designed as a constrained subset of English, which serves domain experts and system architects engaged in analyzing and designing a system. Every OPD construct is expressed by a semantically equivalent OPL sentence or phrase. Designed also for machine interpretation through a well-defined set of production rules, OPL has an XML-based notation that provides a solid basis for automatically generating the designed application. This dual representation of OPM increases the processing capability of humans.

3.2 OPM Refinement and Abstraction Mechanisms

Complexity management aims at balancing the tradeoff between two conflicting requirements: completeness and clarity. Completeness requires that the system details be stipulated to the fullest extent possible, while the need for clarity imposes an upper limit on the level of complexity and does not allow for an OPD (or an OPL paragraph) that is too cluttered or overloaded with entities and links among them. The seamless, recursive, and selective refinement-abstraction mechanisms of OPM enable presenting the system at various detail levels without losing the "big picture" and the comprehension of the system as a whole. The three built-in refinement/abstraction mechanisms are: (1) unfolding/folding, which is used for refining/abstracting the structural hierarchy of a thing and is applied by default to objects; (2) in-zooming/out-zooming, which exposes/hides the inner details of a thing within its frame and is applied primarily to processes; and (3) state expressing/suppressing, which exposes/hides the states of an object. Using flexible combinations of these three mechanisms, the achieved OPM models are consistent by definition.

4 OPM Model of the SMART System

OPM is employed in this research at two levels: one is the specification of the System Model Acquisition from Requirements Text (SMART) system, and the other is an example of the GRACE system, which is the outcome of our proof-of-concept experiment. Having introduced the basics of OPM we proceed to utilize it to model the architecture of the SMART system using OPCAT. The SMART system consists of various software tools that operate cooperatively in order to produce SMART's desired output.

Fig. 1 shows the System Diagram (SD), i.e., the top-level Object-Process Diagram (OPD) of the SMART system. The diagram depicts the high-level structure of the SMART system, its main process, input and output, and the user, as well as their interrelations.

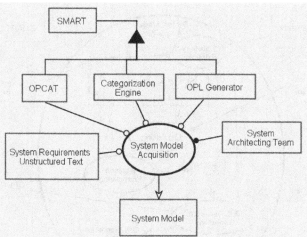

Fig. 1. SD – System Diagram (top-level view) of the SMART system OPM model

The graphical description of SMART—the OPD—is backed by corresponding OPL specification, which OPCAT generates automatically in real time in response to the user's graphic input. Table 1 presents the OPL paragraph that describes the OPD in Fig. 1.

Table 1. The OPL paragraph describing the SMART system whose OPD is in Fig. 1

System Architecting Team handles **System Model Acquisition**.
SMART consists of **Categorization Engine, OPCAT**, and **OPL Generator**.
System Model Acquisition requires **System Requirements Unstructured Text, Categorization Engine, OPCAT**, and **OPL Generator**.
System Model Acquisition yields **System Model**.

The first sentence in the OPL paragraph expresses the fact that the **System Archi-tecting Team** is in charge of, or is involved in the process. As Fig. 1 shows, it is con-nected by an agent link, which triggers the process **System Model Acquisition**. The sec-ond sentence expresses the structure of the SMART system. The major components of the system, **Categorization Engine**, **OPCAT**, and **OPL Generator**, are related to the main **System Model Acquisition** process by instrument links. The fourth and last sentence in the OPL paragraph expresses the fact that **System Model Acquisition** generates as a re-sult of its occurrence a new object called **System Model**.

In order to elaborate on the details of the **System Model Acquisition** process de-picted in Fig. 1 we take advantage of OPM's complexity management capability. Zooming into **System Model Acquisition**, OPCAT creates a new OPD shown in Fig. 2, which is automatically labeled SD1 – System Model Acquisition in-zoomed . SD1 is one level lower than SD in the OPD hierarchy.

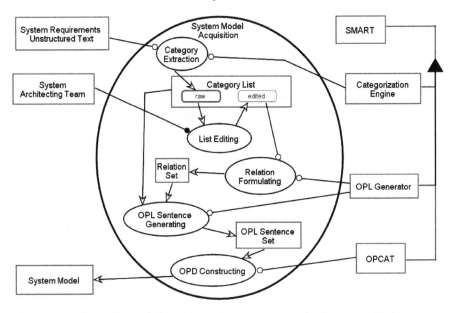

Fig. 2. The in-zoomed **System Model Acquisition** process of Fig. 1 exposes subprocesses and interim objects

The graphical description of SD1 is backed by another corresponding automati-cally-generated OPL paragraph. The major subprocesses of SMART, their order of operation (top to bottom), and the interim objects—**Category List**, **Relation Set**, and **OPL Sentence Set**—are obvious from the diagram. The subprocesses and interim ob-jects are also clearly listed in the third sentence in the OPL paragraph, which reads:

OPM Model Construction zooms into **Category Extraction, List Editing, Relation**

Formulating, OPL Sentence Generating, and **OPD Constructing,** as well as **OPL**

Sentence Set, Relation Set, and **Category List.**

Drilling down into lower levels in the model hierarchy using OPM's abstraction/refinement mechanisms (not shown here due to shortage of space) would reveal further details on the system by showing sub-subprocesses and additional objects' lower level parts and/or attributes. A detailed description of SMART is provided in the next section.

5 The Proof-of-Concept SMART Experiment

Our experiment was aimed to provide proof of concept to the possibility of semi-automatically constructing portions of a model of the system-to-be, as expressed in free text of a corpus of requirement documents. The following is an account of the experimental settings and procedures. As proof of concept, the experiment proceeded while operating various software programs independently in different phases, rather the attempting to produce a unifying application with a user-friendly graphic interface.

5.1 Automatic Extraction of Categories from Unstructured Text

Our document set of unstructured text consisted of half a dozen free text documents from the GRACE corpus, with a total size of about 0.5 MB. We developed a LISP-based, heuristics-directed categorization engine and utilized it to extract categories from our document set. A category in our context is defined as an idiomatic phrase (word sequence) reflecting the underlying topics in a given corpus of documents. Idioms are expressions whose meaning cannot be deduced from the meaning of its individual constituents, but rather from their consistent use in specific contexts.

Table 2 presents a few examples of categories that were automatically extracted from the unstructured GRACE documentation text by our categorization engine.

Table 2. Examples of categories that were automatically extracted from our GRACE documentation

Search Results	Advanced Searching	Knowledge Managing
Content Sources	Web Services	Query Routing
Search Engine	Document Storing	Knowledge Sharing
User Profile	Document Retrieving	Frontend Application
Web Server	Content Source Registering	

Overall, the categorization engine extracted 109 categories, utilizing only its heuristics. Many domains of human knowledge, in particular sciences, have very detailed and precise nomenclatures and dictionaries that could be used for that purpose. We could also calibrate the categorization engine to extract particular categories specified in an external ontology, taxonomy, or thesaurus. Such combination of unconstrained and ontology-guided extraction might generate better results, as the unconstrained categorization could add to the domain vocabulary concepts and expressions that are specific to a document corpus.

5.2 Manual Editing of the Extracted Categories

SMART is intended for use by system engineers with some knowledge domain or previous involvement in similar efforts, since manual category editing requires some domain expertise. The extracted categories were next manually inspected to achieve the following purposes:

Selection of those categories that can serve as things (objects or processes) in the OPM model, and classifying them as either object or processes. For example, about half of the extracted things in

1. Table 2 are objects, while the rest are processes. OPM favors processes in the gerund form, i.e., those that end with the "ing" suffix. Indeed, all the processes in the table have this form, but this is not necessarily the case. Fore example, **Document Retrieval** would be classified as a process, synonym with **Document Retrieving**. A counterexample of the word **Building**, means either the object (house) or the process of constructing the house, shows why automatic object-process classification is difficult (but not impossible) to automate.

2. Clustering alternative formulations for the selected OPM things (for example, **Search Results** and **Retrieved Results**) based on their semantic similarity, and

3. Optionally adding OPM things that did not show up among the extracted categories.

An important assistance to the manual editing of categories is the ability of the categorization engine to present all the sentences from the processed corpus in which a particular category appears. Using this feature, a system engineer can focus on the few really relevant instances, in which a particular category occurs, saving the sifting through hundreds of documentation pages. During this inspection, additional categories that were not automatically extracted but are nonetheless relevant for the design may be detected in the text, or may simply come to mind and be manually added.

The system allows *semantic clustering*, i.e., grouping of categories into clusters that share similar a meaning. This caters to the variety of natural language formulations encountered in actual texts. Our experiment has revealed several typical situations in which such clustering is required:

1. Abbreviations and acronyms (e.g., European Data Grid and EDG),
2. Lexical variations (e.g., search results, retrieved documents, retrieved results),
3. Synonyms (e.g., screen, monitor, display),
4. Morphological variations (e.g., registering, registration), and
5. Orthographic variations (e.g., frontend, front-end, front end).

5.3 Automatic Search of OPM Relations

In order to extract OPL sentences from the unstructured text, SMART utilizes a set of configurable, predefined templates. Each template consists of two things and the relation between them, expressed in alternative ways. For example, the **result** relation between a process and an object, expressed in OPL by the verb *yields*, can also occur as *generates, results in,* etc. SMART currently utilizes 50 predefined general templates and 20 domain-specific templates that were detected by inspecting various contexts in which the selected categories occurred. These 70 templates were applied to 109 categories organized in 46 clusters. Since not all combinations of things and relations are allowed (for example, the OPM relation **result** cannot exist between two OPM objects from the list of 109 categories, but only between a process and an object, and in this order), the original document corpus was tested against a total of 234,320 templates.

We define *second order regular expressions* as regular expressions, in which the basic unit is a word rather than a character. Instead of comparing character strings, a program that uses second order regular expressions compares word sequences. The program is implemented as a finite-state automaton that operates on suffix-tree index consisting of tokens from the processed text. To guarantee the required expressiveness of the framework, SMART manipulates second order regular expressions, allowing them to be defined on any lexical or grammatical attribute of the processed text, such as part-of-speech, capitalization, and punctuation. The extraction of OPM relations is performed with these templates in two modes:

1. Constrained extraction, which is limited only to the pairs of categories defined as OPM things in the manual editing process, systematically generates couples and attempts to detect any possible relation between them in the text, and

2. Unconstrained extraction, which allows selection of any single OPM thing and seeks all possible relations in which it occurs.

5.4 Automatic Generation of OPL Sentences

Since each template has a corresponding OPL formulation, every extracted natural language sentence can be straight-forwardly translated into an OPL sentence. Nonetheless, at this stage it is also possible to reformulate the outcome in order to better reflect the underlying relations. This transformation is performed in two steps:

1. A custom relation is transformed into a process, for example: **cached into** is transformed into **Caching**, and

2. A complex relation, such as **Actual Documents Cached into Document Repositories**, is transformed into two equivalent simple sentences. In our case, (1) **Caching** requires **Actual Documents** and (2) **Caching** yields **Document Repositories**.

These transformations do not modify the underlying semantics of the NL sentences but allow the complex natural language formulations to be and simplified into concise OPL sentences. The output set of the OPL sentences is listed in Table 3.

Table 3. The OPL paragraph describing the GRACE system whose OPD is in Fig. 3.

Search Results consists of **Actual Documents.**
Knowledge Domain consists of **Content Sources.**
EDG Application Layer consists of **Job Management Element** and **Data Management Element.**
Data Management Element retrieves **User Profile.**
Data Management Element and **Document Storage Service** are interfaced.
Data Management Element and **Search Engine** are interfaced.
NDF Repository consists of **Documents NDF.**
Documents NDF are transferred to **Document Storage Service.**
Document Processing Service processes **Actual Documents.**
Frontend Application transfers **Query Request.**
Web Server and **Frontend Application** are interfaced.
Text Indexing requires **Search Engine.**
Query Routing consumes **Query Request, Internal Content Sources,** and **External Content Sources.**
Query Routing yields **Actual Documents.**
Downloading requires **Document Processing Service.**
Downloading consumes **External Content Sources.**
Downloading yields **Actual Documents.**
Cashing consumes **Actual Documents** and **External Content Sources.**
Cashing yields **Content Sources.**
Storing consumes **Actual Documents.**
Storing yields **Internal Content Sources.**
Retrieving requires **Query Request.**
Retrieving yields **Search Results** and **Actual Documents.**
Accessing requires **EDG Application Layer.**
Accessing affects **NDF Repository** and **Document Repositories.**

5.5 Manual Editing of the Results

The OPL sentences were fed into OPCAT one by one to obtain the OPD, which is shown in Fig. 3 after manual beatification.

Both the OPL sentence set and the OPD are significantly simpler and more digestible than the hundreds of NL documentation pages from which the model was extracted. OPCAT allows the results to be edited graphically in order to remove the incorrect relations, organize the things and the relations into more complex (multi-layered) structures, add undetected things and relations, etc. The graphic manipulation is much easier than text editing, and this ability is a great advantage of OPCAT. Since complete equivalence between OPD and OPL presentations is granted, every modification in the OPD is automatically reflected in the corresponding OPL sentence(s). Several operations were applied to the results at this final step:

1. *Corrections*: Some non-semantic corrections were necessary due to the fact that the extraction did not depict all of the existing or implied relations. These corrections fall into the following categories:

    1. Grouping of specialized elements into a general one (e.g., **Internal Content Sources** and **External Content Sources** were grouped into **Content Sources**),

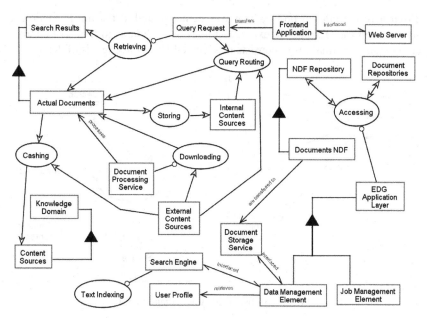

Fig. 3. The OPD that represents the OPL sentences generated from GRACE free text

2. Grouping of specialized elements into a general one (e.g., **Internal Content Sources** and **External Content Sources** were grouped into **Content Sources**),

3. Associating unrelated elements (e.g., **Text Indexing** was associated with the **Document Processing Service**),

4. Renaming elements (e.g., **Storing** was renamed more specifically as **Grid Publishing**),

5. Reapplying a relation transitively from a general object to its specialization or from a whole to a part (e.g., transferring the instrument link attached to **Text Indexing** from **Search Engine** to its **Document Processing Service** part).

2. *Additions and Eliminations*: Unlike corrections, additions and eliminations may semantically modify the original output. Additions aim primarily at improving the detail level and completing the implied structure based on common sense (e.g., by introducing **User** as the human agent that interacts with the system). Eliminations simplify the results by removing superfluous or unessential detail.

3. *Scaling*: Scaling was applied in order to simplify the results without losing details. Inspecting the OPD revealed that the documentation implicitly discusses two main processes: (1) storage of documents into content sources and (2) their retrieval on demand. The first process was conveniently renamed **Grid Publishing** and the second—**Information Retrieval**. Fig. 4 presents the system diagram (SD)—the top-level view that resulted from abstracting the original results.

From here the editing process that was demonstrated at the top level proceeded mostly through transferring the extracted things and relations to the most appropriate level of detail. The final result consists of seven OPDs at three levels of detail.

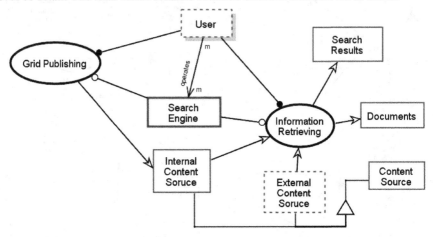

Fig. 4. Manually abstracted system diagram of GRACE

6   Summary and Conclusions

The experiment described in this paper demonstrates the feasibility of automating the most critical step in the system engineering process from unstructured business speci-fication and user requirements to precise and formal system specifications. The ex-periment was designed as a proof-of-concept offering the first hands-on experience required for the development of a future full-scale industrial application. We drew the following be conclusions from the experiment:

1. The proposed methodology significantly reduces the quantity of material that would otherwise need to be processed manually.
2. Translating the original NL sentences into OPL reduces the initial level of con-ceptual complexity. The variety in which a relation may be expressed in NL may be surprisingly broad, leading to confusion, imprecision, and vagueness. This is typical if the documentation was written by many authors from various profes-sional backgrounds. OPL, on the other hand, introduces uniformity, which guar-antees that the relations are expressed in a concise and unambiguous way.
3. The results depend critically on the quality of the processed documentation. The more architectural information is contained in it, the better the results. Relevant system components were often successfully extracted from the text as categories, but very little information regarding their relations with other system components was actually available. Obviously, no system can extract information that is not there.
4. Even when the results still require significant editing, it is so much easier to un-derstand and manipulate the dual OPM graphic or even textual presentations than to work directly with the NL sources.

5. The quality, accuracy, and conciseness of the system architecture obtained following the SMART process is likely to be higher than that obtained through traditional model construction due to the discipline OPM introduces.

In order to become more useful, SMART needs significant improvements, in particular more sophisticated extraction templates and improved performance. Having provided a proof-of-concept to the viability of automated extraction of system model from free text, future research and development efforts will focus on enhancing the level of automation of SMART and testing it against traditional model construction processes in terms of both model quality and resource expenditure.

References

1. Dori, D.: Object-Process Methodology - A Holistic Systems Paradigm. Springer-Verlag, Berlin Heidelberg New York (2002)
2. Dori, D., Reinhartz-Berger, I., Sturm, A.: Developing Complex Systems with Object-Process Methodology using OPCAT. Lecture Notes in Computer Science, Vol. 2813. Springer-Verlag, Berlin Heidelberg New York (2003) 570-572
3. GRACE: Grid Search and Categorization Engine. EU RTD Project in the 2002 Fifth Framework. http://www.grace-ist.org/
4. Nuseibeh, B., Easterbrook, S.: Requirements Engineering: A Roadmap. Proc. Conference on The Future of Software Engineering, Limerick, Ireland (2000) 35-46
5. Egyed, A., Grünbacher, P., Medvidovic, N.: Refinement and Evolution Issues in Bridging Requirements and Architectures - The CBSP Approach. Proc. 1st International Workshops From Requirements to Architecture, co-located with ICSE'01, Toronto, Canada (2001)
6. Grünbacher, P., Egyed, A., Medvidovic, N.: Reconciling Software Requirements and Architectures: The CBSP Approach. Proc. 5th IEEE International Symposium on Requirements Engineering (RE'01), Toronto, Canada (2001)
7. Grünbacher, P., Egyed, A., Medvidovic, N.: Dimensions of Concerns in Requirements Negotiation and Architecture Modeling. The second workshop on multi-dimensional separation of concerns in software engineering, co-located with ICSE'2000, Limerick, Ireland, June 2000
8. Robinson, W., Fickas, S.: Automated Support for Requirements Negotiation. Proc. AAAI-94 Workshop on Models of Conflicts on Conflict Management in Cooperative Problem Solving (1994)
9. Ralyté, J., Rolland, C., Plihon, V.: Method Enhancement by Scenario Based Techniques. Proc. 11th Conference on Advanced Information Systems Engineering (CAiSE'99), Lecture Notes in Computer Science, Vol. 1626. Springer-Verlag, Berlin Heidelberg New York (1999) 103-118
10. Ben Achour, C.: Linguistic Instruments for the Integration of Scenarios in Requirements Engineering. Proc. 3rd International Workshop on Requirements Engineering: Foundations of Software Quality (REFSQ'97), Barcelona (1997)
11. Rolland, C., Proix, C.: A Natural Language Approach for Requirements Engineering. Proc. 4th International Conference on Advanced Information Systems Engineering (CAiSE'92), Lecture Notes in Computer Science, Vol. 593. Springer-Verlag, Berlin Heidelberg New York (1992) 257-277
12. Paik. W., Yilmazel, S., Brown, E., Poulin, M., Dubon, S., Amice, C.: Applying Natural Language Processing (NLP) Based Metadata Extraction to Automatically Acquire User Preferences, Knowledge Capture - K-CAP'01, 2001.

13. Si-Said, S., Rolland, C., Grosz, G.: MENTOR: A Computer Aided Requirements Engineering Environment. Proc. 8th International Conference on Advances Information System Engineering (CAiSE'96), Lecture Notes in Computer Science, Vol. 1080. Springer-Verlag, Berlin Heidelberg New York (1996) 22-43

14. Ambriola, V., Gervasi, V.: Processing Natural Language Requirements. Proc. 12th IEEE Conference on Automated Software Engineering (ASE'97). IEEE Press (1997) 36-45

15. Ryan, K.: The Role of Natural Language in Requirements Engineering. Proc. IEEE International Symposium on Requirements Engineering, San Diego, 1993

16. Goldin, L., Berry, D.M.: A Prototype Natural Language Text Abstraction Finder For Use In Requirements Elicitation. Automated Software Engineering Journal 4, (4) 375-412, 1997

17. Macias, B., Pullman, S.B.: Natural Language Processing for Requirements Specification. Safety-Critical Systems. Chapman and Hall, London (1993) 57-59

18. Fantechi, A., Gnesi, S., Ristori, G., Carenini, M., Vanocchi, M., Moreschini, P.: Assisting Requirement Formalization by Means of Natural Language Translation. Formal Methods in System Design, 4(3), 1994, 243-263

19. Juristo, N., Moreno, A.M., Lopez, M.: How to use Linguistic Instruments for Object-Oriented Analysis. IEEE Software; 17(3), 2000, 80-89

20. Macias, B., Pullman, S.G.: A Method for Controlling the Production of Specifications in Natural Language. The Computer Journal, 38(4), 1995, 310-318

21. Nelken, R., Francez, N.: Automatic translation of natural-language system specifications into temporal logic. Proc. 8th Conference on Computer Aided Verification (CAV'96), Lecture Notes in Computer Science, Vol. 1102. Springer-Verlag, Berlin Heidelberg New York (1996) 360-371

22. Jarke, M., Bubenko, J., Rolland, C., Sutcliffe, A., Vassiliou, Y.: Theories Underlying Requirements Engineering: An Overview of NATURE at Genesis. In: Proc.1st IEEE Symposium on Requirements Engineering, San Diego, 1993

23. Sutcliffe, A.G., Maiden, N.A.M.: Use of Domain Knowledge for Requirements Validation. Proc.Conference on Information System Development Process, 1993

24. Fabbrini, F., Fusani, M., Gervasi, V., Gnesi, S., Ruggirei, S.: Achieving Quality in Natural Language Requirements. Proc. 11th International Software Quality Week, 1998

25. Huyck, C., Abbas, F.: Natural Language Processing and Requirements Engineering: a Linguistics Perspective, Proc 1st Asia-Pacific Conference on Software Quality, 2000

26. Natt, J., Regnell, B., Carlshamre, P., Andersson, M., Karlsson, J.: A Feasibility Study of Automated Natural Language Requirements Analysis in Market-Driven Development, Requirements Engineering 7, 2002, 20-33

27. Gervasi, V., Nuseibeh, B.: Lightweight Validation of Natural Language Requirements. Proc. 4th IEEE International Conference on Requirements Engineering (ICRE), Schaumburg, Il, 2000

28. Genesereth, M.R.: Knowledge Interchange Format (KIF), http://logic.stanford.edu/kif/kif.html, 1998

29. Finin, T., Fritzson, R.: KQML as an Agent Communication Language, Proc. 3rd International Conference on Information and Knowledge Management (CIKM'94), ACM Press (1994)

30. Helbig, H., Hartrumpf, S.: Word Class Functions for Syntactic-Semantic Analysis, Proc. 2nd International Conference on Recent Advances in Natural Language Processing, 1997, 312-317

31. Samuelsson, C., Optimizing Analysis and Generation in Natural Language Processing, Computational Lingustics – ERCIM, 1996.

Workload Balancing on Agents for Business Process Efficiency Based on Stochastic Model

Byung-Hyun Ha[1], Joonsoo Bae[2], and Suk-Ho Kang[1]

[1] Department of Industrial Engineering, Seoul National University,
Seoul 151-742, Republic of Korea
pepper@netopia.snu.ac.kr, shkang@snu.ac.kr
http://ara.snu.ac.kr
[2] Department of Industrial & Information System Eng., Chonbuk National University,
Jeonju, 561-756, Republic of Korea
jsbae@chonbuk.ac.kr
http://prof.chonbuk.ac.kr/~jsbae

Abstract. BPMS (Business Process Management Systems) is a revolutionary information system that supports designing, administrating, and improving the business processes systematically. BPMS enables execution of business processes by assigning tasks to human or computer agents according to the predefined definitions of the processes. In this paper, we model business processes and agents using a queueing network and propose a task assignment algorithm to maximize overall process efficiency under the limitation of agent's capacity. We first transform the business processes into queueing network models, in which the agents are considered as servers. With this complete, workloads of agents are calculated as server utilization and the task assignment policy can be determined by balancing the workloads. This will serve to minimize the workloads of all agents, thus achieving overall process efficiency. Another application of these results can be capacity planning of agents in advance and business process optimization in reengineering context. The simulation results and comparisons with other well-known dispatching policies show the effectiveness of our algorithm.

1 Introduction

Although the productivity of the current enterprises is greatly increased due to advanced technologies and management skills, they cannot avoid the fierce international competition and they have to compete with world's best companies in the same industry area. In order to keep a competitive advantage in today's customer-oriented business environment, business process management is gathering force as an important element in the organization. So, BPMS is becoming an imperative to manage the business process in the proper manner [12,13,25]. The BPMS (Business Process Management System) is introduced as an effort to manage business processes. While the previous WFMS (Workflow Management Systems) provides the basis to develop,

J. Desel, B. Pernici, and M. Weske (Eds.): BPM 2004, LNCS 3080, pp. 195–210, 2004.

execute, and manage the internal business procedure, BPMS is extended to apply the previous efforts to inter-organizational business integration [25].

The critical components of BPMS are business processes, tasks, agents, roles, and relevant elements [9,25]. If a new business process is to be executed, BPMS reads the appropriate tasks that are determined according to the predefined specification. These selected tasks are assigned to agents with the proper roles to execute them. So BPMS controls the process execution efficiently by assigning tasks to agents more appropriately. In particular, the agents who perform tasks are usually human resource, so the reasonable distribution of workloads is a much more critical issue. In general, the resource of agents for a specific task is constrained. So when many tasks arrive at a time, the amount of work is increased to exceed capability. Also, as the appropriate agents for a specific task are defined by the role, a delicate task assignment rule is needed to manipulate the completion of various tasks efficiently.

If business processes are managed utilizing BPMS systematically, the efficiency and execution quality of the process can be improved and customer responsiveness and innovation speed will be augmented. The key performance measure in the execution quality metric of business process is cycle time, and reduction of cycle time is the most important factor in improvement. Reductions in cycle time may be accomplished through efficient scheduling, input control, workload balancing, variability reduction, and etc [20]. Reduction of cycle time by workload balancing in distributing workload to all agents is especially useful for human resources. This method fundamentally prevents the concentration of workload to one agent, therefore guaranteeing performance regardless of the size of the total workload.

In this paper, an analytic process model is presented, which is based on probability and can be used to analyze the performance of execution. However, this analytic process model is still task-based process definition, so in order to transform to agent-based process definition with the same meaning, process queueing network is implemented. This queueing network model represents a dual problem of the analytic process model, in which an agent is regarded as a server. The workload of an agent is considered as server utilization and the task assignment policy can be determined by balancing workloads. This will serve to minimize the workloads of all agents, therefore maximizing the overall process efficiency.

The major contribution of this paper shall be that process execution is analyzed in consideration with agent capacity. Although many researchers used queueing network to analyze processes [1,5,14,20,26,27], so far, most of them have not considered the agent's ability of accomplishing multiple tasks, since modeled queueing network have been based on each task and not on its agent. Another application of the results can include capacity planning of agents in advance and business process optimization in reengineering context.

This paper is organized as follows. Section 2 provides a review of literature on efficient process execution and application of queueing network to BPMS. The significance of business process execution is described in Section 3, and the method of generating analytic process model is presented in Section 4. In Section 5, the analytic process model is transformed into a process queueing network model. Section 6 covers the workload balancing in the process queueing network. The experimental results of the proposed methodology are presented in Section 7, followed by the conclusions.

2 Related Work

There are extensive researches on cycle time reduction in manufacturing systems area. One of them is job shop scheduling problem, in which efficient production schedules are found to optimize performance measures such as flow time and lateness [3,21]. The results of this type of research can be applied to problems in business process, but complexities and probabilistic nature of the business process prohibits straightforward application of the research. Another conventional research area investigating efficient execution of business process is project management. Project management is the effort of planning and administrating special business processes, which are to be carried out only once. It controls progress of the process by using *critical path*. Two typical methods of analyzing critical path are Program Evaluation and Review Technique (PERT) and Critical Path Method (CPM) [17]. PERT/CPM examines critical path with the assumption of infinite resource and makes resource capacity plan to improve the critical path. Therefore, it is difficult to apply the result in case of limited resources such as business process.

In general, we can say that performance of business process depends on the method of assigning tasks to agents. One simple and effective approach is to assign tasks using dispatching rules such as SPT (shortest processing time), EDD (Earliest Due Date), and MST (Minimum Slack Time) [6,23]. The strength of these is that they can be easily employed to almost every system. However the weakness is that they cannot guarantee performance in complex systems such as business process. Another approach is that of using detailed role information to govern the manner of assigning tasks [4,24]. This approach indirectly attempts to enhance the process performance by determining the most suitable agent based on its preference.

Load balancing is a methodology for improving performance of systems with limited resource in various research areas such as distributed systems and parallel computing [7], computational grids [11], database management systems [22], and etc. In relation to workflow, Jin et al. [15] has proposed a means of load balancing among workflow engines to ensure scalability of distributed workflow management systems. Not all aspects of a business process may be automated, or automatable, thus requiring that BPMS should work in partnership with human agents. Therefore, workload balancing of agents is still important irrespective of aim of performance [19]. However, little has been done on the workload of agents

Employing queueing models as analytic models for business process has been well researched for various purposes in numerous ways. Narahari et al. [20] analyzed cycle time of new product development by modeling organization's departments as queueing servers, and proposed several ways of reducing cycle time. Son and Kim [26] suggested a capacity planning scheme for satisfying process due date by modeling tasks of business process as queueing servers. Chang et al. [5] studied techniques of identifying critical path in business process with the same scheme. Stochastic Workflow Net (SWN) is developed for analyzing the business process, which is represented as Petri Net, using queueing theory. Therefore, SWN can be used to analyze process performance and to plan agent capacity. [1,14,27] Probabilistic Timed Graph does not employ queueing models but it is still based on probabilities of events in business process and provides the better way of managing agents' schedules [8].

In most of the studies in business process based on queueing theory, it has been presumed that the capacity of agents is infinite or that one agent is dedicated to only one task. These assumptions may hinder more accurate descriptions of the real business process. Therefore, we are in need of a new model reflecting the fact that real agents have their own capacity and the ability of accomplishing multiple tasks.

3 Business Process Execution and Task Assignment Policies

The three major steps of using BPMS are design of a new process, enactment & management of the process, and analysis of the process by using the execution results [2]. This section presents a specific case of process execution in BPMS. In this case, it can be found that the cycle time of the process may become increased if the process is executed without desirable assignment rule. The solution of this problem is also suggested.

Fig. 1 shows a loan process in online banking, composed of *Application Check, History Review, Credit Inquiry*, and *Loan Granting*. The role and mean processing time are denoted at the bottom of each task. Both *History Review* and *Credit Inquiry* are executed simultaneously, following the completion of *Application Check*. Then the last task, *Loan Granting*, is executed as in the temporal precedence. The roles performing the tasks are *BizApp, Clerk*, and *Manager*, and each role has its own agents, *Srv1, Mary*, and *Bill* respectively.

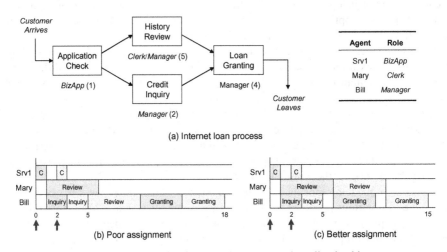

(a) Internet loan process

(b) Poor assignment   (c) Better assignment

Fig. 1. An example of internet loan process in online banking

In Fig. 1, (b) and (c) are real task assignment cases that show how the performance of a system can be deteriorated while using an improper assignment rule. Two orders are generated at time 0 and 2 in both (b) and (c). If we view the situation of task assignments at time 5, the first order has finished *Application Check* and *Credit Inquiry*, and Mary is in the clergy role of doing *History Review*. The second order also has finished *Application Check* and *Credit Inquiry*. At this time, if there is no special task assignment rule in BPMS, *History Review* of the second order will be assigned to Bill because he can perform the task and is now idle. This result is shown at (b) and the completion time of two orders is time 18. However, another case (c) represents a more desirable task assignment in which there is an efficient assignment rule. Although Bill can start *History Review* of the second order at time 5, he will not perform it but rather he will be idle for a short time. However, he will start *Loan Granting* of the first order upon completion of *History Review* by Mary, and Mary will begin *History Review* of the second order. It can be observed that the two orders have a completion time of 15 with this assignment rule. In other word, although there is a variable of idle time in the agents, it can be advantageous in the final outcome. The assignment rule in (c) takes constraints of agents' capacity into consideration, thereby demonstrating that workload balancing can make the execution of process more efficient.

As seen in the above example, process execution in BPMS means a kind of scheduling, which determines which tasks are assigned to which agents. The task assignment rule analyzed in this paper uses proprietary work list and static dispatching rule, FIFO (First In First Out). Although it seems that shared work list and dynamic dispatching have advantages in that shared work list make the assignment more efficient by the common usage of a work list and dynamic dispatching adjusts the sequence of tasks along with time, proprietary work lists can make the assignment more elaborate for each agent and static dispatching can make the scheduling stable in the long run. These advantages are coincident with the insight of the example in this section and will be verified by the experimental simulation in the following section.

4   Analytic Process Model

In this section, we suggest *analytic process model,* which serves as an intermediate model from business process model to process queueing model that is used to analyze the workload in the view of agent. The analytic process model provides the information about business process flow and agents executing tasks. In particular, it focuses on the reporting of the essential information for performance analysis rather than the precise specifications used by BPMS for process execution. These features of the analytic process model can be easily applied to various types of analyses such as simulation for Business Process Reengineering (BPR).

In general, the process model in BPMS includes all of the detailed information for process automation. However, the level of detail required for a process model varies depending on the type of analysis. Furthermore, in order to achieve certain goals, it may be necessary to obtain other information that is not present in the process executing model as well. Suppose a business rule of *exemption of history review* in the process of Fig. 1. The rule of exemption of history review asserts that the applicants who have been issued a loan within the past month are exempted from the 'history review'. BPMS can automatically implement this type of rule with little effort by applying the rules in the composition and design phase of the model. If the aim is to analyze execution behavior of this process, however, the information about the *rate* of applicants exempted from the history review is more useful than the *reason* for the applicants to be exempted from history review. To reflect this kind of requirement, the analytic process model includes three types of statistical information; *customer arrival rate, structural execution probability,* and *average service rate.*

First, the customer arrival rate is the request rate of services embodied by business process. Customers who are requesting the services can be individuals, other companies or even automated systems. Second, the structural execution probability is the probability of representing execution dependency between two tasks. For example, if the task *t*1 and *t*2 are connected with link *l*, structural execution probability e_l is the probability of executing *t*2 when *t*1 is performed. This concept can be applied to loop structure and more general split structures of business process. Third, the average service rate is the ability of an agent to perform a specific task. The statistical information of the analytic process model can be estimated by domain experts at design phase or plainly collected from the execution history of the business process. In the following, we define such model.

Definition 1 (Analytic Process Model). An *analytic process model* for a business process is defined by a 5-tuple (Φ, T, L, A, R) which is characterized by the following.

   i) Φ is customer arrival rate.

   ii) *T* is a set of tasks.

   iii) $L \subseteq T \times T$ is a set of links and e_l is structural execution probability of $l \in L$.

   iv) *A* is a set of agents.

   v) $R \subseteq T \times A$ is a set of responsibilities on an agent for a task and $\mu_{t,a}$ is average service rate of agent *a* at task *t*, where $(t, a) \in R$.

Fig. 2 depicts the analytic process model after adding two more rules to the business process illustrated in Fig. 1. The new rules are i) the exemption of history review stated above and ii) the rework of the previous two tasks (history review and credit inquiry) because of loan granting problems. Here, a set of tasks *T* is $\{t1, t2, t3, t4\}$ = {*Application check, History review, Credit inquiry, Loan granting*} and a set of agents *A* is $\{a1, a2, a3\}$ = {Srv1, Mary, Bill}. From the role information, a set of responsibilities *R* is {(*t*1, *a*1), (*t*2, *a*2), (*t*2, *a*3), (*t*3, *a*3), (*t*4, *a*3)}. We assume customer arrival rate, structural execution probability, and average service rate are collected from the history of former process execution. The value of structural execution probability is labeled near the link. No label indicates the probability is 1.0.

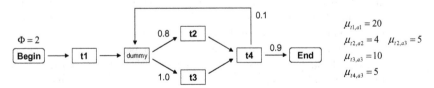

Fig. 2. The analytic process model of the business process in Fig. 1

If we consult this analytic process model, we become aware of some detailed information at execution phase of the business process as follows. For a unit time, there are two customers on the average who request services. After performing task $t1$, task $t3$ is always performed and $t2$ is performed with probability 0.8. There is rework with probability 0.1 after $t4$. In order to model the rework, a *dummy* task is inserted after $t1$. We can perceive that a manager, Bill, could handle the task 'History Review' faster than a clerk, Mary, $(\mu_{t2,a2} < \mu_{t2,a3})$. Again, the information above is only the statistical value for analysis by eliminating details of process execution like the business rules we stated above.

Remark 1. You may refer to Appendix for precise meaning of the split structure of analytic process model.

We transform business process into queueing model from which we can measure the workload of agents. The transformation is carried out based on the analyzed result of information in analytic process model and the information itself. We need to know the total quantity of tasks in order to calculate the workload of agents during the execution of the business process.

Definition 2 (Expected Execution Frequency). *Expected execution frequency* of t, denoted by f_t, is the frequency of performing specific task t when the business process is executed once.

The expected execution frequency is calculated from the structural execution probability of analytic process model. This technique is also based on the research of Eder el al. [8], and we append logic to deal with the loop structure, which is not included in their research. A similar study for loop structure is the research of Chang et al. [5].
When the customer arrival rate is given, the number of occurrences of performing specific tasks per unit time is easily calculated by using expected execution frequency.

Definition 3 (Task Arrival Rate). *Task arrival rate* of t, denoted by λ_t, is the number of occurrences of performing a task t per unit time when the business process is constantly executed by customers. Given the customer arrival rate Φ and the expected execution frequency of task t, the task arrival rate of t is determined as $\Phi \cdot f_t$.

In the example process of Fig. 2, the expected execution frequency, $\{f_{t1}, f_{t2}, f_{t3}, f_{t4}\}$ is computed to $\{1, 8/9, 10/9, 10/9\}$ and the task arrival rate, $\{\lambda_{t1}, \lambda_{t2}, \lambda_{t3}, \lambda_{t4}\}$ is $\{2, 16/9, 20/9, 20/9\}$. The expected execution frequency of $t3$ and $t4$ is greater than 1 because the rework occurs with the probability 0.1 after $t4$.

5 Process Queueing Network

The business processes handled by BPMS should have the characteristics of formality, predictability, and stability in general. The formality in business process enables the analysis of various aspects in detail, and the predictability and stability provides opportunities for building queueing models. In this section, we propose *process queueing network* based on the above characteristics and compute the workload of agents by using the results. The difference between general queueing network and process queueing network is that the model deals with unique properties in business process.

In the process queueing network, agents are modeled as queueing servers and are named *agent server*. If this accomplished, a queueing network can be built by connecting agent servers. The jobs arriving at a queueing server are the tasks assigned to the agent server. The detailed behavior of the process queueing network is determined by the execution manner of business process. The manner follows two rules described in Chapter 3. First, whenever BPMS has a job to process, it explicitly selects one agent, who can perform the task, and assigns the task to the selected agent. Second, an agent performs every assigned task to itself with FIFO rule. At process execution phase, a task is assigned to an agent with predefined probability as defined below.

Definition 4 (Task Assignment Probability). *Task assignment probability* of a task t to an agent a, denoted by $p_{t,a}$, is the probability that an agent a is selected to perform a task t at business process execution, where $(t, a) \in R$ of analytic process model.

Remark 2. At process execution phase, it holds by Definition 3 and Definition 4 that the arrival rate of a task t which is assigned to an agent a becomes $p_{t,a} \cdot \lambda_t$. In addition, tasks to be executed should be executed only once and by one agent. Hence task assignment probability has a following constraint.

$$\sum_{for\ a,(t,a)\in R} p_{t,a} = 1, \qquad t \in T \tag{1}$$

A business process is transformed into process queueing network based on analytic process model and task assignment probability. The first step in the transformation is discovering the execution sequence of tasks using analytic process model. The route between agent servers means passing over a specific task between agents. A route of one task diverges into multiple routes, which are routed to agent servers corresponding to the agents that can execute the task. The probability that the task selects each route is task assignment probability. The split routes join together after departing from the agent servers. The merged route advances toward the next agent servers according to the execution sequence of tasks. The arrival rate of jobs entering into the queueing network from outside is the customer arrival rate of the analytic process model. With a tangible example, we will describe details of the process queueing network. Fig. 3 is process queueing network, which is transformed from the business process of Fig. 2. Agent servers $\{q1, q2, q3\}$ correspond to agents $\{a1, a2, a3\}$. For the purpose of illustration, each route is numbered. In this example, only agent $a1$ can perform task $t1$ and only $a3$ can perform task $t3$ and $t4$, thus task assignment probability $p_{t1,a1}$, $p_{t3,a3}$, and $p_{t4,a3}$ are all 1.0. These probabilities are not shown in Fig. 3.

When a customer requests a service provided by the business process in Fig. 2, a task $t1$ is required to be performed at first. Since only an agent $a1$ has responsibility for a task $t1$, route 1 enters into queueing network in Fig. 3 from outside and proceeds to $q1$. After completion of $t1$ by $a1$, $t2$ and $t3$ are required to be performed. As a result, the route departing from $q1$ diverges into two routes at point (s). One is route 2 for performing $t2$ and the other is route 3 for $t3$. Note that task $t3$ is always performed after $t1$ but $t2$ is conditionally performed with probability 0.8. In this case, structural execution probability is routing probability of the queueing network, and the probabilities are marked near point (s) in Fig. 3. Task $t2$ can be performed by $a2$ or $a3$. Therefore, route 2 diverges into two routes heading for $q2$ and $q3$ and, in this case, routing probability is the task assignment probability $(p_{t2,a2}, p_{t2,a3})$. The two routes that have come in $q2$ and $q3$ merge after departing from each server. Route 2 merges again with route 3, which departing from $q3$ at point (m) and the re-merged route (route 4) proceeds to $q3$ to perform $t4$. Route 5, which departs from $q3$ after finishing $t4$, diverges into two routes again at point (l). One merges with a route before point (s) for rework with probability 0.1. The other leaves the process queueing network with probability 0.9, which means termination of the business process. Each route has a label, which indicates arrival rate and service rate of a task corresponding to the route. For example, on route 2 there is a label $(p_{t2,a2} \cdot \lambda_{t2}$ 4) before $q2$. Route 2 corresponds with task $t2$ and the task arrival rate of $t2$ is λ_{t2} and $a2$ perform $t2$ with probability $p_{t2,a2}$. Therefore, the arrival rate of this route is $p_{t2,a2} \cdot \lambda_{t2}$, and average service rate of $a2$ at $t2$ is $\mu_{t2,a2}$ and its value is 4.

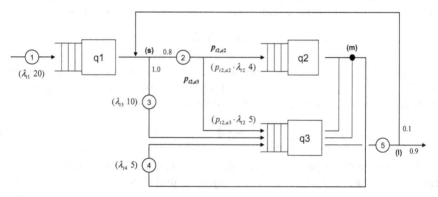

Fig. 3. The process queueing network of the analytic process model in Fig. 2. Task arrival rates, $\{\lambda_{t1}, \lambda_{t2}, \lambda_{t3}, \lambda_{t4}\}$ are equal to $\{2, 16/9, 20/9, 20/9\}$

Business process has several features, which are difficult to be represented by a general queueing network, so we have developed a process queueing network for supporting these features. In business process, upon the completion of a single task, multiple tasks following the task can be performed in parallel (task $t2$ and $t3$ in Fig. 2). In the case of a general queueing network, if there are routes from a server to multiple servers, jobs should select only one route and arrive at the server connected from the route. This constraint of the general queueing network prohibits modeling parallel execution of business process. The process queueing network relaxes the constraint. The split route at point (s) in Fig. 3 is the example of such a routing discipline. In addition, when tasks are performed in parallel in business process, there exists one point at which the parallel execution is terminated (task $t4$). At that point, execution threads are synchronized and the synchronized thread proceeds for performing following tasks. In process queueing network we can express this feature by marking the point (filled circle at point (m) of Fig. 3).

6   Workload Balancing

The workload of an agent can be measured by calculating utilization of a corresponding agent server. In Fig. 3, the types of tasks, which arrived at an agent server, are not identical, as the average service rate depends on the type of task. This means that the arrival pattern of tasks at the agent server is not a simple variable. Suppose that the execution dependency between tasks is static, i.e. it dose not depend on the current state of business process, and an ample number of tasks are performed. Then we could assume that the task types have multinomial distribution. As well, the service rate of an agent is assumed to have exponential distribution in general. The service time of the queueing server having this pattern has hyper-exponential distribution [10]. If there are r types of jobs, and the overall arriving rate of the jobs at a queueing server is λ, and for the type i of jobs the probability of arriving is p_i and the average service rate of the server is μ_i, then the utilization ρ of the server is computed as,

$$\rho = \sum \frac{\lambda \cdot p_i}{\mu_i} = \sum \frac{\lambda_i}{\mu_i}. \tag{2}$$

Equation 2 indicates that the total utilization of a server is the sum of the partial contributions of each type of jobs (λ_i/μ_i). Therefore the workload ld_a of an agent a, i.e. the utilization of an agent server corresponding to a, is as follows.

$$ld_a = \sum_{for\ t,(t,a)\in R} \frac{\lambda_t \cdot p_{t,a}}{\mu_{t,a}} = \Phi \cdot \sum_{for\ t,(t,a)\in R} \frac{f_t \cdot p_{t,a}}{\mu_{t,a}} \tag{3}$$

According to Equation 3, once we calculate average execution frequency f_t and average service rate $\mu_{t,a}$ and decide task assignment probability $p_{t,a}$, the workload of an agent is in proportion to the customer arrival rate Φ. This result comes from using the proprietary work list and static dispatching, which are the manners of executing business process in this research. That is, at process execution phase, the average number of tasks being assigned to an agent per unit time is constant for a sufficient period, and no one other than the agent can undertake the agent's tasks.

Now we can get the task assignment probability $p_{t,a}$ which balances workloads of all agents by solving the mathematical programming formula below. To balance the workloads, the objective of the program is defined as minimizing the maximum workload over all agents. The solution of Equation 4 is the task assignment probability which balance workloads.

$$\min \max_{a \in A} \{ld_a\}$$
$$s.t. \ 0 \leq p_{t,a} \leq 1 \quad (t,a) \in R$$
$$\sum_{a \in A, d_{t,a}} p_{t,a} = 1 \quad t \in T \tag{4}$$

Equation 4 is a linear optimization problem, which can be easily solved using a general OR solver. The expected workload of agents at process execution phase is calculated by using Equation 3 with the solution of Equation 4. If the workload is close to 1 or greater than 1, business process is expected to operate poorly in the real world. This means that the response time of certain agent goes to infinity, thus additional agents are needed for improving performance. It is not difficult to decide which role the new agents are required to possess. We can predict as well the capacity of an organization i.e. the customer arrival rate that the organization can manage.

The workload of each agent in Fig. 2, is obtained as follows:

$$ld_{a1} = \frac{2}{20},$$

$$ld_{a2} = \frac{16/9 \cdot p_{t2,a2}}{5} = \frac{16 p_{t2,a2}}{45}, \tag{5}$$

$$ld_{a3} = \frac{16/9 \cdot p_{t2,a3}}{4} + \frac{20/9}{10} + \frac{20/9}{5} = \frac{4 p_{t2,a3}}{9} + \frac{6}{9}.$$

The solution of Equation 4 with Equation 5 is the task assignment probability $\{p_{t2,a2} = 1, p_{t2,a3} = 0\}$, which is intended to balance workloads. For efficient process execution, as a result, all $t2$ (*History Review*) must be assigned to $a2$ (Mary) even though $a3$ (Bill) can process $t2$ faster than agent $a2$. That is, for a long term performance, it is not preferred that *History Review* is assigned to Bill even when he is idle, since he has the responsibility for not only *History Review* but also *Credit Inquiry* and *Loan Granting*. This result is in accordance with implication of Chapter 3.

7 Experimental Results

In this section we apply the proposed research results to a real business process, and optimal task assignment parameters are determined by using linear programming formula. Following, we confirm that the business process is more efficient than any other task assignment rules by using simulation with the solved task assignment parameters. First of all, an example process model for the validation is Fig. 4, which is composed of 12 tasks and the structural execution probabilities that are collected from execution history data or consultation of process expert.

Table 1 shows the information of agents and mean service time for each task. For example task $t1$ can be assigned to agent $a1$ only and its mean service time is 7. It also shows that task $t2$ can be assigned to agent $a2$ and $a3$, which are taken time 3 and 2 respectively.

In order to balance workload for each agent of example process in Fig. 4 as proposed in this paper, task assignment probabilities are found with the process queueing network and linear programming formula, and the results are Table 2. The meaning of probabilities for each task is the execution assignment ratio of each agent for the task. For example, $t2$ can be assigned to agent $a2$ and $a3$, and their task assignment probabilities should be 0.06 and 0.94 respectively in order to balance workload. This means that $t2$ has to be assigned to $a3$ in order to minimize the cycle time of the total process. In the same manner, $t3$ can be assigned to $a2$, $a3$, $a4$, $a5$, however, it shows that $a2$ is most desirable to perform $t3$. Also it shows that the expected workload of each agent is balanced to 0.878 when customer arrival rate Φ is 1/12.

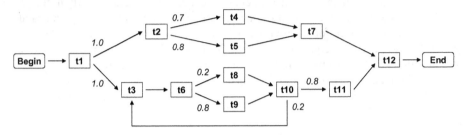

Fig. 4. An example process for simulation

Table 1. Mean service time of each agent for specific task

	$t1$	$t2$	$t3$	$t4$	$T5$	$t6$	$t7$	$t8$	$t9$	$t10$	$t11$	$T12$
$a1$	7	-	-	-	5	8	-	2	4	5	-	6
$a2$	-	3	5	2	-	-	8	1	-	-	3	-
$a3$	-	2	7	2	-	-	8	1	-	-	2	-
$a4$	-	-	6	2	-	6	7	1	-	3	2	-
$a5$	-	-	7	3	5	-	8	1	2	-	1	8

Table 2. Task-Agent Probability for workload balancing

	$t1$	$t2$	$t3$	$t4$	$t5$	$t6$	$t7$	$t8$	$t9$	$t10$	$t11$	$t12$	Load
$a1$	1.00	-	-	-	×	0.10	-	×	×	×	-	0.43	0.878
$a2$	-	0.06	0.95	1.00	-	-	×	×	-	-	1.00	-	0.878
$a3$	-	0.94	0.05	×	-	-	1.00	1.00	-	-	×	-	0.878
$a4$	-	-	×	×	-	0.90	×	×	-	1.00	×	-	0.878
$a5$	-	-	×	×	1.00	-	×	×	1.00	-	×	0.57	0.878

As stated in the previous section, the proprietary work list and static dispatching rules are used to execute the example process using the results of Table 2. The experimental simulations of its operation are performed to obtain the cycle time of the total process and workload for each agent. These results are compared with other task assignment rules to prove the excellence of the proposed assignment rules. The first assignment rule is random task assignment without special rules, the second is Early Due Date (EDD) rule, which maintains the sequence of due date in the work list, and the last one is the assignment rules proposed in this paper. In all three cases, the customer arrival rate Φ are changed from 1/20 to 1/12 in order to simulate the various environments.

Let us compare the three cases in view of cycle time (Fig.5 (a)). In the case that total workload is small, e.g. 1/20, EDD shows the minimum values. However, if the

total workload is large, e.g. 1/12, the cycle times of Random and EDD increase exponentially. (Note that the scale of the cycle time axis is logarithm.) On the contrary, the
cycle time of Load Balancing does not increase greatly. If we compare the three cases
in view of workload balancing (Fig. 5 (b)), Random and EDD do not balance the
workload if the total workload is increased. On the contrary, in the Load Balancing,
the workload of each agent is balanced similarly regardless of the total workload. Also
we can verify the predictability of our method, in that all of workloads are approximately 88% when customer arrival rate is 1/12.

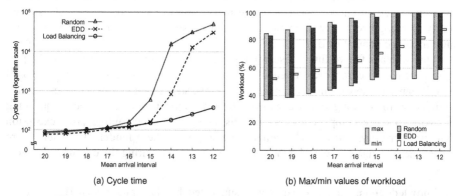

(a) Cycle time   (b) Max/min values of workload

Fig. 5. Experimental results with Random, EDD, and Load balancing rule.

If we summarize the results of experiments, the proposed method in this paper is
superior in the view of cycle time and workload balance of each agent when the total
workload is large. However when the total workload is at low level, the performance
is not significantly enhanced. This is because the objective function is not for the
reduction of cycle time itself, but for the workload balancing. We also find that we can
shorten the cycle time by balancing workload of each agent.

8   Conclusions

In order to execute business process in an efficient way, this paper presents a method
of balancing the workload of agents who perform the tasks in the business process.
There are four principle steps in achieving this. First, analytic process model is presented using process specification and execution history data. This model eliminates
many semantics in the real execution, but includes statistical information of flows that
is found not in the specification but in the execution history data. Second, a process
queueing network is built from the analytic process model in order to establish task
assignment policies for efficient execution of the business process. The process
queueing network is built based on agents, so the agents are regarded as servers. As
far as we know, this is an original work in the sense that the capacity of agents in the
execution phase is considered in the design phase. Third, as a practical use of the
process queueing network, workload balancing is presented to improve overall busi-

ness process efficiency using linear programming formula. Finally, a set of simulation experiments is conducted in order to validate the performance with respect to other task assignment rules, such as random, EDD, etc.

The method presented in this paper possesses the following advantages. First, the resource utilization policies of some business processes already in operation can be established, leading from the local optimum to the global optimum in view of total process. Second, the method is very useful in designing a new business process. When a new business process is launched, the necessary number of agents and their accompanying skills can be determined in advance utilizing this method. Third, the method is useful when an improvement to the current process is needed, because of its capability to recognize problems in the inefficient processes. This advantage is also important in the context of BPR.

This all leads to two future research topics. In the short run, we can extend the performance measure of process queueing network from the workload of agents proposed in this paper to the various performance measures, such as cycle time, tardiness or cost efficiency. In the long run, we will pursue the application of the process queueing network to more complex process models such as flexible routing [16], exception handling, priority, and etc. The collective analyses of these models, will yield more precise knowledge of the problems that can be generated during the execution of business processes.

Acknowledgement. This research was supported by the grant No. R01-2002-000-00155-0 from the Basic Research Program of the Korea Science & Engineering Foundation.

References

1. van der Aalst, W.M.P., van Hee, K.M., Reijers, H.A.: Analysis of Discrete-Time Stochastic Petri Nets. Statistica Neerlandica 54 (2000) 237–255
2. van der Aalst, W.M.P., ter Hofstede, A.H.M., Weske, M.: Business Process Management: A Survey. In: BPM 2003. Lecture Notes in Computer Science, Vol. 2678. Springer-Verlag, Berlin Heidelberg New York (2003) 13–24
3. Baker, K. R.: Introduction to Sequencing and Scheduling. John Wiley & Sons, New York (1974)
4. Bussler, C., Jablonski, S.: Policy Resolution in Workflow management Systems. In: Proceedings of the 28th Hawaii International Conference on System Sciences (HICSS-28), Hawaii (1995) 831–840
5. Chang, D., Son, J., and Kim, M.: Critical Path Identification in the Context of a Workflow. Information and Software Technology 44 (2002) 405-417
6. Cichocki, A., Helal, A.A., Rusinkiewicz, M., Woelk, D.:, Workflow and Process Automation: Concepts and Technology. Kluwer Academic Publishers, Boston (1998)
7. Culler, D.E., Singh, J.P., Gupta, A.: Parallel Computer Architecture: a Hardware/Software Approach. Morgan Kaufmann Publishers, San Francisco (1999)
8. Eder, J., Pichler, H., Gruber, W., Ninaus, M.: Personal Schedules for Workflow Systems. In: BPM 2003. Lecture Notes in Computer Science, Vol. 2678. Springer-Verlag, Berlin Heidelberg New York (2003) 216–231

9. Georgakopoulos, D., Hornick, M., Sheth, A.: An Overview of Workflow Management: From Process Modeling to Workflow Automation Infrastructure. Distributed and Parallel Databases 3 (1995) 119–153

10. Gross, D., Harris, C.M.: Fundamentals of Queueing Theory. John Wiley & Sons, New York (1998)

11. Grosu, D., Chronopoulos, A.T.: Algorithmic Mechanism Design for Load Balancing in Distributed Systems. In: Proceedings of 2002 IEEE International Conference on Cluster Computing, Chicago (2002) 445–450

12. Hammer, M., The Agenda: What Every Business Must Do to Dominate the Decade. Crown Business, New York (2001)

13. Hammer, M., Champy, J.:, Reengineering the Corporation: A Manifesto for Business Revolution. HarperBusiness, New York (1993)

14. van Hee, K.M., Reijers, H.A.: An Analytical Method for Computing Throughput Times in Stochastic Workflow Nets. In: Proceedings of the 11th European Simulation Symposium, Delft (1999) 635–643

15. Jin, L.-J., Casati, F., Sayal, M., Shan, M.-C.: Load Balancing In Distributed Workflow Management System. In: Proceedings of the 2001 ACM Symposium on Applied computing (SAC'01), Las Vegas (2001) 522–530

16. Kumar, A., Zhao, J.L.: Dynamic Routing and Operational Controls in Workflow Management Systems. Management Science 45 (1999) 253–272

17. Lewis, J.P.: Fundamentals of Project Management: Developing Core Competencies to Help Outperform the Competition, 2nd edt., AMACOM, New York, (2002)

18. Milojicic, D.S., Pjevac, M.: LoadBalacing Survey. In: Proceedings of the Autumn 1991 EurOpen Conference, Budapest (1991)

19. Myers, K.L., Berry, P.M.: At the Boundary of Workflow and AI. In: Proceedings of the 16th National Conference on Artificial Intelligence (AAAI-99) Workshop on Agent Based Systems in Business, Orlando (1999)

20. Narahari, Y., Viswanadham, N.: Lead Time Modeling and Acceleration of Product Design and Development. IEEE Transaction on Robotics and Automation 15 (1999) 882–896

21. Pinedo, M.: Scheduling: Theory, Algorithms and Systems. Prentice-Hall, Englewood Cliffs (1995)

22. Rahm, E.: Dynamic Load balancing in Parallel Database Systems. In: Proceeding of Euro-Par 96 Conference. Lecture Notes in Computer Science, Vol. 1123. Springer-Verlag, Berlin Heidelberg New York (1996)

23. Rhee, S.-H., Bae, H., Seo, Y.: Efficient Workflow Management through the Introduction of TOC Concepts. In: Proceedings of the 8th Annual International Conference on Industrial Engineering Theory, Las Vegas (2003)

24. Shen, M., Tzeng, G.-H., Liu, D.-R.: Multi-Criteria Task Assignment in Workflow Management Systems. In: Proceedings of the 36th Hawaii International Conference on System Sciences (HICSS-36), Hawaii (2002) 202–210

25. Smith, H., Fingar, P.:, Business Process Management: The Third Wave. Meghan-Kiffer, Tampa (2003)

26. Son, J., Kim, M.: Improving the Performance of Time-Constrained Workflow Processing, Journal of Systems and Software 58 (2001) 211-219.

27. Zerguini, L., van Hee, K.M., A New Reduction Method for the Analysis of Large Workflow Models. In: Proceedings of the Joint Annual Conference of the GI Special Interest Groups "Petrinetze und verwandte Systemmodelle" and EMISA (Promise 2002), Potsdam (2002) 188-201

Appendix: Split Structure of Analytic Process Model

Since more than one task in business process can be executed in parallel, split structure has to be used to represent dependency between tasks. Without loss of generality, we will use an example of split structure having two branches and describe the meaning of structural execution probability e_l.

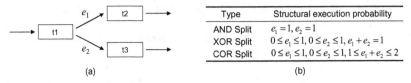

Type	Structural execution probability
AND Split	$e_1 = 1, e_2 = 1$
XOR Split	$0 \le e_1 \le 1, 0 \le e_2 \le 1, e_1 + e_2 = 1$
COR Split	$0 \le e_1 \le 1, 0 \le e_2 \le 1, 1 \le e_1 + e_2 \le 2$

(a)   (b)

Fig. 6. An example of the split structure of analytic process model

Fig. 6 (a) is a fragment of process flow that designed with split structure. Structural execution probability is marked on a link and it shows that if task $t1$ is performed, then the probability of performing $t1$ is e_1 and $t2$ is e2. In this split structure, there occur three exclusive events after finishing task $t1$. These events are i) performing both $t2$ and $t3$, and ii) performing only $t2$, and iii) performing only $t3$. The probabilities of the events are calculated based on the structural execution probability e_1 and e2, in the following. Define T_1, T_2, and T_3 as representing events of performing $t1$, $t2$, and $t3$ respectively. From the definition of structural execution probability, following holds.

$$Pr\{T_2|T_1\} = e_1, Pr\{T_3|T_1\} = e_2 \tag{6}$$

In business process there is no case that neither $t2$ nor $t3$ is performed after performing $t1$ in ordinary case. Define $(T_2 \cup T_3)$ as an event of performing T_2 or T_3, and T^C as a complement event of T, and following holds.

$$Pr\{(T_2 \cup T_3)^C|T_1\} = 0 \tag{7}$$

Therefore, if we define $(T_2 \cap T_3)$ as the event that T_2 and T_3 occur at the same time, then the probability of performing both $t2$ and $t3$ after finishing $t1$ is,

$$Pr\{T_2 \cap T_3|T_1\} = Pr\{T_2|T_1\} + Pr\{T_3|T_1\} - Pr\{T_2 \cup T_3|T_1\} = e_1 + e_2 - 1 . \tag{8}$$

Define $(T_2 - T_3)$ as the event of T_2 occurring without T_3, and $(T_3 - T_2)$ as the opposite event of the event, then the probability of performing either only $t2$ or only $t3$ is,

$$Pr\{T_2 - T_3|T_1\} = 1 - Pr\{(T_2 \cup T_3)^C|T_1\} - Pr\{T_3\} = 1 - e_2 ,$$

$$Pr\{T_3 - T_2|T_1\} = 1 - e_1 . \tag{9}$$

Fig. 6 (b) shows the types of split structures that employed by process model of commercial BPMS products, and the relation with our split model. 'AND split' in the figure means that after finishing $t1$, always both $t2$ and $t3$ are required to performed. 'XOR split' means either only $t2$ or only $t3$ is required to performed and 'COR' (Conditional OR) means $t2$ and $t3$ are required to performed according to the context of process execution.

Interactive Workflow Mining

Markus Hammori[1], Joachim Herbst[1], and Niko Kleiner[2]

[1] DaimlerChrysler AG, Research & Technology, P.O. Box 2360, 89013 Ulm,
Germany, {Markus.Hammori, Joachim.J.Herbst}@DaimlerChrysler.com
[2] University of Ulm, Faculty for Computer Science, 89069 Ulm, Germany,
Nikolaus.Kleiner@informatik.uni-ulm.de

Abstract. Workflow or process mining is concerned with deriving a
workflow model from observed behavior described in a workflow log.
Experience from applying our workflow mining system InWoLvE in experiments and practical applications has shown that workflow mining is a
highly interactive process. The mining expert iteratively approaches the
result by varying the parameters of the mining tool and verifying the mined models. Our tool InWoLvE was not designed for intensive interactive
usage making practical usage more than difficult. In this contribution
we describe the main requirements for an interactive workflow mining
system and how we derived these. We outline two selected concepts: a
special layout algorithm that is stable against small changes of the model thus allowing the workflow mining expert to maintain a mental map
of the workflow and a validation procedure helping the mining expert
in his decision for the final result. These and other important concepts
have been implemented in the first prototype of an interactive workflow
mining system called ProTo.

1 Introduction

Explicit workflow models are the basis for many advanced technologies like process oriented information systems or business process performance management.
In highly dynamic environments with ever changing processes such as the product development domain in the automotive industry acquiring and representing this process knowledge is one of the main bottlenecks for applying these
advanced technologies. Recently there has been an increasing interest in using
techniques from data mining and machine learning to support this task [1,2,3].
This approach has also been termed as process or workflow mining. The basic
idea of the workflow mining approach is to collect traces of executions and to
derive a workflow model from these observations. This is useful for example if
some information system supporting the process, that logs all relevant events,
is already in place before the workflow model is defined. Furthermore workflow
mining techniques and advanced workflow technology, which is moving towards
more operational flexibility [4,5,6], enable an evolutionary approach to the development of workflow applications.

Experiences with our workflow mining tool InWoLvE [7,3,8] have shown that
workflow mining is a highly interactive process. The mining expert iteratively

J. Desel, B. Pernici, and M. Weske (Eds.): BPM 2004, LNCS 3080, pp. 211–226, 2004.
© Springer-Verlag Berlin Heidelberg 2004

approaches the result by varying the parameters of the mining tool and verifying the mined models. As our tool InWoLvE is command-line oriented, producing text-files as output, it is not really suited for intensive interactive usage. This paper is the first contribution dealing with those aspects of the workflow mining process, that require user interaction. This leads to a number of new requirements, not yet addressed in this research field. In the course of our work we were able to solve some of the more challenging ones, as we will discuss below.

This paper is organized as follows: Section 2 gives a short overview of the InWoLvE workflow mining system. In section 3 we explain, how we systematically gathered requirements for an interactive workflow mining tool, before we outline two of the mayor concepts needed for interactive workflow mining in section 4. These concepts have been implemented in a first prototype called ProTo, which is presented in section 5. We conclude discussing related work in section 6 and giving an outlook on future work in section 7.

2   The InWoLvE Workflow Mining System

In this section we give a short overview of the InWoLvE (*Inductive Workflow Learning via Examples*) workflow mining system [7,3]. InWoLvE solves the workflow mining task in two steps: the induction and the transformation step.

In the induction step a stochastic activity graph (SAG) [7,3] is induced from the workflow log. The induction algorithm can be described as a graph generation algorithm that is embedded into a search procedure.

The search procedure borrows ideas from machine learning and grammatical inference [9]. It searches for a mapping from activity instances in the workflow log to activity nodes of a workflow model. The search space can be described as a lattice of such mappings. Between the mappings there is a partial ordering (more general than/more specific than). The lattice is limited by a top or most general mapping (all activity instances with name X are mapped to one single activity node with name X) and a bottom or most specific element (the mapping is a bijection between activity instances in the log and activity nodes of a workflow model). Our search algorithm searches top down starting with the most general mapping for an optimal mapping. More specific mappings are created using a split operator. The graph generation algorithm uses a fixed mapping from instances to activity nodes as input and it generates a stochastic activity graph for this mapping. For the search algorithm we selected beam-search. It is guided by the log likelihood (LLH) of the SAG per sample.

In the transformation step the SAG is transformed into a block-structured workflow-model in the ADONIS definition language (ADL) [10,3]. This step is needed because the stochastic activity graph provided by the induction phase does not explicitly distinguish alternative and parallel routing. The transformation phase can be decomposed into three main steps: The analysis of the synchronization structures of the workflow instances in the workflow log, the generation of the synchronization structure of the workflow model and the generation of the model. Details of the transformation steps are given in [7,3].

The induction and the transformation algorithms outlined above - which are called `splitPar` and `SAGtoADL` - have been implemented in the InWoLvE prototype. InWoLvE was completely realized in Microsoft Visual C++. It understands input files containing the example set in three different formats. It accepts event traces in the APF-format, which is the native format of the ADONIS [11] business process management system, it accepts simple ASCII-files, where each workflow instance is encoded as a character string and it supports the common XML-format described in [1]. As output InWoLvE produces files in the ADL format, which can be imported by ADONIS.

3   Requirements Analysis

For our requirements analysis we used three different approaches: We conducted a series of experiments using the combined system based on InWoLvE and ADONIS, we analyzed other workflow mining tools for interactive aspects and finally evaluated methods dealing with interactivity in the related research area of data mining. In this contribution we will present only results obtained using the first approach, since it provided nearly all of the relevant requirements. The other two approaches are addressed in [8]. For a more complete description of the conducted experiments we refer to [8], [7] and [3].

This section is organized as follows. The experimental work with our existing prototype resulted in a kind of standard workflow mining process. This process is roughly described in the next subsection. In the following subsections we deduce requirements for each of the three major steps of this workflow mining process. The identified requirements are highlighted using italics.

3.1   The Workflow Mining Process

The series of experiments with our prototype based on InWoLvE and ADONIS indicate that workflow mining is not a completely automatic task but rather a highly interactive process requiring many decisions by the mining expert. The general workflow mining process that best represents the way we worked with our prototype consists of three mayor steps:

1. Choosing the initial parameters for InWoLvE
2. Visualizing and evaluating the result in ADONIS
3. Deciding on the next step:
    a) Modifying parameters for a new iteration
    b) Choosing a result model

3.2   Choosing the Initial Parameters

In order to start the mining process a first set of parameters is needed. These parameters among others include the number of examples to be used, the number of beams of the search algorithm and a variable, that determines the degree of specialization (see [7] for details). The selection of the settings depends to some extent on the amount and quality of the available log-data and the size and complexity of the workflow model. Some useful measures for the selection of initial parameters are implicitly stored in the workflow-log. *We demand from an interactive workflow mining tool that it should provide log statistics helping the mining expert to select good starting parameters. These should include:*

- *The total number of traces.*
- *The number of different traces.*
- *A rough estimation of the maturity of the log by setting the total number of traces in relation with the number of different traces.*
- *The average number of events per trace as a rough estimation of the complexity of the workflow.*

3.3   Visualizing and Evaluating the Result

The next main step is to examine the results and to understand the mined workflow models to get an impression of the calculation's success. A result consists of a number of models, marking the path in the search tree according to the chosen parameters. As InWoLvE writes its results into text-files after finishing a calculation, every result the user wants to view has to be manually imported to ADONIS. In this setup there exist a number of problems, that make the mining process tiresome and can prevent the user from working efficiently:

1. Loading every single result into an external visualization component is time consuming and characterized by repetitive user interactions. *Therefore we require that there should be a much deeper integration of calculation and visualization.*
2. There exists no means to follow a calculation's progress. The user has no means to estimate the quality of the ongoing calculation and he has no indication of how long it will take until the calculation is finished. *We require that mining tool should allow a visualization of intermediate results as soon as they are available and not only at the end of a complete calculation. Furthermore the mining tool should provide the user some measure of progress and allow him to influence a running calculation.*
3. Managing the results on a text-file basis in a way that preserves them for later usage requires a lot of discipline. *The workflow mining tool should help the user in maintaining a history of calculations and allow him to revisit results at a later point in time.*
4. The layout mechanisms provided by ADONIS do not support the mining process in an optimal way:
   - Small differences between two models often cause unnecessary drastic changes in the layout
   - Restrictions of the ADL language, which in our opinion enable a more concise layout are not exploited

An example of this is shown in Fig. 1 where we highlighted the unnecessary changes between two successive models. *As a consequence we require that an interactive workflow mining tool should provide a special layout component, which is more stable against changes and which provides a more concise layout. In addition a mechanism helping the user to locate differences between two models would be helpful.*

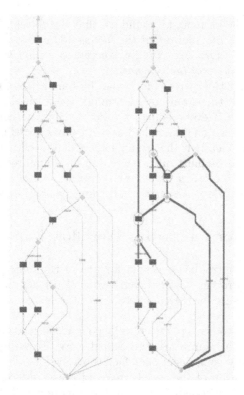

Fig. 1. Unnecessary changes in the layout

3.4   Deciding on the Next Step

Based on the information obtained from evaluating the results the user then has
to decide if another iteration with modified parameters is needed. The decision
for the final result is the hardest task in the workflow mining process. There are
three main problems that need to be considered:

1. Selecting the right model involves finding the right tradeoff between size
   of the model and the LLH. Our experiments showed, that the human eye
   usually outperforms the simple stopping criterion of InWoLvE based on the
   LLH. Experts use not only the LLH but also the model as a criterion for
   the decision. Over-generalization for example can sometimes be recognized if
   the model contains spaghetti-like links between its elements. Many repetitive
   patterns on the other hand may indicate over-specialization. *We demand that
   in addition to the visualization of models (see previous section) the workflow
   mining tool should provide an LLH-graph for the search path.*
2. The result is an element of the search space explored by InWoLvE. The
   users confidence in a selected result is influenced by the number of trials
   that were made by InWoLvE to further improve the LLH. If the system has
   performed huge number of trials without being able to improve the LLH

significantly, the user can be confidend that the choice of the result model is good. *Therefore we require that the tool should provide a graphical overview of the complete search tree with direct access to the models and an association with the parameters of the calculation.*

3. Whether or not the correct model can be found depends on the structural completeness of the examples. Informally the examples can be considered to be complete, if every behavior described by the correct model can be observed in at least one example. For a more precise definition we refer to [7]. In practical applications the mining expert does not know if the example set is complete. But he must make a decision for a final result. *For this purpose we require that the tool provides the user some measure of completeness that indicates how likely it is that further examples will introduce new behaviors.*

4   Concepts for Interactive Workflow Mining

In this section we introduce concepts for two of the more challenging requirements. First we introduce an improved layout algorithm and second we present an additional measure for the completeness of the mined models. For a detailed description we refer to [8].

Beyond these two concepts we developed various solutions to support those requirements, which require less theoretical work. These include post pruning of models, a history component that facilitates working with a large number of results, a visualization of the search tree and a user interface that enables the user to influence an ongoing calculation. For a more detailed discussion of these solutions we refer to [8].

4.1   Layout – The MaximumRecognitionLayout Algorithm

From the layout component we required that it should

1. generate layouts for successive results with maximum similarity
2. exploit the language restrictions of ADL

The first problem is special to workflow mining. Suppliers of workflow management systems and business process modelling tools usually provide layout algorithms optimized for static layout generation. The second problem is special to the modelling language we use.

Scientifically the first problem is related to the dynamic graph layout problem which has already been investigated by a number of authors [12,13] outside the business process domain. An evaluation of the various approaches showed, however, that none of them could be applied in our case (see Sect. 6), we therefore decided to develop a special layout algorithm to suit our needs.

Exploited Language Restrictions of ADL. The language restrictions of ADL that we exploited for a better layout algorithm can be summarized as follows:

- splits and joins are block-structured and thus form a subgraph with only one incoming and one outgoing edge
- the branches of a split are not connected amongst each other
- process start, activity and join vertices have exactly one successor

A more extensive explanation of properties of the ADL language can be found in [8].

Basic Principle of the MaximumRecognitionLayout Algorithm. Since the split operator of InWoLvE is not defined directly on the model but on the examples requiring a complex induction and transformation operation, there is no simple way to identify the incremental changes between two successive models. For this reason we decided to develop a static layout algorithm that deals with dynamic changes by using a very strict set of rules:

R1 Ignore edges that are part of a loop during the calculation of the layout.
R2 The process start vertex is always placed in the top level.
R3 The process stop vertex is always placed in a separate level below all other levels.
R4 Each branch of a decision is treated as a separate substructure with the maximum width of the branch.
R5 The split vertex is placed in a level above its successors.
R6 The join vertex is placed in a separate level below those of its predecessors.
R7 Each branch of a split is treated as a separate substructure with the maximum width of the branch.
R8 The successors of split and decision vertices are sorted according to a well-defined ordering.
R9 Edges are drawn around intermediate vertices
R10 Place the process stop vertex in the way that promises the least possible edge crossings.

As in many other layout algorithms [12] we divide the layout area into levels and columns, and try to find the best positions for the vertices. The algorithm can be split into three main steps

1. Calculating the level for each vertex
2. Setting the column for the vertices
3. Refining the layout in respect to edge-crossing and overlapping

Arranging the Vertices in Levels. The algorithm starts by sorting the vertices into levels. This is done using a breadth-first search on the graph. During this search we number the vertices in the order that they are visited, and assign them their levels. In this step we assure that the rules R2, R3, R5, R6 and R8 are met.

Rule R2 is automatically fulfilled by using the process start vertex as first vertex in the breadth-first search. We just assign it to level number one, and all other vertices will be placed in subsequent levels. In the same way rule R5 is automatically fulfilled, since all successors of a split vertex are automatically placed in a new level. In order to fulfill rule R6 we need to make sure that the level of a join vertex is set via the longest path towards it. We accomplish this by adjusting the level of the join vertex every time it is reached over a longer path. After calculating the levels for all vertices we make sure that rule R3 is fulfilled by putting the stop vertex in a separate level. Finally it is easy to modify the breadth-first search, to process the children in sorted order, thus implementing rule R8.

Computing the Column of the Vertices. The second important part of the layout algorithm is the calculation of a paths's width, and the assignment of the columns. For that purpose the algorithm traverses the graph in a depth-first search, while recursively calculating the width of the segments and setting their position at the same time.

The basic idea of calculating the width and assigning columns is shown in Fig. 2. The algorithm starts by splitting the graph into subgraphs. The width of each of those subgraphs is calculated and passed on upwards. In Fig. 2 the width of a subgraph is shown in the top left corner of the rectangle surrounding it. The value it passes on is noted just above that. In the given example the first split has an internal width of two, but will pass on a width of three because of its successors, thus setting the width of the left path to the correct value of three.

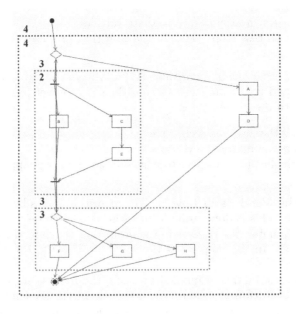

Fig. 2. Schematic split of the graph into subgraphs during the calculation.

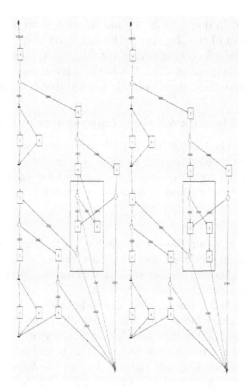

Fig. 3. Successive layouts generated by the MaximumRecognitionLayout Algorithm

The goal of this step is to assign each path of the graph its maximum width, thus implementing rules R4 and R7. By marking visited vertices we can locate and then ignore loops during this calculation, thus implementing rule R1.

Refinements. The goal of the final step of the layout algorithm is to implement a concept for preventing edge crossings and edges crossing vertices as far as possible. The requirement for change resistance gives us even less opportunities for optimization than in the general unrestricted setting. To this end the rules R9 and R10 are realized, as follows.

The most common solution to prevent edge crossings would be to move the vertices in a level into the position that causes the least number of crossings. We could not apply this approach because of rule R8. Furthermore we not only want to minimize edge crossings but also try to prevent edges from crossing vertices. At this stage there exists only a best practice method: using the location data computed in the previous steps we find the relevant areas, and draw edges not as straight lines but around intermediate vertices.

In order to implement R10 we need to find the placement for the process stop vertex that causes the least edge crossings. Due to some properties of the algorithm described in detail in [8] a good solution is to place the process stop vertex in the column of the shortest path connected to it.

Fig. 3 shows the effect of applying the MaximumRecognitionLayout Algorithm to the example given in Fig. 1. Changes in the layout are now limited to those are areas where they are absolutely needed due to structural changes.

4.2   Creating a Measure for the Completeness of a Model

In order to support the user in his decision for a result we developed a measure that estimates the completeness of a model. Incomplete models (models where certain paths or behaviors are missing) are found for example if the workflow changes frequently or in a young system, where only few traces are available and some actions have not yet occurred.

Basic Concept. For our basic concept we borrowed some ideas from data mining. In data mining different methods for evaluating the predictive accuracy of a model e.g. a classifier are used. Three common approaches are holdout, cross-validation and bootstrap (see e.g. [14]).

The holdout method is the simplest method of measuring predictive accuracy. The examples are partitioned into two mutually exclusive subsets called the training and the test or holdout set. A common partitioning is two thirds for the training set and the rest for the test set. The model is then learned from the training set, and validated against the test set. For the following explanations we define D as the training set and D_t as the test set. Furthermore we define $S(D)$ as the size of a training set, and $V(D_1, D_2)$ is the number of traces successfully validated when using D_1 as training set and D_2 as test set. Using this definition the accuracy estimation for the holdout method is defined as:

$$acc_h = \frac{V(D \backslash D_t, D_t)}{S(D_t)}$$

In k-fold cross-validation the examples are randomly split into k mutually exclusive subsets (the folds) $D_1, D_2, ...D_k$ of approximately equal size. For the calculation of the measure k steps are needed. In each of these steps one subset is chosen as the test set, and the others are used as training set.

The bootstrap method differs from the other two methods because it uses all examples as training set and a part of the examples as the test set. In data mining this is especially useful, when there exists only a very small example set.

All three methods have in common that we need a validation mechanism that determines, whether or not a certain workflow instance can be generated by a given model. This validation method is outlined in the following section.

Among these three methods cross-validation seems to be the most advanced. For practical reasons we selected the holdout method. As the intended use of the result is a quality-measure for the ongoing calculation process, a drawback of applying the cross-validation approach to our problem is time needed to learn k different models. Mining k different training sets may require up to k different parameter settings or even user interaction. Furthermore the result of cross-validation cannot be associated with a special model. It is more a measure for the quality of the examples than for a specific model.

Although the bootstrap method is not faced with such problems it has an even more serious drawback in our setup. In [7] we have proven that all (block-structured) examples that are used by InWoLvE for learning are covered by the result model. Thus the bootstrap method would in our case always result in a 100 percent accuracy estimation.

Developing an Approach for Validation. In our opinion there are basically two ways to realize a validation procedure. The first is a brute force approach, where all possible mappings of workflow instance vertices to activity vertices of the model are tested one after the other. If one of these mappings represents a valid path through the model, we have validated the trace. This method seems ideal if the vertex names are unique, because then only one test with a fixed mapping - which of course is still not trivial due to loops and concurrency - is necessary.

The second possibility is to use a more constructive approach, that tries to match the actions in the trace step by step to activity vertices. This approach seems more promising when we are dealing with models having non-unique activity names, because it excludes some invalid mappings right away. We therefore decided to focus on this technique.

The basic idea is to walk a path through the model step by step according to the trace. To this end we first need to sort the action instances in the trace according to their end times. The validation of a trace is done by trying to map the instances time-ordered on the vertices of a model. Every time an instance is successfully mapped onto a vertex we look at the successor of the vertex, and try to match the next instance against it.

We now explain the algorithm in more detail, starting with strictly sequential models without decisions, which are easiest to understand, and then we explain what additional difficulties emerge when dealing with decisions and splits.

Strictly Sequential Models without Decisions. When dealing with strictly sequential models without decisions we begin by validating the initial state against the process start vertex. Since the process start vertex is always valid, we can continue with its successor. We now have to validate the state against an action vertex (we know there are no decision and split vertices in this model). The validation state is valid with respect to the action vertex if its current action instance matches the action vertex. In this case we can continue the validation with the vertex's successor. If the state cannot be validated the validation has failed, because there exist no other possibilities to continue.

In order to be successful, the validation not only needs to reach the process stop vertex, but also must match all the available action instances. Without the second condition, an endless trace could be validated against a model containing only one action vertex, if only the first action instance is matching.

Models Containing Decisions. Dealing with decisions only introduces little additional complexity. The validation algorithm simply tries to validate one path after the other. Because each path needs to be validated with the current state, the algorithm makes a copy of the current validation state for each path, and remembers the original state.

This procedure is also unproblematic when dealing with loops since there exists only a limited number of action instances. An exception is a model containing an empty loop (contains only two decision vertices), which would capture the validation in an endless loop. These loops can be located, however by logging the visited vertices.

Models Containing Concurrency. The naive approach to validate a split vertex would be to do it analogously to the validation of the decision vertex. The only difference is that not only one branch must be validated, but all the branches that are assigned a probability of one.

This approach is, however, severely flawed because of two reasons:

1. only the sequence of actions on the same branch is fixed; actions on different branches may occur in any sequence
2. branches with a probability less than one may be included or not, opening up two separate branches in the calculation space of the validation.

Because of the first problem we need to adapt the validation to try all valid sequences of the actions. We achieve this using a backtracking algorithm with special treatment for nested splits, and loops within the split / join blocks. Details of the algorithm are given in [8].

A split join block is successfully validated if all its branches with a probability of one and at least one branch have been validated.

An example with a step by step explanation of the validation can be found in [8] along with a more detailed explanation of the validation algorithm itself.

5   Prototypical Implementation

The concepts mentioned above have been implemented in a prototypical implementation called "ProTo - The Process Tool". The tool is implemented in JAVA. It uses a modified InWoLvE kernel to perform the actual mining computation. To this end interfaces were embedded into the InWoLvE code. These pass data during a running calculation, enabling the user to follow and control the state of the calculation.

Because of the usage of InWoLvE as kernel, ProTo accepts the same input formats. For performance reasons ProTo internally manages the data using a SQL database.

The graphical user interface of ProTo shown in Fig. 4 is separated into three subpanels. On the left side a representation of the search tree is shown, in which every node represents one model, and is labelled with its LLH. Every leaf is the end of one search path. The currently selected model is shown in the upper panel on the right. It is automatically layouted, and can be manipulated in various ways for better understanding. The panel below this window graphically depicts the measures for the models, ordered by their time of occurrence. The bars represent the LLH of each model with the selected model marked in a different color. The curve depicts the reliability measure that we introduced above.

All these components are linked, so that the current model is always selected in each window. This enables the user to browse the models either using the search tree or the project history. During a mining calculation the results are displayed as soon as they are found, and all panels are updated.

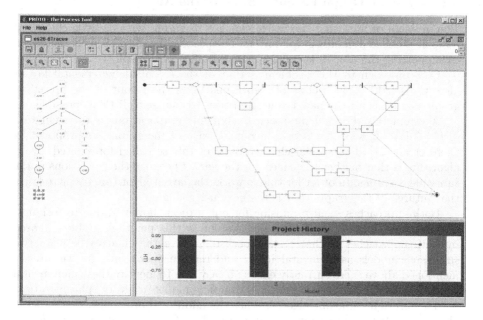

Fig. 4. Screenshot of the ProTo user interface

6   Related Work

6.1   Workflow Mining

Other workflow mining algorithms presented in the literature such as [15], [16] and [17] are restricted to workflow models with unique activity names. This simplifies the workflow mining problem in a way that there is no need for a search procedure. As a consequence these approaches do not require the same amount of user interaction as InWoLvE. Thus none of these approaches provides a special solution for interactive workflow mining.

A completely different approach for workflow mining is presented by Schimm [18]. The idea is to start with a workflow model that basically represents an enumeration of all observed workflow instances and then to apply rewriting rules that preserve behavioral equivalence. A notable difference to InWoLvE is that there is no effort to generalize. The approach can be considered as a transformation between behaviorally equivalent representations. As this transformation is a deterministic process it also does not require heavy user interaction.

For a detailed discussion of the strengths and weaknesses of these different basic mining algorithms, which is beyond the scope of this paper, because we are only interested in concepts supporting interactivity, we refer to [1] or [3].

6.2   Dynamic Graph Layout – State of the Art

The problem of layouting successive changes to graphs with as little change as possible is called dynamic graph layout. The problem has also been characterized as supporting the user in keeping a "mental map" of a graph [19].

One approach to this problem is that of the so called incremental layout algorithms [20,12]. This class of algorithms takes the layout of the preceding graph as a basis for the new layout, and tries to change as little as possible.

A completely different approach to dynamic graph layout is to calculate a "global" layout, which induces a layout for each of the graphs, as proposed by Diehl et al. [21]. The special characteristic of this so called foresighted layout algorithm is that neither the edges nor the vertices change their positions in the subsequent graphs. In order for this to work, the layout algorithm needs to know the "future" of the graph, that is the next n-1 changes.

Both approaches seem promising for our project, however, due to technical reasons they can't be applied in our system at this point. A problem shared by both approaches is that they expect to receive the changes between two successive models as elemental insert and remove operations. As we already mentioned above there currently exists no easy way to identify these incremental changes in InWoLvE, since it produces complete models at every split operation.

The foresighted layout algorithm has the additional drawback, that it needs all the models to compute its global layout. This fact makes it worthless for on the fly layout of the intermediate result during a mining calculation.

6.3   Validation

The question if a trace can be generated as a model can also be formulated as the question if the trace is contained in the language described by the model. This question has already been evaluated to some extent for message systems [22] which can be converted into petri nets [23]. However the semantics described in these papers do not match those specified by the ADL. An approach that is very similar to validation is presented in [24]. Here the workflow-log is replayed in the mined workflow model to calculate sojourn times, probabilities, flow times, and other metrics.

7   Conclusion and Outlook

This paper describes the first analysis of the interactive aspects of the workflow mining process and the first solution for some of the problems that became obvious under this focus. To this end we systematically gathered requirements, and then selectively developed solutions. Among others we developed a special layout algorithm that provides a structured and change resistant layout. Furthermore we defined a measure for the reliability of mined models based on validation, and devised several methods of supporting the user in the decision for a final result.

Most of the concepts were implemented in the ProTo tool in order to prove their feasibility. First working experiences with this tool have been very promising, surpassing the possibilities of a combined system of a non-interactive workflow mining tool and a "normal" workflow tool by far.

A real estimation of the value of the developed concepts can only be made after putting the system to work in a realistic scenario. Also the feedback from non-developing users will bring invaluable information about the deficiencies of the tool.

Further future work also includes the improvement of the InWoLvE mining algorithms. Improvements will include the mechanisms for dealing with loops and for the detection of dependencies.

In parallel to ProTo, InterPoL [25] has been developed. InterPoL supports the task of comparing actual work practice with the intended business process (also called Delta-Analysis). Both approaches complement each other since ProTo contributes to a better understanding of the actual work practice. Thus, we built them on the same code basis to make a future integration easy.

References

[1] van der Aalst, W., van Dongen, B., Herbst, J., L. Maruster, G.S., Weijters, A.: Workflow mining: A survey of issues and approaches. Journal of Data and Knowledge Engineering **47** (2003) 237–267

[2] van der Aalst, W., Weijters, A.J.M.M.: Process mining: a research agenda. Computers in Industry. Special Issue: Process/Workflow Mining **53** (2003) 231–244

[3] Herbst, J., Karagiannis, D.: Workflow mining with InWoLvE. Computers in Industry. Special Issue: Process/Workflow Mining **53** (2003) 245–264

[4] van der Aalst, W., Desel, J., Oberweis, A.: Business Process Management: Models, Techniques, and Empirical Studies. Springer-Verlag (2000)

[5] Klein, M., Dellarocas, C., Bernstein, A.: Introduction to the Special Issue on Adaptive Workflow Systems. Computer Supported Cooperative Work **9** (2000) 265–267

[6] Reichert, M.: Dynamische Ablaufänderungen in Workflow-Management-Systemen. PhD thesis, Fakultät für Informatik, Universität Ulm (2000)

[7] Herbst, J.: Ein induktiver Ansatz zur Akquisition und Adaption von Workflow-Modellen. PhD thesis, Universität Ulm (2001)

[8] Hammori, M.: Interactive Workflow Mining. Diploma thesis, University of Ulm (2003)

[9] Parekh, R., Honavar, V.: Automata Induction, Grammar Inference, and Language Acquisition. In Dale, Moisl, Somers, eds.: Handbook of Natural Language Processing. New York: Marcel Dekker (2000)

[10] BOC: ADONIS Version 3.0 - Users Guide. BOC GmbH, Vienna (1999)

[11] Junginger, S., Kühn, H., Strobl, R., Karagiannis, D.: Ein Geschäfts-prozessmanagement-Werkzeug der nächsten Generation – ADONIS: Konzeption und Anwendungen. Wirtschaftsinformatik **42** (2000) 392–401

[12] Battista, G.D., Eades, P., Tamassia, R., Tollis, I.: Algorithms for drawing graphs: an annotated bibliography. In: Computational Geometry: Theory and Applications. (1994) 235–282

[13] Branke, J.: Drawing Graphs. (2001) Dynamic Graph Drawing, pages 228–246.

[14] Kohavi, R.: A study of cross-validation and bootstrap for accuracy estimation and model selection. In: Proceedings of the IJCAI. (1995) 1137–1145

[15] Agrawal, R., Gunopulos, D., Leymann, F.: Mining Process Models from Workflow Logs. In: Proc. of the 6th International Conference on Extending Database Technology (EDBT). (1998) 469–483

[16] Cook, J., Wolf, A.: Event-Based Detection of Concurrency. Technical Report, CU-CS-860-98, Department of Computer Science, University of Colorado (1998)

[17] van der Aalst, W., Weijters, A., Maruster, L.: Workflow mining: Which processes can be rediscovered? Beta working paper series, wp 74, Eindhoven University of Technology (2002)

[18] Schimm, G.: Process mining elektronischer Geschäftsprozesse. In: Proceedings Elektronische Geschäftsprozesse. (2001)

[19] Eades, P., Lai, W., Misue, K., Sugiyama, K.: Preserving the mental map of a diagram. In: Proc. of Compugraphics 91. (1991) 24–33

[20] North, S.C.: Incremental Layout in DynaDAG. In: Lecture Notes in Computer Science, vol. 1027. Springer (1996) 409–418

[21] Diehl, S., Görg, C., Kerren, A.: Preserving the mental map using foresighted layout. In: Proceedings of Joint Eurographics - IEEE TCVG Symposium on Visualization (VisSym '01), Eurographics, Ascona, Schweiz, Springer (2001) 175–184

[22] Riddle, W.: The Modeling and Analysis of Supervisory Systems. Stanford, California: Stanford University, Computer Science Department, PhD Thesis (1972)

[23] Peterson, J.L.: Petri Net Theory and the Modeling of Systems. Englewood Cliffs, New Jersey: Prentice Hall, Inc. (1981)

[24] van der Aalst, W., van Dongen, B.: Discovering workflow performance models from timed logs. In: International Conference on Engineering and Deployment of Cooperative Information Systems (EDCIS 2002). Lecture Notes in Computer Science Nr. 2480, Springer-Verlag (2002) 45–63

[25] Kleiner, N.: Supporting Usage-Centered Workflow Design: Why and How? In: Proceedings of the 2nd International Business Process Management Conference. (2004)

Supporting Usage-Centered Workflow Design: Why and How?

Niko Kleiner

Dept. of Programming Methodology, Faculty of Computer Science
D-89069 University of Ulm, Germany
nikolaus.kleiner@informatik.uni-ulm.de

Abstract. One of the most difficult tasks in the development of Process-aware Information Systems (*p*-IS) is the design of the related workflow. Methods and tools to support this design process are an emerging trend in Business Process Management research. Despite the many approaches already presented it is unclear on what researchers should focus.

Hence, in this paper, I first undertake *a* sound problem analysis of the workflow design process. With respect to this analysis, workflow design should primarily be informed of the study of the 'where' and 'why' of deviations of the work practice — which emerges with the deployment and use of the new *p*-IS — and the initially intended business process.

Secondly, I describe log-based Delta-Analysis, a new concept to study process deviations using data logged during operational *p*-IS-usage. InterPoL, a tool to support log-based Delta-Analysis, is also presented.

Finally, I report about results of a feasibility as well as a detailed case study with real-world projects.

1 Introduction

The introduction and/or reengineering of business processes is usually supported by an Information System (IS). IS that are designed and deployed with the goal to support business processes are often called Process-aware Information Systems (*p*-IS). One of the most difficult and time consuming tasks in *p*-IS development is the design of the related workflow [1,2].

This fact has been recognized for a while. As van der Aalst et al. [3] point out, the methods and tools that support *p*-IS development are mainly concerned with business process modeling, model analysis and implementation issues (e.g., Workflow Management Systems). Only few tools support simulation, validation or collection and interpretation of event-data. Emerging research areas like Business Activity Monitoring and Workflow Mining concentrate more on the latter aspects.

The variety of solutions brings up the question which methods and tools are the most promising ones. Thus, in the first part of this paper, I undertake an analysis of the workflow design process to better understand the crucial problems related with this task.

J. Desel, B. Pernici, and M. Weske (Eds.): BPM 2004, LNCS 3080, pp. 227–243, 2004.
© Springer-Verlag Berlin Heidelberg 2004

For a problem analysis I have to foreground certain aspects and neglect others. This does not mean that other aspects are less important. For the purpose of this paper, I focus the goal of a p-IS to change/to improve an existing work practice process, that is, the ability of a p-IS to influence process participants' working habits.

With respect to these assumptions and to the conducted analysis, the most important result is that researchers should put more emphasis on the study of *operational p-IS-usage* and, in particular, on the study of the *where* and *why* of deviations of work practice from the intended business process.

Section 2 reports about the problem analysis and its implications on the workflow design process. In the second part (section 3), I present a new concept to study process deviations based on event-data logged during p-IS-usage: log-based Delta-Analysis. Further, I present InterPoL, a tool from the University of Ulm that supports log-based Delta-Analysis. Finally, in section 4 and 5 report about a feasibility as well as a case study of these ideas.

Note that the focus of this paper is on problem analysis and the feasibility study of the presented ideas. Emphasizing these aspects, the sound technical description of the concept is not within the scope of this paper.

Before going into more detail, I want to define some important terminology. The definitions are close to the definitions of the WfMC [4]. A *business process* is a set of activities that collectively realize a business objective within an organizational context. Activities can be *manual* or can be computer supported (in the following called *workflow*-activities). The distinguishing criteria is if the activity is known by the p-IS or not and does not necessarily imply its automatic execution[1]. The term *workflow* refers to the projection of the business process to its workflow-activities. A *Process-aware Information System (p-IS)* refers to any IS that is designed to support a business process. In contrast, a Workflow Management System is a p-IS with a specific architecture.

2   Analysis of the Workflow Design Process

This section analyzes the workflow design process. For this purpose, I focus the goal of a p-IS to change/to improve an existing work practice process, that is, the ability of a p-IS to influence process participants' working habits. Like already mentioned, this does not imply that other aspects are less important.

Section 2.1 describes the research methodology applied for problem analysis. Section 2.2 explains why Giddens' structuration theory and Orlikowski's Technologies-in-Practice are appropriate theories to analyze the p-IS-domain. Section 2.3 uses these theories to derive general domain properties. The consequences for the workflow design process are described in section 2.4.

---

[1] For example, the activity 'sign the contract' can be a workflow-activity — the p-IS just informs the process participant — but cannot be executed automatically

2.1   Applied Research Methodology

Different research methodologies can be applied to analyze a development process. Two strategies are common: an inductive or a deductive one. Using an inductive strategy presupposes a statistically significant number of comparable project histories. Then, one can search for common problems and/or characteristics. On the other hand, a deductive approach presupposes an appropriate and well-accepted theory for the domain of interest. Then, one can assume the domain to behave like described by the theory and derive characteristics. In this paper, I use a deductive approach.

2.2   Which Theory Is Appropriate?

Understanding the influence of a p-IS on working processes requires a sound understanding of the role of a p-IS in an organization. The more general problem — understanding the role of IT in an organization — has been a long standing research question in Organizational Sciences.

The fundamental results relate to very basic insights from Social Sciences. According to [5], Social Science researchers can be roughly distinguished as being subjectivists or objectivists. Subjectivists explain the behaviour of a social system (e.g. an organization) by focusing on the situated acting individuals. In contrast, objectivists concentrate on institutional properties, like, for example, existing norms or resources. The assumption that the two scholars exclude each other has divided researchers from Social and Organizational Sciences and the IT-field.

More recent work in Social Sciences (cf [6,7,8,9,10]) and Philosophy [11,12] propose integrating meta-theories that respect both views at the same time. One such meta-theory is Giddens' structuration theory [9,13,10]. His theory has been extensively applied to analyze organizational and social processes (cf [14,15,16, 17,18,19,20,21,22,23,24,25]).

IT-research has been criticized for their inconsistent research results regarding the definition of the role of IT in organizations [26,27,28,29,30,31,32]. Markus and Robey show in a fundamental paper [27] that IT-research, concerning this topic, is subject to the same dualistic view as has been Social and Organizational Sciences. According to their research IT-research has neglected the analysis of its fundamental philosophical standpoints. This has resulted in oversimplified and therefore unsatisfying and inconsistent theories about the role of IT in organization.

Based on these insights, Orliskowski and Robey reconceptualized the role of IT using Giddens' structuration theory [33]. Orlikowski further developed this theory [34,35]. In this paper, I am using Giddens' structuration theory and Orlikowski's Technologies-in-Practice [35], her most recent theory.

2.3 p-IS Domain Properties

Figure 1 illustrates Giddens'/Orlikowski's theory applied to our problem. For more explanations on the original findings, the reader is referred to [10] and [35].

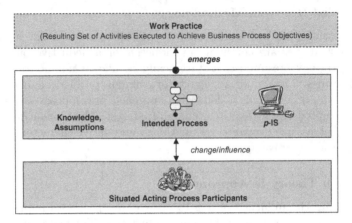

Fig. 1. A Model of the p-IS-Domain

The model distinguishes three layers. The bottom-layer represents the process participants. The process participants do not act in a vacuum but in a context. The middle-layer represents this context. It is one of Giddens' contributions that there are exactly three classes of social action influencing factors: knowledge and assumptions of the actors, norms and resources. Giddens mentions that in an analysis with his model one should foreground some aspects and background others [9]. Since we want to study the role of work practice process influencing factors, we focus on specific representatives. In Orlikowski's Technologies-in-Practice, IT is defined as a resource in Giddens' sense. So, in the case of a p-IS, the three representatives are: the knowledge and assumptions related to the execution of the business process and p-IS-usage, the intended business process (the norm), and the p-IS itself (the resource that supports process execution). The top-layer symbolizes the resulting work practice. Since we focus on process, the work practice can be seen as the set of executed activities to achieve the business process objectives.

Giddens explains the dynamics of a social system as a recursive process (symbolized by the double arrow between the bottom- and middle-layer in figure 1): while people act, they are influenced by their context. On the other hand, with every action, people change this context. They learn, they save data, they write documents etc. This changed context is then the starting point for the following actions, and so on (*recursiveness of actions*).

Although this context has a certain influence, it is non-deterministic. People have the given norms in mind and resources at hand, but they still have a certain degree of freedom to choose to do otherwise. For example, everybody has a more or less personal way of using MS Word. Regarding the p-IS, it follows that its usage is neither independent from its context nor does it have a deterministic influence on work practice process. Work practice emerges and can usually not be foreseen — at least not in its entirety (*emergence of work practice*).

Further, a p-IS is only one influencing factor. But the work practice that we want to change/improve depends on all three. In general, work practice cannot be improved by just improving the p-IS-influenced part of it. In figure 1, the black frame and outgoing arrow indicate that work practice is a result of the interplay between situated acting process participants and the whole context (*work practice completeness*).

Further, in the sense of Giddens' theory, work practice is immaterial. It is only visible in the current actions and p-IS-usage. In figure 1 this is depicted by the dotted line around the work practice (*immateriality of work practice*).

2.4   Consequences for the Workflow Design Process

According to van der Aalst, ter Hofstede and Weske [3] the BPM lifecycle comprises the four main activities process design, system configuration, process enactment and diagnosis. I will explain the consequences with respect to these activities.

Usage-centeredness. Since work practice emerges, the definition of the intended business process and the implementation of the corresponding workflow must always be seen as preliminary objects. Consequently, more emphasis should be put in the study of the newly emerged work practice. With respect to the workflow design process, this shifts the focus from initial design and configuration to diagnosis (compare also [36]).

Continuous Learning. Even though there were an optimal process design and we knew how to implement it, the resulting work practice would most probably deviate (emergence). But even though work practice would not deviate, every action changes the context and thus the conditions under which the optimum was defined. Hence, improving work practice means continuously looking for required changes.

Focusing on Delta-Analysis. But what is the most important information for a process/workflow redesign? Considering the BPM lifecycle, we started with a definition of the intended process design and ended up with the newly emerged work practice. Thus, to improve work practice, we first need to understand *what* this work practice looks like. Then, we are interested *where* work practice deviates from the intended process. Finally, to be able to make the right decisions in redesign, we need to know *why* process participants did not follow our definitions. We call the diagnosis-activity of finding the 'where' and 'why' of such deviations *Delta-Analysis*.

Inseparability of Business Process and Workflow Design. Since work practice is complete, only redesigning the workflow might not improve it. Thus, when redesigning the workflow, one always needs to take the whole business process into account, that is, workflow- *and* manual activities. Changes in the business process usually imply changes in the workflow, but they do not need to.

3   Semi-automatic, Log-Based Delta-Analysis

With respect to the results of section 2.4, the primary diagnosis activity of the workflow design process is Delta-Analysis — the study of the 'where' and 'why' of deviations of work practice from the intended business process. Figure 2 shows the context of Delta-Analysis. The intended process has been defined and the corresponding p-IS implemented and deployed. Through the enactment of the p-IS the new work practice emerges. For the purposes of this paper, work practice can be seen as a set of timestamped activities. In figure 2 MA1 and MA2 depict manual and WA1, WA2 and WA3 workflow-activities.

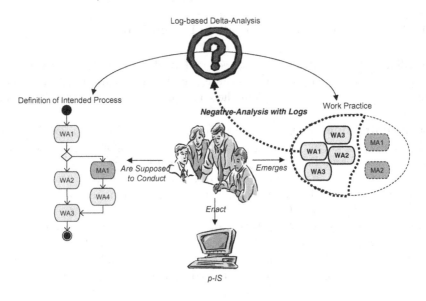

Fig. 2. Context of the Log-based Delta-Analysis

3.1   Using Log-Data for Delta-Analysis

According to section 2.3, work practice is immaterial. It can only be observed in the actions of the process participants. Similar to Workflow Mining (cf [1]), I use log-data gathered by the p-IS to get an objective data basis for Delta-Analysis. This yields the following advantages:

- *Logs partially materialize work practice*
  Data logged about p-IS-usage is a materialization of work practice. Since work practice comprises manual as well as workflow-activities (completeness property), such data is usually only a partial image of the eventual conducted activities. Only workflow-activities can be captured. In figure 2, this materialization is illustrated by solid lines around workflow-activities.

– *Logs can be used for negative-analysis*
Although those logs are only a partial image of work practice, a negative
analysis can be done. If the analyst finds a log sequence that contradicts
the intended business process, he found a deviation for sure. The reverse
cannot be concluded. The fact that there are no such log sequences does not
necessarily entail that the work practice follows the intended process.

When the analyst found deviations it is still necessary to talk to the process
participants and find out why they deviated. So, log-based Delta-Analysis must
be seen as a pre-analysis and does not replace interviews. But this new process
step improves the quality of the subsequent interviews and provides *objective
data* as a basis for discussions.

3.2   Why *Semi*-automation?

Using logs to check for process deviations means relating logs with workflow-
activities of a corresponding business process definition. Hereby, one of the main
problems is the difference in the levels of abstraction between the logs and the
business process. Business process activities are usually described on a considerable higher level. In general, the reverse can also be true. Hence, these different
levels make a direct comparison impossible. Either we need additional semantic
information or user interaction is required.

But the situation is not hopeless. If there are logs that occur over and over
again, a supporting system can learn from previous relations, make suggestions
or even try to automate this process over time. In face of 10000s of logs and with
respect to the continuous learning process, this is a very desirable feature of a
supporting tool.

When a relationship between a log and a workflow-activity is defined, I express that there is an execution of the activity that produced this log (maybe
among others). Such a relationship is defined between a specific log-entry and a
specific activity and is not a relationship of log- and/or activity-names. When
defining such a relationship the following cases must be taken into account:

– *Granularity of Logs/Activities*
Case 1: Logs are more fine grained than activities
Then either a subset of logs needs to be related to exactly one workflow-
activity or there is no workflow-activity the subset can be related to. In
the latter case, either the *p*-IS logged something that is irrelevant for our
purposes, or there is a gap in the business process definition.
Case 2: Logs are more coarse grained than activities
Then either a subset of workflow-activities needs to be related to exactly
one log or there is no log the activities can be related to. If there is no such
log then there is a gap in the log sequence. Note that manual activities can
never have logs.
In general, there is a relation between one subset of logs to another subset
of workflow-activities.

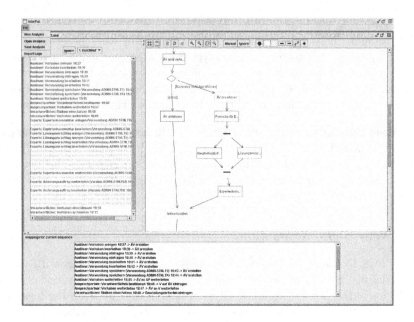

Fig. 3. Screenshot of InterPoL

- *Multiple Executions of Workflow-Activities*
  As soon as loops are considered in the business process definition workflow-activities can be executed several times. Then, two further cases must be taken into account. Either, the workflow-activity outputs exactly the same logs (also in the same order) or not. In the latter case, the execution of the workflow-activity might output a different subset of logs or the same subset but with a different ordering.

In my current research, the problem of relating logs and workflow-activities is fully formalized and machine learning algorithms are considered to support the semi-automated mapping process. But within this paper, the focus is on a rational for Delta-Analysis, an initial concept and the feasibility of the approach.

3.3 A Prototype to Support Log-Based Delta-Analysis: InterPoL

InterPoL (Inter-active PrOcess EvoLution) is a Java-based tool from the University of Ulm that supports Log-based Delta-Analysis. Figure 3 is a screenshot of InterPoL. InterPoL consists of three frames. A process modeling frame (the upper right frame of figure 3) that supports modeling and automatic layout of UML activity diagrams. With this component the intended business process is documented. Second, InterPoL has a component that can import logs and visualize a log ordered by business process instance and within each instance ordered by time (upper left frame). The logs are assumed to be given in the common XML-log-format as suggested by van der Aalst et. al. [1]. Third, there is a component that manages mappings between logs and business process activities (lower frame). The main goal of InterPoL is to help the analyst to map logs to business process activities and manage and analyze these relations. During this 'mapping-process' the analyst searches for process deviations. Section 5 describes a more detailed application scenario and case study results.

4 Feasibility: Data Availability, Quality, and Appropriateness

Before going into a detailed case study this section reports about the overall feasibility of the approach. This study was conducted with respect current practice and to see if the preconditions to be able to apply the approach are too restrictive. Three feasibility criteria guided this study: data availability, quality and appropriateness.

Table 1. Summary of Results of the Feasibility Study

Project	Business Process	Logs	Delta-Analysis	Problem
DC Project 1	0	+	0	BP too Coarse
DC Project 2	+	+	-	Hard Coded Workflow
DC Project 3	0	0	+	—
DC Project 4	0	+	0	BP too Coarse
SCM Workflow	+	+	-	Hard Coded Workflow
SCM Designer	+	+	+	—

Log-based Delta-Analysis presupposes an explicit business process definition and a log of p-IS-usage containing information about executed workflow-activities. The process documentation should be sufficiently detailed. All important activities should be documented as well as their relationships. Further, we also want documentation of alternatives and loops etc. Few knowledge about those relationships makes it difficult to say something about valid process execution paths — but this is what we are interested in. A log-file must contain information about the executed activity, the execution date and time and information about the process instance it belongs to.

Table 1 summarizes the results. A '+' for a business process documentation means all criteria are met. A '0' indicates that the activities and/or relationships are not sufficiently detailed. For example, only rough process phases are described. If there is a '−' then there is almost no or a very poor process documentation. A log has a '+' if all data is available and the log data is accessible. A log is accessible if there is a single log-file that only needs to be converted into the XML format. If there is a '0' then the data is still available but not accessible without further effort. A '–' means that not all needed data is logged. Note that this first analysis only assures the necessary preconditions. The business process and log data still can be inappropriate. For example, logs might not be comparable to process activities etc. At the end of this section we deal with this topic.

We studied six projects. Four of them are real world projects from DaimlerChrysler (DC). The remaining two are two different implementations of one further DC project. The latter two mainly differ in implementation technology: one is implemented using Lotus Domino Designer and the other one using Lotus Domino Workflow.

The results related to data availability and quality are positive (compare table 1). One of the DC projects has a complete process documentation in the above sense. Two other projects have a fairly good process documentation. Only some alternative paths are missing. Only one project has just an overview documentation, that is, only process phases are described. The two university projects also have a sufficient process documentation. No project has a complete graphical process model. It is also interesting to mention that the business process documentations are better the more recent the projects are. This indicates a trend towards more detailed descriptions.

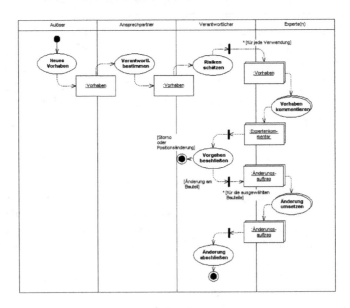

Fig. 4. SCM Overview Process Model

Figure 4 exemplifies a business process description. It shows an UML activity diagram with document flow and swimlanes of the university project SCM. Each activity is detailed with a use case description.

All log-files contained the necessary data. Not all logs are fine-grained enough to track all interesting activities. Two DC systems just log coarse grained process states. One project logs detailed process states and one process as well as document states (a notes application). Although this last system has the best-grained logs (with respect to the comparability to the business process description) the logs are spread over the documents that are produced during the execution of the business process. One would need to compile the separate logs into one log-file manually.

Table 2. Example Logs

SCM Lotus Domino Designer Implementation
18:38:15,Ausloeser,Vorhaben-5TVNNT,Vorhaben weiterleiten 18:38:23,Ansprechpartner,Vorhaben-5TVNNT,Verantwortlichen bestimmen 18:38:40,Verantwortlicher,Vorhaben-5TVNNT,Risiken einschaetzen 18:38:44,Verantwortlicher,Vorhaben-5TVNNT,Vorhaben weiterleiten 18:38:50,Experte,Vorhaben-5TVNNT,Expertenkommentar anlegen

SCM Lotus Domino Workflow Implementation
Activity#UQ47ZQAI|1#UQ4RZQDP| 12.12.03 18:21 Vorhaben kommentieren Activity#UQ47ZQAG|1#UQ4RZQDP| 12.12.03 18:22 Vorgehen beschliessen Activity#UQ47ZQAK|1#UQ4RZQDP| 12.12.03 18:23 Aenderung umsetzen Activity#UQ47ZQAE|1#UQ4RZQDP| 12.12.03 18:24 Aenderung abschliessen

Table 2 shows two example logs. The first is a log of the SCM implementation with Domino Designer. The second is a log of the SCM implementation with Domino Workflow. In the Domino Designer implementation we have a custom logging mechanism to demonstrate the ideal for a Delta-Analysis. The log of the Domino Workflow implementation comes with the workflow component.

Having good data is the first and necessary condition to be able to apply Log-based Delta-Analysis. Second, the levels of abstraction and the granularities of the logs and business process activities must be of the kind such that an analyst can relate them to each other. This is possible in all inspected projects. Section 5 discusses some problems that one has to deal with anyways.

Third, Delta-Analysis only makes sense in a context where the supporting system allows deviating working styles. With respect to the results of section 2, a p-IS should not have a 'hard' coded workflow implementation, because in this case nothing interesting can be concluded from the logs. For example, if the workflow implementation only allowed paths through the business process as modeled in figure 4, the corresponding log only yields data about which path has been chosen most often. But no information can be gathered about other — maybe preferred — working styles. In this case nothing can be *learned* from the logs. A workflow implementation only should include some rules that are for sure and then add more rules — if necessary — over time. This criteria is not met by two DC projects, as can be seen in table 1[2]. Only one DC project is ideal. The second ideal candidate, SCM Designer, is an artificial BPM project, constructed by us to demonstrate the ideal situation. DC project 1 and 4 are fairly good with respect to the workflow implementation. The logs contain the necessary data and are sufficiently expressive to be comparable to business process activities but are pretty coarse grained. So, only rough information can be gathered about preferred working styles.

In summary, the data availability and quality is good. The main problem in practice seems to be the appropriate workflow implementation. Too often, this workflow is assumed to be the ideal one and 'hardly' implemented instead of giving the process participants — and other stakeholders — the chance to learn.

5   Case Study

This section reports about a detailed case study with InterPoL. Section 5.1 introduces an application scenario and section 5.2 briefly summarizes our results.

5.1   Application Scenario

For our first case study we chose the most simple scenario with respect to section 3. First, we assume the logs to be always of finer granularity than the activities. From section 4 we already know that this is the more common case. Second, we omit loops. So, we do not have to deal with multiple executions of an activity.

A Delta-Analysis with InterPoL is divided in three major steps: Initialize, Analyze, and Evolve. Before an analysis can be started, the intended business process must be explicitly defined and the p-IS implemented and put into operational use. In the following, I explain the separate steps:

Initialize: If this is the first analysis, the business process is modeled with InterPoL's UML modeling component. Otherwise, a model already exists (see also analysis step 'evolve'). Further, the analyst needs to get the most recent log-file and convert it into the XML-log-format as mentioned in section 3. Then, the logs are imported into InterPoL.

Analyze: An analysis starts with the choice of a specific log sequence. Such a sequence represents timely ordered logs belonging to a specific process instance. Now, the analyst drags a log to the business process model and drops it onto an activity. InterPoL stores this mapping. During this 'mapping-process' the analyst can step into the following cases:

---

[2] A hard workflow implementation can be due to several reasons. One might be simply an unawareness of the problem or the (usually wrong) assumptions that the prescribed business process is the optimal one. But also political or governmental reasons might be the cause. Then process participants must not deviate but are supposed to adapt to this prescribed working style. But the introduction of such processes and related systems is not the topic of this paper.

Case 1: All logs could be mapped to activities. Then, two further sub-cases can be distinguished. First, the log sequence describes a full path through the process model. Then, there are no deviations and the analysis can proceed with another log sequence. Second, all logs can be mapped in the correct timely order but they do not cover a full path of the business process model. Then, there is a *log-gap*. Either, logs are missing, that is, a workflow-activity does not output a log, or a workflow-activity was not executed (but should have been), or there is a manual activity in the business process model. Then, there cannot be any log for this activity. InterPoL allows a marking of these activities. Either, an activity is marked as *'ignored'* or as *'manual'*. Marking it as 'ignored means that a log is missing and the analyst does not know how to deal with it in the moment.

Case 2: There are logs that could not be mapped to activities. Again, two sub-cases can be distinguished. First, there is no activity in the process model the log can be mapped to. Then, there is a *process-gap*. In this case, the relevant logs would be marked as *'ignored'* (compare the discussion of a log-gap). Second, there is an activity the log could be mapped to but not in this timely order. Then, either the analyst has chosen a wrong path in the business process model (for example, taken the wrong path at a decision point) or there is a true deviation. In the first case, the analyst can *roll back* his mappings up to the last decision point. In the second case, the deviation is documented and analysis stops for this sequence.

Evolve: After several log sequences have been analyzed, the found deviations are used as a data basis for discussions. Then, process/workflow changes are negotiated and implemented. In InterPoL, the business process model is updated accordingly. This step finishes an analysis cycle.

According to this scenario we conducted several case studies with the SCM Designer project.

5.2 Case Study Results

It was one of the crucial questions addressed by the case study, if the described mapping-process is sufficiently supported by InterPoL. For example, it might be that the levels of abstraction between the logs and the business process activities are too different, the logs are hard to interpret or too many logs need to be inspected in order to get some reasonable results. The case studies did not yield such negative results. The simple drag and drop mechanism worked fine. Even larger log sequences could be managed. The provided marking mechanisms were sufficient for the simple scenario. Some suggestions for further markings have been made (for example, in case of a log-gap, a marking to distinguish if a workflow-activity should have produced a log or should not be in the business process model). But more markings yield a more complicated model the analyst has to deal with. Further case studies will show if more markings or just additional documentation is appropriate.

Some minor extensions would be useful: One should be able to attach a note to ignored logs or activities and found deviations. Further, InterPoL should provide an appropriate printing feature such that documents for discussions can be provided.

Beside those trivial enhancements two advanced features were identified. In case an analyst does not map logs according to their sequence but decides to proceed in a more 'chaotic' style it is sometimes not obvious if he defines a correct mapping with respect to timely ordering. InterPoL could provide a validation mechanism. Further, when going through several sequences, pretty often the same logs are mapped to the same business process activities. InterPoL could provide an appropriate learning mechanism to propose mappings automatically.

My current research deals with these weaknesses. I also include loops in my ongoing work. Further, to be able to provide a validation and learning mechanism I will need to formalize the syntax and semantics of our business process modeling component and the semantics of the log-activity relation.

6   Related Work

Workflow Mining is a new emerging area that is concerned with the acquisition of process models out of workflow-logs. It presupposes an already deployed Information System from which transactional data can be collected (the workflow-logs). Workflow Mining uses different techniques to derive a (mostly) graphical representation of work practice process. Van der Aalst et al. [1] give an overview over available approaches. Like Workflow Mining, Log-based Delta-Analysis uses workflow-logs as information source to make conclusions about the actual work practice process. The presented approach differs in some points (compare also figure 2 for this discussion). I do not want to discover a graphical process model out of workflow-logs but use these logs to find deviations from the prescribed business process model. Workflow Mining can also be used for Delta-Analysis. But the activities of a 'mined' process model are usually on a low level of abstraction since their granularity and names correspond to the logs. Usually, for a Delta-Analysis, an analyst must match (in his mind) this low level model with the high level business process definition. It is one of the goals of Log-based Delta-Analysis to support this task. Further, I also take care of manual activities. When looking for deviations from the business process model such manual activities can additionally complicate a comparison of workflow-log sequences and the high level process model: whole parts of the process model might consist of manual activities or at least comprise many of them. I believe that Workflow Mining and Log-based Delta-Analysis complement each other.

Cook and Wulf [37] presented a tool supported approach in the context of software processes to compare logs to a process model. Like Workflow Mining they neither take the problem of different levels of abstraction nor the existence of manual activities into account. Based on these assumptions they use enhanced string matching and AI algorithms to detect deviations. Further, they define different measures to express the quantity of such deviations.

Adaptive Workflow Research (cf. [38,39,40]) also considers the problem of process changes and evolution. Two fundamental classes of changes are usually distinguished [41]: changes on the a running workflow (workflow instance) and changes on the workflow type (also called 'schema changes'). Changing a workflow type (in our terms the workflow) poses the problem which and how changes to running workflow instances must be propagated. So, adaptive workflow research deals with the question of 'top-down' changes (from the model to its instances). In contrast, Log-based Delta-Analysis focuses on 'bottom-up' changes (using workflow-logs to evolve the business process model).

7 Summary

The presented research was conducted with the hypothesis that a p-IS is designed and deployed with the goal to help to improve work practice process. A rigorous problem analysis of the corresponding workflow design process was presented. According to the conducted problem analysis, one of the crucial results is that designers should focus on the work practice process that emerges with the deployment and operational p-IS-usage and that the most important information to further optimize the worklfow is 'where' and 'why' process participants deviate from the intended business process. This is a shift from user-centered to usage-centered workflow design.

Log-based Delta-Analysis is a new concept that uses workflow-logs to analyze such deviations. InterPoL is a prototype that supports this kind of Delta-Analysis. Log-based Delta-Analysis presupposes some conditions about business process documentation and the nature of workflow-logs. Therefore, a feasibility study was conducted to check if these assumptions are unrealistic. Further, a reported about a detailed case study with InterPoL. The majority of the results were positive. The approach only makes sense in a 'workflow learning friendly' environment, that is, the corresponding workflow implementation must allow alternative working styles. Further, the case study brought two important new requirements to light: the need for a validation mechanism that checks if log-activity relations are valid with respect to timely ordering and the need for a learning mechanism that partially supports the automatic mapping of logs to activities. The latter two insights drive my current research.

Acknowledgements. Many thanks to Joachim Herbst and Kurt Schneider for fruitful discussions. I'm also thankful to Markus Hammori for his provision of the business process modeling component. Finally, I would like to thank the anonymous reviewers who helped to improve an earlier version of this paper.

References

1. W.M.P. van der Aalst, B.F. van Dongen, Herbst, J., Maruster, L., Schimm, G., Weijters, A.: Workflow mining: A survey of issues and approaches. Data and Knowledge Engineering **47** (2003) 237–267
2. Herbst, J.: Ein induktiver Ansatz zur Acquisition und Adaption von Workflow-Modellen (in german). PhD thesis, University of Ulm (2003)

3. W.M.P. van der Aalst, A. ter Hofstefe, Weske, M.: Business process management: A survey. In: Proceedings of the 2nd International Business Process Management Conference (BPM'2003), Berlin, Heidelberg, Springer (2003) 369–380

4. Lawrence, P., ed.: Workflow Handbook 1997, Workflow Management Coalition. Jon Wiley and Sons, New York (1997)

5. Burrell, G., Morgan, G.: Sociological Paradigms and Organizational Analysis. Heinemann, London, UK (1979)

6. Bernstein, R.: The Restructuring of Social and Political Theory. University of Pennsylvania Press, Philadelphia, PA (1978)

7. Bernstein, R.: Beyond Objectivism and Relativism. University of Pennsylvania Press, Philadelphia, PA (1983)

8. Giddens, A.: New Rules of Sociological Method. Basic Books, New York (1976)

9. Giddens, A.: Central Problems in Social Theory: Action, Structure and Contradiction in Social Analysis. University of California Press, Berkley, CA (1979)

10. Giddens, A.: The Constitution of Society: Outline of the Theory of Structure. University of California Press, Berkley, CA (1984)

11. Bhaskar, R.: A Realist Theory of Science. Harvester Press, Brighton, UK (1978)

12. Bhaskar, R.: Beef, structure and place: Notes from a critical naturalist perspective. Journal for the Theory of Social Behaviour **13** (1983) 81–95

13. Giddens, A.: Profiles and Critiques in Social Theory. University of California Press, Berkley, CA (1982)

14. Barley, S.: Technology as an occasion for structuring: Evidence from observations of ct scanners and the social order of radiology departments. Administrative Science Quarterly **31** (1986) 78–108

15. Manning, P.: Organizational work: Structuration of environments. British Journal of Sociology **33** (1982) 118–134

16. Manning, P.: Symbolic Communication. MIT Press, Cambridge, MA (1989)

17. McPhee, R.: Formal structure and organizational communication. In McPhee, R., Tompkins, P., eds.: Organization Communication: Traditional Themes and New Directions, Beverly Hills, CA, Sage Publications (1985) 79–108

18. Pettigrew, A.: Contextualist research: A natural way to link theory and practice. In E.E. Lawler III, et al., eds.: Doing Research That is Useful for Theory and Practice, San Francisco, CA, Jossey-Bass (1985) 222–248

19. Poole, M.: Communication and organizational climate: Review, critique and a new perspective. In McPhee, R., Tompkins, P., eds.: Organization Communication: Traditional Themes and New Directions, Beverly Hills, CA, Sage Publications (1985) 79–108

20. Ranson, S., Hinings, B., Greenwood, R.: The structuring of organizational structures. Administrative Science Quarterly **25** (1980) 1–17

21. Riley, P.: A structurationist account of political culture. Administrative Science Quarterly **28** (1983) 347–414

22. Roberts, J., Scapens, R.: Accounting systems and systems of accountability: Understanding accounting practices in their organizational context. Accounting, Organizations and Society **10** (1985) 443–456

23. Smith, C.: A case study of structuration: A pure-bred beef business. Journal for the Theory of Social Behaviour **13** (1983) 3–18

24. Spybey, T.: Traditional and professional frames of meaning in management. Sociology **18** (1984) 550–562

25. Willmott, H.: Studying managerial work: A critique and a proposal. Journal of Management Studies **24** (1987) 249–270

26. Attewell, P., Rule, J.: Computing and organizations: What we know and what we don't know. Communications of the ACM **27** (1984) 1184–1192

27. Markus, L., Robey, D.: Information technology and organizational change: Causal structure in theory and research. Management Science **34** (1988) 583–598

28. Davis, L., Taylor, J.: Technology, organization and job structure. In Dubin, R., ed.: Handbook of Work, Organization and Society, Chicago, IL, Rand McNelly (1986) 379–419

29. Hodson, R., Parker, R.: Work in high-tech settings: A review of the empirical literature. Research in the Sociology of Work **4** (1988) 1–30

30. Perrow, C.: The organizational context of human factors engineering. Administrative Science Quarterly **28** (1983) 521–541

31. Powell, W.: Review essay: Explaining technological change. American Journal of Sociology **93** (1987) 185–197

32. Sabel, C.: Work and Politics. Cambridge University Press, New York (1982)

33. Orlikowski, W., Robey, D.: Information technology and the structuring of organizations. Information Systems Research **2** (1991) 143–169

34. Orlikowski, W.: The duality of technology: Rethinking the concept of technology in organizations. Organization Science **3** (1992) 398–427

35. Orlikowski, W.: Using technology and constituting structures: A practice lens for studying technology in organizations. Organization Science **11** (2000) 404–428

36. Kleiner, N.: The focus of requirements engineering in workflow application development. In: CAiSE'03 Workshop Proceedings, Workshop Requirements Engineering for Business Process Support (REBPS'03), Aachen, Technical University of Aachen (RWTH) (2003) 372–378

37. Cook, J., Wulf, A.: Software process validation: Quantitatively measuring the correspondence of a process to a model. ACM Transactions on Software Engineering and Methodology **8** (1999) 147–176

38. Ellis, C., Maltzahn, C.: The chautauqua workflow system. In: Proceedings of the International Conference on System Science, Maui, Hawaii (1997)

39. Sadiq, S., Marjanovic, O., Orlowska, M.: Mananging change and time in dynamic workflow processes. IJCIS **9** (2000) 93–116

40. Reichert, M., Dadam, P.: ADEPT$_{flex}$ — supporting dynamic changes of workflows without losing control. JIIS **10** (1998) 93–129

41. Rinderle, S., Reichert, M., Dadam, P.: Correctness criteria for dynamic changes in workflow systems — a survey. (To Appear in 'Data and Knowledge Engineering')

Mining Social Networks: Uncovering Interaction Patterns in Business Processes

Wil M.P. van der Aalst[1] and Minseok Song[1,2]

[1] Department of Technology Management, Eindhoven University of Technology, P.O. Box 513, NL-5600 MB, Eindhoven, The Netherlands.
w.m.p.v.d.aalst@tm.tue.nl

[2] Dept. of Industrial Engineering, Pohang University of Science and Technology, San 31 Hyoja-Dong, Nam-gu, Pohang, 790-784, South Korea.
mssong@postech.ac.kr

Abstract. Increasingly information systems log historic information in a systematic way. Workflow management systems, but also ERP, CRM, SCM, and B2B systems often provide a so-called "event log", i.e., a log recording the execution of activities. Unfortunately, the information in these event logs is rarely used to analyze the underlying processes. Process mining aims at improving this by providing techniques and tools for discovering process, control, data, organizational, and social structures from event logs. This paper focuses on the mining social networks. This is possible because event logs typically record information about the users executing the activities recorded in the log. To do this we combine concepts from workflow management and social network analysis. This paper introduces the approach, defines metrics, and presents a tool to mine social networks from event logs.

1 Introduction

Sociometry, also referred to as sociography, refers to methods presenting data on interpersonal relationships in graph or matrix form [9,22,23]. The term sociometry was coined by Jacob Levy Moreno who conducted the first long-range sociometric study from 1932-1938 at the New York State Training School for Girls in Hudson, New York [17]. As part of this study, Moreno used sociometric techniques to assign residents to various residential cottages. He found that assignments on the basis of sociometry substantially reduced the number of runaways from the facility. Many more sociometric studies have been conducted since then by Moreno and others. In most applications of sociometry, the assessment is based on surveys (also referred to as sociometric tests). With the availability of more electronic data, new ways of gathering data are enabled [11]. For example, BuddyGraph (http://www.buddygraph.com/) and MetaSight (http://www.metasight.co.uk/) are tools that use logs on e-mail traffic as a starting point for sociometric analysis. Similarly, information on the Web can be used for such an analysis. For the analysis of social networks in organizations such approaches are less useful, since they are based on unstructured information. For example, when analyzing e-mail it is difficult, but also crucial, to distinguish between e-mails corresponding to important decisions (e.g., allocation of

J. Desel, B. Pernici, and M. Weske (Eds.): BPM 2004, LNCS 3080, pp. 244–260, 2004.

resources) and e-mails representing less relevant operational details (e.g., schedu-ling a meeting). Fortunately, many enterprise information systems store relevant events in a more structured form. For example, workflow management systems like Staffware register the start and completion of activities [2]. ERP systems like SAP log all transactions, e.g., users filling out forms, changing documents, etc. Business-to-business (B2B) systems log the exchange of messages with other parties. Call center packages but also general-purpose CRM systems log interac-tions with customers. These examples show that many systems have some kind of *event log* often referred to as "history", "audit trail", "transaction file", etc. [3,6,14,21].

When people are involved, event logs will typically contain information on the person executing or initiating the *event*. We only consider events referring to an *activity* and a *case* [3]. The case (also named process instance) is the "thing" which is being handled, e.g., a customer order, a job application, an insurance claim, a building permit, etc. The activity (also named task, operation, action, or work-item) is some operation on the case, e.g., "Contact customer". An event may be denoted by (c, a, p) where c is the case, a is the activity, and p is the per-son. Events are ordered in time allowing the inference of causal relations between activities and the corresponding social interaction. For example, if (c, a_1, p_1) is directly followed by (c, a_2, p_2), there is some handover of work from p_1 to p_2 (note that both events refer to the same case). If this pattern (i.e., there is some handover of work from p_1 to p_2) occurs frequently but there is never a handover of work from p_1 to p_3 although p_2 and p_3 have identical roles in the organization, then this may indicate that the relation between p_1 and p_2 is stronger than the relation between p_1 and p_3. Using such information it is possible to build a *social network* expressed in terms of a graph ("sociogram") or matrix.

Social Network Analysis (SNA) refers to the collection of methods, techniques and tools in sociometry aiming at the analysis of social networks [9,22,23]. There is an abundance of tools allowing for the visualization of such networks and their analysis. A social network may be dense or not, the "social distances" between individuals may be short or long, etc. An individual may be a so-called "star" (directly linked to many other individuals) or an "isolate" (not linked to others). However, also more subtle notions are possible, e.g., an individual who is only linked to people having many relationships is considered to be a more powerful node in the network than an individual having many connections to less connected individuals.

The work presented in this paper applies the results from sociometry, and SNA in particular, to events logs in today's enterprise information systems. The main challenge is to derive social networks from this type of data. This paper presents the approach, the various metrics that can be used to build a social network, and our tool *MiSoN* (Mining Social Networks).

The paper is organized as follows. Section 2 introduces the concept of process mining. Section 3 focuses on the mining of organizational relations, introducing concepts from SNA but also showing which relations can be derived from event logs. Section 4 defines the metrics we propose for mining organizational relations. We propose metrics based on (possible) causality, metrics based on joint cases, metrics based on joint activities, and metrics based on special event types (e.g., delegation). Then we present our tool MiSoN, a small case study, and related work. Finally, Section 8 concludes the paper.

2   Process Mining: An Overview

The goal of process mining is to extract information about processes from transaction logs [3]. We assume that it is possible to record events such that (i) each event refers to an *activity* (i.e., a well-defined step in the process), (ii) each event refers to a *case* (i.e., a process instance), (iii) each event refers to a *performer* (the person executing or initiating the activity), and (iv) events are totally ordered. Any information system using transactional systems such as ERP, CRM, or workflow management systems will offer this information in some form [2]. Note that we do not assume the presence of a workflow management system. The only assumption we make, is that it is possible to collect logs with event data. These event logs are used to construct models that explain some aspect of the behavior registered. The term *process mining* refers to methods for distilling a structured process description from a set of real executions [3,6,14,21]. The term "structured process description" may be interpreted in various ways, ranging from a control-flow model expressed in terms of classical Petri net to a model incorporating organizational, temporal, informational, and social aspects. In this paper we focus on the social aspect. However, we first provide an example illustrating the broader concept of process mining.

2.1   An Example of a Staffware Log

Table 1 shows a fragment of a workflow log generated by the Staffware system. In Staffware events are grouped on a case-by-case basis. The first column refers to the activity (description), the second to the type of event, the third to the user generating the event (if any), and the last column shows a time stamp. The corresponding Staffware model is shown in Figure 1. Case 10 shown in Table 1 follows the scenario where first activity *Register* is executed followed by *Send questionnaire*, *Receive questionnaire*, and *Evaluate*. Based on the evaluation, the decision is made to directly archive (activity *Archive*) the case without further processing. For Case 9 further processing is needed, while Case 8 involves a timeout and the repeated execution of some activities. Someone familiar with Staffware will be able to decide that the three cases indeed follow a scenario possible in the Staffware model shown in Figure 1. However, three cases are not sufficient to automatically derive the model of Figure 1. Note that there are many Staffware models enabling the three scenarios shown in Table 1. The challenge of process mining is to derive "good" process, organizational, and social models with as little information as possible.

2.2   Discovering Control-Flow Structures

To illustrate the principle of process mining in more detail, we consider the event log shown in Table 2.3 and focus on the *control flow* (cf. [1,3,5,6,10]). This log

Table 1. A Staffware log.

```
Case 10
Directive Description   Event           User        yyyy/mm/dd hh:mm
-------------------------------------------------------------------------
                        Start           John        2003/11/26 09:02
Register                Processed To    John        2003/11/26 09:02
Register                Released By     John        2003/11/26 09:09
Send questionnaire      Processed To    Clare       2003/11/26 09:23
Evaluate                Processed To    Sue         2003/11/26 09:58
Send questionnaire      Released By     Clare       2003/11/26 10:11
Receive questionnaire   Processed To    John        2003/11/26 13:05
Receive questionnaire   Released By     John        2003/11/26 13:06
Evaluate                Released By     Sue         2003/11/26 15:23
Archive                 Processed To    Mary        2003/11/26 16:20
Archive                 Released By     Mary        2003/11/26 16:21
                        Terminated                  2003/11/26 16:21
Case 9
Directive Description   Event           User        yyyy/mm/dd hh:mm
-------------------------------------------------------------------------
                        Start           Mike        2003/11/25 11:25
Register                Processed To    Mike        2003/11/25 11:25
Register                Released By     Mike        2003/11/25 11:37
Send questionnaire      Processed To    Mary        2003/11/25 11:51
Evaluate                Processed To    Sue         2003/11/25 11:52
Send questionnaire      Released By     Mary        2003/11/25 13:10
Receive questionnaire   Processed To    Mike        2003/11/25 15:02
Receive questionnaire   Released By     Mike        2003/11/25 15:20
Evaluate                Released By     Sue         2003/11/25 15:31
Process complaint       Processed To    Peter       2003/11/25 16:37
Process complaint       Released By     Peter       2003/11/25 16:51
Check processing        Processed To    Sue         2003/11/25 17:03
Check processing        Released By     Sue         2003/11/25 17:12
Archive                 Processed To    Mary        2003/11/25 17:38
Archive                 Released By     Mary        2003/11/25 17:41
                        Terminated                  2003/11/25 17:41
Case 8
Directive Description   Event           User        yyyy/mm/dd hh:mm
-------------------------------------------------------------------------
                        Start           John        2003/11/25 10:36
Register                Processed To    John        2003/11/25 10:36
Register                Released By     John        2003/11/25 10:40
Send questionnaire      Processed To    Mary        2003/11/25 10:50
Evaluate                Processed To    Sue         2003/11/25 11:25
Send questionnaire      Released By     Mary        2003/11/25 11:51
Receive questionnaire   Processed To    John        2003/11/26 09:36
Receive questionnaire   Expired         John        2003/11/26 09:52
Receive questionnaire   Withdrawn       John        2003/11/26 09:53
...
```

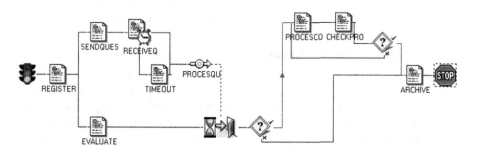

Fig. 1. The staffware model

abstracts from the time, date, and event type, and limits the information to the order in which activities are being executed. The log shown in Table 2.3 contains information about five cases (i.e., process instances). The log shows that for four cases (1, 2, 3, and 4) the activities A, B, C, and D have been executed. For the fifth case only three activities are executed: activities A, E, and D. Each case starts with the execution of A and ends with the execution of D. If activity B is executed, then also activity C is executed. However, for some cases activity C is executed before activity B. Based on the information shown in Table 2.3 and by making some assumptions about the completeness of the log (i.e., assuming that the cases are representative and a sufficient large subset of possible behaviors is observed), we can deduce the Petri net shown in Figure 2(a) (cf. [20]).

2.3   Discovering Organizational Structures

Table 2. An event log.

case identifier	activity identifier	performer
case 1	activity A	John
case 2	activity A	John
case 3	activity A	Sue
case 3	activity B	Carol
case 1	activity B	Mike
case 1	activity C	John
case 2	activity C	Mike
case 4	activity A	Sue
case 2	activity B	John
case 2	activity D	Pete
case 5	activity A	Sue
case 4	activity C	Carol
case 1	activity D	Pete
case 3	activity C	Sue
case 3	activity D	Pete
case 4	activity B	Sue
case 5	activity E	Clare
case 5	activity D	Clare
case 4	activity D	Pete

Figure 2(a) does not show any information about the performers, i.e., the people executing activities. However, Table 2.3 shows information about the performers. For example, we can deduce that activity A is executed by either John or Sue, activity B is executed by John, Sue, Mike or Carol, C is executed by John, Sue, Mike or Carol, D is executed by Pete or Clare, and E is executed by Clare. We could indicate this information in Figure 2(a). The information could also be used to "guess" or "discover" organizational structures. For example, a guess could be that there are three roles: X, Y, and Z. For the execution of A role X is required and John and Sue have this role. For the execution of B and C role Y is required and John, Sue, Mike and Carol have this role. For the execution of D and E role Z is required and Pete and Clare have this role. For five cases these choices may seem arbitrary but for larger data sets such inferences capture the dominant roles in an organization. The resulting "activity-role-performer diagram" is shown in Figure 2(b). The three "discovered" roles link activities to performers.

2.4   Discovering Social Networks

When deriving roles and other organizational entities from the event log the focus is on the relation between people or groups of people and the process. Another perspective is not to focus on the relation between the process and individuals but on relations among individuals (or groups of individuals). Consider for example Table 2.3. Although Carol and Mike can execute the same activities (B and C), Mike is always working with John (cases 1 and 2) and Carol

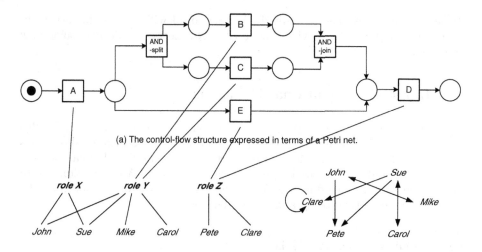

(a) The control-flow structure expressed in terms of a Petri net.

(b) The organizational structure expressed in terms of a activity-role-performer diagram.

(c) A sociogram based on transfer of work.

Fig. 2. Three models (control-flow, organizational, and social network structures) based on the event log shown in Table 2.3.

is always working with Sue (cases 3 and 4). Probably Carol and Mike have the same role but based on the small sample shown in Table 2.3 it seems that John is not working with Carol and Sue is not working with Carol.[1] These examples show that the event log can be used to derive relations between performers of activities, thus resulting in a sociogram. For example, it is possible to generate a sociogram based on the transfers of work from one individual to another as is shown in Figure 2(c). Each node represents one of the six performers and each arc represents that there has been a transfer of work from one individual to another. The definition of "transfer of work from A to B" is based on whether there for the same case an activity executed by A is directly followed by an activity executed by B. For example, both in case 1 and 2 there is a transfer from John to Mike. Figure 2(c) does not show frequencies. However, for analysis proposes these frequencies can added. The arc from John to Mike would then have weight 2. Typically, we do not use absolute frequencies but weighted frequencies to get relative values between 0 and 1. Figure 2(c) shows that work is transferred to Pete but not vice versa. Mike only interacts with John and Carol only interacts with Sue. Clare is the only person transferring work to herself.

For a simple network with just a few cases and performers the results may seem trivial. However, for larger organizations with many cases it may be possible to discover interesting structures. Sociograms as shown in Figure 2(c) can be used as input for SNA tools that can visualize the network in various ways, compute metrics like the density of the network, analyze the role of an individual in the network (for example the "centrality" or "power" of a performer), and identify

---

[1] Clearly the number of events in Table 2.3 is too small to establish these assumptions accurately. However, for the sake of argument we assume that the things that did not happen will never happen.

cliques (groups of connected individuals). Section 3 will discuss this aspect in more detail and Section 4 will provide concrete metrics to derive sociograms from event logs.

3 Mining Organizational Relations

In the previous section, we provided an overview of process mining. In this section, we focus on the main topic of this paper: mining organizational relations as described in Section 2.4. The goal is to generate a sociogram that can be used as input for standard software in the SNA (Social Network Analysis) domain. In this section we first introduce the fundamentals of SNA and then focus on the question how to derive sociograms from event logs.

3.1 Social Network Analysis

Applications of SNA range from the analysis of small social networks to large networks. For example, the tool InFlow (http://www.orgnet.com/) has been used to analyze terrorist network surrounding the September 11th 2001 events. However, such tools could also be used to analyze the social network in a classroom. In literature, researchers distinguish between *sociocentric* (whole) and *egocentric* (personal) approaches. Sociocentric approaches consider interactions within a defined group and consider the group as a whole. Egocentric approaches consider the network of an individual, e.g., relations among the friends of a given person. From a mathematical point of view both approaches are quite similar. In both cases the starting point for analysis is graph where nodes represent people and the arcs/edges represent relations. Although this information can also be represented as a matrix, we use the graph notation. The graph can be undirected or directed, e.g., A may like B but not vice versa. Moreover, the relations may be binary (they are there or not) or weighted (e.g., "+" or "-", or a real number). The weight is used to qualify the relation. The resulting graph is named a *sociogram*.

In a mathematical sense such a sociogram is a graph (P, R) where P is the set of individuals (in the context of process mining referred to as performers) and $R \subseteq P \times P$. If the graph is undirected, R is symmetric. If the graph is weighted, there is an additional function W assigning a value to all elements of R. When looking at the graph as a *whole* there are notions like *density*, i.e., the number of element in R divided by the maximal number of elements, e.g., in a directed graph there are n^2 possible connections (including self loops) where n is the number of nodes. For example the density of the graph shown in Figure 2(c) is $8/(6 * 6) = 0.22$. Other metrics based on weighted graphs are the maximal geodesic distance in a graph. The geodesic distance of two nodes is the distance of the shortest path in the graph based on R and W.

When looking at one specific individual (i.e., a node in the graph), many notions can be defined. If all other individuals are in short distance to a given node and all geodesic paths (i.e., shorted path in the graph) visit this node, clearly the node is very central (like a spider in the web). There are different metrics for this intuitive notion of *centrality*. The Bavelas-Leavitt index of centrality is a well-known example that is based on the geodesic paths in the graph [7]. Let i be an individual (i.e., $i \in P$) and $D_{j,k}$ the geodesic distance from an individual j to an individual k. The Bavelas-Leavitt index of centrality is defined as $BL(i) = (\sum_{j,k} D_{j,k})/(\sum_{j,k} D_{j,i} + D_{i,k})$. Note that the index divides the sum of all geodesic distances by the sum of all geodesic distances from and to a given resource. Other related metrics are *closeness* (1 divided by the sum of all geodesic distances to a given resource) and *betweenness* (a ratio based on the number of geodesic paths visiting a given node) [9,12,13,22,23]. Other notions include the *emission* of a resource (i.e., $\sum_j W_{i,j}$), the *reception* of a resource (i.e., $\sum_j W_{j,i}$), and the *determination degree* (i.e., $\sum_j W_{j,i} - W_{i,j}$) [9,22,23]. Another interesting metric is the *sociometric status* which is determined by the sum of input and output relations, i.e., $\sum_j D_{j,i} + D_{i,j}$. All metrics can be normalized by taking the size of the social network into account (e.g., divide by the number of resources). Using these metrics and a visual representation of the network one can analyze various aspects of the social structure of an organization. For example, one can search for densely connected clusters of resources and structural holes (i.e., areas with few connections), cf. [9,22,23].

Let us apply some of these notions to the sociogram shown Figure 2(c) where the arcs indicate (unweighted) frequencies. The sociometric status of Clare is 2 (if we include self-links), the sociometric status of Pete is 4, the emission of John is 5, the emission of Pete is 0, the reception of Pete is 4, the reception of Sue is 2, the determination degree of Mike is 0, etc. The Bavelas-Leavitt index of centrality of John is 4.33 while the same index for Sue is 3.25. The numbers are unweighted and in most cases these are made relative to allow for easy comparison. Tools like AGNA, NetMiner, Egonet, InFlow, KliqueFinder, MetaSight, NetForm, NetVis, StOCNET, UCINET, and visone are just some of the many SNA tools available. For more information on SNA we refer to [8,9, 22,23].

3.2   Deriving Relations from Event Logs

After showing the potential of SNA and the availability of techniques and tools, the main question is: *How to derive meaningful sociograms from event logs?* To address this question we identify four types of metrics that can be used to establish relationships between individuals: (1) metrics based on (possible) causality, (2) metrics based on joint cases, (3) metrics based on joint activities, and (4) metrics based on special event types.

Metrics based on (possible) causality monitor for individual cases how work moves among performers. One of the examples of such a metric is *handover of work*. Within a case (i.e., process instance) there is a handover of work from individual i to individual j if there are two subsequent activities where the first is completed by i and the second by j. This notion can be refined in various ways. For example, knowledge of the process structure can be used to detect whether there is really a causal dependency between both activities. It is also possible to not only consider direct succession but also indirect succession using a "causality fall factor" β, i.e., if there are 3 activities in-between an activity completed by i and an activity completed by j, the causality fall factor is β^3. A related metric is *subcontracting* where the main idea is to count the number of times individual j executed an activity in-between two activities executed by individual i. This may indicate that work was subcontracted from i to j. Again all kinds of refinements are possible.

Metrics based on joint cases ignore causal dependencies but simply count how frequently two individuals are performing activities for the same case. If individuals work together on cases, they will have a stronger relation than individuals rarely working together.

Metrics based on joint activities do not consider how individuals work together on shared cases but focus on the activities they do. The assumption here is that people doing similar things have stronger relations than people doing completely different things. Each individual has a "profile" based on how frequent they conduct specific activities. There are many ways to measure the "distance" between two profiles thus enabling many metrics.

Metrics based on special event types consider the type of event. Thus far we assumed that events correspond to the execution of activities. However, there are also events like reassigning an activity from one individual to another. For example, if i frequently delegates work to j but not vice versa it is likely that i is in a hierarchical relation with j. From a SNA point of view these observations are particularly interesting since they represent explicit power relations.

The sociogram shown Figure 2(c) is based on the causality metric handover of work. In the next section, we will define the metrics in more detail.

4   Metrics

In this section, we define some of the metrics we have developed to establish relationships between individuals from event logs. We address only examples of the first three types introduced in Section 3.2. Before we define these examples in detail, we introduce a convenient notation for event logs.

Definition 4.1. (Event log) Let A be a set of activities (i.e., atomic workflow/process objects, also referred to as tasks) and P a set of performers (i.e., resources, individuals, or workers). $E = A \times P$ is the set of (possible) events, i.e., combinations of an activity and a performer (e.g. (a, p) denotes the execution of activity a by performer p). $C = E^*$ is the set of possible event sequences (traces describing a case). $L \in \mathcal{B}(C)$ is an *event log*. Note that $\mathcal{B}(C)$ is the set of all bags (multi-sets) over C.

Note that this definition of an event slightly differs from the informal notions used before. First of all, we abstract from additional information such as time stamps, data, etc. Secondly, we do not consider the ordering of events corresponding to different cases. For convenience, we define two operations on events: $\pi_a(e) = a$ and $\pi_p(e) = p$ for some event $e = (a, p)$.

4.1   Metrics Based on (Possible) Causality

Metrics based on causality take into account both handover of work and subcontracting. The basic idea is that performers are related if a case is passed from one performer to another. For both situations, three kinds of refinements are applied. First of all, one can differentiate with respect to the degree of causality, e.g., the length of handover. It means that we can consider not only direct succession but also indirect succession. Second, we can ignore multiple transfers within one instance or not. Third, we can consider arbitrary transfers of work or only consider those where there is a casual dependency (for the latter we need to know the process model). Based on these refinements, we derive $2^3 = 8$ variants for both the handover of work and subcontracting metrics. These variant metrics are all based on the same event log. Before defining metrics, the basic notions applied to a single case $c = (c_0, c_1, \dots)$ are specified.

Definition 4.2. ($\triangleright, \trianglerighteq$) Let L be a log. Assume that $\rightarrow$ denotes some causality relation derived from the process model. For $a_1, a_2 \in A$, $p_1, p_2 \in P$, $c = (c_0, c_1, \dots) \in L$, and $n \in \mathbb{N}$:

- $p_1 \triangleright^n_c p_2 = \exists_{0 \leq i < |c|-n} \; \pi_p(c_i) = p_1 \; \wedge \; \pi_p(c_{i+n}) = p_2$

- $|p_1 \triangleright^n_c p_2| = \sum_{0 \leq i < |c|-n} \begin{cases} 1 \text{ if } \pi_p(c_i) = p_1 \; \wedge \; \pi_p(c_{i+n}) = p_2 \\ 0 \text{ otherwise} \end{cases}$

- $p_1 \trianglerighteq^n_c p_2 = \exists_{0 \leq i < |c|-n} \; \pi_p(c_i) = p_1 \; \wedge \; \pi_p(c_{i+n}) = p_2 \; \wedge \; \pi_a(c_i) \rightarrow \pi_a(c_{i+n})$

- $|p_1 \trianglerighteq^n_c p_2| = \sum_{0 \leq i < |c|-n} \begin{cases} 1 \text{ if } \pi_p(c_i) = p_1 \; \wedge \; \pi_p(c_{i+n}) = p_2 \; \wedge \; \pi_a(c_i) \rightarrow \pi_a(c_{i+n}) \\ 0 \text{ otherwise} \end{cases}$

$p_1 \triangleright^n_c p_2$ denotes the function which returns *true* if within the context of case c performers p_1 and p_2 both executed some activity such that the distance between these two activities is n. For example, for case 1 shown in Table 2.3, *John* $\triangleright^1_c$ *Mike* equals 1 and *John* $\triangleright^3_c$ *Pete* equals 1. In this definition, if the value of n equals 1, it refers to direct succession. If n is greater than 1, it refers to indirect succession. However, it ignores both multiple transfers within one instance and casual dependencies. $|p_1 \triangleright^n_c p_2|$ denotes the function which returns the number of times $p_1 \triangleright^n_c p_2$ in the case c. In other words, it considers multiple transfers within one instance. $p_1 \trianglerighteq^n_c p_2$ and $|p_1 \trianglerighteq^n_c p_2|$ are similar to $p_1 \triangleright^n_c p_2$ and $|p_1 \triangleright^n_c p_2|$ but in addition they take into account whether there is a real casual dependency. For example, consider case 1 shown in Table 2.3. The order of events is: A (John), B (Mike), C (John), and D (Pete). If we calculate the relationships among activity B, C, and D, *Mike* $\triangleright^1_c$ *John* equals 1 and *Mike* $\triangleright^1_c$ *Pete* equals 0. However, *Mike* $\trianglerighteq^1_c$ *John* equals 0 and *Mike* $\trianglerighteq^2_c$ *Pete* equals 1, because activity B and C do not have a casual dependency but activity B and D do (see Figure 2(a); B and C are in parallel but are both causally followed by D).

Using such relations, we define handover of work metrics. The following metrics only deal with first and second refinements. If we replace $\triangleright$ with $\trianglerighteq$, we can calculate the relationships considering only real casual dependencies and thus deal with the third refinement.

Definition 4.3. (Handover of work metrics) Let L be a log. For $p_1, p_2 \in P$ and some β ($0 < \beta < 1$):

$- p_1 \rhd_L p_2 = (\sum_{c \in L} |p_1 \rhd_c^1 p_2|)/(\sum_{c \in L} |c| - 1)$

$- p_1 \dot{\rhd}_L p_2 = (\sum_{c \in L \wedge p_1 \rhd_c^1 p_2} 1)/|L|$

$- p_1 \rhd_L^\beta p_2 = (\sum_{c \in L} \sum_{1 \le n < |c|} \beta^{n-1} |p_1 \rhd_c^n p_2|)/(\sum_{c \in L} \sum_{1 \le n < |c|} \beta^{n-1}(|c| - n))$

$- p_1 \dot{\rhd}_L^\beta p_2 = (\sum_{c \in L} \sum_{1 \le n < |c| \wedge p_1 \rhd_c^n p_2} \beta^{n-1})/(\sum_{c \in L} \sum_{1 \le n < |c|} \beta^{n-1})$

$p_1 \rhd_L p_2$ means dividing the total number of direct successions from p_1 to p_2 in a process log by the maximum number of possible direct successions in the log. For example, in Table 2.3, $John \rhd_L Mike$ equals 2/14. $p_1 \dot{\rhd}_L p_2$ ignores multiple transfers within one instance (i.e., case). $p_1 \rhd_L^\beta p_2$ and $p_1 \dot{\rhd}_L^\beta p_2$ deal with indirect succession by introducing a "causality fall factor" β in this notation. If within the context of a case there are n events in-between two performers, the causality fall factor is β^n. $p_1 \rhd_L^\beta p_2$ consider all possible successions, while $p_1 \dot{\rhd}_L^\beta p_2$ ignores multiple transfers within one case.

In the case of subcontracting, we only describe a basic relation and a basic metrics, i.e., again there are 8 variants but we only consider the basic one.

Definition 4.4. (In-between metrics) Let L be a log. Assume that $\rightarrow$ denotes some causality relation. In the context of L and $\rightarrow$, we define a number of relations. For $a_1, a_2 \in A$, $p_1, p_2 \in P$, $c = (c_0, c_1, \ldots) \in L$, $|c| > 2$, $n \in \mathbb{N}$, and $n > 1$:

$- p_1 \diamondsuit_c^n p_2 = \exists_{0 \le i < j < i+n < |c|} \pi_p(c_i) = p_1 \wedge \pi_p(c_j) = p_2 \wedge \pi_p(c_{i+n}) = p_1$

$- p_1 \diamondsuit_L p_2 = (\sum_{c \in L} |p_1 \diamondsuit_c^2 p_2|)/(\sum_{c \in L} (|c| - 2))$

In subcontracting, the three refinements mentioned can also be applied. However the concept of direct and indirect succession is changed. Direct succession means there is only one activity in-between two activities executed by one performer. While indirect succession means, there are multiple activities in-between two activities executed by one performer. We also introduce causality fall factor β for indirect succession. For example, assume that there are four activities. Both first and fourth activity are executed by a performer i, while the second and third activity are executed by performer j and k respectively. In this situation, we can derive two relations which are from a performer i to a performer j and from a performer i to a performer k. Again we use a causality fall factor β. The second and third refinements are the same as for handover of work.

4.2   Metrics Based on Joint Cases

For this type of metric we ignore causal dependencies and simply count how often two individuals are performing activities for the same case.

Definition 4.5. (Working together metrics) Let L be a log. For $p_1, p_2 \in P$:
$p_1 \bowtie_L p_2 = \sum_{c \in L} p_1 \bowtie_c p_2 / \sum_{c \in L} g(c, p_1)$ if $\sum_{c \in L} g(c, p_1) \neq 0$, otherwise $p_1 \bowtie_L p_2 = 0$, where for $c = (c_0, c_1, \ldots) \in L$: $p_1 \bowtie_c p_2 = 1$ if $\exists_{0 \le i,j < |c| \wedge i \neq j} \pi_p(c_i) = p_1 \wedge \pi_p(c_j) = p_2$, otherwise $p_1 \bowtie_c p_2 = 0$: $g(c, p_1) = 1$ if $\exists_{0 \le i < |c|} \pi_p(c_i) = p_1$, otherwise $g(c, p_1) = 0$

Note that, in this definition we divide the number of joint cases by the number of cases which p_1 appeared, since the appearance is relative to the performers. Let us apply this metric to analyze the relationship between John and Pete based in the log shown in Table 2.3. *John* $\bowtie_L$ *Pete* equals 2/2 and *Pete* $\bowtie_L$ *John* equals 2/4.

Moreover, alternative metrics can be composed by taking the distance between activities into account, e.g., use variants like $(p_1 \rhd_L^\beta p_2 + p_2 \rhd_L^\beta p_1)/2$ or $(p_1 \dot\rhd_L^\beta p_2 + p_2 \dot\rhd_L^\beta p_1)/2$.

4.3   Metrics Based on Joint Activities

To calculate the metrics based on joint activities, first we make a "profile" based on how frequent individuals conduct specific activities. In this paper, we use a *performer by activity matrix* to represent these profiles. This matrix simply records how frequent each performer executes specific activities.

Definition 4.6. ($\triangle$) Let L be a log. For $p_1 \in P$, $a_1 \in A$, and $c = (c_0, c_1, \dots) \in L$:

$$- \; p_1 \triangle_c a_1 = \sum_{0 \le i < |c|} \begin{cases} 1 \text{ if } \pi_a(c_i) = a_1 \; \wedge \; \pi_p(c_i) = p_1 \\ 0 \text{ otherwise} \end{cases}$$

$$- \; p_1 \triangle_L a_1 = \sum_{c \in L} p_1 \triangle_c a_1$$

Note that $\triangle$ defines a matrix with rows P and columns A. Table 3 shows a part of the performer by activity matrix derived from Table 2.3.

Table 3. A part of the performer by activity matrix.

performer	activity A	activity B	activity C	activity D	activity E
Sue	3	1	1	0	0
Carol	0	1	1	0	0
Clare	0	0	0	1	1

Based on this matrix, we defined several metrics to measure the distance between two performers. These metrics are all based on a comparison of the corresponding row vectors.

In this section we introduced only some of the metrics we have developed. It is important to note that each of the metrics is derived from some log L and the result can be represented in terms of a weighted graph (P, R, W), where P is the set of performers, R is the set of relations, and W is a function indicating the weight of each relation (see Section 3.1). For example, the basic handover of work metric $\rhd_L$ defines $R = \{(p_1, p_2) \in P \times P \mid p_1 \rhd_L p_2 \neq 0\}$ and $W(p_1, p_2) = p_1 \rhd_L p_2$. In other words, given an event log L each metric results in a sociogram that can be analyzed using existing SNA tools.

5   MiSoN

This section introduces our tool MiSoN (Mining Social Networks). MiSoN has been developed to discover relationships between individuals from a range of enterprise information systems including workflow management systems such as Staffware, InConcert, and MQSeries, ERP systems, and CRM systems. Based on the event logs extracted from these systems MiSoN constructs sociograms that can be used as a starting point for SNA. The derived relationships can be exported in a matrix format and used by most SNA tools. With such tools, we can apply several techniques to analyze social networks, e.g., find interaction patterns, evaluate the role of an individual in an organization, etc.

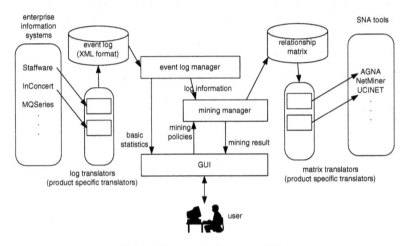

Fig. 3. The architecture of MiSoN

MiSoN has been developed using Java including XML-based libraries such as JAXB and JDOM, and provides an easy-to-use graphical user interface. Figure 3 shows the architecture of MiSoN. The mining starts from a tool-independent XML format which includes information about processes, cases, activities, event times, and performers. MiSoN provides functionalities for displaying user statistics and event log statistics. Using the metrics defined in Section 4, MiSoN constructs relationships between individuals. When calculating the relationships, the user can select suitable metrics and set relevant options. The result can be displayed using a matrix representation and a graph representation, but it can also be exported to SNA tools. Exported data contains the number of performers, names of performers, and a relationship matrix.

6   Example: Applying MiSoN to a Staffware Log

Although MiSoN and the underlying analysis routines are tool-independent, we focus on a concrete system to illustrate the applicability of the results presented in this paper. The Staffware audit trail referred to by Table 1 is converted by MiSoN to the XML format described in the previous section. In this sample data, we only consider the "released by" event type to make sociograms. We have tested MiSoN with several metrics mentioned in previous section. Figure 4 shows a screenshot of MiSoN when displaying the mining result of handover of work metrics. MiSoN can export the mining result using the

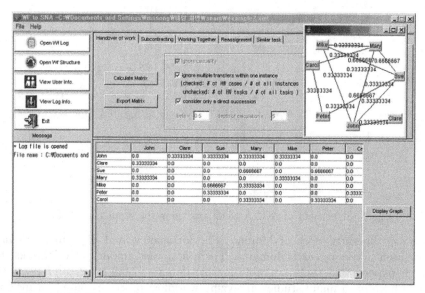

Fig. 4. MiSoN screenshot showing a sociogram based on the Staffware log

AGNA-translator (but also other tools like UCINET and NetMiner). AGNA (cf. http://www.geocities.com/imbenta/agna/) is an SNA tool that allows for a wide variety of sociometric analysis techniques. For example, AGNA supports various notions of centrality including the Bavelas-Leavitt index described in Section 3.1. John and Sue have the highest Bavelas-Leavitt index (the value is 4.2), while Clare has the smallest value (2.8). Figure 5 shows the analysis using the tool AGNA. It also shows the network structure of result.

7   Related Work

Related work can be divided in two categories: process mining and SNA.

The idea of process mining is not new [1,3,5,6,10,15,16,18,21,24] but has been mainly aiming at the control-flow perspective. In this paper, it is impossible to do justice to the work done in this area. Therefore, for more information on process mining we refer to a special issue of Computers in Industry on process mining [4] and the survey paper [3]. Note that although quite some work has been done on process mining from event logs none of the approaches known to the authors have incorporated the social dimension as discussed in this paper.

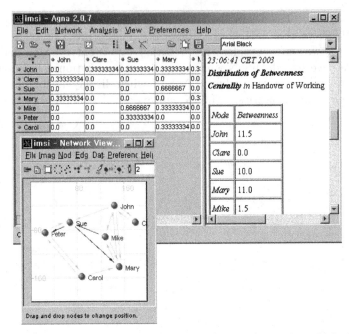

Fig. 5. Screenshot of AGNA when analyzing the input from MiSocN

Since the early work of Moreno [17], sociometry, and SNA in particular, have been active research domains. There is a vast amount of textbooks, research papers, and tools available in this domain [7,8,9,11,12,13,17,19,22,23]. There have been many studies analyzing workflow processes based on insights from social network analysis. However, these studies typically have an ad-hoc character and sociograms are typically constructed based on questionnaires rather than using a structured and automated approach as described in this paper. Most tools in the SNA domain take sociograms as input. MiSoN is one of the few tools that generate sociograms as output. The only comparable tools are tools to analyze e-mail traffic, cf. BuddyGraph (http://www.buddygraph.com/) and MetaSight (http://www.metasight.co.uk/). However, these tools monitor unstructured messages and cannot distinguish between different activities (e.g., work-related interaction versus social interaction).

8   Conclusions

This paper presents an approach, concrete metrics, and a tool to extract information from event logs and construct a sociogram which can be used to analyze interpersonal relationships in an organization. Today many information systems are "process aware" and log events in some structured way. As indicated in the introduction, workflow management systems register the start and completion of activities, ERP systems log all transactions (e.g., users filling out forms), call center and CRM systems log interactions with customers, etc. These examples have in common that there is some kind of event log. Unfortunately, the information in these logs is rarely used to derive information about the process, the organization, and the social network. In this paper we focus on the latter aspect and present an approach to discover sociograms. These sociograms are based on the observed behavior and may use events like the transfer of work or delegation from one individual to another. MiSoN can interface with commercial systems such as Staffware and standard SNA tools like AGNA, UCINET and NetMiner, thus allowing for the application of the ideas presented in this paper.

At this point in time we are applying MiSoN to a real data set, and we plan to report on this in a future paper. We also investigate extensions of the approach using filtering techniques and more advanced forms clustering. For example, we now abstract from the results of activities. If activities or cases can be classified as successful or unsuccessful, important or unimportant, standard or special, etc., this information could be used when building sociograms.

Acknowledgement. Minseok Song is visiting Department of Technology Management at Eindhoven University of Technology with fund by BK21 program. He would like to thank the Ministry of Education of Korea for its financial support through the BK21 program.

References

1. W.M.P. van der Aalst and B.F. van Dongen. Discovering Workflow Performance Models from Timed Logs. In Y. Han, S. Tai, and D. Wikarski, editors, *International Conference on Engineering and Deployment of Cooperative Information Systems (EDCIS 2002)*, volume 2480 of *Lecture Notes in Computer Science*, pages 45–63. Springer-Verlag, Berlin, 2002.
2. W.M.P. van der Aalst and K.M. van Hee. *Workflow Management: Models, Methods, and Systems*. MIT press, Cambridge, MA, 2002.
3. W.M.P. van der Aalst, B.F. van Dongen, J. Herbst, L. Maruster, G. Schimm, and A.J.M.M. Weijters. Workflow Mining: A Survey of Issues and Approaches. *Data and Knowledge Engineering*, 47(2):237–267, 2003.
4. W.M.P. van der Aalst and A.J.M.M. Weijters, editors. *Process Mining*, Special Issue of Computers in Industry, Volume 53, Number 3. Elsevier Science Publishers, Amsterdam, 2004.
5. W.M.P. van der Aalst, A.J.M.M. Weijters, and L. Maruster. Workflow Mining: Discovering Process Models from Event Logs. QUT Technical report, FIT-TR-2003-03, Queensland University of Technology, Brisbane, 2003. (Accepted for publication in IEEE Transactions on Knowledge and Data Engineering.).
6. R. Agrawal, D. Gunopulos, and F. Leymann. Mining Process Models from Workflow Logs. In *Sixth International Conference on Extending Database Technology*, pages 469–483, 1998.
7. A.A. Bavelas. A Mathematical Model for Group Structures. *Human Organization*, 7:16–30, 1948.
8. H.R. Bernard, P.D. Killworth, C. McCarty, G.A. Shelley, and S. Robinson. Comparing Four Different Methods for Measuring Personal Social Networks. *Social Networks*, 12:179–216, 1990.

9. R.S. Burt and M Minor. *Applied Network Analysis: A Methodological Introduction.* Sage, Newbury Park CA, 1983.

10. J.E. Cook and A.L. Wolf. Discovering Models of Software Processes from Event-Based Data. *ACM Transactions on Software Engineering and Methodology,* 7(3):215–249, 1998.

11. M. Feldman. Electronic mail and weak ties in organizations. *Office: Technology and People,* 3:83–101, 1987.

12. L.C. Freeman. A Set of Measures of Centrality Based on Betweenness. *Sociometry,* 40:35–41, 1977.

13. L.C. Freeman. Centrality in Social Networks: Conceptual Clarification. *Social Networks,* 1:215–239, 1979.

14. D. Grigori, F. Casati, U. Dayal, and M.C. Shan. Improving Business Process Quality through Exception Understanding, Prediction, and Prevention. In P. Apers, P. Atzeni, S. Ceri, S. Paraboschi, K. Ramamohanarao, and R. Snodgrass, editors, *Proceedings of 27th International Conference on Very Large Data Bases (VLDB'01),* pages 159–168. Morgan Kaufmann, 2001.

15. J. Herbst. A Machine Learning Approach to Workflow Management. In *Proceedings 11th European Conference on Machine Learning,* volume 1810 of *Lecture Notes in Computer Science,* pages 183–194. Springer-Verlag, Berlin, 2000.

16. IDS Scheer. ARIS Process Performance Manager (ARIS PPM). http://www.ids-scheer.com, 2002.

17. J.L. Moreno. *Who Shall Survive?* Nervous and Mental Disease Publishing Company, Washington, DC, 1934.

18. M. zur Mühlen and M. Rosemann. Workflow-based Process Monitoring and Controlling - Technical and Organizational Issues. In R. Sprague, editor, *Proceedings of the 33rd Hawaii International Conference on System Science (HICSS-33),* pages 1–10. IEEE Computer Society Press, Los Alamitos, California, 2000.

19. H. Nemati and C.D. Barko. *Organizational Data Mining: Leveraging Enterprise Data Resources for Optimal Performance.* Idea Group Publishing, Hershey, PA, USA, 2003.

20. W. Reisig and G. Rozenberg, editors. *Lectures on Petri Nets I: Basic Models,* volume 1491 of *Lecture Notes in Computer Science.* Springer-Verlag, Berlin, 1998.

21. M. Sayal, F. Casati, and M.C. Shan U. Dayal. Business Process Cockpit. In *Proceedings of 28th International Conference on Very Large Data Bases (VLDB'02),* pages 880–883. Morgan Kaufmann, 2002.

22. J. Scott. *Social Network Analysis.* Sage, Newbury Park CA, 1992.

23. S. Wasserman and K. Faust. *Social Network Analysis: Methods and Applications.* Cambridge University Press, Cambridge, 1994.

24. A.J.M.M. Weijters and W.M.P. van der Aalst. Rediscovering Workflow Models from Event-Based Data using Little Thumb. *Integrated Computer-Aided Engineering,* 10(2):151–162, 2003.

Model-Driven Approach to Workflow Execution

Wonchang Hur[1], Jae-yoon Jung[1†], Hoontae Kim[2], and Suk-Ho Kang[1]

[1] Department of Industrial Engineering, Seoul National University,
San 56-1, Shinlim-dong, Kwanak-gu, Seoul, Korea
{bethoven,jyjung}@ara.snu.ac.kr, shkang@cybernet.snu.ac.kr
[2] Department of Industrial and Systems Engineering, Daejin University,
San 11-1, Sundan-dong, Poch'on-si, Kyonggi-do, Korea
hoontae@daejin.ac.kr

Abstract. Workflow execution is usually accomplished by a central enactment engine that interprets a process definition and dispatches activities as specified in the definition. In practice, this type of workflow execution is successfully automated for such processes that involve routine activities. However, today's business processes don't seem to be manageable, compared to the traditional workflows. Particularly, with explosion of e-business, the processes sometimes span multiple companies, and interoperability among distributed process-centric systems has become an important issue. Therefore, the conventional execution framework may not effectively handle the complicated business processes for collaboration any more. In this article, we deliberate on realizing the vision of Model-Driven Architecture (MDA) for workflow systems and make an effort to build up a concrete process model reflecting on whole life cycle of workflow processes. The process model will improve interchangeability and portability of workflow processes, which requires that the executable components be generated from the model regardless of the variety of run-time architecture.

1 Motivation

In general, a workflow management system (WFMS) is characterized as providing support in two functional areas; build-time functions and run-time functions. The build-time functions are concerned with defining, and possibly modeling, workflow processes and their constituent activities. The run-time functions are concerned with managing the workflow processes in an operational environment and sequencing the various activities to be handled as parts of each process [10, 16].

In many WFMS's, the relationship between these two functional areas is mediated by a description of workflow processes, which are subject to be exploited by an enactment service to execute the workflow. The description of workflow provides the enactment service with relatively abstract instruction based on process semantics to determine what the next activities to dispatch are and who is responsible for them.

---

† Corresponding author. Tel.:+82-2-880-7180; fax.+82-2-889-8560

J. Desel, B. Pernici, and M. Weske (Eds.): BPM 2004, LNCS 3080, pp. 261–273, 2004.
© Springer-Verlag Berlin Heidelberg 2004

In this article we envision a new framework of workflow execution where the description of the process is transformed, either automatically or manually, into a platform specific executable model that contains specifications about run-time components as well as the description of the process itself. We argue that model-driven approach, if properly applied to the proposed framework, can articulate a systematic development of WMFS starting from the design of a platform independent model for workflow processes [11].

2 Lessons Learned

We have developed SNUFlow, which is a web-based WFMS since 1997[10]. The first version of SNUFlow was built on top of CORBA and RDBMS platform. However, as WfMC standards for process model and relevant technologies evolve, our workflow engine was required to be completely re-implemented in order to be compatible with the new standards. This is mainly because a model-driven concept did not exist in the course of WFMS development. From the experience, we have identified several elements that must be considered in the development of WFMS.

(1) Level of abstraction in process design
The first important element is notion of abstraction level in the design of a process model. WfMC has announced XPDL schema designed to represent an interchangeable process definition. To keep up with the standard, there seems to be two possible solutions. One is to re-design and re-implement the workflow engine according to XPDL schema, and the other is to transform all the definitions stored in database into XPDL style. Which one is more reasonable?

We have concluded that the most reasonable approach for XPDL support is to allow different abstraction levels of a workflow process. For example, we can start the process design from an abstract process model described using a language-independent meta-model. Then, the abstract process model may be mapped to a language-specific process model through a possible model mapping approach.

(2) Mapping from build-time process to run-time process
As stated before, run-time aspect of WFMS is confronting a challenge of shifting from simple routing and dispatching by a central enactment system to coordination of communication between distributed and autonomous software components. With proliferation of middleware technologies promising interoperability of the components, it has become technically possible to make them cooperate with each other.

Current workflow process model is more focused on representation of logical sequence of works than detailed specification of participants or communication infrastructure. For a workflow process defined in build-time to be executable during run-time, all the components participating in the process need to be able to interact with workflow engine.

For example, our workflow engine may not handle a web service activity that is performed by invoking a predefined web service. This problem becomes more serious if the process is composed of activities that span multiple companies, requiring both a web service and a CORBA object to be invoked.

From these considerations, we have realized the necessities of a new design framework based on model-driven paradigm that covers the whole life cycle of a workflow process. The design framework would support various levels of process definitions that enable language independence, and build-time and run-time mapping that enables interchangeability and portability of a workflow process.

3 Process Modeling Languages

We take a look at the plethora of process definition languages that has been issued recently. Table 1 gives brief information about these languages. For more detailed information, readers can refer to the related literature [17,14,13,1,5,3].

Table 1. Process modeling languages

Specifications	Involved parties	Domain	Modeling language	Control flow
XPDL	WfMC	Workflow Definition	XML	Graph-structured
BPSS	ebXML	B2B collaboration	UML/XML	Sequence diagram
PIP	RosettaNet	B2B collaboration	UML	Sequence diagram
BPML	BPMI	Web service Orchestration	XML	Block-structured
BPEL4WS	IBM, BEA, Microsoft, etc.	Web service Orchestration	WSDL/XML	Block-, graph-structured
WSCI	SUN, Intalio, BEA, etc.	Web service Orchestration	WSDL/XML	Block-structured

These modeling languages are all intended for providing a data model to specify business processes, but arguably, they relatively pay little attention to how the data model can be realized in a certain type of run-time architecture. We have reviewed this new family of languages by grouping them into three categories according to their application domains; workflow, B2B transaction, and web service choreography.

(1) Workflow: XPDL, which is announced by WfMC, is a standard process description language specified in XML Schema. Since XPDL was originally created in an effort to establish an interchangeable process definition format, it focuses on interpretable description of a workflow process, assuming that a dedicated enactment service handles the process.

(2) B2B transactions: The aim of this group of languages is to provide for the nominal set of specification elements necessary to specify collaboration between business partners, and to provide configuration parameters for the partners' run-time systems in order to execute that collaboration between a set of e-business software components.

(3) Web service choreography: The process models in this group are introduced for orchestration of web services. They provide a descriptive process model usually built on top of the WSDL schema, and describe how the web services in the process are collaborated and coordinated to provide services to users.

4 Run-Time Architecture for Process Execution

There may be a variety of structural designs for a run-time environment where a workflow process can be executed, but they can be categorized into three types of architecture in terms of how process definitions are handled and how participants communicate with each other in the course of the process execution.

Fig. 1 shows the conceptual illustrations of these three types of run-time architecture; (a) execution through a shared space, (b) execution through a global coordinator, and (c) execution through message exchange.

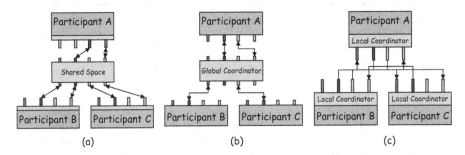

Fig. 1. Run-time architecture for process execution

(1) Execution through a shared space

In this architecture, communication is realized through writing and reading data in a shared repository. It was first introduced as a coordination model for collaborating agents in the context of traditional distributed systems. This can be further classified into two categories; data-associative and event-based. In a data-associative model agents are coordinated by producing, consuming, and testing for the presence of data objects, called 'tuples' in a shared repository [6]. In event-based model, communication takes place through the raising of events performed by the agents via publish or subscribe operation [4].

One of the noticeable features of this architecture is that participants are timely and spatially uncoupled. This implies that they are implemented to behave autonomously and independently and communicate usually in an asynchronous manner without explicit naming of each other. Therefore, in order to execute a workflow in this architecture, it may be required to introduce another participant that is specially designed to perform only a coordination activity.

(2) Execution through a global coordinator

This is a conventional type of run-time architecture for process execution that is based on traditional client-server framework. In this architecture, the process execution is performed by a global coordinator, which is responsible for creating and controlling operational instances of the process, scheduling the various activities steps within the process, and invoking the appropriate participants.

Since the coordinator exclusively possesses process definitions and intervene with every interaction between participants, they are more or less loosely coupled within the context of a certain process. This type of process execution is inefficient for handling such processes that necessitate frequent interactions between the participants.

(3) Execution through point-to-point message exchange

In this architecture, without a particular service for coordination, processes are executable by their participants that communicate directly with each other. The participants implement their own services for handling message exchange, and invoke the services to send or receive messages required to perform execution of the process.

Since the participants actively take part in the process execution, the definition of the process is distributed and shared among them and they get tightly coupled with each other in the context of the process. To execute a workflow process in this type of run-time architecture, a sophisticated approach need to be taken considering how to decompose and distribute a portion of the process model to corresponding software components representing participants, and how to configure the process logics in them.

5 Model-Driven Approach to Workflow Execution

We are interested in a model-driven approach to the development of process enactment systems. The approach needs to be preceded by establishing a well-structured model for collaborative processes.

Above all, for successful application of model-driven approach to process execution in WFMS, it is necessary to create a concrete process model reflecting on all the entities related with the whole life cycle of the process. As a modeling method for the process model we have considered the Workflow Meta-Model (WMM) of WfMC [17] and EDOC profile of OMG [12]. Though the WMM itself has very limited modeling capability, we think that it can be augmented by the UML profiles for EDOC (Enterprise Distributed Object Computing). The profiles provide many useful modeling elements to simplify the development of component based enterprise-wide software systems by means of a modeling framework, based on UML 1.4 and conforming to the OMG Model Driven Architecture [11]. At the core of the profile is the Enterprise Collaboration Architecture (ECA). The ECA is composed of four UML profiles (Entity profile, Business Process profile, Events profile, and Relationship profile) derived from the Component Collaboration Architecture (CCA). The CCA details how the UML concepts of classes, collaborations and activity graphs can be used to model, at varying and mixed levels of granularity, the structure and behavior of the components that comprise a system. The CCA meta-model is divided into four sub meta-models according to semantics of each component: Structural Specification, Choreography, Composition, and Document meta-models [12].

The *Structural Specification* meta-model represents the physical structure of the component contract, defining the component and its ports. The *Choreography* meta-model specifies how messages will flow between PortUsages. The choreography may be externally oriented, specifying the contract a component will have with other components or, it may be internally oriented, specifying the flow of messages within a composition. External choreographies are shown as an activity graph while internal choreography is shown as part of collaboration. An external choreography may be defined for a protocol or a ProcessComponent. The *Composition* meta-model is an abstract capability that is used for ProcessComponents and for community processes. Compositions show how a set of components can be used to define and perhaps to implement a process. Finally, the *Document* meta-model defines the information that can be transferred and manipulated between ProcessComponents. It also forms the basis for information in entities.

5.1 EDOC-Based Workflow

The EDOC-based workflow adopts a data model described by UML profiles, which have their foundation derived from the CCA meta-model of EDOC. The process model can be designed from the ECA that already has predefined profiles, such as business process profiles and entity profiles, for modeling enterprise components. Otherwise, one can devise a specific profile for WFMS based on CCA meta-model, and then the process model can be described using the newly designed UML profile.

The EDOC-based workflow model has several advantages over the existing XML-based process models. First of all, it is possible to design a process model incorporating detailed specifications of its run-time components, such as events, messages, and protocols. It facilitates representation of interaction between these components, by means of inheriting the already established relationships that the CCA meta-model provide. One of the other benefits is that it provides a recursive composition of a process model. It allows zooming of the process model so that one can easily grasp an abstract structure of the process.

Above all, the EDOC-based workflow is basically a UML model by itself, which implies that through a sophisticatedly devised mapping process the workflow model can be ported to a specific platform. That is, skeleton codes for software components required to execute the workflow model can be generated from the workflow model itself. The skeleton codes can be implemented to fit the target platform.

Fig. 2 illustrates conceptual schema for an EDOC-based workflow. The schema consists of three sub-models that are tightly coupled with each other: Process, Enactment, and Component meta-models. The *Process* meta-model is used to describe a logical structure of a workflow process with execution rules. The *Component* meta-model describes software components representing workflow participants, and models schema of relevant data. Finally, the *Enactment* meta-model specifies software objects used to execute the workflow process. The objects play a role of state management of processes, message exchange, and event monitoring.

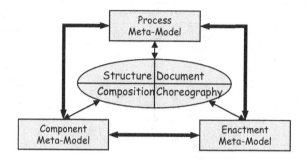

Fig. 2. Conceptual schema for an EDOC-based workflow

5.2 Extended Workflow Meta-model

The WMM of WfMC describes the basic set of entities contained within a workflow process, its relationships, and attributes. The entities include processes, activities, transition information, participant specification, application declaration, and relevant data. Because WMM is originally created in consideration for XPDL, the modeling capability is more or less insufficient for representing the whole aspects of a workflow process, including its run-time entities. A good way to supplement the semantics of WMM is to incorporate the modeling constructs provided by Component Collaboration Architecture (CCA) of EDOC profile.

The CCA details how the UML concepts of classes, collaborations, and activity graphs can be used to model, at varying and mixed levels of granularity, the structure and behavior of the components that comprise a system [12]. It provides many useful modeling constructs that enable us to define a UML profile for representing domain specific systems like WFMS.

Fig. 3 shows an overall structure of an Extended Workflow Meta-Model (EWMM) for workflow execution, which is incorporated with the four sets of components in CCA. In the EWMM, the existing entities are redefined using stereotypes in CCA, and new entities are brought in to represent the run-time entities including events and messages. Then, the newly introduced entities make associations with other existing entities based on the relationships specified in CCA. EWMM may be thought of as a new UML profile for WFMS based on CCA.

EWMM redefined by adopting the CCA can inherit several advantages of the CCA. This includes

• Recursive component composition, allowing an effective representation of nested processes,
• Support for event-driven systems to represent run-time entities,
• Integration of process and document models, and

- Technology independence, allowing implementation of a design using different technologies.

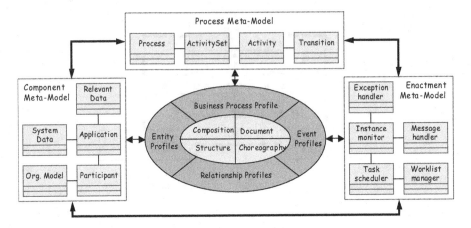

Fig. 3. Extended Workflow Meta-Model for workflow execution

5.3 Model Mapping from PIM to PSM

A workflow model is not an executable process model by itself, because it represents only platform independent model. For the process model to be executed in a specific run-time environment, the components defined in the model must be transformed into platform specific components through a mapping procedure. The mapping procedure generates interfaces used for communication among the transformed components. The interfaces are implemented to enable run-time interactions among the components to execute the workflow process specified in the workflow process model.

Fig. 4 outlines the model mapping procedure. At first, a process designer generates a Platform Independent Model (PIM) for the workflow using the Extended Workflow Meta-Model. If the designed process should require interactions among multiple companies, several designers on behalf of each partner may be involved in the design process. Noticeably, some elements in the *Process* meta-model, which is designed for a process definition, may be reusable for the design of another process definition. The PIM that represents choreography among activities of components may be different from process definitions, but some components of the component model and enactment model, such as relevant data or events, may be shared among the process definitions.

The generated PIM then is transformed to a Platform Specific Model (PSM) to target run-time architecture. The elements in the *Enactment* Meta-model generate components for implementing process coordinator. The elements in the *Component* meta-model are mapped to software components representing relevant data, such as documents or forms. It also generates software agents on behalf of the participants.

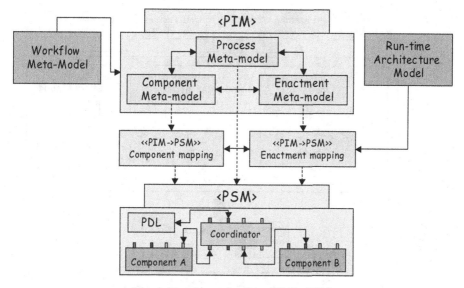

Fig. 4. Model mapping from PIM to PSM

In the PSM model, three types of interfaces are contained: process-enactment, process-component, and component-enactment interfaces. *Process-enactment interfaces* are used for the components involved in enacting a process to interpret sequence or rules for process execution. *Process-component interfaces* define job assignment or message exchange in the process. Finally, *component-enactment interfaces* are invoked to generate particular events for the enactment system or to notify the events to participants. After all of these interfaces are implemented, the workflow process model can be executed.

5.4 Model-Driven Framework for Workflow Execution

The essence of model-driven workflow execution is that a workflow definition is not handled as just a description to provide semantics of the workflow process to an enactment system. Instead, the definition is regarded as a concrete process model that can be actively used to configure run-time software components that execute the process. Fig. 5 illustrates the conceptual procedure of the model-driven approach for workflow execution in WFMS.

In the figure, the arrows tagged with (a) and (b) depict the procedure of deriving the PSM that specifies entities responsible for run-time functions of WFMS. The PSM is designed with a consultation on what type of run-time architecture our WFMS will take. Basically, our EWMM is based on an event-driven computing paradigm where interaction among components is performed by notification of events, but the components can be configured to communicate with each other in a mixture of several types of architecture including publish-and-subscribe, asynchronous point-to-point, and client-server remote invocation styles.

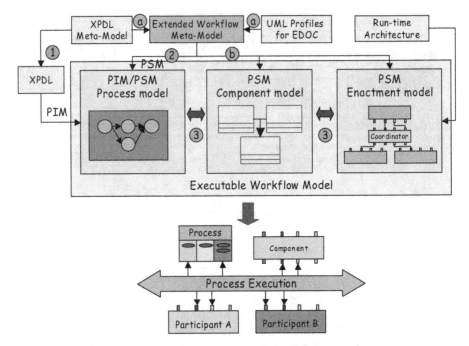

Fig. 5. Model-driven framework for workflow execution

On the other hand, the arrows tagged with (1) and (2) show the path along which a workflow process is eventually executed in the model-driven framework. At first, a process definition to describe the process is first created in XPDL. The definition is turned into the PIM by redesign, using the EWMM, and then the PIM is finally mapped to PSM. The mapping procedure, tagged with (3) in the figure, associates every entity in the PIM with corresponding target entities in the PSM, and also generates some new proxy entities that operate on behalf of the participants in the PIM. After the mapping procedure is created, the whole workflow model is executable at the target run-time platform.

The PSM itself does not change as long as a type of run-time platform is fixed, whereas the PIM must be recreated every time a new process definition is created. The main architectural principle of PSM is that individual components modeled in the PIM are kept as autonomously as possible, and that through the sophisticatedly-devised mapping procedure the components are rapidly reconfigured to perform an execution of a specific process model.

6 The Purchasing Process Example

The model-driven approach to workflow execution facilitates rapid and flexible design of business process in a distributed component environment. For this approach we can adopt the Extended Workflow Meta-Model, which is composed of three sub-models:

Process, *Enactment*, and *Component* meta-models. Each sub-model can include a variety of platform independent models to express the specific modules of workflow processes. For example, *Process* meta-model can have the graph-structured control-flow model for XPDL [17] or the block-structured one for BPML [1]. *Component* meta-model may include document models such as the form-based document model or the document-process association model [7], or vendor-specific organizational models [8,2]. *Enactment* meta-model may also describe various coordination models in Section 4 as well as various message models, choreography models, and exception models.

Fig. 6 illustrates an example for purchasing process. The purchasing process scenario in the light-bottom of the figure contains mixed components of the three sub-models. To extract the PIM of the process, designers can adopt a kind of specific models. The figure shows only a model for each sub-model. The Activity model in the *Process* meta-model followed Business Process Profile of EDOC, the Document model in the *Component* meta-model used the document-process association model [7], and the message model in *Enactment* meta-model adopted the Business Process Choreography model [9]. The three models are mapping to EJB and Java models as the PSM, shown in the right of the figure. The example process may be described more in detail by using other models for specific workflow functions.

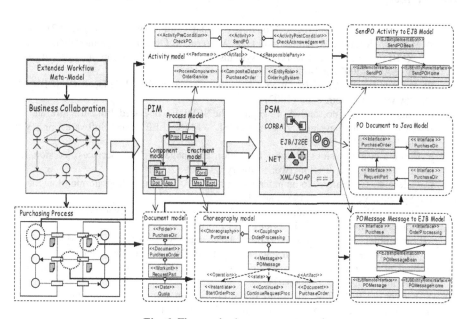

Fig. 6. The purchasing process example

7 Summary and Discussions

The purpose of this article is to examine model-driven architecture as a new framework for workflow execution and to describe a possible approach for realizing the model-driven architecture for workflow systems. As a potential solution, we suggest a procedure to design an executable workflow model that incorporates all the entities related with not only the definition of a workflow process but also the execution of it.

In this article, we dealt with a workflow process model in terms of its execution, but there are some other issues from different points of view. First issue is about evaluating a process model in terms of its performance. For possible performance measures, there are message complexity and time complexity. Message complexity is concerned with how many message exchanges are required to complete the process, and time complexity represents an approximate completion time of the process model through simulating its execution. Another issue is about design of a process model through assembling elementary process blocks representing stereotyped workflow patterns. Finally, we are concerned with supporting dynamic modification of a workflow process based on the runtime encapsulation concept [10].

Acknowledgements. This work was supported by the Korean Science and Engineering Foundation (KOSEF) under grant number R01-2002-000-00155-0.

References

1. A. Arkin et al.: Business Process Modeling Language. http://www.bpmi.org (2002)
2. W.M.P. van der Aalst, A. Kumar, and H.M.W. Verbeek: Organizational modeling in UML and XML in the context of workflow systems. Proc. 2003 ACM Symp. on Applied Computing (SAC), (2003) 603-608.
3. BEA et al.: WSCI 1.0: Web Services Choreography Interface (WSCI) 1.0. http://www.intalio.com/wsci/ (2002)
4. G. Cugola, E.D. Nitto, and A. Fuggetta: The JEDI Event-Based Infrastructure and Its Application to the Development of the OPSS WFMS. IEEE Trans. Software Eng., Vol. 27, no. 9 (2001) 827-850.
5. F. Curbera et al.: Business Process Execution Language for Web Services: Version 1.0. http://www.ibm.com/developerworks/library/ws-bpel/ (2002)
6. D. Gelernter: Generative Communication in Linda. ACM Trans. Programming Languages and Systems, Vol. 7, no. 1 (1985) 80-112.
7. H. Bae and Y. Kim: A document-process association model for workflow management. Computers in Industry, Vol. 47, issue 2 (2002) 139-154.
8. M. zur Mühlen: Evaluation of Workflow Management Systems Using Meta Models. Proc. 32rd Int. Hawaii Conf. on Systems Sciences (HICSS32), Vol. 5 (1999) 5060.
9. J. Jung et al.: Business Process Choreography for B2B Collaboration. IEEE Internet Computing. Vol. 8. no. 1 (2004) 37-45.
10. Y. Kim et al.: WW-Flow: Web-Based Workflow Management with Runtime Encapsulation. IEEE Internet Computing, Vol. 4, no. 3 (2000) 55-64.
11. ormsc/2001-07-01: Model Driven Architecture (MDA). Object Management Group (OMG) (2001)
12. ptc/02-02-05, UML Profile for Enterprise Distributed Object Computing Specification. Object Management Group (OMG) (2002)
13. RosettaNet: RosettaNet Implementation Framework: Core Specification (2002)
14. UN/CEFACT and OASIS: ebXML Business Process Specification Schema Version 1.01. http://www.ebxml.org/specs/ebBPSS.pdf (2001)

15. W3C Note: WSDL 1.1: Web Services Description Language (WSDL) 1.1. World Wide Web Consortium. http://www.w3.org/TR/wsdl.html (2001)
16. WfMC-TC-1003: The Workflow Reference Model. Workflow Management Coalition, Lighthouse Point, Fla. (1995)
17. WFMC-TC-1025: Workflow Process Definition Interface - XML Process Definition Language. Workflow Management Coalition, Lighthouse Point, Fla. (2002)

On Dealing with Structural Conflicts between Process Type and Instance Changes[*]

Stefanie Rinderle, Manfred Reichert, and Peter Dadam

University of Ulm, Faculty of Computer Science,
Dept. Databases and Information Systems
{rinderle, reichert, dadam}@informatik.uni-ulm.de

Abstract. Adaptive process management systems must be able to support changes of single process instances as well as modifications at the process type level and their propagation to a collection of related process instances. So far, these two kinds of dynamic process changes have been mainly considered in an isolated manner. However, especially for long-running processes, it must be possible to handle the interplay between process type and instance changes as well, but without running into trouble at runtime. This paper presents an extended criterion for correctly *propagating* process type changes to both, instances which are still running according to their original schema and instances which have been individually modified. In this context, we discuss and categorize structural conflicts potentially occuring between concurrent process changes. We show that our considerations are applicable to different process meta models and present tests for quickly detecting such structural conflicts.

1 Introduction

Adaptivity in process management systems (PMS) is key to flexible enterprise information systems. Basically, changes in process-oriented applications can take place at two levels – the process type or the process instance level.

A *process type* represents a particular business process (e.g., handling of a purchase order or treatment of a patient). It is described by a *process schema* which defines a collection of activities and sets out the control as well as data flow between them. Based on such a process schema, new *process instances* can be created and executed according to the defined process logic. *Process type changes* become necessary, for example, to adapt the process-oriented information system to optimized business processes or to new laws. They are handled by (structurally) modifying the respective process schema, which leads to a new schema version of the respective type. Particularly for long-running processes (e.g., handling of leasing contracts or medical treatments) it is desired to *propagate* a process type change to already running process instances as well. Process instances for which this is possible are *compliant* with the new schema and can therefore be *migrated* to it. As opposed to process type changes, *changes of*

---

[*] This work was done within the research project "Change management in adaptive workflow systems", which is funded by the German Research Community (DFG).

J. Desel, B. Pernici, and M. Weske (Eds.): BPM 2004, LNCS 3080, pp. 274–289, 2004.
© Springer-Verlag Berlin Heidelberg 2004

single process instances (e.g., to insert or skip an activity) are often carried out in an ad-hoc manner in order to deal with an exceptional situation. Adapting a single process instance during runtime, in turn, results in an instance-specific schema (also called *instance execution schema* in the following), which differs from the original schema this instance was created from. In the following, we denote such individually modified process instances as *biased*.

In the literature [1,2,3,4,5,6,7,8,9,10] process type and instance changes have been an important research topic for several years. However, there are only few adaptive PMS which support both kinds of changes in one system [10,11]. All of them have in common that once an instance has been individually modified (i.e., it possesses an instance-specific process schema), it cannot longer benefit from process type changes; i.e., changes of the schema they were originally created from. In $WASA_2$ [10], for example, an instance change is carried out by deriving a new schema version to which the instance is migrated. In the sequence, this instance is excluded from further adaptations of its original schema version at the process type level. However, doing so is not sufficient in many cases, especially in connection with long-running processes. Therefore, it must be possible to propagate process schema changes at the type level to such biased instances as well.

This paper focuses on the interplay of process type and instance changes under appropriate correctness constraints. Such constraints are necessary since an uncontrolled propagation of process type changes to biased instances may raise severe errors at runtime. A first contribution is to present a **correctness criterion** for propagating process type changes to both unbiased and biased process instances. This criterion is independent of the used process meta model. Furthermore, it excludes *state-related*, *structural*, and *semantical* conflicts between concurrent process type and instance changes. A second contribution deals with **structural correctness** of concurrent process type and instance changes. A simple example for such a structural conflict is depicted in Fig. 1. Here, propagating the process type change (cf. Fig. 1a) to biased instance I in an uncontrolled manner would lead to a deadlock causing cycle in the resulting process instance schema (cf. Fig. 1b). A naive solution to overcome this undesired behavior would be to simulate the process type change on each instance-specific schema (i.e., to materialize the resulting instance schema) and then to verify control and data flow correctness. Doing so may become very critical regarding performance, especially in conjunction with a large number of biased instances. An alternative solution is to check for process schema and instance changes whether they are in conflict or not. Our ambition is to exclude structural conflicts for as much (biased) instances as possible by the use of simple and easy to check tests. In any case expensive control and data flow analyses shall be avoided to a large degree. This paper presents appropriate tests to detect control flow as well as data flow conflicts between process schema and instance changes.

In Section 2, a general correctness criterion handling both process type and instance changes is introduced. Section 3 provides necessary background information for our concrete solution approach. In Section 4 we present structural conflict tests which are illustrated by an example in Section 5. Section 6 discusses related work and Section 7 closes with a summary of the presented results.

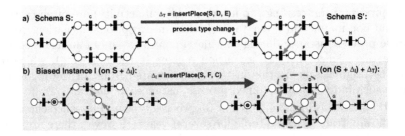

Fig. 1. Structural Conflict in Petri Nets (Deadlock)

2   A General Correctness Criterion for Process Type and Process Instance Changes

In this section we present a criterion for correctly propagating process type changes to both unbiased and biased process instances (cf. Axiom 1).

Axiom 1 (Propagating Type Changes To Biased Instances) *Let T be a process type with actual schema version S. Assume that a new (correct) schema version S' is derived from S by applying type change Δ_T to it. Then: Δ_T may be propagated to instance I (with type T and current instance execution schema $S_I := S + \Delta_I$) :$\Leftrightarrow$*

1. **Structural Correctness:** *$S_I^* := (S + \Delta_I) + \Delta_T$ is a correct schema according to the structural correctness constraints set out by the used process meta model; i.e., Δ_T can be correctly applied to $S_I = (S + \Delta_I)$.*
2. **State-Related Correctness:** *I is compliant with S_I^* (cf. 2); i.e., the execution history $\mathcal{H}_{red}$ of I can be produced on S_I^* as well.[1]*
3. **Semantical Correctness:** *Δ_T and Δ_I are semantically conflict-free.*

Axiom 1 is valid for unbiased as well as for biased process instances. More precisely, it handles unbiased instances as a special case; i.e., for an unbiased instance we obtain $S_I^* = S'$ whereby S' is correct according to the assumption of Axiom 1 and Δ_T and Δ_I are semantically conflict-free. Consequently, only state-related correctness has to be checked what exactly corresponds to the well-known compliance criterion [3,9,12]; i.e., an unbiased instance I is compliant with a changed schema S' if its previous execution trace on S is also a possible execution trace on S' (cf. Requirement 2 in Axiom 1).

Regarding Requirement 1 of Axiom 1 we first have to ensure that Δ_T is actually applicable to the instance-specific execution schema $S_I := S + \Delta_I$.

---

[1] An execution history $\mathcal{H}$ of instance I on S usually logs all start and end events generated during the execution of I. The reduced execution history $\mathcal{H}_{red}$ is determined by logically discarding all entries from $\mathcal{H}$ which have been produced by another than the actual loop iteration for each loop contained in S. The reduction from $\mathcal{H}$ to $\mathcal{H}_{red}$ is necessary in order to avoid restrictiveness in conjunction with loops [12]).

Therefore, generally, all "pre-conditions" of Δ_T on S_I must be fulfilled. How these change pre-conditions exactly look like depends on the respective change operations. However, a common claim for all kinds of change operations is that all schema objects manipulated by Δ_T should be present in S_I. An example for a process type change Δ_T not applicable to S_I is depicted in Fig. 2: Δ_T deletes activity D which has already been deleted at the instance level. Intuitively, Δ_T cannot be applied to the instance-specific schema S_I.

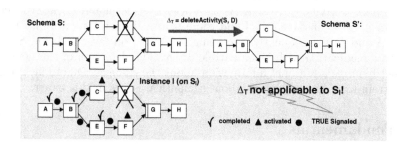

Fig. 2. Process Type Change Not Applicable to Instance-Specific Schema

If, in contrast, Δ_T is applicable to S_I, target schema $S_I^* := (S + \Delta_I) + \Delta_T$ can be produced. However, the resulting instance-specific schema S_I^* may still contain control and data flow errors (like deadlock-causing cycles or missing input data). We therefore must analyze S_I^* with respect to its structural correctness properties (e.g., absence of cycles except loop bodies) by the corresponding "post-conditions" of Δ_T on S_I. The core problem addressed in this paper is how to (efficiently) ensure that S_I^* does not contain any control or data flow errors, i.e., to (efficiently) ensure that there are no structural conflicts between process schema and instance changes (cf. Requirement 2 of Axiom 1). Obviously, an appropriate approach for this problem has to work for a large number of biased process instances as well. As mentioned in the introduction, a naive solution would be to first materialize schema $S_I^* := (S + \Delta_I) + \Delta_T$ for each (biased) instance I and then to apply respective correctness checks on S_I^*. However, this may result in a serious performance problem caused by the expensive materialization of S_I^* on the one hand and the subsequent complex control and data flow correctness checks on S_I^* on the other hand. Again note that these two steps would have to be applied to each biased instance to be migrated.

Therefore, in this paper, we show how expensive correctness tests (based on materialized schemes S_I^* for each biased instance I) can be avoided. The key idea behind is to detect potential control and data flow errors in $S_I^* := S + (\Delta_I) + \Delta_T$ solely based on the applied changes Δ_T and Δ_I, and the original schema S. More precisely, we elaborate quickly checkable conflict tests by exploiting the semantics of the applied changes Δ_T and Δ_I. Respective conflict tests either yield that there would be definitely no control or data flow error in schema S_I^* or they indicate that a possible structural conflict between Δ_T and Δ_I (potentially leading to such an error) may occur.

How to check state-related correctness (cf. Requirement 2 of Axiom 1) has been described in another paper of our group [12]. We have developed a set of compliance rules which can be used for checking state-related compliance of unbiased as well as of biased process instances with a modified schema. More precisely, these compliance rules define efficiently checkable conditions on activity node markings for each applicable change operation.

A semantical conflict (cf. Requirement 3 of Axiom 1) may occur, for example, if Δ_T inserts activity "give drug A" at process type level and Δ_I inserts activity "give drug B" at instance level and there is a medical incompatibility between drugs A and B. Consequently, executing instance I on target schema S_I^* would lead to a medication with incompatible drugs. The detection of this semantical conflict requires additional information about the changes. Due to lack of space we obstain from further details about semantical issues in this paper.

3   Fundamentals

In order to be able to precisely define structural conflicts tests for concurrent process type and instance changes we need a formal process meta model. In this paper, we exemplarily use WSM-Nets (as for example applied in ADEPT [13]) and the change operations based on them for this purpose. However, similar conflict tests can be developed for other process meta models as well.

Definition 1 (WSM-Net). *A tuple S = (N, D, NT, CtrlE, SyncE, LoopE, DataE) is called a WSM-Net if the following holds:*

- *N is a set of activities and D a set of process data elements*
- *NT: $N \mapsto$ {StartFlow, EndFlow, Activity, AndSplit, AndJoin, XOrSplit, XOrJoin, StartLoop, EndLoop}*
  NT assigns to each node of the WSM-Net a respective node type.
- *CtrlE $\subset N \times N$ is a precedence relation*
- *SyncE $\subset N \times N$ is a precedence relation between activities of parallel branches*
- *LoopE $\subset N \times N$ is a set of loop backward edges*
- *DataE $\subseteq N \times D \times$ {read, write} is a set of read/write data links between activities and data elements*

Thus, a process schema is represented by attributed serial-parallel graphs with additional sync links. A WSM-Net S is *structurally correct* if the following constraints hold:

1. S has a unique start node *Start* and a unique end node *End*.
2. Except for nodes *Start* and *End* each activity node of S has at least one incoming and one outgoing control edge $e \in$ CtrlE.
3. $S_{block} := (N, CtrlE, LoopE)$ is structured following a block concept, for which control blocks (sequences, branchings, loops) can be nested but must not overlap.

4. S_{fwd} = (N, CtrlE, SyncE) is an acyclic graph, i.e., the use of control and sync edges must not lead to deadlock-causing cycles.
5. Sync links must not cross the boundary of a loop block; i.e., an activity from a loop block must not be connected with an activity from outside the loop block via a sync link (and vice versa).
6. For activities for which a mandatory input parameter is linked to a data element $d \in D$ it has to be ensured that d will be always written at runtime independently of which execution path will be chosen.
7. Parallel write accesses on data elements (and consequently lost updates) have to be avoided.

Taking a correct WSM Net S new instances can be created and started. Logically, each process instance I is associated with an instance-specific schema $S_I := S + \Delta_I$ (for unbiased instances $S_I = S$ holds). The control state of I is captured by a marking function M^{S_I} =(NS^{S_I}, ES^{S_I}). It assigns to each activity n its current status $NS(n)$ and to each control and loop edge its marking $ES(e)$. These markings are determined according to well defined marking rules [8], whereas markings of already passed regions and skipped branches are preserved (except loop backs). Concerning data elements, different versions of a data object may be stored, which is important for the context-dependent reading of data elements and the handling of (partial) rollback operations. Formally:

Definition 2 (Process Instance). *A process instance I is defined by a tuple $(S, \Delta_I, M^{S_I}, Val^{S_I}, \mathcal{H})$ where*

- *S = (N, D, NT, CtrlE, SyncE, ...) denotes the process schema I was derived from. We call S the original schema of I.*
- *Δ_I comprises instance-specific changes $op_1^I, \ldots, op_m^I$ that have been applied to I so far. Schema $S_I := S + \Delta_I$, which results from the application of Δ_I to S, is called the instance execution schema of I.*
- *M^{S_I} = (NS^{S_I}, ES^{S_I}) describes node and edge markings of I:*
  NS^{S_I}:   N $\mapsto$ {NotActivated, Activated, Running, Completed, Skipped}
  ES^{S_I}: (CtrlE $\cup$ SyncE $\cup$ LoopE) $\mapsto$
                  {NotSignaled, TrueSignaled, FalseSignaled}
- *Val^{S_I} is a function on D. It reflects for each data element $d \in D$ either its current value or the value UNDEFINED (if d has not been written yet).*
- *$\mathcal{H}$ = < $e_0, \ldots, e_k$ > is the execution history of I. $e_0, \ldots, e_k$ denote the start <u>and</u> end events of activity executions. For each started activity X the values of data elements read by X and for each completed activity Y the values of data elements written by Y are logged.*

Activities marked as Activated are ready to fire and can then be worked on, i.e., their status changes to Running. As an example take instance I in Fig. 3: Activity A is completed whereas activity B is activated. Activities with marking Skipped cannot longer be selected for execution.

Table 1 presents a selection of *high-level operations* which can be used to define or change WSM-Nets. We distinguish between *basic* and *high-level change operations.* Examples for basic change operations are insertion/deletion of activity nodes or control edges. Such basic change operations can be applied to a process schema; afterwards structural correctness of the resulting schema has to be checked. In contrast, high-level change operations include formal pre- and post-conditions and automatically perform the necessary schema transformations such that schema correctness can be ensured. An example is process type change Δ_T in Fig. 3: Δ_T serially inserts activity X into S by automatically embedding X between activities D and G. (For more complex examples see [8]).

Table 1. *A Selection of High-Level Change Operations on WSM-Nets*

Change Operation Δ Applied to Schema S	Effects on Schema S
Additive Change Operations	
serialInsert(S, X, A, B)	serial insertion of activity X between activities A and B
parallelInsert(S, X, CtrlBlock)	insertion of activity X parallel to control block CtrlBlock
insertSyncEdge(S, src, dest)	insertion of sync edge linking two parallel nodes src and dest
Subtractive Change Operations	
deleteActivity(S, X)	deletes activity X from schema S
deleteSyncEdge(S, edge)	deletes edge $\in$ SyncE from schema S
Order-Changing Operations	
serialMoveActivity(S, X, A, B)	moves activity X from current position to position between activities A and B
parallelMoveActivity(S, X, CtrlBlock)	moves activity X to position parallel to control block CtrlBlock
Attribute Changing Operations	
changeActivityAttribute(S, X, attr, nV)	changes value of attribute attr of activity X to nV
changeEdgeAttribute(S, edge, attr, nV)	changes value of attribute attr of edge $\in$ CtrlE $\cup$ SyncE to nV
Data Flow Change Operations	
addDataElement(S, d, dom, defVal)	adds data element d with domain dom and default value defVal to S
deleteDataElement(S, d)	deletes data element d from S
addDataEdge(S, (X, d, mode))	adds data edge (X, d, mode) to S (mode $\in$ {read, write})
deleteDataEdge(S, dL))	deletes data edge dL from S

4   Structural Conflict Tests

In this section, we provide simple but effective tests for detecting potential conflicts between concurrently applied control and/or data flow changes. In particular, respective tests can be used in connection with the common support of process type and process instance changes.

4.1   On Detecting Control Flow Conflicts

A serious problem which may arise from the uncontrolled propagation of a process type change Δ_T to a biased instance (on instance-specific schema $S_I := S + \Delta_I$) is the occurence of deadlock-causing cycles (for an example see Fig. 1). As mentioned before, a naive solution would be to first materialize the target schema $S_I^* := (S + \Delta_I) + \Delta_T$ and then to carry out respective cycle checks on S_I^*. Since these materialization and validation steps would have to be applied for each biased instance I, this approach would cause severe performance problems. Thus, our ambition is to perform an appropriate deadlock test based on information given by the process type and instance changes themselves and the original process schema S. A first version of a deadlock tests satisfying these claims is given in Proposition 1 [13]:

Proposition 1 (Basic Deadlock Prevention). *Let S be a WSM-Net and I be a biased instance with starting schema S and execution schema $S_I := S + \Delta_I = (N_I, D_I, NT_I, CtrlE_I, SyncE_I, \ldots)$. Assume that type change Δ_T transforms S into a correct schema $S' = (N', D', NT', CtrlE', SyncE', \ldots)$. Then: $S_I^* = (S + \Delta_I) + \Delta_T$ does not contain deadlock-causing cycles if the following condition holds:*

$$\forall (s_1, d_1) \in \mathcal{AS}(S, \Delta_T), \forall (s_2, d_2) \, \mathcal{AS}(S, \Delta_I):$$
$$d_1 \notin (pred^*(S, s_2) \cup \{s_2\}) \vee d_2 \notin (pred^*(S, s_1) \cup \{s_1\}) \, (\Psi)$$

whereas

- $\mathcal{AS}(S, \Delta_T) := SyncE' \setminus SyncE$
- $\mathcal{AS}(S, \Delta_I) := SyncE_I \setminus SyncE$
- $pred^*(S, n)$ *denotes all direct and indirect predecessors of activity n when considering both control and sync edges of S.*

By simply applying condition Ψ from Proposition 1 we can exclude deadlocks when propagating a type change to a biased instance. Note that condition Ψ is based on the original process schema S. Consequently, an easy conflict test can be derived which avoids the materialization of any other schema (S_I or S_I^*).

In general, the quality of a conflict test can be measured according to how efficiently it can be applied to concurrent process type and instance changes. Another important quality factor is the number of "uncritical" instances I for which conflicts between process type and instance changes can be definitely excluded. The deadlock test derived from Proposition 1 is a "good" test with respect to efficiency. However, it still scores lower regarding the second quality factor. Reason is that for particular instance changes Δ_I this test indicates conflicts with type change Δ_T although the target schema $S_I^* := (S + \Delta_I) + \Delta_T$ will not contain any deadlock causing cycle. An example is depicted in Fig. 3: Instance change Δ_I inserts a sync edge between activities C and F already contained in S whereas type change Δ_T inserts a sync edge between also newly inserted activites X and Y. From the applied changes we derive $\mathcal{AS}(S, \Delta_T) = \{(X, Y)\}$ and $\mathcal{AS}(S, \Delta_I) = \{(C, F)\}$ (cf. Proposition 1). The expression yielding from applying condition Ψ from Proposition 1 to these sets cannot be evaluated due to the absence of activites X and Y in S. Consequently, the respective conflict test is unable to exclude the occurence of a deadlock-causing cycle in S although in fact there is none.

At first glance it seems that we must materialize and validate target schema S_I^* in order to overcome this problem. This approach, however, offends against the efficiency quality factor. Fortunately, there is another solution avoiding materialization of S_I^* and excluding deadlock conflicts for "uncritical" instances.

Consider again the example given in Fig. 3: Here we cannot evaluate condition
Ψ based on sync edge (X, Y) since its source and destination activities have been
newly inserted by Δ_T as well. However, the insertion of sync edge (X, Y) does
not only set out the direct order relation "X before Y" but also, for example, the
transitive order relation "D before E". Since D and E are present in S we are
able to verify condition Ψ for a respective sync edge (D, E). Based on this consideration we try to virtually re-link the actual sync edge (X, Y) to the virtual
sync edge (D, E). The challenge is to determine the virtual sync edge(s) based
on which condition Ψ can be evaluated on S. Then solely based on S we can
determine whether S_I^* will contain a deadlock-causing cycle or not. From Δ_T we
know which activities have been inserted and into which context they have been
embedded (*insertion context*). For serial insertion of activities, for example, the
insertion context includes the direct predecessor and successor of the newly inserted activity. For the newly inserted activity X in Fig. 3, for example, insertion
context (D, G) includes the direct predecessor D of X in S' and for the newly
inserted activity Y its insertion context (B, E) includes the direct successor E of
Y in S'. Altogether, this is the information we need for determining the virtual
sync edges between activities present in S. In our example (cf. Fig. 3) we get
the virtual sync egde (D, E) instead of (X, Y).

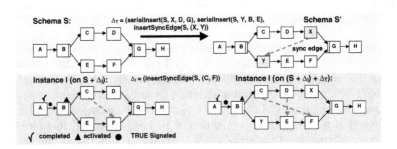

Fig. 3. Insertion of Sync Edges on Process Type and Instance Level

Thus, the idea behind is to first transfer the order relations set out by the
newly inserted sync edges to starting schema S by applying "virtual" graph
reduction rules and then to apply condition Ψ of Proposition 1 to the reduced
graph. The respective graph reduction approach applicable in connection with
the composed insertion of activities and sync edges is given in Algorithm 1:

Algorithm 1 (Graph Reduction Rules (Deadlock Prevention)) *Let* S
$= (N, D, NT, CtrlE, SyncE, ...)$ *be a WSM-Net and* Δ *be a type change which
transforms S into a correct schema $S' = (N', D', NT', CtrlE', SyncE', ...)$. Let
further*
- $\mathcal{AS}(S, \Delta) := SyncE' \setminus SyncE$ *and*
- $\mathcal{AA}(S, \Delta) := \{(X, (src, dest)) \mid X \in N', src, dest \in N, X \text{ serially inserted}$
between src and dest by $\Delta\}$.

```
GraphRed(N, AS(S, Δ), AA(S, Δ)) ⟶ (ASred(S, Δ))
```

```
ASred(S, Δ):=∅
forall (src, dest) ∈ AS(S, Δ) do
    while src ∉ N do
        find (src, (pSrc, sSrc)) ∈ AA(S, Δ);
        src := pSrc;
    done
    while dest ∉ N do
        find (dest, (pDest, sDest)) ∈ AA(S, Δ);
        dest := sDest;
    done
    ASred(S, Δ) := ASred(S, Δ) ∪ {(src, dest)}
done
```

Algorithm 1 works by replacing the source (destination) nodes of the newly inserted sync edges by their direct predecessors (successors) if these nodes have not been present in the original schema S. If several activities are inserted in a row Algorithm 1 iteratively replaces them by their direct predecessors/successors until we find an adequate predecessor/successor also present in S. In the following Prop. 2, condition Ψ of Prop. 1 is applied based on the graph reduction of Algorithm 1. A deadlock test derived from this proposition fulfills both desired quality factors: It is efficiently applicable based on original schema S and it does not indicate deadlocks for target schema S_I^* if S_I^* is actually deadlock-free.

Proposition 2 (Deadlock Prevention (2)). *Let the assumption be as in Proposition 1. Let further* $AS_{red}(S, \Delta_T)$ *and* $AS_{red}(S, \Delta_I)$ *be the sync edge reductions after applying Algorithm 1.*
Then: $S_I^* = (S + \Delta_I) + \Delta_S$ *does not contain deadlock-causing cycles iff the following condition holds:*

$$\forall \ (s_1, d_1) \in AS_{red}(S, \Delta_T), \ \forall \ (s_2, d_2) \in AS_{red}(S, \Delta_I):$$
$$d_1 \notin (pred^*(S, s_2) \cup \{s_2\}) \lor d_2 \notin (pred^*(S, s_1) \cup \{s_1\}) \ (\Psi)$$

As already mentioned, the reduction rules of Algorithm 1 are necessary in order to transfer the order relations set out by the newly inserted sync edges to the original schema S. As decribed in Proposition 2, we apply Algorithm 1 to the sync edges and activities newly inserted by Δ_T and Δ_I. Based on the resulting sets $AS_{red}(S, \Delta_T)$ and $AS_{red}(S, \Delta_I)$ condition Ψ from Proposition 1 can be applied to S. Doing so saves us from expensive checks on S_I^*.

In general, there are further constraints set out by the particular process meta model. In block-structured meta models like BPEL4WS [14] or ADEPT [8], for example, it is forbidden that sync links cross the boundaries of loop blocks. However, uncontrolled propagation complex process type changes to biased instances may result in such undesired sync links. Therefore we have made formal propositions for respective cases as well from which quick conflict tests can be derived. Due to lack of space we obstain from further details here.

4.2   On Detecting Data Flow Conflicts

An uncontrolled propagation of process type change Δ_T to biased instance I on $S_I = S + \Delta_I$ may not only cause control flow errors as described above but also severe data flow problems. The detection of data flow conflicts based on the materialization of schema $S_I^* := (S + \Delta_I) + \Delta_T$ has at least the same complexity as respective control flow checks. Our data flow constraints from Def. 1 forbid activities with missing input data and lost updates on data elements. Respective problems may occur for S_I^* if both instance and type change delete write data links on the same data element read by other activities in the sequel. An example is depicted in Fig. 4 where Δ_T and Δ_I delete write data links related to the same data element d_1 which causes missing input data of activity G in $S_{incorrect}^*$.

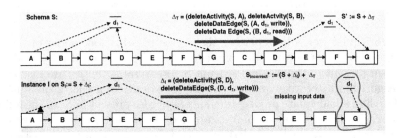

Fig. 4. Deleting All Necessary Write Accesses on Instance Data (Example)

Therefore, in the following we provide a formal proposition to exclude data flow errors for S_I^* for a magnitude of instances solely on basis of Δ_T and Δ_I.

Proposition 3 (Avoiding Missing Input Data and Lost Updates).
Let S be a WSM-Net and I be a biased instance with starting schema S and execution schema $S_I := S + \Delta_I = (N_I, D_I, NT_I, CtrlE_I, SyncE_I, \ldots)$. Assume that type change Δ_T transforms S into a correct schema $S' = (N', D', NT', CtrlE', SyncE', \ldots)$. Then: Propagating Δ_T to I neither results in missing input data nor in lost updates if

$$\forall \ mDL_1 = (d_1, mode_1, ["add"|"delete"]) \in \mathcal{AD}(S, \Delta_T) \cup \mathcal{DD}(S, \Delta_T),$$
$$\forall \ mDL_2 = (d_2, mode_2, ["add"|"delete"]) \in \in \mathcal{AD}(S, \Delta_I) \cup \mathcal{DD}(S, \Delta_I)$$
$$\text{with } mode_i \in \{read, write\} \ (i = 1, 2):$$
$$d_1 \neq d_2 \ \vee$$
$$mode1 = mode2 = read \ \vee$$
$$mDL_1 = (d_1, "read", "delete") \vee mDL_2 = (d_2, read, "delete") \ (\clubsuit)$$

whereas
- $\mathcal{AD}(S, \Delta_T) := \{(d, mode, "add") \in DataE' \setminus DataE, mode \in \{read, write\}\}$
- $\mathcal{DD}(S, \Delta_T) := \{(d, mode, "delete") \in DataE \setminus DataE', mode \in \{read, write\}\}$
- $\mathcal{AD}(S, \Delta_I) := \{(d, mode, "add") \in DataE_I \setminus DataE, mode \in \{read, write\}\}$
- $\mathcal{DD}(S, \Delta_I) := \{(d, mode, "delete") \in DataE \setminus DataE_I, mode \in \{read, write\}\}$

In Fig. 5, Δ_T deletes activities B and F together with data edges $(B, d_2, write)$ and $(F, d_2, read)$. At the instance level, Δ_I serially inserts activity Y between activities D and E with a read data link connected to data element d_2 $(\Delta_I = \{addDataEdge(S, (Y, d_2, read))\})$. Obviously, propagating Δ_T to S_I

leads to the problem of missing input data regarding the newly inserted activity Y. Condition ♣ from Proposition 3 indicates this conflict since both type and instance change, work on the same data element d_2 by deleting write data links and inserting new read data links for this data element. Such critical instances can be easily detected by a test derived from Proposition 3. Note that otherwise expensive data flow analyses on S_I^* would become necessary.

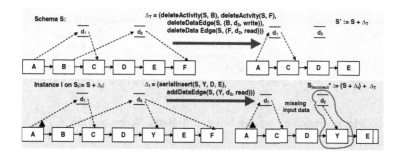

Fig. 5. Deleting Write Accesses on Data Read by Newly Inserted Activity (Example)

For a few special cases, a conflict test derived from Propostion 3 may identify potential conflicts which would not lead to a violation of the data flow constraints set out in Def. 1. Nevertheless, the presented propositions and the respective tests are very helpful to quickly and efficiently detect conflicts between concurrent data flow changes at the type and instance level.

4.3   Structural Conflicts for Seleted Process Meta Models

Some of the potential conflicts between concurrent process type and instance changes as introduced in Section 4.1 are present for other process meta models as well. One example is the deadlock-causing cycle contained in a Petri Net after the uncontrolled insertion of new order relations by process and instance changes (cf. Fig. 1). Of course a conflict test derived from Proposition 2 may be easily transferred to Activity Nets as used by WebSphere MQWorkflow [15] as well.

For other process meta models additional conflicts between process type and instance changes may occur. In the following, we exemplarily consider Activity Nets [15]. One reasonable control flow constraint for this process meta model may be to require the absence of isolated activity nodes in order to ensure clearly defined process start and end states. An example for an Activity Net containing an isolated activity node after an uncontrolled application of concurrent process type and instance changes is depicted in Fig. 6: Δ_T deletes control link (C, E) whereas Δ_I has already deleted control link (E, I). The uncontrolled propagation of Δ_T to instance-specific schema S_I leads to target schema $(S + \Delta_I) + \Delta_T$ containing isolated activity node E. Consequently, it would be a good idea to find an appropriate formal proposition setting out conditions to detect isolated activity nodes based on the applied change operations. Based on this an efficient conflict test could be derived.

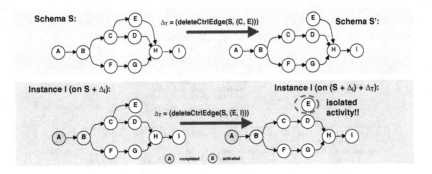

Fig. 6. Changes Causing Isolated Activity Nodes in Activity Nets

Interestingly, the test detecting isolated activities does not depend on the underlying process meta model but on the kind of applied change operation. As we have discussed in Section 3, generally, there are two levels for defining change operations. On the basis level change primitives may be carried out without special pre- and post-conditions. This is the reason why we get an isolated activity node in Fig. 6. When applying change operations on a higher semantical level, as for example defined for WSM-Nets (cf. Table 1) this specific problem is prohibited. Another problem arising in connection with basis change primitives is present for block-structured process meta models, like BPEL4WS [14] and ADEPT, namely the violation ot the block structure.

5   Illustrating Example

To summarize the results presented in this paper and to show the whole migration process followed in our approach we provide an illustrating example. In Fig. 7 process type change Δ_T transforms schema S into new schema version S' by serially inserting activites X and Y and by connecting them via a sync link (X, Y). Furthermore Δ_T deletes activities F and H together with their respective data links dL_6 and dL_7. Based on original schema S two instances have been started. Instance I_1 is biased and therefore runs according to its instance-specific schema S_{I_1} whereas I_2 is an unbiased instance still running according to S. If now type change Δ_T shall be propagated to these instances we have to check structural as well as state-related compliance for the running instances. Instance change Δ_{I_1} has serially inserted two activites U and T and sync link (T, U) between them. At first, the deadlock test derived from Proposition 2 is carried out to detect whether target schema S_1^* will contain a deadlock-causing cycle or not. After applying the graph reduction rules of Algorithm 1 we obtain that S_1^* will actually contain a deadlock-causing cycle and therefore I_1 cannot migrate to S' (and remains running according to S). For unbiased Instance I_2 we only have to check state-related compliance as described in Section 2. Since the previous execution of I_2 can be replayed on S', I_2 is compliant with S' and therefore migrates to S' by applying appropriate marking adaptation rules [13].

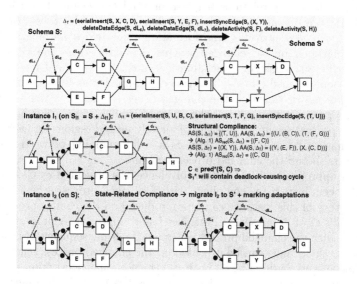

Fig. 7. Process Type Change and Instance Migration

6   Related Work

Today's workflow technology is rather weak with respect to dynamic process changes [16]. Particularly, it is unsuited for supporting long-running processes. As a consequence, process descriptions are often split into a series of smaller, short-running process fragments that are maintained as separate schemes and correlated through application data at runtime. Such a fragmented representation, however, does not provide a natural view of the process and is also unfavorable in other respects. In particular, it does not abolish the need for dynamic instance migrations (even if techniques such as late binding are applied).

Adaptive workflows have been addressed in many research papers so far [1,2, 3,5,6,7,10]. The main focus was put on providing appropriate correctness criteria for deciding about compliance of <u>unbiased</u> process instances with a changed process schema. More precisely, these criteria solely aim on <u>state-related</u> correctness when propagating a process type change to an instance. There are only few approaches [10,11] to allow process type and changes within one PMS. However, there is no **interplay** between process type and instance changes. WASA$_2$ [10], for example, realizes changes of single process instances by deriving a new schema version with one running instance. Consequently, individually modified instances are totally excluded from further process type optimizations.

For unbiased process instances, correctness criteria range from graph equivalence [1,2,10] to trace equivalence [3,5,6,7]:

In [1], v.d. Aalst and Basten base correctness of dynamic process change on special inheritance relations between original and changed process schema. Compliance can be ensured by checking easy conditions on these two schemes. This approach also provides transformation rules which automatically adapt instance markings on the changed schema. For correctness checking, Agostini and De Michelis [2] construct reachability graphs for the original and the changed process schema. Based on this, it can be determined whether a process instance is in a state which exists on the changed process schema as well. In contrast, Weske [10] proposes to construct the purged instance graph – a subgraph of the respective process schema consisting of already passed regions for each instance. Then it has to be analyzed if there is a valid mapping between the purged instance graph and the changed process schema.

A first approach based on trace equivalence was presented by Casati et al [3]. Here a process instance is compliant with a changed process schema if the execution history of this instance can be reproduced on the change process schema as well. Ellis et al [5] present a Petri-Net based approach. A process instance is compliant with the changed process schema if the firing sequence of this instance previous to the change can be executed on the changed process schema as well. Kradolfer [6] and Sadiq et al [7] both use the compliance criterion presented in [3]. Thereby Kradolfer [6] provides conditions based on the instance execution history and the applied change operation to check compliance whereas Sadiq et al [7] focus on the treatment of non-compliant instances and temporal aspects in conjunction with dynamic change.

The described WSM-Nets are somewhat comparable to BPEL4WS (Business Process Execution Language for Web Services) [14], but with a better understanding and formal foundation regarding the use of links (called sync links in our approach). Though there is some work on exception handling in BPEL4WS [17], dynamic change issues have been completely factored out.

A detailed discussion of all these approaches can be found in [16]. It would be very interesting to learn more about the definition of change operations and the use of their specific semantics for the different process meta models.

7   Summary and Outlook

We have introduced basic work on the challenging question of how to correctly deal with concurrent process type and instance changes. At first, a comprehensive correctness criterion has been presented including structural, state-related and semantical correctness when propagating process type changes to biased process instances. Furthermore, we have derived formal propositions for constructing efficient tests which allow us to quickly and efficiently detect potential conflicts between changes at the type and instance level. These tests are based on WSM-Nets. However, we have discussed possible conflicts between process type and instance changes for other process meta models like Petri-Nets and

Activity Nets as well. In our future work on adaptive processes, we will consider semantical conflicts between concurrent process changes and their treatment as well. Furthermore, we will fully implement both, structural as well as semantical conflict tests in our current proof-of-concept prototype for process schema evolution. Hereby, it is very important to think about implementation issues like locking of instances or the order in which structural, state-related and semantical correctness is checked. In any case, the support of process type and instance changes would benefit by a more intense study of the research community.

References

1. van der Aalst, W., Basten, T.: Inheritance of workflows: An approach to tackling problems related to change. Theoretical Computer Science **270** (2002) 125–203
2. Agostini, A., De Michelis, G.: Improving flexibility of workflow management systems. In: Proc. BPM '00. LNCS 1806, Springer (2000) 218–234
3. Casati, F., Ceri, S., Pernici, B., Pozzi, G.: Workflow evolution. Data and Knowledge Engineering **24** (1998) 211–238
4. Edmond, D., ter Hofstede, A.: A reflective infrastructure for workflow adaptability. Data and Knowledge Engineering **34** (2000) 271–304
5. Ellis, C., Keddara, K., Rozenberg, G.: Dynamic change within workflow systems. In: Proc. COOCS '95, Milpitas, CA (1995) 10–21
6. Kradolfer, M., Geppert, A.: Dynamic workflow schema evolution based on workflow type versioning and workflow migration. In: Proc. CoopIS '99, Edinburgh (1999) 104–114
7. Sadiq, S., Marjanovic, O., Orlowska, M.: Managing change and time in dynamic workflow processes. IJCIS **9** (2000) 93–116
8. Reichert, M., Dadam, P.: ADEPT$_{flex}$ - supporting dynamic changes of workflows without losing control. JIIS **10** (1998) 93–129
9. Rinderle, S., Reichert, M., Dadam, P.: Evaluation of correctness criteria for dynamic workflow changes. In: Proc. Int'l Conf. on Business Process Management (BPM '03). LNCS 2678, Eindhoven, The Netherlands, Springer (2003) 41–57
10. Weske, M.: Formal foundation and conceptual design of dynamic adaptations in a workflow management system. In: HICSS-34. (2001)
11. Kochut, K., Arnold, J., Sheth, A., Miller, J., Kraemer, E., Arpinar, B., Cardoso, J.: IntelliGEN: A distributed workflow system for discovering protein-protein interactions. Distributed and Parallel Databases **13** (2003) 43–72
12. Rinderle, S., Reichert, M., Dadam, P.: Flexible support of team processes by adaptive workflow systems. Distributed and Parallel Databases (to appear)
13. Reichert, M., Rinderle, S., Dadam, P.: On the common support of workflow type and instance changes under correctness constraints. In: Proc. CoopIS '03, Catania, Italy (2003) 407–425
14. Curbera, F., Goland, Y., Klein, J., Leymann, F., Roller, D., Thatte, S., Weerawarana, S.: Business Process Execution Language for Web Services, Version 1.0. (2002) http://www.ibm.com/developerworks/library/ws-bpel/.
15. Leymann, F., Altenhuber, W.: Managing business processes as an information ressource. IBM Systems Journal **33** (1994) 326–348
16. Rinderle, S., Reichert, M., Dadam, P.: Correctness criteria for dynamic changes in workflow systems – a survey. Data and Knowledge Engineering (to appear)
17. Curbera, F., Khalaf, R., Leymann, F., Weerawarana, S.: Execption handling in the BPEL4WS language. In: BPM'03, Eindhoven (2003) 276–290

Cohesion and Coupling Metrics for Workflow Process Design

Hajo A. Reijers and Irene T.P. Vanderfeesten

Department of Technology Management, Eindhoven University of Technology,
PO Box 513, NL-5600 MB Eindhoven, The Netherlands
H.A.Reijers@tm.tue.nl, I.T.P.Vanderfeesten@student.tue.nl

Abstract. Workflow designers experience considerable freedom in designing the smaller steps (or activities) within a process. An operational notion of activity cohesion and coupling may help them to design more well-structured workflow activities. Inspired by resemblances between software programs and workflow processes, this paper gives an overview of software quality metrics and their applicability to workflow process design. New cohesion and coupling metrics – inspired by these software metrics – are introduced, which are integrated in a design heuristic. This heuristic can be used by workflow designers to identify the strongly cohesive and weakly coupled process design among several alternatives. The paper includes an application of this heuristic in a realistic workflow process setting.

1 Introduction

Administrative business processes are considerably more flexible in their lay-out than manufacturing processes, because their focus is on the processing of *information* instead of physical parts (see e.g. [14]). While this may be exploited to improve the performance of administrative business processes (see e.g. [2]), it may be difficult to cope with this freedom in other respects. One issue is the proper size of the individual activities in a process (the process granularity). Badly chosen boundaries between activities may affect process performance negatively. For example, small activities increase the number of hand-offs between activities, with a corresponding increase of errors ([19]). On the other hand, activities that are too large may cause inflexibility, since their underlying operations must be performed regardless of their merits under specific circumstances ([2]).

This paper addresses the issue of activity design in administrative processes, or *workflow processes*, using cohesion and coupling metrics. By focusing on the content of an activity, i.e. its underlying operations, it can be quantitatively expressed how these operations "belong" to each other within one activity or, in other words, how *cohesive* such an activity is. In addition, it is also important to what extent the activities are independent from each other or, conversely, how much they are *coupled*.

The inspiration for these metrics comes from software engineering, where an old aphorism is to strive for "strong cohesion, loose coupling". Baresi et al. already

J. Desel, B. Pernici, and M. Weske (Eds.): BPM 2004, LNCS 3080, pp. 290–305, 2004.

suggested applying this principle to workflow process design ([6]). Moreover, this application seems justified by the fact that workflow processes are quite similar to software programs in some respects:

- They both focus on *information processing*. Within each step, one or more outputs are produced on the basis of one or more inputs.
- They are alike in their *structure of components*. Workflow processes and software programs have a similar compositional structure. A program – functional or object-oriented – can be split up into respectively modules or classes. Every module consists of a number of statements, and every statement has a number of variables and constants. Likewise, a workflow process has activities. Every activity is built out of a number of elementary operations and each operation uses one or more information elements.
- Their *dynamic execution* follows a static structure. In instantiating either a software program or a workflow process, an execution flow of their elements takes place in accordance with their static representation. This flow may involve consecutive executions, concurrency, conditional routings, etc.

Although the metrics in software engineering try to give an indication of the overall quality of a program design, we aim for a more modest goal with respect to workflow process design. Clearly, an overall quality concept of a workflow design must encompass elements such as implementability and its effect on customer satisfaction. We will, however, focus on a particular part, i.e. the execution of a workflow process design. Similar to the advantages of a well-designed software program (see [9]), we think that a workflow process that consists of loosely coupled activities will experience fewer errors during runtime, because less communication and exchange of information is needed. The execution of cohesive activities will result in higher quality, because each of them is a coherent part. From an organizational perspective, it should become clearer what it is that needs to be done and who or which department is responsible for it. Several researchers already indicated that intra-organizational dependencies and shared responsibilities should be avoided in workflow (re)design (see for example [7] and [18]). Besides these high-level advantages, we also expect that employees who work within a well-designed process on well designed activities may like their work more and can work more efficiently.

In a previous paper ([17]), we compared the application of a simple workflow quality metric to various design dilemma's with the decisions of 14 experienced workflow designers. The outcomes matched, supporting the validity of the metric and the viability of the underlying idea. This metric, however, lacked facilities to handle conditional alternatives to achieve the same output (XOR-construction), a construct very common in business processes and in administrative processes in particular ([5]). Neither could we balance this quantitative notion of cohesion with a similar notion of coupling, a more or less natural span. Finally, we did not extensively study whether existing metrics in the software engineering domain could be applied in workflow design. These three issues are addressed in this paper, resulting in an extended workflow cohesion metric and the addition of a workflow coupling metric, inspired by thorough research of quality metrics from software engineering literature.

The structure of this paper is as follows. First, we will introduce a new way of looking at a workflow process, considering a structure of information processing underneath the workflow model. We will introduce a realistic example and explain the new concepts using this example. Following is a short overview of important literature on software engineering metrics, the formal introduction of our cohesion and coupling metrics and an application within a realistic workflow setting. The paper ends with a discussion of the limitations of the presented approach and directions for further research.

2   An Input-Output Perspective on Workflow Processes

As we stated in the introduction, workflow processes process information. In this paper, we will consider the smallest, meaningfully distinguishable portions of information that are being processed and refer to them as *information elements*. Examples of information elements are given in Table 1. A number of information elements is needed as input to the process. Subsequently, in the activities of the process these information elements are used to produce new information elements and, in the end, the workflow's output is produced, usually in the form of a single information element. An *activity* in a workflow process consists of a number of *operations* on information elements. Each operation has one or more input information elements and one output information element. An operation is a basic processing step and cannot have "half-assembly" products, i.e. intermediate information element values, itself. An activity, on the contrary, is built out of one or more operations. The output of one of the operations can be the input of another operation of that activity. Therefore the activity can have "half-assembly" products. The issue we raised of defining activities can now be reformulated as the proper clustering of information elements and operations into activities. Or from another point of view: the proper distribution of operations across a workflow's activities.

This information input-output perspective on workflow processes we adopt here is similar to that of the methodology of product based workflow design (PBWD) [1, 15, 16]. Also, some contemporary Workflow Management Systems adopt a comparable information-centered modeling and execution approach (see e.g. [3]).

As a running example for the application of our cohesion and coupling metrics and as an illustration for the concepts we introduced, we will present here both a workflow process model and a so-called *information element structure*. The latter model expresses the formal dependencies between the various information elements. Both models deal with the way how requests for governmental student grants are handled in the Netherlands. The presented workflow is a simplified version of the actual procedure as implemented by the Informatie Beheer Groep (IBG) under the authority of the Ministry of Education, Culture and Science. The essential output of the workflow process is the calculation of the scholarship a new student will get from the government. The amount of money is dependent on the student's background, his parents income, his living situation, the type of health insurance and the kind of study grant he applied for. The total amount of student grant is composed of three parts (the amount of basic scholarship, the amount of supplementary scholarship and the loan amount).

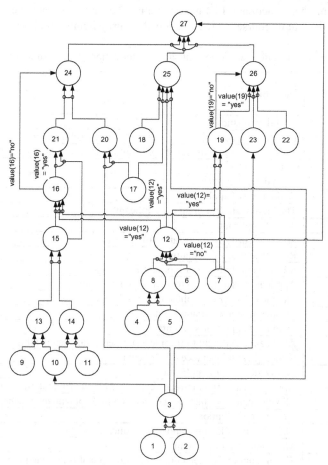

Fig. 1. Information element structure for the process "Request for governmental student grant".

In Figure 1, the complete information element structure for this calculation can be found. Information elements are represented as circles, operations as one or more arrows between information elements. The individual information elements are described in Table 1. Now, as an example, we will focus on the part which calculates the parents' income, to understand the concept of information elements, operations and activities. The total income of both parents (information element '15') is composed of the total income of the father ('13') plus the total income of the mother ('14') of the applicant. Both information elements '13' and '14' are needed to produce the outcome of the calculation ('15'). Therefore, the two arrows are linked to each other. In our information element structure view, this can be distinguished as one operation, containing two input elements ('13' and '14') and one output element ('15'). To determine the father's income another operation has to be executed. The amount of income ('13') is inquired from the tax authority, requiring the social security number of the father ('9') and the reference year ('10'). The operation to retrieve the mother's income ('14') uses as inputs the same reference year for the tax authority ('10'), but of course, a different social security number ('11').

Table 1. Description of information elements of the information element structure in figure 2.

Information element number	Description
1	First day of study
2	Date from which applicant wants to receive a scholarship
3	Period or year for which the applicant requests a student grant
4	Date of request
5	Birth date of applicant
6	Nationality of applicant
7	The kind of student grant the applicant requests
8	Age of applicant
9	Social Security Number father of applicant
10	Reference year for tax authorities
11	Social Security Number mother of applicant
12	Applicant has a right to receive a student grant
13	Income of father of applicant
14	Income of mother of applicant
15	Income of applicant's parents
16	Applicant has a right to receive a supplementary scholarship
17	Kind of health insurance of applicant
18	Living situation of applicant
19	Applicant has a right to receive a loan from the student grant institute
20	Maximum amount that can be received for supplementary scholarship
21	Parental contribution
22	The amount of loan the applicant requests
23	Maximum amount of loan
24	The amount of supplementary scholarship that is assigned to applicant
25	The amount of basic scholarship that is assigned to applicant
26	The amount of loan that is assigned to applicant
27	The total amount of student grant that is assigned to applicant

Now, the determination of the parent's income can be seen as one activity in the workflow process, containing exactly the three operations as described above. Information elements '13' and '14' can be distinguished as "half-assembly" products, because they are output elements of two different operations and input elements of another operation. An information element structure as we presented here, is rather similar to a Bill Of Material (BOM), (see [305]).

Note that the presented information element structure incorporates an interesting characteristic, namely a *conditional alternative*. In general, this means that depending on a specific condition, i.e. the value of an information element, different routes have to be followed to produce the end product. The notion of the conditional alternative is represented in the information element structure by using different notations. In Figure 2 this is clarified. The structure on the left-hand side is an AND-construction. All three input elements are needed to determine the value of the output element of this operation. On the contrary, the structure on the right-hand side is a so-called eXclusive OR-construction (XOR). The output information element can be produced either out of "a" or out of "b" and "c" together.

Having explained this notation, it may now become clear from Figure 1 that the value of information element '27' can be determined in two different ways. If the value of information element '12' is "no", information element '27' can be produced directly. When the value of '12' is "yes", a number of other steps have to be executed before the value of information element '27' can be determined.

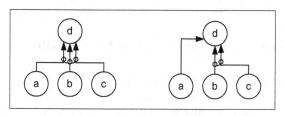

Fig. 2. Representation of an information element structure with AND- and XOR-construction. The structure on the left-hand side is the AND-construction: "a", "b" and "c" are needed to get "d". The right-hand structure is the XOR-construction. To make "d" information element "a" is needed or information elements "b" and "c" are needed.

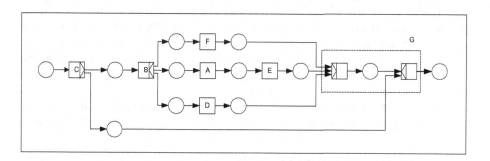

Fig. 3. The workflow net of "Request for governmental student grant"

In Figure 3, the current workflow process that implements the information structure of Figure 1 is represented as a workflow net ([4]). Individual activities, as described in Table 2, are represented as rectangles. We will explain the exact relation between the operations of the information element structure and the workflow process after we have formally defined both concepts in a later section.

Table 2. Description of the activities in the workflow net of Figure 4.

Activity	Description
A	Determine the income of the parents of the applicant
B	Determine the period/year of student grant and the reference year for tax authorities
C	Determine if the applicant has a right to receive governmental student grant
D	Determine the amount of basic scholarship
E	Determine the amount of supplementary scholarship
F	Determine the amount of loan
G	Determine the total amount of student grant

3   A Cohesion and Coupling Notion for Workflow Activities

Because of the resemblances between software programs and workflow processes as mentioned in the introduction, we studied various software quality metrics in software engineering and their applicability to workflow process design. According to [9] and [22] the quality of a design is related to five design principles: coupling, cohesion, complexity, modularity and size, of which the first two are the most important ones ([12] and [22]). These concepts can be implemented in several ways (see for example: [8], [10], [11] and [21]). Due to space limitations, we cannot describe these metrics in detail, but we concluded that because of subtle differences between software programs and workflow processes none of the existing cohesion metrics seem to be directly applicable to workflow design. However, we were inspired by the idea of the coupling metric by Selby and Basili ([20]) and Xenos et al ([23]). Also, we adopted the combined use of a cohesion and coupling metric as in [20]. As an extension of earlier work ([17]), we will now present a formalization of the design problem and new and extended cohesion and coupling metrics.

First of all, the job of process design is to impose on a set of operations and its accompanying information elements a number of activities that partition it. Therefore, we introduce the concept of an operations structure.

Definition 1 (Operations Structure). An *operations structure* is a tuple (D, O) with:
- D: the set of *information elements* that are being processed,
- $O = \{(p, cs) \in D \times P(D)\}$ is a set of *operations* on the information elements, such that there are no 'dangling' information elements and no value of an information element depends on itself:
  - $R = \{(p, c) \in D \times D \mid \exists (p, cs) \in O: c \in cs\}$ is connected and acyclic,

where p denotes the output information element of the operation and cs the input elements of the operation.

We have to remark here that the conditional alternative construction as introduced previously is represented by multiple operations with the same output element (as many as there are alternatives). The formalization of the operations of the situations given in Figure 2 is then as follows. The construction on the left is built of one operation that is represented by the tuple: $\{(d, \{a, b, c\})\}$. The XOR-construction on the right is built out of two operations that can be formalized by $\{(d, \{a\}), (d, \{b, c\})\}$.

The activities that partition an operations structure should satisfy a basic notion of correctness.

Definition 2 (Valid Activity). Given an operations structure (D, O), any subset $t \subseteq O$ is a *valid activity* on the operations structure, or simply an *activity*.

Definition 3 (Valid Activity Ordering). Given an operations structure (D, O), the tuple (T, F) is a valid activity ordering on that operations structure iff:

- T is a set of valid activities, $T \subseteq P(O)$, such that:

$$\forall o \in O : \left(\exists t \in T : o \in t \right). \tag{1}$$

- F is a partial ordering on T, $F \subseteq T \times T$, such that:

$$\forall t, u \in T : \left(\left(\exists (p, cs) \in t, (q, ds) \in u : q \in cs \right) \Rightarrow (u, t) \in F^* \right) \tag{2}$$

Within this definition it is expressed by (1) that all operations from the operation structure should appear at least once in an activity. This condition ensures the completeness of the activity design. Condition (2) enforces that when one operation depends on the output of another operation, then the respective activities they are part of are ordered such that they respect this dependency. In other words, if the execution of an activity requires the value of an information element for one of its operations to be executed, this information element has been established as part of executing a preceding activity. This condition ensures the correctness of the ordering.

A new cohesion metric, which allows for the assessment of conditional alternatives in an information element structure, can now be defined as follows. Its first component, the *relation cohesion*, quantifies how much the different operations within one activity are related. It does so by determining for each operation of an activity with how many other operations it overlaps by sharing an input or output, i.e. a non-empty intersection. In this determination conditional alternatives are treated as separate operations, because in an instantiation only one of the alternatives will be executed. The overlap between these operations (they have the same output element) is therefore not considered. This explains why the expression $p \neq q$ is in the formula. Then, the average overlap per operation is computed by dividing the total amount of overlaps by the number of operations. Finally, note that all overlaps are counted twice, because we considered all pairs of operations separately (distinguishing as different pairs for example (p, cs), (q, ds) and (q, ds), (p, cs)). Therefore, to get a relative metric between 0 and 1, the average overlap per operation over all operations within an activity is divided by the maximal overlap, i.e. the number of operations minus 1.

Definition 4 (Activity Relation Cohesion). For a valid activity t on an operation structure (D, O), its relation cohesion $\lambda(t)$ is defined as follows:

$$\lambda(t) = \begin{cases} \dfrac{\displaystyle\sum_{(p,cs)\in t} \left|\left\{(q,ds)\in t \mid (\{p\}\cup cs)\cap(\{q\}\cup ds) \neq \varnothing \wedge (p \neq q)\right\}\right|}{|t|\cdot(|t|-1)}, & \text{for } |t| > 1 \\[4mm] 0, & \text{for } |t| \leq 1 \end{cases} \tag{3}$$

The other component of our cohesion metric, the activity information cohesion, focuses on all information elements that are used either as input or output by any operation within the respective activity. It determines how many information elements are used more than once in proportion to all the information elements used. It does so by counting all different information elements that appear in the intersection of a pair of operations, considering all pairs. Again, in case of conditional alternatives, the overlapping element is left aside. This number is divided by the total number of information elements in the activity.

Definition 5 (Activity Information Cohesion). For a valid activity t on an operation structure (D, O), its information cohesion $\mu(t)$ is defined as follows:

$$\mu(t) = \begin{cases} \dfrac{\left|\left\{d \in D \mid \exists(p,cs),(q,ds)\in t : d \in (\{p\}\cup cs)\cap(\{q\}\cup ds) \wedge (p \neq q)\right\}\right|}{\left|\left\{d \in D \mid \exists(p,cs)\in t : d \in (\{p\}\cup cs)\right\}\right|}, & \text{for } |t| > 0 \\[4mm] 0, & \text{for } |t| = 0 \end{cases} \tag{4}$$

The total cohesion of an activity is now given as the product of both the relation and information cohesion. This is to reflect that in our opinion an activity has to score high on both cohesion metrics to say it is cohesive in total. In other words, the operations should be inter-related to each other and information should be shared.

Definition 6 (Activity Cohesion). For a valid activity t on an operation structure (D, O), its cohesion $c(t)$ is defined as follows:

$$c(t) = \lambda(t)\cdot\mu(t) . \tag{5}$$

The cohesion of the process in total can then be determined by the average activity cohesion.

Definition 7 (Process Cohesion). For a process, which consists of a number of valid activities on the operations structure (D, O), the average cohesion, or process cohesion (c), is defined as follows:

$$c = \frac{\displaystyle\sum_{t\in T} c(t)}{|T|} \tag{6}$$

As an extension and a natural counterpart of cohesion we also define a metric for coupling in a process. Coupling focuses on how much the activities in a process are related, or connected, to each other. A certain activity is connected to another iff they share one or more information elements.

The coupling metric determines the number of related activities for each activity. First the average coupling is determined by adding up the number of connections for all activities and dividing this number by the total number of activities. Now, all pairs of activities have been counted twice. To get a relative metric, the average coupling is divided by the maximal number of coupling, i.e. the number of activities minus 1.

Definition 8 (Process Coupling). For a process, which consist of a number of valid activities on the operations structure (D, O), the process coupling k is defined as follows:

$$k = \begin{cases} \dfrac{\displaystyle\sum_{s,t \in T} connected(s,t)}{|T| \cdot (|T| - 1)} & , \text{for } |T| > 1 \\[2mm] 0 & , \text{for } |T| \leq 1 \end{cases} \tag{7}$$

where

$$connected(s,t) = \begin{cases} 1, & \text{if} (s \neq t) \wedge (\exists (p,cs) \in s \wedge (q,ds) \in t : (\{p\} \cup cs) \cap (\{q\} \cup ds) \neq \varnothing) \\ 0, & \text{otherwise} \end{cases} \tag{8}$$

Inspired by the work of Selby and Basili ([20]), we also define a coupling/cohesion ratio. This ratio enables the comparison between various design alternatives.

Definition 9 (Process Coupling/Cohesion Ratio). For a process, which consists of a number of valid activities on an operations structure (D, O), the process coupling/cohesion ratio ρ is defined as follows:

$$\rho = \frac{k}{c}. \tag{9}$$

The previously defined metrics can be used to find the best workflow design among a number of alternative designs. The design with the minimal process coupling/cohesion ratio, is the best design. Note that we do not describe how the alternative designs can be determined. The ratio can only help to choose the best alternative between already devised options.

4   Application

In this section we will show an application of our above presented heuristic. We will use the example of the request for student grant introduced earlier. First we will compute the process cohesion of the partitioning of activities as given in the workflow net of Figure 3. Afterwards, we will give two alternative designs, one with smaller activities and one with larger activities. Our heuristic will help to determine which of the three designs is best, implementing our hypothesis that activities should neither be too small nor too large. This is the insight which we derived from our experiences with workflow designers (see [17]).

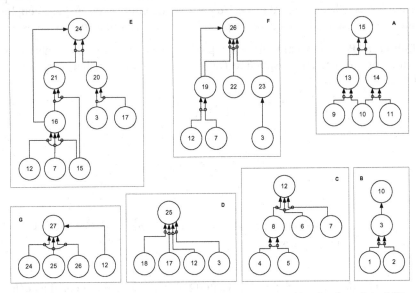

Fig. 4. Partitioning of the information element structure in activities for the original "Request for student grant" process.

4.1   The Original Process Design

The original process design is a division of the information element structure into 7 activities, as displayed in the process model of Figure 3. The accompanying information element structures of the activities are shown in Figure 4. The formalization of the structure is as follows:

$$D_A = \{9, 10, 11, 13, 14, 15\}$$
$$O_A = \{ (13, \{9, 10\}), (14, \{10, 11\}), (15, \{13, 14\}) \}$$
$$D_B = \{1, 2, 3, 10\}$$
$$O_B = \{ (3, \{1, 2\}), (10, \{3\}) \}$$
$$D_C = \{4, 5, 6, 7, 8, 12\}$$
$$O_C = \{ (8, \{4, 5\}), (12, \{6, 7, 8\}) \}$$
$$D_D = \{3, 12, 17, 18, 25\}$$
$$O_D = \{ (25, \{3, 12, 17, 18\}) \}$$
$$D_E = \{3, 7, 12, 15, 16, 17, 20, 21, 24\}$$
$$O_E = \{ (16, \{7, 12, 15\}), (20, \{3, 17\}), (21, \{15, 16\}), (24, \{20, 21\}),$$
$$(24, \{16\}) \}$$
$$D_F = \{3, 7, 12, 19, 22, 23, 26\}$$
$$O_F = \{ (19, \{7, 12\}), (23, \{3\}), (26, \{19, 22, 23\}), (26, \{19\}) \}$$

$D_G = \{12, 24, 25, 26, 27\}$
$O_G = \{ (27, \{24, 25, 26\}), (27, \{12\}) \}$

The activity relation cohesion, the activity information cohesion and the activity cohesion are computed for all seven activities (see Table 3). Next the process cohesion is calculated. The process cohesion of the original process design is:

$$c = \frac{0.5 + 0.25 + 0.167 + 0 + 0.222 + 0.143 + 0}{7} \approx 0.183 \ . \tag{10}$$

Table 3. The activity relation cohesion, the activity information cohesion and the activity cohesion for all activities in the original process design.

Activity	Activity relation cohesion	Activity information cohesion	Activity cohesion
A	1	0.5	0.5
B	1	0.25	0.25
C	1	0.167	0.167
D	0	0	0
E	0.5	0.444	0.222
F	0.5	0.286	0.143
G	0	0	0

Table 4. The connections between activities from the original process design.

	A	B	C	D	E	F	G	
A	0	1	0	0	1	0	0	2
B	1	0	0	1	1	1	0	4
C	0	0	0	1	1	1	1	4
D	0	1	1	0	1	1	1	5
E	1	1	1	1	0	1	1	6
F	0	1	1	1	1	0	1	5
G	0	0	1	1	1	1	0	4
	2	4	4	5	6	5	4	30

As an illustration of the computation of the coupling metric for this process a table (see Table 4) is given, containing all relations between activities (when two activities are connected the value is 1, when they are not connected the value is 0). The coupling value can now be calculated as follows:

$$k = \frac{2 + 4 + 4 + 5 + 6 + 5 + 4}{7 * 6} = \frac{30}{42} \approx 0.714 \ . \tag{11}$$

Based on these values for cohesion and coupling for the process we can compute the coupling/cohesion ratio:

$$\rho = \frac{0.714}{0.183} \approx 3.9 \ . \tag{12}$$

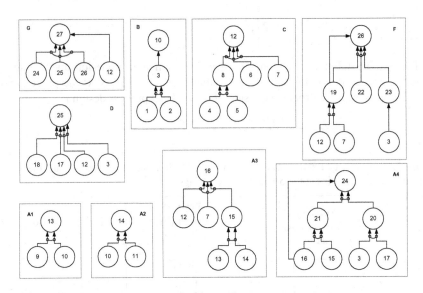

Fig. 5. The partitioning of the information element structure in smaller activities.

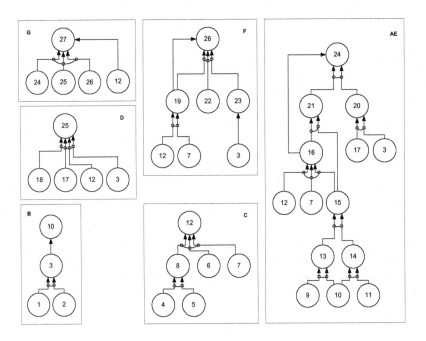

Fig. 6. The partitioning of the information element structure in larger activities. Compared to the original structure activities A and E are merged.

4.2   The First Alternative Process Design: Smaller Activities

In the first alternative design the activities are considerably smaller (see Figure 5). Activities A and E are split up into four new activities: A1, A2, A3, and A4. The total number of activities in this first alternative design is now nine. The process cohesion value for this first alternative process design is 0.104. The value for coupling is 0.611. The resulting process coupling/cohesion ratio is 5.8.

4.3   The Second Alternative Process Design: Larger Activities

In the second, alternative process design we merged activities A and E from the original design together (see Figure 6). This process design has six activities. The value for the process cohesion metric is 0.123, the process coupling is 0.867 and the coupling/cohesion ratio is 7.0.

Now we know the value for the coupling/cohesion ratio of each process design, we can apply our heuristic. When we compare the coupling/cohesion ratio of the original design to that of the first alternative design we can conclude that the original design is best, because its coupling/cohesion ratio is lower. In the first alternative, various very small activities have been defined that seem to lead to a very fragmented workflow model, which is not something to aim for.

Then, comparing the original design to the second alternative, the heuristic indicates that the original design again is best (lower coupling/cohesion ratio). This appeals to our intuition that the very large activity AE is not very attractive, because of its relatively high complexity and incohesive structure.

In conclusion, the heuristic points out the original design as the most favorable one, which is confirmed by our intuition. Moreover, it seems to be in line with earlier findings where activities which were not too large and not too small were favored by experienced workflow designers ([17]).

5   Conclusion / Future Work

In this paper we discussed the applicability and development of cohesion and coupling metrics in workflow process design. We defined cohesion and coupling metrics for the design of activities in a workflow design, based on an information processing perspective on workflow processes. Although existing software quality metrics inspired us, none of these seemed directly applicable to the workflow process domain. Based on our newly introduced coupling and cohesion metrics, we also defined a ratio that allows for a comparison between alternative designs to decide which one is best.

Obviously, the information processing perspective we took is but one of the views on workflow design. An important limitation of the metric in isolation is its abstraction from *resources*. Only qualified and authorized employees may execute specific operations (see e.g. [4]). Therefore, two operations with different resource requirements can not be clustered within the same activity. Resource restrictions limit the freedom in distributing operations over activities and should therefore precede the application of a heuristic as discussed in this paper. A similar argument may be raised for the *performance* aspect of the operations. We abstracted, for example, from timing information on the various operations, although this may be essential information to come up with a well-structured workflow design. When certain operations take a lot of time compared to other activities, it is not sensible to put them together in one activity. We feel that this is one of the most pressing issues for further research in extending our – as of yet – purely logic view on the operations.

Many more possibilities to extend this research exist. On a higher level, we aim for the testing of our hypothesis on the quality of workflow designs. This will require the further involvement of actual workflow models, the knowledge of workflow designers, and end-users.

Finally, the cohesion and coupling metrics and heuristic can only support the workflow designer in making decisions with respect to activity definition. The heuristic does not suggest any clustering or ordering of information elements itself. An extension of the heuristic so that it efficiently generates (semi-)optimal activity definitions itself will be an ultimate and challenging next step in this domain.

References

1. W.M.P. van der Aalst. On the Automatic Generation of Workflow Processes Based on Product Structures. Computers in Industry, 39(2):97-111, 1999.
2. W.M.P. van der Aalst. Reengineering Knock-out Processes. Decision Support Systems, 30(4):451-468, 2001.
3. W.M.P. van der Aalst and P.J.S. Berens. Beyond Workflow Management: Product-Driven Case Handling. In S. Ellis, T. Rodden, and I. Zigurs, editors, International ACM SIGGROUP Conference on Supporting Group Work (GROUP 2001), pages 42-51. ACM Press, New York, 2001.
4. W.M.P. van der Aalst and K.M. van Hee. Workflow Management: Models, Methods, and Systems. MIT press, Cambridge, MA, 2002.
5. W.M.P. van der Aalst, A.H.M. ter Hofstede, B. Kiepuszewski, and A.P. Barros. Workflow Patterns. Distributed and Parallel Databases, 14(1):5-51, 2003.
6. L. Baresi, F. Casati, S. Castano, M. Fugini, I. Mirbel, and B. Pernici. WIDE Workflow Development Methodology. Proceedings of International Joint Conference on Work Activities Coordination and Collaboration., pp. 19-28, 1999.
7. A. van den Berg, P. Pottjewijd. Workflow: Continuous Improvement by Integral Process Management. Academic Service, 1997 (page 77). (In Dutch)
8. J.M. Bieman, B-K Kang. Measuring Design-level Cohesion. IEEE Transactions on Software Engineering, 24(2): 111-124, 1998.
9. S.D. Conte, H.E. Dunsmore, V.Y. Shen. Software Engineering Metrics and Models. Benjamin/Cummings Publishing Company, Inc., 1986.
10. T.J. Emerson. A Discriminant Metric for Module Cohesion. Proceedings of the 7th International Conference on Software Engineering (ICSE-7), pages 294-303, 1984.
11. N. Fenton, A. Melton. Deriving Structurally Based Software Measures. Journal of Systems and Software, 12: 177-187, 1990.
12. G.J. Myers. Composite/Structured Design. Van Nostrand Reinhold, New York NY, 1978.

13. A. Orlicky. Structuring the Bill of Materials for MRP. Production and Inventory Management, December, pp.19-42, 1972.

14. E.A.H. Platier. A Logistical View on Business Processes: Concepts for Business Process Redesign and Workflow Management. PhD thesis, Eindhoven University of Technology, Eindhoven, 1996.

15. H.A. Reijers, S. Limam, W.M.P. van der Aalst. Product-Based Workflow Design. Journal of Management. Information Systems, 20(1): 229-262, 2003.

16. H.A. Reijers. Design and Control of Workflow Processes: Business Process Management for the Service Industry. Lecture Notes in Computer Science 2617. Springer-Verlag, Berlin, 2003.

17. H.A. Reijers. A Cohesion Metric for the Definition of Activities in a Workflow Process. Proceedings of the Eighth CAiSE/IFIP8.1 International Workshop on Evaluation of Modeling Methods in Systems Analysis and Design 2003, pages 116-125, 2003.

18. R.O. Rupp, J.R. Russell. The Golden Rules of Process Redesign. Quality Progress, 27(12): 85-92, 1994.

19. A. Seidmann and A. Sundararajan. The Effects of Task and Information Asymmetry on Business Process Redesign. International Journal of Production Economics, 50(2-3): 117-128, 1997.

20. R.W. Selby, V.R. Basili. Analyzing Error-Prone System Structure. IEEE Transactions on Software Engineering, 17(2):141-152, 1991.

21. F. Simon, S. Löffler, C. Lewerentz. Distance Based Cohesion Measuring. Proceedings of the 2nd European Software Measurement Conference (FESMA) 1999, pages 69-83, 1999.

22. D.A. Troy, S.H. Zweben. Measuring the Quality of Structured Designs. Journal of Systems and Software, 2: 113-120, 1981.

23. M. Xenos, D. Stavrinoudis, K. Zikouli, D. Christodoulakis. Object-oriented Metrics – A Survey. Proceedings of the Federation of European Software Measurement Association (FESMA) 2000, pages 1-10, 2000.

Author Index

Lecture Notes in Computer Science

For information about Vols. 1–3007

please contact your bookseller or Springer-Verlag

Vol. 3054: I. Crnkovic, J.A. Stafford, H.W. Schmidt, K. Wallnau (Eds.), Component-Based Software Engineering. XI, 311 pages. 2004.

Vol. 3053: C. Bussler, J. Davies, D. Fensel, R. Studer (Eds.), The Semantic Web: Research and Applications. XIII, 490 pages. 2004.

Vol. 3052: W. Zimmermann, B. Thalheim (Eds.), Abstract State Machines 2004. Advances in Theory and Practice. XII, 235 pages. 2004.

Vol. 3051: R. Berghammer, B. Möller, G. Struth (Eds.), Relational and Kleene-Algebraic Methods in Computer Science. X, 279 pages. 2004.

Vol. 3050: J. Domingo-Ferrer, V. Torra (Eds.), Privacy in Statistical Databases. IX, 367 pages. 2004.

Vol. 3049: M. Bruynooghe, K.-K. Lau (Eds.), Program Development in Computational Logic. VIII, 539 pages. 2004.

Vol. 3047: F. Oquendo, B. Warboys, R. Morrison (Eds.), Software Architecture. X, 279 pages. 2004.

Vol. 3046: A. Laganà, M.L. Gavrilova, V. Kumar, Y. Mun, C.K. Tan, O. Gervasi (Eds.), Computational Science and Its Applications – ICCSA 2004. LIII, 1016 pages. 2004.

Vol. 3045: A. Laganà, M.L. Gavrilova, V. Kumar, Y. Mun, C.K. Tan, O. Gervasi (Eds.), Computational Science and Its Applications – ICCSA 2004. LIII, 1040 pages. 2004.

Vol. 3044: A. Laganà, M.L. Gavrilova, V. Kumar, Y. Mun, C.K. Tan, O. Gervasi (Eds.), Computational Science and Its Applications – ICCSA 2004. LIII, 1140 pages. 2004.

Vol. 3043: A. Laganà, M.L. Gavrilova, V. Kumar, Y. Mun, C.K. Tan, O. Gervasi (Eds.), Computational Science and Its Applications – ICCSA 2004. LIII, 1180 pages. 2004.

Vol. 3042: N. Mitrou, K. Kontovasilis, G.N. Rouskas, I. Iliadis, L. Merakos (Eds.), NETWORKING 2004, Networking Technologies, Services, and Protocols; Performance of Computer and Communication Networks; Mobile and Wireless Communications. XXXIII, 1519 pages. 2004.

Vol. 3040: R. Conejo, M. Urretavizcaya, J.-L. Pérez-de-la-Cruz (Eds.), Current Topics in Artificial Intelligence. XIV, 689 pages. 2004. (Subseries LNAI).

Vol. 3039: M. Bubak, G.D.v. Albada, P.M. Sloot, J.J. Dongarra (Eds.), Computational Science - ICCS 2004. LXVI, 1271 pages. 2004.

Vol. 3038: M. Bubak, G.D.v. Albada, P.M. Sloot, J.J. Dongarra (Eds.), Computational Science - ICCS 2004. LXVI, 1311 pages. 2004.

Vol. 3037: M. Bubak, G.D.v. Albada, P.M. Sloot, J.J. Dongarra (Eds.), Computational Science - ICCS 2004. LXVI, 745 pages. 2004.

Vol. 3036: M. Bubak, G.D.v. Albada, P.M. Sloot, J.J. Dongarra (Eds.), Computational Science - ICCS 2004. LXVI, 713 pages. 2004.

Vol. 3035: M.A. Wimmer (Ed.), Knowledge Management in Electronic Government. XII, 326 pages. 2004. (Subseries LNAI).

Vol. 3034: J. Favela, E. Menasalvas, E. Chávez (Eds.), Advances in Web Intelligence. XIII, 227 pages. 2004. (Subseries LNAI).

Vol. 3033: M. Li, X.-H. Sun, Q. Deng, J. Ni (Eds.), Grid and Cooperative Computing. XXXVIII, 1076 pages. 2004.

Vol. 3032: M. Li, X.-H. Sun, Q. Deng, J. Ni (Eds.), Grid and Cooperative Computing. XXXVII, 1112 pages. 2004.

Vol. 3031: A. Butz, A. Krüger, P. Olivier (Eds.), Smart Graphics. X, 165 pages. 2004.

Vol. 3030: P. Giorgini, B. Henderson-Sellers, M. Winikoff (Eds.), Agent-Oriented Information Systems. XIV, 207 pages. 2004. (Subseries LNAI).

Vol. 3029: B. Orchard, C. Yang, M. Ali (Eds.), Innovations in Applied Artificial Intelligence. XXI, 1272 pages. 2004. (Subseries LNAI).

Vol. 3028: D. Neuenschwander, Probabilistic and Statistical Methods in Cryptology. X, 158 pages. 2004.

Vol. 3027: C. Cachin, J. Camenisch (Eds.), Advances in Cryptology - EUROCRYPT 2004. XI, 628 pages. 2004.

Vol. 3026: C. Ramamoorthy, R. Lee, K.W. Lee (Eds.), Software Engineering Research and Applications. XV, 377 pages. 2004.

Vol. 3025: G.A. Vouros, T. Panayiotopoulos (Eds.), Methods and Applications of Artificial Intelligence. XV, 546 pages. 2004. (Subseries LNAI).

Vol. 3024: T. Pajdla, J. Matas (Eds.), Computer Vision - ECCV 2004. XXVIII, 621 pages. 2004.

Vol. 3023: T. Pajdla, J. Matas (Eds.), Computer Vision - ECCV 2004. XXVIII, 611 pages. 2004.

Vol. 3022: T. Pajdla, J. Matas (Eds.), Computer Vision - ECCV 2004. XXVIII, 621 pages. 2004.

Vol. 3021: T. Pajdla, J. Matas (Eds.), Computer Vision - ECCV 2004. XXVIII, 633 pages. 2004.

Vol. 3019: R. Wyrzykowski, J.J. Dongarra, M. Paprzycki, J. Wasniewski (Eds.), Parallel Processing and Applied Mathematics. XIX, 1174 pages. 2004.

Vol. 3018: M. Bruynooghe (Ed.), Logic Based Program Synthesis and Transformation. X, 233 pages. 2004.

Vol. 3017: B. Roy, W. Meier (Eds.), Fast Software Encryption. XI, 485 pages. 2004.

Vol. 3016: C. Lengauer, D. Batory, C. Consel, M. Odersky (Eds.), Domain-Specific Program Generation. XII, 325 pages. 2004.

Vol. 3015: C. Barakat, I. Pratt (Eds.), Passive and Active Network Measurement. XI, 300 pages. 2004.

Vol. 3014: F. van der Linden (Ed.), Software Product-Family Engineering. IX, 486 pages. 2004.

Vol. 3012: K. Kurumatani, S.-H. Chen, A. Ohuchi (Eds.), Multi-Agnets for Mass User Support. X, 217 pages. 2004. (Subseries LNAI).

Vol. 3011: J.-C. Régin, M. Rueher (Eds.), Integration of AI and OR Techniques in Constraint Programming for Combinatorial Optimization Problems. XI, 415 pages. 2004.

Vol. 3010: K.R. Apt, F. Fages, F. Rossi, P. Szeredi, J. Váncza (Eds.), Recent Advances in Constraints. VIII, 285 pages. 2004. (Subseries LNAI).

Vol. 3009: F. Bomarius, H. Iida (Eds.), Product Focused Software Process Improvement. XIV, 584 pages. 2004.

Vol. 3008: S. Heuel, Uncertain Projective Geometry. XVII, 205 pages. 2004.